Friedrich Schiller.

Heath's Modern Language Series

Schillers

Wilhelm Tell

*EDITED WITH AN INTRODUCTION, NOTES
AND VOCABULARY*

BY

ROBERT WALLER DEERING, Ph. D.

PROFESSOR OF GERMANIC LANGUAGES IN WESTERN RESERVE UNIVERSITY

———◆———

BOSTON, U. S. A.

D. C. HEATH & CO., PUBLISHERS

1911

Wilhelm Tell is published
both with and without a vocabulary. In ordering please
specify which edition is desired.

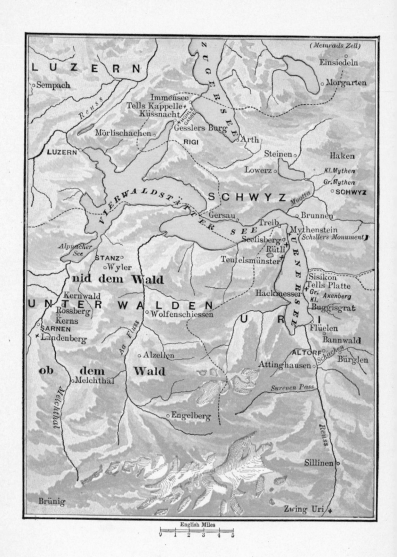

English Miles
0 1 2 3 4 5

PREFACE.

THERE is, perhaps, no German play better suited to the needs of students than Schiller's 𝔚𝔦𝔩𝔥𝔢𝔩𝔪 𝔗𝔢𝔩𝔩. Its noble theme, simple style, lofty poetic tone and wonderful dramatic power make it in every way an admirable text for class use. The writer's purpose in the present volume has been to prepare an adequate, yet convenient edition of the play for school and college. The book claims no special originality, but is simply an attempt to provide the text with such practical commentary as will best meet the needs of the student who would not only read, but also understand and appreciate Schiller's great drama.

The *Text* is that of the first Cotta edition (1804), the only one Schiller corrected, with such minor changes as seemed necessary on comparison of this original with the Berlin, Hamburg and Aschaffenburg MSS., which have been carefully collated by Maltzahn, Oesterley and Vollmer. For obvious reasons orthography and punctuation have been conformed to modern standards.

The *Introduction* has been made as short as possible in justice to the subject. After some hesitation, a sketch of Schiller was included; not, of course, because of any lack of 'lives' of Schiller, but because even the best known of these sketches, Carlyle's for instance, are unfortunately not

(iii)

always accessible to students, and again because students
rarely read a detailed biography, even when it is accessible.
Other chapters of the Introduction are devoted to the
systematic treatment of the more important dramatic, historical and legendary questions connected with the play,
which could not be properly discussed in the Notes. The
sometimes rather detailed statement has seemed necessary,
since any real appreciation of Tell is impossible until such
vital points are clearly understood.

Designed for two very different kinds of students — for
such as may read Tell as a first classic, early in their German
course, as well as for more advanced pupils who may wish
to use the play for rapid reading later — the *Notes* have
of necessity a two-fold character, so that elementary points
are often explained side by side with matters more difficult.

In preparing the commentary, the editor has made free use
of all the material available and desires to express here his
sense of general obligation to Bellermann, Birlinger, Breul,
Buchheim, Dierauer, Düntzer, Funke, Oechsli, Vischer and
other predecessors in the same field. Particular indebted-
ness is frankly acknowledged in its proper connection.
Heartiest thanks are also due to Professor E. S. Joynes of
South Carolina College for many valuable suggestions, and
to Dr. Lewis A. Rhoades of Cornell University for careful
reading of the proofs.

R. W. DEERING.

CLEVELAND, January, 1894.

INTRODUCTION.

I. SKETCH OF SCHILLER'S LIFE AND WORKS.

THERE is no writer so well known, none so honored among the masses of German people as Friedrich Schiller. Not Luther, nor Goethe, nor anyone has ever got so close to the great, honest German *heart* as he. His name is a household word with every class. The rich and cultured honor the genius with which he embodied his lofty ideals ; the poor and humble love him for his childlike simplicity and genuineness, for his broad and tender human sympathies, for his noble life — in spite of its sore trials and bitter disappointments, to them an inspiring example of all that is best and noblest in German character. His splendid genius, his sterling manhood, his tireless energy, his unflinching courage command the esteem and admiration of all men.

He descended from the sturdy stock of the middle classes. His ancestors were doughty village bakers and inn-keepers, holding office also as magistrates. His father was first barber's apprentice, then surgeon, soldier and finally major in the army of the Duke of Würtemberg. He was a man of considerable culture, of positive character, blunt and imperious in manner, but the soul of honor and kindness. The rugged soldier found a fitting helpmeet in Elisabeth Dorothea Kodweiss, the slender, blond-haired daughter of 'mine host of the Golden Lion' in Marbach in Würtemberg — a glad-hearted girl of seventeen, whom time soon developed into a noble, womanly woman of excellent tact and judgment, of singularly gentle and happy disposition, of finest sense and feeling. The eldest son and second child of this worthy couple was Johann Christoph Fried-rich Schiller, born in Marbach on Saturday, Nov. 10, 1759 — thirty years after Lessing, ten years after Goethe, two hundred and seventy-six years, to the day, after Luther. Unlike the precocious wonder-child Goethe, Schiller was an average boy, like other boys. Unlike Goethe, he inherited the physique of his mother, even to her soft blue eyes and red-blond hair. He combined the mental qualities of both parents — his father's restless energy and ambition and his mother's gentle dignity, happy disposition, refined feeling and decided literary taste. The mother's influence, especially during his earlier years, when the father was away with the army, cannot be overestimated in its wholesome effect upon the boy's character. His first teacher was good old pastor Moser in the neighboring village of Lorch, whom the poet afterward honored in Mojer, the priest, in the Räuber.

By nature devout, inspired by the example of his teacher and warmly encouraged by his parents, the boy early decided to be-come a clergyman and devoted some time to preparatory classical studies in the Latin School at Ludwigsburg. These cherished plans were broken up, however, by Duke Karl Eugen, who wanted the already promising student for his new military academy, the later Karlsschule, near his country residence, 'Soli-tude.' He offered a free education on condition that Schiller then devote himself to the service of Würtemberg. Limited in means and afraid to refuse, his parents reluctantly consented, and in Jan. 1773, not yet fourteen, the boy entered the school as a student of Law, since Theology was not taught there. The step was soon bitterly regretted, for the government of the school, a rigorous military discipline, which made machines of the students, cut off the outside world and regulated work and play and even prayers and meals " by word of command," was in the highest degree galling to Schiller's impulsive, sensitive nature. The fault was partly his own, however. Having come against his wish, he was prepared to be displeased. Expecting, as every boy does, greater freedom at school than at home, he was disappointed to find even more exacting rules. He naturally resented such restraint and received only too ready encouragement from his fellows. He soon developed decided aversion to Law, and within two years, on the removal of the school to Stuttgart, changed to Medicine. This was less irksome, yet his heart was not in it. His chief interest centered in literature, especially poetry, and, in spite of the rules, the works of Rousseau, Ossian, Shakespeare (Wieland's translation), Klopstock's Messias, Goethe's Götz and Werther, and other foreign and German classics, were eagerly devoured, like forbidden fruit, in secret with a few chosen friends. Such reading at once awakened his own poetic impulse. He said later: "I would have gladly given my last shirt for a subject on which to practice my youthful ambitious spirit." He did find themes for short poems, for epic and dramatic sketches —all more or less the extravagant expression of a morbidly sensitive imagination, and none of them important as literature, "but enough," says Carlyle, "to show that his mind had already dimly discovered its destination and was striving with restless vehemence to reach it, in spite of every obstacle."

These early efforts soon gave place to his first larger work, a revolutionary drama, Die Räuber, begun at eighteen and published, at his own expense, in 1781, after he had left the Karlsschule to become regimental surgeon, in the service of the Duke, at Stuttgart. At the instance of Dalberg, theater-manager at Mannheim, it was soon prepared for the stage and, in Jan. 1782, was performed. Eager to see his first drama played, but unable to go without special permission, which he knew would be refused, Schiller went secretly to see it. A second similar offence led to his arrest for a fortnight and to the Duke's positive command that in future he cease "all literary work and all communication with other countries." He pleaded in vain, endured for a while and then, irritated beyond control by such senseless restraint, determined on flight as a last resort.   In the night of Sept. 22, 1782, in company with his musician friend, Andreas Streicher, he left position, home and country, and fled, under the assumed name of Dr. Ritter, to Mannheim.   By repeated promises Dalberg had led him to hope for help towards pacifying the Duke and securing the post of theatre-poet and critic.   Dalberg had promised much, but, fearing the Duke's displeasure, did little, even refusing to accept Fiesco, a second drama Schiller had just finished and hoped soon to see performed.   Disheartened, almost penniless and fearing that even in Mannheim he was not safe from the Duke's anger, he pawned his watch, changed his name again and wandered about, undecided what to do, seeking relief from his trouble in revising Fiesco and sketching another play, Louise Müllerin, later called Kabale und Liebe (*Plot and Passion*).

Finally in his distress he turned to his friend, Frau von Wolzogen, the widowed mother of two of his Stuttgart fellow-students, who had offered him a home at her house in Bauerbach, near Meiningen.   Kindly received there, he forgot his griefs, found leisure for work on Kabale und Liebe, and even planned another drama, Don Carlos.   Too proud to accept longer the support of his hostess and unhappy in a love-affair with her daughter, he returned the next summer to Mannheim, where Dalberg, seeing that the Duke intended no persecution of Schiller or his family, felt free to help by giving him the wished-for position of theater-poet, with small, but assured salary.   Schiller contracted to furnish Fiesco, Kabale und Liebe, and one other play during the year.   This agreement soon proved a burden; petty jealousies among the actors worked against him and rendered his position unpleasant.   After one year he gave it up.

Again adrift, in great pecuniary distress, broken in health and out of heart, he turned next to journalism and founded a periodical — Die Rheinische (later Die Neue) Thalia, devoted to literature in general and drama in particular.   The venture increased his literary influence, but was not a success financially.   The future

seemed darker than ever.   Karl August of Weimar had heard
him read parts of Don Carlos and had made him Hofrat (Court
Councillor); but such empty honor, however appreciated for the
social prestige it gave, could not relieve his need or make Mannheim a congenial home.   He keenly felt the narrowness of his
sphere and yearned for better opportunities and conditions for
work.   With unalloyed pleasure, therefore, did he receive " the
most glorious surprise in the world " — an invitation to make his
home in Leipzig with one of several ardent admirers, Christian
Gottfried Körner, later a high government official in Dresden
and father of the poet, Theodor Körner.

In April 1785 he went to Leipzig and, generously helped by
Körner, began the second " period " of his life.   For two years,
spent in Leipzig, Gohlis, Dresden, he was busy with many plans.
He wrote for the Thalia, finished Don Carlos, and composed a
number of fine lyrics, of which his *Ode to Joy* is especially
popular.   He became interested also in history, and began his
Geschichte des Abfalls der Niederlande (*Revolt of the Netherlands*).
In July 1787, hoping to make influential connections, which
might help to permanent position, he visited Weimar, the university town of Jena, and other places.   He met prominent scholars
and court officials, the dowager Duchess Amalia, and, in Rudol-
stadt, became acquainted in the family of Frau von Lengefeld,
whose youngest daughter Charlotte (Schiller's ' Lotte ') afterwards became his wife.   Here, too, about a year later, he met
Goethe, who, though not at once an intimate friend, felt interest
in him and helped him to the chair of History, nominally Philosophy, in the University of Jena in May 1789.   The position
paid little at first, but soon, with a salary of two hundred thalers
and a pension yielding the same amount from the ever generous
Karl August, he felt able to marry and have a home of his own.
Feb. 22, 1790 is the date of the wedding.   He owed much to
Lotte.   A noble heart, a sunny nature, a most lovable woman
in heartiest sympathy with him and his plans, she was just the

wife for him. With her help he soon found what he needed most
— the quiet, contented happiness that only a happy home and
settled work can bring. He devoted himself with enthusiasm to
his history lectures, began his Geſchichte des dreißigjährigen Krieges,
and for once the future was all bright. His prospects were soon
blighted, however. Within a year his health failed, and long
and serious illness brought direst need. Fortunately help came
from the Prince of Holstein-Augustenburg and the Danish
Minister, Count Schimmelmann, who generously and delicately
offered him a thousand thalers a year for three years. A trip
to Karlsbad had benefited his health, and now a visit of nearly a
year to his old Swabian home gave him rest and made glad his
heart, but his enfeebled body was not yet restored to normal
strength. Still he continued to study and to write, finished his
Thirty Years' War, read Kant and occupied himself much with
philosophy and æsthetics.

May 1794 he returned to Jena, where he soon received a visit
from Goethe, whom he invited to become co-editor of a new
periodical, Die Horen, for which arrangements had already been
made with Cotta, the great South-German publisher. Goethe
readily accepted, and from this time dates their intimate friendship, which became the pride of the nation and was so fruitful
of good to its literature. Schiller's enthusiasm inspired Goethe
to effort, while Goethe's calmer judgment had most wholesome
influence on Schiller's impulsive nature. In spite of excellent
prospects the Horen met a cold reception; many contributors
lacked interest, and the public failed to appreciate its high standards of taste. Literary jealousy inspired attacks by mediocre
writers, which injured the paper, and its issue was stopped. Retribution soon came in the Xenien, a collection of cutting epi-
grams, in which both poets took revenge upon the writers and
critics of the day. In the Horen, and more especially in the
Muſenalmanach, his new annual, founded 1795, Schiller published
many of his finest lyrics and ballads, written in friendly rivalry

with Goethe, Der Handschuh, Der Spaziergang, Der Ring des Poly=
krates, Der Taucher, Die Bürgschaft, Die Kraniche des Jbykus, and
many others, of which Das Lied von der Glocke, published in 1800,
is the longest and best.

Meanwhile Schiller had "shut up the philosophy shop" and
returned to the drama. He was busy with Wallenstein, the idea of
which he had found in his studies for the *Thirty Years' War*,
and which had developed during his visit to Karlsbad in 1791.
He saw it performed in Weimar, and in Dec. 1799, wishing to
be nearer Goethe and the theater, he moved permanently to
Weimar, and spent there the last five years of his life. These
last years were the happiest, busiest and most successful of all.
Material affairs took a turn for the better; his salary was doubled;
his income from his publishers was considerable; he bought a
house; he became co-director of the theater with Goethe and
was happy in his home and in the brother poet, who had grown
mentally, socially and professionally so necessary to him. He
was influential at court and among "such friends," says Bulwer,
"as genius rarely finds — men alike dear to his heart and worthy
of his intellect." After years of trial, he was at last honored as
he deserved. Queen Luise of Prussia tried in vain to draw him to
Berlin as director of a magnificent theater. In 1802 Franz II.
gave him a patent of nobility, a distinction he neither sought
nor desired, but which he accepted "to please Lotte and the
children." At the height of his literary fame, just as he was
ready to live, he had to prepare to die. His feeble body grew
rapidly weaker, yet with a mighty energy which no infirmity
checked and no glory could satisfy, he worked on as if he knew
his days were numbered. His persevering courage, his lofty
poetic inspiration rose superior to every obstacle. Though his
health was gone, he wrote in quick succession and, as it were,
with his heart's blood, that splendid array of dramas, Wallenstein,
Maria Stuart, Die Jungfrau von Orleans, Die Braut von Messina,
Wilhelm Tell, which made him Germany's greatest dramatist and

made his name a household word in every German home. Important translations from French and classic authors engaged him, ambitious literary plans were going through his mind, when on May 9, 1805, death overtook him in the midst of what promised to be his greatest work thus far, a drama from Russian history, called Demetriuß. He was cut off by consumption in the prime of his noble manhood, when not yet forty-six years old.

In personal appearance, to quote Carlyle in substance, 'Schiller was tall, bony, very thin, with pale face, hollow cheeks, aquiline nose and reddish hair. At no time handsome, his form and features were much wasted by disease and overwork, but his high, thoughtful brow, his finely shaped mouth, soft kindling eyes and pale cheeks gave him withal an attractive appearance and a certain manly beauty. In manner he was plain and unassuming, modesty and childlike simplicity itself. Somewhat shy with strangers, he was, at home and among his friends, light-hearted and gay, everywhere patient, buoyant, calm, cheerful, never morose, never complaining. With no parade or display, he simply rated himself an honest man and a good citizen. He was the greater for having forgotten that he was great.'

Schiller's literary career may be conveniently divided into three periods, determined largely by the external circumstances of his life : (1) the formative stage, from his first work to his removal to Leipzig-Dresden, 1777–1785, is devoted to drama and lyrics; (2) with greater maturity the author and professor writes history and is busy with æsthetic and philosophical studies, 1785–1794; (3) his ripest years, spent in close friendship with Goethe; he returns to poetry and writes his greatest lyrics and dramas, 1794–1805.

His earliest important works were three plays, Die Räuber (1781), Fiesco (1783), and Kabale und Liebe (1784), all three written in prose and of decided revolutionary tendency. Die Räuber, he confesses, was the 'product of his liberty-loving genius in union with the thralldom' of the Karlsschule, a true type of the 'Storm and Stress' play, crude in plan, extravagant in expression, but intensely tragic, in spite of many unnatural scenes and distorted characters. In substance it is a violent, unreasoning attack upon existing social evils. Older people were scandalized, but the young were inspired to wildest enthusiasm by its stirring scenes. It was and has remained very popular and marks a distinct epoch in the poet's development as well as in the literature of his time. Fiesco embodies a political revolution in Genoa, and though much less violent, it attempts by shrewdness and stratagem the same end, freedom, attained by brute force in the Räuber It is inferior in animation, yet is notable as Schiller's first historical drama. Kabale und Liebe protests against abuses in society, especially against the privileged position of the upper classes. Its greater simplicity and more natural tone make it dramatically and artistically far the best of the three. All show poetic fire and dramatic talent, but a talent that has not yet found its true path. The lyrics of this period are much like the dramas — boldly, vividly conceived and full of "deep, though overdrawn, poetic feeling and impatient impulse."

The transition to the second period is Don Carlos, in which the extravagant, unreasoning passion of earlier plays becomes the calmer expression of riper thought. Though, as a result of long delay in its composition, 1784–1787, it lacks dramatic unity, it is notable as Schiller's first drama in verse, as the poet's own political confession of faith, and as marking a turning-point in his literary career. He is now a mature man, no longer a gifted youth. Based on important events in Spanish history, it involved careful study of the political movements of those times. Such study soon led Schiller away from poetry, and for years he devoted himself almost entirely to prose and especially to history. Besides a number of shorter essays and sketches, he produced two larger works, the above-mentioned Abfall der Niederlande (1788) and Die Geschichte des dreißigjährigen Krieges (1792), both faithful, often vivid pictures of the times they describe, most remarkable, perhaps, for the characteristic epic method, by which details are conveniently grouped around well-drawn central characters, like Orange, Egmont and Wallenstein. The philosophical and æsthetic studies of this period resulted in a number of shorter essays, such as his Ästhetische Erziehung des Menschen, Über Anmut und Würde, and his later Naive und sentimentalische Dichtung.

His last ten years form a third period, filled and inspired by his friendship for Goethe, and one of great lyric and dramatic activity. His growing epic interest in Wallenstein, developed by his studies for the *Thirty Year's War*, brought him back to poetry. The Wallenstein trilogy (1798–99) — Wallensteins Lager, Die Piccolomini, Wallensteins Tod — is an historical drama in the best sense, based upon those great movements of the Thirty Years' War in which Wallenstein took part. Free from the faults of earlier plays, it is considered by some his best work. Its images are no longer distorted; they are faithful, vivid pictures from a master hand. After Schiller's removal to Weimar almost every year brought a new drama. Wallenstein was followed by Maria Stuart (1800), which deals with the imprisonment and death of Mary Queen of Scots, at the hands of Elizabeth. Turning then to France for a theme, he wrote Die Jungfrau von Orleans (1801), a classic account of the career of the beautiful and terrible Joan of Arc, in her struggle against the English invaders of her country, in her tragic struggle with herself, when love for her enemy enters her heart. Die Braut von Messina (1803), a "drama of fate," is an unsuccessful attempt to combine the Classic and the Romantic, by bringing the Greek chorus into a modern play, thus giving it an antique dress; an awful destiny keeps two brothers at war with each other, which results in ruin and death. There is but little action in the play, and the chorus is a disturbing element, so that it has never been popular on the stage, yet many of the lyric passages are of unrivaled beauty and tenderness. In his last drama, Wilhelm Tell (1804), Schiller "completes the circle," says

Bulwer, "in which genius often seems to move and returns to those longings for liberty, now idealized and tempered by riper years, which once prompted the *Robbers*." It is the story of the Swiss struggle for liberty, and is in many respects the finest work of his life. The lyrics and ballads of this last period are among the best in German literature. For bold conception, graphic description, deep poetic feeling and rich fancy, Schiller is unsurpassed as a ballad-writer. Even Goethe acknowledged his own inferiority to him. In order to help supply the Weimar stage, Schiller was also busy during these last years with translations and adaptations, notably from Euripides, Jphigenie in Aulis, Shakespeare, Macbeth, Picard, Der Parafit and Der Neffe als Onkel, Gozzi, Turandot, and Racine, Phädra. His last complete work was a lyric festival play, Die Huldigung der Künfte (*Homage to the Arts*), containing "his poetic confession of faith," and written in honor of the marriage of the hereditary Grand Duke of Weimar to a Russian princess, Nov. 1804. In a review of Schiller's literary life we are surprised at the great *amount* of his work. He was allowed about 25 years, and into this time, by untiring industry, he crowded the work of a long life. Again there is the greatest *variety* in his productions. As student, surgeon, theater director and critic, editor, professor, historian, philosopher, essayist, dramatic and lyric poet, he was always busy, and despite the great amount and the great variety of his literary work, he attained a degree of *excellence* truly remarkable — and that in the face of poverty and life-long ill health. What might he not have been and become, if he could have lived out a happy, green old age!

II. FACT AND FABLE.

The real difficulties in Schiller's Tell are rarely points of grammar or style. They lie rather in the many historical, legendary and local allusions, which occur on every page. The play

has to do not only with the famous archer, but also, and
especially, with the Swiss struggle for liberty, and the poet,
closely following native chroniclers, presents genuine history so
blended with local tradition that the necessary separation of the
two is very difficult. Moreover, the early history of the Forest
Cantons, especially in their political relation to Austria and the
German Empire, is, in itself and without the admixture of tradition, often very incomplete and indefinite. After bitter partisan
disputes, for more than two centuries, over the story of Tell and
the beginnings of the Swiss Republic, impartial historians, both
Swiss and German, have established what is now generally con-
ceded to be the truth. Knowledge of the facts they have
gathered, by most searching examination and careful deduction,
from the authentic documents preserved, is absolutely necessary,
if one would understand and appreciate Schiller's play. The
following sketch attempts to embody, clearly though briefly, the
results of the most recent and reliable investigation on the chief
points involved, viz., the settlement and early history of the
Forest Cantons, their relation to the German Empire and to the
House of Habsburg-Austria, their finally successful struggle for
liberty and the establishment of their independent government.

Though the play has a certain historical background, it is by
no means history. The poet-artist was concerned that his
picture be true to Swiss life and character; he did not care for
historical accuracy of time, or place, or fact. He took, therefore,
from local tradition, as he found it in old chronicles, whatever
material suited his purpose best — in substance as follows:

The people of the Waldstätte were descendants, tradition
says, of Scandinavian ancestors, who, driven by famine from
their northern home, Sweden, had forced their way south and
settled the uninhabited shores of Lake Lucerne (Tell, ll. 1167-
1203). From the first they had been free men, acknowledging
only the authority of the German Emperor, giving their voluntary allegiance in return for his royal protection (Tell, 1211-

1227). They managed their own affairs, save in extraordinary cases of penal jurisdiction, when an imperial delegate was called in (Tell, 1233–1242). All went well until a grasping Habsburg-Austrian emperor, Albrecht, ignoring their true relation to the Empire, endeavored, with the help of tyrannical bailiffs, Gessler and others, whose cruelty is described in detail, to subjugate them and add the Forest Cantons to his own, Austrian, private possessions (Tell, 1257 ff.). After patient endurance and vain entreaty (Tell, 1325–1349), the people in Uri, Schwyz and Unterwalden conspired against their governors (Act II., Sc. 2), and, in open revolt on New Year's Day 1308, destroyed their castles (Tell, 2873 ff.), killed some and drove out others (Tell, 2903 ff.). The worst of the tyrants, Gessler von Bruneck, fell by the hand of Wilhelm Tell, a worthy man of Uri (Act IV. 3). This union of the three cantons was the origin of the independent Swiss Confederation.

Thus in brief the legend. For the most part, however, these events are not founded on fact. The Swiss did not descend from famine-stricken Swedes, nor were they free from obligation to Habsburg. Albrecht did not send tyrants to grind the people, nor was any bailiff, Gessler, ever shot by a Tell. Authentic history knows no Wilhelm Tell. The Swiss Confederacy was not established by any sudden uprising, but by a long, stubborn struggle with Austria.

On each point, therefore, it is necessary first to find out actual fact and then to note how, in the hands of the chroniclers, this fact has been gradually mingled with fable, by the addition of whatever new feature seemed good to each successive writer.

Though the presence of prehistoric races, lake-dwellers and nomad hunters, in the Waldstätte has been sufficiently established by the remains found there, the origin and fate of these ancient peoples are still in doubt. The earliest inhabitants of Switzerland, definitely known to history, were several Keltic tribes, notably Helvetians and Rhætians, who were conquered and half civilized by the Romans early in the Christian era. Remains of this rude Roman-Keltic culture have been found in abundance. From the third to the fifth century Helvetia was gradually overrun by Germanic tribes from the north. Forced south by the migration of races, some penetrated even to the shores of Lake Lucerne. About 406 the Alamanni spread over north-east Switzerland, destroying all civilization, enslaving the Kelts and forcing upon them their own Teutonic speech and pagan religion. A generation later, about 443–450, the less numerous Burgundians occupied the south-west, where, though victors, they gradually adopted the language, religion and culture of the conquered race. To this day French predominates there, while German is spoken in the north-east. The Forest Cantons were settled very slowly ; latest investigation seems to indicate that the colonization, by straggling Alamanni gradually forced out of more fertile lowland districts, was not complete until the ninth century, though begun in the fifth.

By the treaty of Verdun, in 843, after three centuries of Frankish overlordship, Alamannic (Eastern) Helvetia became part of the empire of Ludwig the German, and from 1032, when Burgundian (Western) Helvetia was added, all Switzerland belonged directly to the German Empire. The population included various elements; some were free men (Tell, 1366), others were serfs (eigne Leute, 1081) attached to the soil, while others owed more or less allegiance to individual lords, lay and clerical (Tell, 1360 ff.). Rich monasteries, especially, early acquired great power and important privileges. Thus the Abbey of Our Lady in Zürich (die Große Frau zu Zürch, Tell, 1364) was endowed by Ludwig the German with large estates in Uri, together with his rents, his serfs and privileges of exemption from all authority save that of the Emperor. The monasteries of Murbach, Einsiedeln (Tell, 1248) and Engelberg (Tell, 1080), are other important instances. Many free towns and communities, as well as petty nobles, enjoyed special privileges, holding lands in fief directly from the Empire. In the eleventh and twelfth centuries the imperial power was represented in these remote districts by the Dukes of Zäringen, but on the extinction of this family, in 1218, the greatest confusion prevailed. Naturally a few rich and prominent nobles increased their power at the expense of the others, and gradually gained control. This is true especially of the Counts of Savoy in the south-east and of those of Kiburg and Habsburg in the north and east. Above all the Habsburgs, insatiably land-hungry, forced their way up with restless energy. By inheritance, by purchase, by force, by well-planned marriages and political cunning, they rapidly absorbed the power of the Kiburgs, Lenzburgs, Laufenburgs and others, and gained virtual control, either as private landowners or as Reichsvögte (or Schirmvögte, i. e. rulers in the Emperor's name and stead), in the Forest Cantons. The latter, fearing lest this Habsburg 'protectorate' (Vogtei) be forcibly changed into absolute ownership, sought refuge in charters (Freiheitsbriefe, Tell, 311) promising the protection of the Emperor. In Uri Habsburg possessions were small, the canton having been settled largely by dependents of the abbey of Zürich and by free nobles and peasants. Moreover, Ludwig the German had already granted, in 843, special privileges. In 1231, therefore, the canton readily obtained from Heinrich, the rebellious son of Friedrich II., an imperial charter attesting its Reichsunmittelbarkeit.[1]

In Schwyz the case was different. Though most of the people were free, large estates and many serfs were owned by monasteries and by the Habsburgs, who claimed, moreover, to be "by lawful inheritance the rulers and 'protectors' of the canton."

---

[1] That is — its dependence directly on the Empire and not on a feudal lord. The protectorship (governorship), thus in the Emperor's hands, could not become hereditary in any family. Often no governor was appointed, affairs being administered by a local magistrate (Ammann) or, in special cases, by an imperial delegate (Graf). Rudolf of Habsburg served as such in Altorf in 1256-7.

Though without prior claim, such as Uri's just mentioned, Schwyz sought a similar charter. Shrewdly seizing their opportunity they sent messengers and troops to Emperor Friedrich II., then besieging Faenza in North Italy, offering their services in return for the desired charter. Though conflicting with certain Habsburg rights, it was granted, in doubtful terms at least, in Dec. 1240, and the Schwyzer were taken under the immediate and especial protection of the Empire.

Unterwalden was not so fortunate. Without organic union between Ob- and Nidwalden, with fewer free men and owned so largely by ecclesiastical and secular lords, chief among which were the Habsburgs, it had no charter. Watching their opportunity during the Guelph-Ghibelline conflicts between Emperor and Pope, Schwyz, Luzern and Unterwalden, i. e. Stanz and Sarnen, met in 1246–7 and formed the first Swiss league for mutual defence (cf. the uralt Bündnis, Tell, 1157). For so doing they were promptly put under the ban by Pope Innocent IV. on Aug. 28, 1247. Soon after Uri joined them and for years a stubborn fight was kept up. This struggle furnished, perhaps, the historical basis upon which tradition built up all the later stories of Habsburg cruelty told in Tell. After the extinction of the Hohenstaufens and during the long interregnum (1254–1273), the Habsburgs regained and even increased their old authority, especially in Schwyz and Unterwalden.

When Rudolf of Habsburg was elected Emperor in 1273, the situation changed. Their Vogt and enemy became their sovereign. As such he confirmed the charter of Uri in 1274, but refused to accept that of Schwyz, since it had come (1240) from an excommunicated emperor (Friedrich II. was excommunicated 1239) and violated Habsburg *private* rights. Schwyz felt the danger and urged union with Uri and Unterwalden. On Aug. 1, 1291, soon after Rudolf's death, they formed that memorable offensive and defensive alliance which is aptly called their Magna Charta, the basis of their later Confederacy. This document, preserved with religious care in Schwyz, though independent in tone, is very conservative. It pledges resistance to "attacks from without and dissensions within," and will tolerate no feudal lord, but, far from suggesting the establishment of any independent federal state, urges continued adherence to their lawful sovereign, the Emperor.

Nov. 30, 1297, Rudolf's successor, Adolf of Nassau, granted to Uri and Schwyz charters identical with that of Friedrich II., but these availed little, since Adolf was soon afterward killed in battle. His rival and successor, Rudolf's son Albrecht of Austria,[1] during whose reign the play passes, refused charters to both Schwyz and Uri. Though he was a stern, grasping ruler, determined to maintain and increase his *private* power (here using his imperial veto as a means to this end), tradition makes him much worse than he really was. He refused the charters, yet the cantons were practically reichsunmittelbar, being governed by native magistrates. Wernherr Attinghausen was Landammann in Uri, Rudolf Stauffacher in Schwyz, Rudolf Ödisried in Unterwalden. Albrecht was too busy elsewhere to send tyrannical bailiffs, nor was there any uprising during his reign. Not until 250 years after was such ascribed to his time. Murdered May 1, 1308, Albrecht was succeeded by Heinrich (VII.) of Luxemburg (1308–1313), the enemy and rival of the Habsburg Dukes of Austria, Albrecht's sons. He not only confirmed, in 1309, the charters of Schwyz and Uri, but gave a similar one to Unterwalden. The next rivals for the crown were Ludwig of Bavaria and Friedrich of Austria, son of Albrecht and grandson of Rudolf of Habsburg. The Swiss naturally declared for Ludwig, whereupon Friedrich's brother, Leopold, equipped a splendid army and set out to subdue the cantons and enforce all old

---

[1] Emperor Rudolf had, in 1278, invested his sons with the conquered duchy of Austria, the Counts of Habsburg thus becoming the Dukes of Austria. Hence allegiance to Östreich (Tell, 184) meant submission to their hated enemies the Habsburgs.

Habsburg rights. He was met on Nov. 15, 1315, in the pass of Morgarten and signally defeated by the Swiss. Ludwig confirmed their charters, and the League of 1291 was renewed at Brunnen, Dec. 9, 1315. Other cantons, Luzern, Zürich, Zug, etc., admitted later, and other victories won from Austria (Sempach, 1386; Näfels, 1388) only served to extend and strengthen the confederation thus begun.

Such the genuine history, as drawn from the scanty records preserved. It is now important to trace the gradual intermingling of this history with fable, in the direction (1) of the origin of the Confederation and (2) of the union of this story with the Tell legend.

Strange to say, nearly a hundred years pass by after Morgarten without even the slightest mention of Habsburg oppression or Swiss resistance. *Contemporary* record says nothing of the events described in the later chronicles. The supposed Scandinavian ancestry of the Swiss is first mentioned by Johann Püntiner, in 1414, who makes the Urner descendants of Alaric's Goths. Other chroniclers, impelled by local or political prejudice, change the story to suit themselves or their cantons; thus we find Swedes, Frisians, Cimbrians, 'heathen Saxons' etc., instead of Goths. The dates of the supposed settlement vary from the fourth to the ninth century. The name, too (Swiss from Schwyz), is dragged through many shrewd and amusing etymological processes.[1] It is plain that these stories, though steadfastly believed by the common folk, are pure fable. Such a Norse people in the Waldstätte would have been mentioned in the earliest records, would at least have left its impress on the language of the country. This is not to any degree the case. The fact is, no doubt, that the Alamanni, coming south from the Elbe and the Oder, kept alive the memory of their "northern

---

[1] Rochholz gives detailed accounts of these versions in his *Tell und Gessler*, pp. 64 ff., 148. Oechsli derives the name from *Suites* (gen. of *Suito*), i. e. *the men* (descendants) *of Suito*.

home," which the later legend purposely construed to mean Sweden or Frisia, lest the admission of their German descent should weaken their case in their quarrel with Habsburg.

Of bailiff tyranny and Swiss resistance the earliest records say nothing. They merely mention Morgarten as the result of Habsburg-Austrian effort to assert authority which the Swiss resented. Conrad Justinger, official chronicler of Bern, gives the first account of the cruel 'governors' (about 1420). With verbal tradition as authority, he writes of old struggles with Habsburg leading up to Morgarten, and gives two reasons for them : (1) Habsburg attempts to assert and increase authority ('mortgaged to them by the Empire') never wholly denied, but always stubbornly resisted by the Swiss ; (2) insolent conduct of Habsburg bailiffs towards worthy men and women. The statement is perfectly general ; *all particulars, names and dates are, as yet, wanting.*

The real ground for these conflicts — a political one, the extent of Habsburg rights — was soon forgotten, and only the tyranny of the bailiffs was remembered as the cause of the struggle. Meanwhile legend, ever ready to develop general statement into definite details, was not slow to invent in each canton special stories of *individual acts* of cruelty, not failing gradually to assign name and place and time. These were believed by the common people and then further embellished by whatever additions best accorded with the personal taste or local prejudice of each chronicler. Hemmerlin of Zürich records, in 1450, one of the oldest of these special stories : two brothers kill a Habsburg bailiff (no names given), living on *Lake Lowerz* in Schwyz, for having insulted their sister ; punishment is threatened, friends come to their help, the bailiff's castle is destroyed ; thereupon the Unterwaldner revolt, destroy *Burg Sarnen*, expel *Landenberg* and league with the Schwyzer. The 'White Book' of Sarnen, an anonymous chronicle of about 1470, has several of these stories, and contains, in fact, all the main features of the later legend. Each canton is represented. Thus in *Obwalden* a Vogt, Landenberg (the original *hill*, ber Landenberg, near Sarnen, has thus already become a *grim tyrant*), sends a servant to take a pair of fine oxen from a "man in the Melchi" (not named as yet); the man's son breaks the servant's finger and flees, whereupon Landenberg puts out the father's eyes and takes all his property (Tell, 561 ff.). For *Nidwalden* Hemmerlin's Lowerz incident is transferred to 'Altsellen' (for Alzellen) and becomes the later Baumgarten story (Tell, 68 ff.), though as yet *without names*. Then for *Schwyz*: '*der Gessler*' whose name is probably borrowed from the Gesslers of the neighboring Meyenberg or Aargau, covets the 'stone house of *Stoupacher*' in *Steinen;* the 'wise wife' of the latter inspires a compact (not merely with friends in Schwyz, as in the Lowerz story above, but with representatives of the other cantons) with 'him from the Melche in Underwalden' and 'one of the *Fürsts* of Uri'; these meet in league at night 'im Rübli' (Tell, 195–348, 656–745, II. 2). *Uri*, not mentioned by Hemmerlin, probably because not so controlled by Habsburg as the others, is, of course, anxious, now that the others are so honorably mentioned, to get the most credit possible for *her* part in the struggle, and claims for her hero the most important place. The Tell story, no doubt already current in Uri, is brought in *here*, and the two once totally distinct versions of the legend (Tell and Rütlibund) are quietly melted together: 'der Gessler' demands obeisance to the hat, a worthy man named *Tall* also (*Thall, der Thäll*; Tell's first appearance in the legend) refuses, is arrested and punished (here follow *particulars* of the Apfelschuß, cf. Tell, III. 3); in a great storm he escapes from Gessler's boat (IV. 1) at 'ze Tellen blatten' (evidently so named *before* Tell's escape, but later, as Tellsplatte, derived from Tell's own name); he then kills Gessler (here Uri, not Schwyz as in Hemmerlin, gets credit for killing the Vogt) near *Küssnach* (probably a reminiscence of early fourteenth century conflicts with the Ritter von Küßnach) and 'runs home.' After this 'Stoupacher's company becomes powerful,' destroys

'*Twing Uren*' and other castles in *Switz* and *Stans*' (cf. Tell,
V. 1); *Rotzberg* is taken with the help of a maiden (Tell, 1414
ff.); the Confederation is formed. Notably the stories from
Schwyz and Uri begin to assign *definite names*, but no exact
date is yet attempted. It is very probable that the still remembered struggles of 1247 and later years furnished a sort of historical germ or nucleus about which ever growing tradition built
up these tales.

This the substance of the legend. Later chronicles spread it
among wider circles and naturally changed minor points. Thus
the Tellenlied (Lucerne, about 1470) calls the famous archer
'*Wilhelm* Tell, the first Confederate' and makes his daring shot
the chief cause of the uprising which brought freedom. Melchior
Russ (Lucerne, 1482) is also thus partial to Uri and Tell; he
makes *Thell* (no longer *Tall*, *Thall*) the real founder of the
league, whereas the 'White Book' had given 'Stoupacher's
company' most of the credit. Petermann Etterlin (Lucerne,
1507) was the first to spread among wider circles the account of
Tell and 'Geissler,' or 'Gryssler,' which he had copied with few
changes from the 'White Book.' The Hübsch Spyl . . . von dem
Wilhelm Tellen, etc., a play written about 1512, adds other features: 'he of the Melchi' becomes *Erny vom Melchthal*, the
Biedermann von Altzellen is now *Cuno Abatzellen* (= Ab Altzellen,
i. e. *from Alzellen*), 'Stoupacher' is now *Stouffacher*; Tell
arouses the people and founds the league. Uri's predomi-
nance over Schwyz is assured and the account of 'Stoupacher's
company' becomes a mere episode in the now greater Tell story.
Here, too, definite dates are first attempted: in 1243 the cantons
accept Rudolf's 'protectorate'; 1296 is the date of their liberation. Johann Stumpff puts the beginning of the Habsburg
quarrel in 1260, the banishment of the governors in 1314.
Gessler sets up the hat in order to find out who were the Rütli
conspirators.

The form in which Schiller used the legend is substantially

that given by Aegidius Tschudi (or Gilg Schudy), a learned man and high official in Glarus, who diligently collected original documents, other chronicles and verbal traditions, and constructed, about 1569, from the sometimes vague and contradictory versions of the legend, especially as he found them in the ' White Book ' and in Etterlin, an account so systematic in arrangement, so vivid in description, so definite and plausible in statement as to inspire the utmost confidence. His rich fancy, fine command of language and wonderful narrative talent make the whole resemble an historical novel. He not only uses previous accounts, but generously offers his pen to record anything the cantons will send him. He " received many stories," he says, which, though obliged greatly to alter his work, " he could not refuse," since they " would enhance the honor of the Confederacy and do no harm whatever." Supplying needful details, he sends these stories forth as authentic history. He preserves the main features of the legend, but most *arbitrarily assigns names and dates :* Landenberg becomes *Beringer* von Landenberg; his victim is *Heinrich vom Melchthal*, whose son is *Arnold*, date 1307 ; Cuno Abatzellen becomes *Konrad Baumgarten von Alzellen*, date 1306 ; Gessler, coming to Uri in 1304, builds *Zwing Uri* in *Altorf ;* ' Stoupacher ' becomes first *Johans (Hans)* then *Wernher;* ' one of the Fürsts ' is now *Walther Fürst ;* other names, wherever wanting, are supplied at random from any old document. The Rütli oath, taken by ten of each canton, falls on Nov. 8, the Apfelſchuß, Nov. 18, 1307, the expulsion of the governor, Jan. 1, 1308. Other particulars were added later. Stauffacher's ' wise wife ' is named *Margaretha Herlobig* (Schiller calls her *Gertrud*) ; Tell fought at Morgarten in 1315 and was drowned, 1354, in the Schächen, while trying to rescue a child.

The legend received still more definite form (1786–95) at the hands of Schiller's friend, the eminent Swiss historian, Johannes von Müller. He made but few real changes (for instance, following an old play, he calls Gessler *Hermann* Gessler *von*

Bruneck), but he further systematized and settled what was handed down. He knew it was fiction, yet he sacrificed critical method to patriotic and rhetorical ends in order to please his people and promote his own republican views.

At last the poet, with Tschudi and Müller as chief authorities, made whatever changes seemed required by dramatic expediency, inventing thus the *roles* of *Bertha* and *Rudenz*, *Kunz von Gersau* and others, naming Tell's wife *Hedwig*, Stauffacher's, *Gertrud*, etc. Particulars are mentioned in the Notes.

The Swiss have always loved their Tell. To this day many firmly believe in him. Yet as early as 1607 scholars began to doubt his existence. During two centuries of bitter dispute, zealous Swiss partisans resorted to every means possible, even to forgeries in old documents (thus changing *Trullo* to *Tello*, *Näll* to *Thäll*), in order to establish his identity, but the searching investigations of modern scholars have shown him to be a myth, and as such the story is and must be regarded. Yet we honor him and his people none the less for the undaunted spirit he represents. He will live as long as the love of liberty has a place in the hearts of men.

Having traced to their source the stories of the Rütlibund and of the Scandinavian origin of the Swiss, it remains to inquire how the Tell myth became part of the national legend. It appears, already well developed, in the ' White Book ' of Sarnen, yet the famous archer is by no means the exclusive property of the Swiss. Very similar stories have been found among all Germanic peoples — in Denmark, Norway, Sweden, Iceland, England, Germany, etc. — as well as in India, Persia, Greece, Italy and even among the Turks and Mongolians. The target, not always an apple, is often a nut, a ring, a coin laid on the head or held in the hand. The story most like Tell is that first recorded by the Danish historian Saxo Grammaticus (died 1204): Toko (also Tokko, Palnatoki) boasted great skill in archery, whereupon his king, Harald Blaatand (Bluetooth), ordered him to shoot an apple from his son's head. Allowed only one shot, he was to die if he missed. Taking three arrows Toko commanded the boy to stand still, and hit the apple with the first arrow. When asked the purpose of the other arrows, he said they were meant for the king if he had missed the apple. Toko afterwards killed Harald, from ambush in the forest, for cruelty to himself and his friends. In the likewise thoroughly Germanic *Thidrek* (or *Wilkina*) *Saga*, the caprice of King Nidung requires the same shot of Eigil, brother of Weland the Smith; the king also receives, and this time approves, the same answer about the other arrows. These ancient stories were transplanted in quite similar form to England by the Anglo-Saxons, where they still live in the legends of Robin Hood, Adam Bell, Clym of the Clough and William of Cloudesly (cf. Percy's *Reliques*). The latter is much like Tell, save that the shot is his own suggestion and not the king's order. Any connection between *William* of Cloudesly and *Wilhelm* Tell is uncertain. The word *Tell*, both as surname and as nickname, has been variously explained; Grimm derives it from *telum*, 'arrow,' Simrock from Eigil's son Oren*del*, later Ern*thelle*, others from *dalen*, 'to be foolish,' hence Wilhelm Tell = 'William the Simple' etc., etc. The original source of these wide-spread archer stories is thought to be a nature-myth, common to all Aryan races, an allegorical struggle in which the grim tyrant *Winter* is driven from his stronghold and slain by the unerring arrows of the *Summer Sun* (beam = Strahl = arrow). Thus in Germanic mythology, Wotan struggling with the Winter tyrant at first lies bound in a cloud (the symbol of a ship), but he suddenly springs out, draws his (rain) bow and sends the deadly (thunder) bolt into the (cloud) ship and into the heart of the Winter giant. Such mythological ideas transferred to men (heroes) may readily have furnished the nucleus necessary for a Tell legend.

Whatever its origin, it is clear that the legend is common Germanic, even Aryan, property and, as such, it was, no doubt, taken to Switzerland by the original Alamannic settlers.   Later, in developed form, it served in the Swiss-Austrian campaigns and found its way into the 'White Book,' and through Tschudi into Schiller's Tell.

III. SCHILLER'S TELL.

Wilhelm Tell, Schiller's last finished drama, though composed in a few months, really occupied the poet's attention for several years.   The idea of writing the play was due, *very indirectly* however, to Goethe, who had once intended to use the subject himself.   On his third and last trip to Switzerland, late in 1797, Goethe again visited the Forest Cantons and spent some days in the Tell country.   In a letter to Schiller, Oct. 14, 1797, describing his experiences and impressions, he wrote that he had found a subject — the story of Tell — which he "felt would suit *for an epic poem*," adding that he had very carefully studied the country and people and that "good luck" must now determine "whether anything should ever come of the undertaking." Schiller was pleased and warmly encouraged this "very happy idea" of his friend.   Though much interested at first in the plan, Goethe made but little progress with his Tell.   He sketched the outlines of the first cantos, but, in doubt about the verse-form and soon busy with other things, he delayed work on it until, he confesses later, "it had lost the charm of novelty" and until *he* had lost that interest, that proper mood, always so nec-essary to his success.   He gave it up, as he had given up other subjects, neglected in the same way.

Nothing more is said of Tell until early in 1801, when the rumor became current that *Schiller* was writing a Tell, and not an epic but a *drama*.   Many inquiries were made regarding this — a work he had not yet thought of undertaking.   His conversations with Goethe, about the proposed epic, had no doubt inspired him with deeper interest in Tell.   He seems to have even then considered it a better dramatic than epic subject, and this opinion, very probably expressed to others, may have given rise to the rumor just mentioned. It is to this false report that we owe the play. Schiller himself admits as much in letters to various friends. Thus he wrote his publisher, Cotta (March, 1802), asking for "a good map of Lake Lucerne and the adjacent cantons" and confessing that this "false rumor" had called his attention to the subject and led him to read Tschudi's chronicle, which had so attracted him that he "now in all earnestness meant to write a 𝔚𝔦𝔩𝔥𝔢𝔩𝔪 𝔗𝔢𝔩𝔩." He also wrote his Dresden friend, Körner, that he had not before thought of writing such a play.

Though delayed for some time by other plans, he never lost his interest, and finally, on Aug. 25, 1803, he began his 𝔗𝔢𝔩𝔩. He soon realized the peculiar difficulties of the subject, especially to one who had never been in Switzerland and yet who felt obliged to embody as many purely local features as possible. Not in the least discouraged, however, he asked his friends again and again for maps, pictures, books and other material on Switzerland, with which to make himself thoroughly familiar with Swiss scenery and manners and character. With untiring industry, though slowly at first, he gathered from every available source [1] the information he needed. His severer historical studies in other years, his history lectures in Jena, his *Thirty Year's War*, *Revolt of the Netherlands*, *Don Carlos*, *Wallenstein*, had given him great skill in using such material, while his native energy and enthusiastic sympathy with the subject, so congenial to his own liberty-loving soul, enabled him soon to progress more rapidly. His intuitive genius was, moreover, inspired by

---

[1] He studied several maps of Lake Lucerne and, besides Tschudi's Chronicon Helveticum (his principal authority), the chronicles of Etterlin and Stumpf (see above, p. xxv), Johannes von Müller's Geschichte der Schweizerischen Eidgenossenschaft, Scheuchzer's Naturgeschichte des Schweizerlandes, Ebel's Schilderung der Gebirgsvölker der Schweiz, Fäsi's Staats- und Erdbeschreibung der helvetischen Eidgenossenschaft, Schmidt's Geschichte der Deutschen, Meiners' Briefe über die Schweiz.

the vivid descriptions of his wife, of Goethe and of other friends, who had seen Switzerland and could tell him more of places and people than he could find in books. Oct. 1, 1803 he saw *Julius Cæsar* played in Weimar and derived important indirect help from it. He wrote Goethe: "For my Tell this play was invaluable; my own little craft was floated by it; yesterday it at once put me in a most productive frame of mind."

In spite of many interruptions, business engagements, the death of Herder and the chatter of Madame de Stael, then on a visit in Weimar, he was able to send the first act to Goethe on Jan. 12, 1804. The others followed soon, and on Feb. 18, 1804 the whole was finished. Preparations were begun at once to have it played before Easter. As far as poor health permitted, Schiller superintended the rehearsals and in his absence Goethe took his place. The first performance was in the Court Theater in Weimar, March 17, 1804, and during the next few months it was given repeatedly in Berlin, Breslau and other large cities.

After all the labor and enthusiasm bestowed upon Tell, Schiller naturally expected much of the play. He had written Körner: "If the gods favor me . . . it shall be a mighty thing and shake the German stage." His hopes were more than realized. Its effect was greater than that of any of his other plays. Goethe, Körner and Iffland were delighted, Schlegel called it Schiller's finest work and praised especially its wonderful fidelity in local matters. Indeed contemporary criticism was almost universally favorable. The first edition (of seven thousand copies), issued October 1804, was soon exhausted and before the year was out a second (three thousand copies) was printed. On sending out the first edition Cotta wrote: "Tell now goes into all the world." He spoke wiser than he knew. In translations it has gone throughout the civilized world and has done more than anything else to spread the name and the fame of the Swiss and their hero as well as of its author. Above all, in Germany it is his best known, most popular play. Especially in times of political unrest, as during the wars with France, it has been a great source of patriotic enthusiasm, an inspiring lesson to the little German states to hold together — feſt unb einig — in their resistance to their common enemy.

Closely following Tschudi, Schiller has laid all the scenes of Tell on or near the shores of Lake Lucerne. Tschudi's dates, however, — for the Baumgarten incident the autumn of 1306, the Rütli oath Nov. 8, 1307, Gessler's death Nov. 19 (for 20), 1307, the destruction of Rossberg and Sarnen Jan. 1, 1308, the murder of Albrecht May 1, 1308 — are so changed that the events of the play occur on four different days, at intervals within a period of three weeks, as follows: Act I. on Oct. 28, 1307, Act II. on Nov. 8, Acts III. and IV. on *one* day, Nov. 19 (Tschudi says 18 *and* 19, by mistake for 19 and 20), Act V. on the morning of the following day.

The Swiss struggle for independence naturally attracted the Freiheitsbichter, Schiller; the same love of freedom that had once prompted the Räuber, Fiesco, Don Carlos and others found here a most congenial, yes, inspiring theme. He saw its dramatic possibilities and devoted to it the last great effort of his life. His "object," of course, was not deliberately "to teach Germany the lesson of national unity" or any other "lesson" — though many lessons have, no doubt, been drawn from the play — but simply to write a great drama, to nobly embody the noble theme, which had so strongly appealed to his own liberty-loving nature. Better than all the critics, he himself has expressed his plan and purpose in the lines he wrote on sending a manuscript copy of Tell to the Prince Elector Karl von Dalberg, brother of his old friend, the theater manager in Mannheim:

> Wenn rohe Kräfte feindlich ſich entzweien
> Und blinde Wut die Kriegesflamme ſchürt;
> Wenn ſich im Kampfe tobender Parteien
> Die Stimme der Gerechtigkeit verliert;

Wenn alle Laster schamlos sich befreien,
Wenn freche Willkür an das Heilige rührt,
Den Anker löst, an dem die Staaten hängen:
Da ist kein Stoff zu freudigen Gesängen.

Doch wenn ein Volk, das fromm die Heerden weidet,
Sich selbst genug, nicht fremden Guts begehrt,
Den Zwang abwirft, den es unwürdig leidet,
Doch selbst im Zorn die Menschlichkeit noch ehrt,
Im Glücke selbst, im Siege sich bescheidet:
Das ist unsterblich und des Liedes wert.
Und solch ein Lied darf ich dir freudig zeigen,
Du kennst's, denn alles Große ist dein eigen.

The theme of Tell is thus, briefly, the lawful and successful
uprising of a united people against cruel oppression. The hero
of the play is, therefore, not Tell alone, but the whole Swiss
people in close and faithful union against a common enemy.
Though above all the most interesting character, Tell is but one
individual element. Herein lay a great dramatic difficulty, and
one not entirely overcome, namely, to preserve the unity of
action and yet to separate the very important *individual* cause
of Tell from that of the whole people, without giving the former
undue prominence. Such separation was required, for in order to
justify the killing of Gessler, to make it appear not murder, but,
as the poet intended it, a just and necessary deed of self-defense,
Schiller felt, and so did Goethe, that " Tell must stand alone in
the drama, that his cause is and must remain a private one,
entirely without political character, till at the close it coincides
with that of the people," as represented by the men of the Rütli.
Moreover Tell, the individual, must be a type of the whole Swiss
people, a simple-hearted nature folk, brave yet gentle, slow to
speak, but quick to act when once aroused. For such dramatic
reasons, therefore, Tell is made a quiet unobtrusive man of few
words, unwilling to be present at the Rütli or to take part in any
of the deliberations of his friends (which, of course, would have

lent his later action a political character), preferring to pursue
the even tenor of his way, so long as he is let alone, yet strong
in his love of liberty, resolute and ready to fight, when he must,
in defense of his home, his friends, his honor or his rights.
With great physical strength, he is daring and fearless, yet
modest and gentle as he is brave. He shows the tenderest love
for wife and children, and with most unselfish sympathy is ever
ready to help his neighbor in distress, without asking why or
wherefore. His skillful hand, his generous heart, his blameless
life win him the love and admiration of all, who know him : Es
giebt nicht zwei wie der ist im Gebirge ! (Tell, 164.)

While in Tell we have thus the purest type of the Swiss
nature in general, other characters give us types of different and
special classes, occupations, rank and age in society. Thus
Melchthal, Stauffacher and Fürst are splendid types of the better
classes of citizens; each represents one of the three cantons —
Unterwalden, Schwyz and Uri — each, too, a different age and
temper — rash, excitable youth, calm, mature manhood, and
anxious, over-cautious age. Rudenz and Attinghausen stand for
the young and old among the native Swiss nobility; the latter
a class living like loved patriarchs among their people, the
former a class, young and ambitious, coquetting at first with
Austria, but finally awakening to their true duty and character
and supporting the people against a common enemy. The
women are especially well portrayed. Gertrud is the ' pleasant
hostess,' the courageous, patriotic matron, standing in telling
contrast by the side of her hesitating, less confident husband,
Stauffacher. Hedwig, the anxious wife, the loving mother,
whose chief concern is the welfare and safety of husband and
children, ever seeks to restrain the daring, over-confident Tell.
Bertha is the high-minded, fearless girl, who, though noble in
rank and related to Gessler, gives her sympathy to her people
and her heart to the lover whom she brings back to his country
and his duty. All three, and in them all classes of Swiss

womanhood, maidens, wives and mothers, noble and peasant alike, resent and resist the tyrants' oppression.

Gessler, the governor, is the worst enemy of Swiss liberty. He is a typical tyrant, cowardly, coarse and cruel, faithless and vindictive, — a stranger to every impulse of gentleness and kindness. He is the stern, inflexible ruler, with great political plans for extending the power of Habsburg, and determined to carry them out, though it means the stifling of every impulse of liberty in the Swiss people. Angered by their resistance, he resorts to the most cruel and inhuman means of enforcing his authority.

The lower classes, too, hunters, herdsmen, laborers and even serfs, all have their types, well drawn and true to nature, in Werni, Kuoni and the rest, and all making common cause against their common enemy. This union of all classes only makes the justice of their cause the more evident. It is not the rash hot-headedness of youth, not the mere discontent of laborers — it is the common uprising of a whole people, whose most sacred rights have been ruthlessly outraged.

In its dramatic character the play is quite too serious for comedy, nor is it altogether tragedy, for it ends too happily; its theme is, moreover, too epic, and its personal action and passion too often secondary to the general welfare. An individual is better than a people as the hero of a tragedy. Schiller wisely called it ein Schauspiel — ' an epic drama, in which the force of outward circumstances and conditions as well as of innate character determines the action' (Carriere).

As a piece of art Tell is, Wallenstein not excepted, the poet's best work. The first act, in Goethe's opinion ' not a first act simply, but a whole play in itself,' has always been considered a masterpiece of dramatic ' exposition,' or preface, setting forth, as it does, at once and most clearly the conditions under which the play is to proceed. The lyric introduction shows at a glance the idyllic character of country and people and induces just the proper mood of appreciative sympathy for what follows. We

then meet the chief actors and through them, as types, learn how
the different classes of Swiss people feel and think; we see the
just cause of their discontent in the ever increasing cruelty of the
governors in every canton, as well as their determined courage
and their ever growing purpose to resist.   A passing glance at
Tell, in his prompt rescue of Baumgarten, suffices to show his
character and to inspire confidence in him for the future.   Act
II. scene 1, put in II. and not in I. on account of its length,
also belongs to the 'exposition' and shows the attitude of the
Swiss nobility towards the people's cause.   Thus all classes, in
all three cantons, feel the weight of the tyrannical yoke, and
three representative men, Fürst, Stauffacher and Melchthal,
have combined to shake it off.   Thus, side by side, the poet
develops the plans and character of Volf and Vögte; sympathy
for the people is at once awakened, while the introduction
of the younger nobility, in their adherence to Austria (Act
II. 1), adds a new element of uncertainty and danger for
the people's cause, which invests the already doubtful issue with
still further interest.   The plan thus outlined is carried out in a
manner worthy of the poet and his great theme.   Many passages
in Tell equal in force and beauty anything in German literature,
while contrast, rhyme and scenic arrangement are frequently and
most skillfully used to show increasing intensity of feeling and to
heighten the dramatic effect.   Nowhere has Schiller shown the
power of his splendid genius so well as in his faithful reproduc-
tion in Tell of purely local features of Swiss scenery and character.   The glowing descriptions of others were helpful, but the
secret of his success lies rather in his patient study of even the
smallest details, in his intuitive appreciation of his sources, and
in his wonderful skill in using this material.   His rich imagination freely invented what he found wanting, but in many places
he follows his sources so closely as to transfer to his play not
only the subject-matter of whole passages, but to adopt even the
old and peculiar words and all the native simplicity of the Swiss

dialect, thus securing, in spite of unusual difficulties, the most natural local coloring. "One who has read Teℓℓ and then visits Switzerland feels as if he had already seen it all, and that which seemed an ideal picture of the imagination, becomes actual and living reality" (Carriere).

The play has its faults, of course. Chief among these has been urged the want of dramatic unity, due to the relation of the individual cause of Tell to that of the whole people. The poet's sources, however, and not his dramatic method, are to blame, for, as we have seen, the old chronicles present the story of Tell in very loose connection with that of the Rütli men. Within the play there are really three smaller dramas, for convenience named from their chief characters, the Rütli (or People's) drama, the Tell drama and the Rudenz drama. The first begins with accounts of suffering in the three cantons (I.), has its climax in the Rütli meeting (II. 2), and ends with sweeping away the last remnants of tyranny in Act V.; the second, beginning with Tell's rescue of Baumgarten (I. 1), developed in the scene of the Apfelſchuß (III. 3), has its climax in the death of Gessler (IV. 3); the third begins with the allegiance of Rudenz to Austria (II. 1), is developed by Bertha (III. 2), and ends with the storming of Rossberg and Sarnen (IV. 2); all three coincide at the end (V. 3), (Kuenen). Schiller attempted the dramatic union of these three by giving each set of characters (1) a common enemy, the tyrants, (2) a common object, resistance and the freedom of the cantons, (3) a common motive, self defense, and lastly by bringing them together at important points and uniting them all at the end. Though the difficulty was not entirely overcome, so that some parts of the play are but loosely connected with others, we must wonder at the skill with which it was met. "It is as if three independent springs were finally brought together into one stream" (Kluge).

The so-called "Bertha-Rudenz episode," Schiller's own invention, has been considered unnecessary, and condemned as lack-

ing in force and animation and unimportant for the dramatic
development.   True, it is weaker than other parts of the play,
yet it is more than an 'episode,' it is skillfully woven into the
whole action of the play.   This romantic love idyll brightens
and relieves the grim seriousness of the action, and both characters are needed as types of the younger Swiss nobility.   Moreover, Bertha wins over Rudenz to the people's cause, he lends
material assistance in resisting the tyrant, and is the first to
abolish serfdom among his own dependents.   The character of
Attinghausen, too, one of the finest in the play, would lose
much of its force and interest if Rudenz were absent   He is
indeed an essential part of that action. (Buchheim, Tell, xxxiv.)

The killing of Gessler has been criticized as a cowardly as-
sassination.   That it was not such must be evident from his
own inhuman cruelty, from the logic of Tell's monologue, and
from the interview with Parricida (V. 1).   Though he shudders
at it, Tell believes that he may, yes, must kill the tyrant, not for
political or patriotic reasons, — such are not mentioned once —
but in lawful self defense, to protect his home and family, and to
keep a sacred oath, wrung from him in the agony of most
terrible provocation.   Tell is no coward, no assassin; he merely
planned his attack in a manner certain to succeed.

The addition of Act V., with its less animated action, has
been called a mistake.   Some think the play should end with
Gessler's death.   Yet Act V. seems necessary, for, in the capture
of the castles, it shows the *results* of the work of resistance, the
certainty that Swiss liberty is complete, while, in the news of
the Emperor's death, it brings the assurance that their independence may be permanently safe from outside interference.   Tell's
interview with Parricida, the Emperor's murderer, was intended,
by sharp contrast, to excuse and justify the one and to condemn
the other.   Yet it seems out of place; the provocation to Tell's
deed is its own defense, he needs no further justification, and the
scene is greatly weakened by Parricida's presence.

Such are the merits, such the faults of Tell. In summing up an estimate of the play, Gustav Freytag has aptly said : "Whatever may be said against the dramatic structure of Tell, there is a charm in the individual scenes (as I. 1, 3, III. 1, 3, II. 2 etc.) that ever compels admiration," while Börne remarked that "the faults of the play are the virtues of the poet." What is lost in loose dramatic structure is gained in the wonderful power and beauty of the individual scenes.

As the poet of freedom, Schiller has achieved in Tell his greatest triumph. More than any of his other plays does it appeal to the great masses of German people ; more than all the others has it furnished favorite sayings, almost become proverbs, ever remembered and quoted by prince and peasant alike ; in it the prose of his early dramas has given place to his best, his noblest verse ; the extravagant rhetoric and unreasonable theories of the young enthusiast have here become the calmer thought, the riper convictions of the mature man ; the narrower social or political freedom which formed the theme of Fiesco, Kabale und Liebe, Carlos and others, has been broadened, till freedom everywhere — in the home, in society, in thought, in government — the freedom of a whole people is the theme of Tell ; the effort of individual fanatics or revolutionists to overthrow all law and order in attaining an imaginary freedom has become in Tell the uprising of a whole brave and patient people to defend and preserve their real liberty from the attacks of foreign tyrants.

ERZÄHLEN WIRD MA
VON DEM SCHÜZEN
TELL

SO LANG DIE BERGE
STEHN AUF IHREM
GRUNDE

WILHELM TELL

1895

THE NEW TELL STATUE AT ALTORF. Cf. ll. 2041–2.

Wilhelm Tell

Schauspiel

von

Schiller.

———

Zum Neujahrsgeschenk

auf 1805.

———

Tübingen,

in der J. G. Cotta'schen Buchhandlung.

1804.

Personen.

Hermann Geßler, Reichsvogt in Schwyz und Uri.
Werner, Freiherr von Attinghausen, Bannerherr.
Ulrich von Rudenz, sein Neffe.

Werner Stauffacher,
Konrad Hunn,
Itel Reding,
Hans auf der Mauer,
Jörg im Hofe,
Ulrich der Schmid,
Jost von Weiler,
} Landleute aus Schwyz.

Walther Fürst,
Wilhelm Tell,
Rösselmann, der Pfarrer,
Petermann, der Sigrist,
Kuoni, der Hirt,
Werni, der Jäger,
Ruodi, der Fischer,
} aus Uri.

Arnold vom Melchthal,
Konrad Baumgarten,
Meier von Sarnen,
Struth von Winkelried,
Klaus von der Flüe,
Burkhart am Bühel,
Arnold von Sewa,
} aus Unterwalden.

Pfeifer von Luzern.
Kunz von Gersau.
Jenni, Fischerknabe.
Seppi, Hirtenknabe.

Perſonen.

Gertrud, Stauffachers Gattin.
Hedwig, Tells Gattin, Fürſts Tochter.
Bertha von Bruneck, eine reiche Erbin.
Armgard,
Mechthild, } Bäuerinnen.
Elsbeth,
Hildegard,
Walther, } Tells Knaben.
Wilhelm,
Frießhardt, } Söldner.
Leuthold,
Rudolph der Harras, Geßlers Stallmeiſter.
Johannes Parricida, Herzog von Schwaben.
Stüſſi, der Flurſchütz.
Der Stier von Uri.
Ein Reichsbote.
Fronvogt.
Meiſter Steinmetz, Geſellen und Handlanger.
Öffentliche Ausrufer.
Barmherzige Brüder.
Geßleriſche und Landenbergiſche Reiter.

Viele Landleute, Männer und Weiber aus den Waldſtätten.

Jägerliedchen für
Walther Sale
mit Actus III. anzufangen.

Mit dem Pfeil, dem Bogen
Durch Gebirg und Thal
Kommt der Schütz gezogen,
Früh im Morgenstrahl!

Wie im Reich der Lüfte
König ist der Weih.
Durch Gebirg und Klüfte
Herrscht der Schütze frei.

Ihm gehört das Weite,
Was sein Pfeil erreicht,
Das ist seine Beute,
Was da fleugt und kreucht.

Erster Aufzug.

Erste Scene.

Hohes Felsenufer des Vierwaldstättersees, Schwyz gegenüber.

Der See macht eine Bucht ins Land, eine Hütte ist unweit dem Ufer, Fischerknabe fährt sich in einem Kahn. Über den See hinweg sieht man die grünen Matten, Dörfer und Höfe von Schwyz im hellen Sonnenschein liegen. Zur Linken des Zuschauers zeigen sich die Spitzen des Haken, mit Wolken umgeben; zur Rechten im fernen Hintergrund sieht man die Eisgebirge. Noch ehe der Vorhang aufgeht, hört man den Kuhreihen und das harmonische Geläut der Herdenglocken, welches sich auch bei eröffneter Scene noch eine Zeit lang fortsetzt.

Fischerknabe (singt im Kahn).

Melodie des Kuhreihens.

Es lächelt der See, er ladet zum Bade,
Der Knabe schlief ein am grünen Gestade,
    Da hört er ein Klingen,
    Wie Flöten so süß,
    Wie Stimmen der Engel
    Im Paradies.
Und wie er erwachet in seliger Lust,
Da spülen die Wasser ihm um die Brust,
    Und es ruft aus den Tiefen:
    Lieb Knabe, bist **mein**!
    Ich locke den Schläfer,
    Ich zieh' ihn herein.

5

Hirt (auf dem Berge).

Variation des Kuhreihens.

Ihr Matten, lebt wohl,
Ihr sonnigen Weiden!
15   Der Senne muß scheiden,
Der Sommer ist hin.

Wir fahren zu Berg, wir kommen wieder,
Wenn der Kuckuck ruft, wenn erwachen die Lieder,
Wenn mit Blumen die Erde sich kleidet neu,
20 Wenn die Brünnlein fließen im lieblichen Mai.
Ihr Matten, lebt wohl,
Ihr sonnigen Weiden!
Der Senne muß scheiden,
Der Sommer ist hin.

Alpenjäger

(erscheint gegenüber auf der Höhe des Felsens).

Zweite Variation.

25   Es donnern die Höhen, es zittert der Steg,
Nicht grauet dem Schützen auf schwindlichtem Weg;
Er schreitet verwegen
Auf Feldern von Eis;
Da pranget kein Frühling,
30   Da grünet kein Reis;
Und unter den Füßen ein neblichtes Meer,
Erkennt er die Städte der Menschen nicht mehr;
Durch den Riß nur der Wolken
Erblickt er die Welt,
35   Tief unter den Wassern
Das grünende Feld.

(Die Landschaft verändert sich, man hört ein dumpfes Krachen von
den Bergen, Schatten von Wolken laufen über die Gegend.)

Ruodi der Fischer kommt aus der Hütte, Werni der Jäger

steigt vom Felsen, Kuoni der Hirt kommt mit dem Melknapf auf
der Schulter. Seppi sein Handbube, folgt ihm.

Ruodi.

Mach' hurtig, Jenni! Zieh die Naue ein!
Der graue Thalvogt kommt, dumpf brüllt der Firn,
Der Mythenstein zieht seine Haube an,
40 Und kalt her bläst es aus dem Wetterloch;
Der Sturm, ich mein', wird da sein, eh' wir's denken.

Kuoni.

's kommt Regen, Fährmann. Meine Schafe fressen
Mit Begierde Gras, und Wächter scharrt die Erde.

Werni.

Die Fische springen, und das Wasserhuhn
45 Taucht unter. Ein Gewitter ist im Anzug.

Kuoni (zum Buben).

Lug, Seppi, ob das Vieh sich nicht verlaufen.

Seppi.

Die braune Lisel kenn' ich am Geläut.

Kuoni.

So fehlt uns keine mehr, die geht am weitsten.

Ruodi.

Ihr habt ein schön Geläute, Meister Hirt.

Werni.

50 Und schmuckes Vieh — Ist's Euer eignes, Landsmann?

Kuoni.

Bin nit so reich — 's ist meines gnäd'gen Herrn,
Des Attinghäusers, und mir zugezählt.

Ruodi.

Wie schön der Kuh das Band zu Halse steht!

Kuoni.

Das weiß sie auch, daß sie den Reihen führt,
55 Und nähm' ich ihr's, sie hörte auf zu fressen.

Ruodi.

Ihr seid nicht klug! Ein unvernünft'ges Vieh—

Werni.

Ist bald gesagt. Das Tier hat auch Vernunft,
Das wissen wir, die wir die Gemsen jagen.
Die stellen klug, wo sie zur Weide gehn,
60 'ne Vorhut aus, die spitzt das Ohr und warnet
Mit heller Pfeise, wenn der Jäger naht.

Ruodi (zum Hirten).

Treibt Ihr jetzt heim?

Kuoni.

                    Die Alp ist abgeweidet.

Werni.

Glückse'ge Heimkehr, Senn!

Kuoni.

                        Die wünsch' ich Euch;
Von Eurer Fahrt kehrt sich's nicht immer wieder.

Ruodi.

65 Dort kommt ein Mann in voller Hast gelaufen.

Werni.

Ich kenn' ihn, 's ist der Baumgart von Alzellen.

Konrad Baumgarten (atemlos hereinstürzend).

Baumgarten.

Um Gottes willen, Fährmann, Euren Kahn!

Ruodi.

Nun, nun, was giebt's so eilig?

Baumgarten.

Bindet los!
Ihr rettet mich vom Tode! Setzt mich über!

Kuoni.

70 Landsmann, was habt Ihr?

Werni.

Wer verfolgt Euch denn?

Baumgarten (zum Fischer).

Eilt, eilt, sie sind mir dicht schon an den Fersen!
Des Landvogts Reiter kommen hinter mir;
Ich bin ein Mann des Tods, wenn sie mich greifen.

Ruodi.

Warum verfolgen Euch die Reisigen?

Baumgarten.

75 Erst rettet mich, und dann steh' ich Euch Rede.

Werni.

Ihr seid mit Blut befleckt, was hat's gegeben?

Baumgarten.

Des Kaisers Burgvogt, der auf Roßberg saß —

Kuoni.

Der Wolfenschießen! Läßt Euch d e r verfolgen?

Baumgarten.

D e r schadet nicht mehr, ich hab' ihn erschlagen.

Alle (fahren zurück).

80 Gott sei Euch gnädig! Was habt Ihr gethan?

Baumgarten.

Was jeder freie Mann an meinem Platz!
Mein gutes Hausrecht hab' ich ausgeübt

Am Schänder meiner Ehr' und meines Weibes.

Kuoni.

Hat Euch der Burgvogt an der Ehr' geschädigt?

Baumgarten.

85 Daß er sein bös Gelüsten nicht vollbracht,
Hat Gott und meine gute Axt verhütet.

Werni.

Ihr habt ihm mit der Axt den Kopf zerspalten?

Kuoni.

O, laßt uns alles hören, Ihr habt Zeit,
Bis er den Kahn vom Ufer losgebunden.

Baumgarten.

90 Ich hatte Holz gefällt im Wald, da kommt
Mein Weib gelaufen in der Angst des Todes.
„Der Burgvogt lieg' in meinem Haus, er hab'
Ihr anbefohlen, ihm ein Bad zu rüsten.
Drauf hab' er Ungebührliches von ihr
95 Verlangt, sie sei entsprungen, mich zu suchen."
Da lief ich frisch hinzu, so wie ich war,
Und mit der Axt hab' ich ihm 's Bad gesegnet.

Werni.

Ihr thatet wohl, kein Mensch kann Euch drum schelten.

Kuoni.

Der Wüterich! Der hat nun seinen Lohn!
100 Hat's lang' verdient ums Volk von Unterwalden.

Baumgarten.

Die That ward ruchtbar; mir wird nachgesetzt —
Indem wir sprechen — Gott — verrinnt die Zeit —

(Es fängt an zu donnern.)

Kuoni.

Frisch, Fährmann — schaff' den Biedermann hinüber!

Ruodi.

Geht nicht. Ein schweres Ungewitter ist
105 Im Anzug. Ihr müßt warten.

Baumgarten.

Heil'ger Gott!
Ich kann nicht warten. Jeder Aufschub tötet —

Kuoni (zum Fischer).

Greif an mit Gott! Dem Nächsten muß man helfen;
Es kann uns allen Gleiches ja begegnen.

(Brausen und Donnern.)

Ruodi.

Der Föhn ist los, Ihr seht wie hoch der See geht;
110 Ich kann nicht steuern gegen Sturm und Wellen.

Baumgarten (umfaßt seine Kniee).

So helf' Euch Gott, wie Ihr Euch mein erbarmet —

Werni.

Es geht ums Leben. Sei barmherzig, Fährmann!

Kuoni.

's ist ein Hausvater und hat Weib und Kinder!

(Wiederholte Donnerschläge.)

Ruodi.

Was? Ich hab' auch ein Leben zu verlieren,
115 Hab' Weib und Kind daheim, wie er — Seht hin,
Wie's brandet, wie es wogt und Wirbel zieht
Und alle Wasser aufrührt in der Tiefe.
— Ich wollte gern den Biedermann erretten;
Doch es ist rein unmöglich, Ihr seht selbst.

Baumgarten (noch auf den Knieen).

120 So muß ich fallen in des Feindes Hand,
     Das nahe Rettungsufer im Gesichte!
     — Dort liegt's! Ich kann's erreichen mit den Augen,
     Hinüberdringen kann der Stimme Schall,
     Da ist der Kahn, der mich hinübertrüge,
125 Und muß hier liegen, hilflos, und verzagen!

Kuoni.

Seht, wer da kommt!

Werni.

              Es ist der Tell aus Bürglen.

Tell mit der Armbrust.

Tell.

Wer ist der Mann, der hier um Hilfe fleht?

Kuoni.

's ist ein Alzeller Mann; er hat sein' Ehr'
Verteidigt und den Wolfenschieß erschlagen,
130 Des Königs Burgvogt, der auf Roßberg saß —
     Des Landvogts Reiter sind ihm auf den Fersen.
     Er fleht den Schiffer um die Überfahrt;
     Der fürcht't sich vor dem Sturm und will nicht fahren.

Ruodi.

Da ist der Tell, er führt das Ruder auch,
135 Der soll mir's zeugen, ob die Fahrt zu wagen.

Tell.

Wo's not thut, Fährmann, läßt sich alles wagen.
     (Heftige Donnerschläge, der See rauscht auf.)

Ruodi.

Ich soll mich in den Höllenrachen stürzen?
Das thäte keiner, der bei Sinnen ist.

Baumgarten auf der Flucht

Face p. 12.

Tell.

Der brave Mann denkt an sich selbst zuletzt.
140 Vertrau' auf Gott und rette den Bedrängten!

Ruodi.

Vom sichern Port läßt sich's gemächlich raten.
Da ist der Kahn, und dort der See! Versucht's!

Tell.

Der See kann sich, der Landvogt nicht erbarmen.
Versuch' es, Fährmann!

Hirten und Jäger.

Rett' ihn! Rett' ihn! Rett' ihn!

Ruodi.

145 Und wär's mein Bruder und mein leiblich Kind,
Es kann nicht sein; 's ist heut' Simons und Judä,
Da rast der See und will sein Opfer haben.

Tell.

Mit eitler Rede wird hier nichts geschafft;
Die Stunde dringt, dem Mann muß Hilfe werden.
150 Sprich, Fährmann, willst du fahren?

Ruodi.

Nein, nicht ich!

Tell.

In Gottes Namen denn! Gieb her den Kahn!
Ich will's mit meiner schwachen Kraft versuchen.

Kuoni.

Ha, wackrer Tell!

Werni.

Das gleicht dem Weidgesellen!

Baumgarten.

Mein Retter seid Ihr und mein Engel, Tell!

Tell.

155 Wohl aus des Vogts Gewalt errett' ich Euch,
Aus Sturmes Nöten muß ein Andrer helfen.
Doch besser ist's, Ihr fallt in Gottes Hand
Als in der Menschen!

(Zu dem Hirten.)

Landsmann, tröstet Ihr
Mein Weib, wenn mir was Menschliches begegnet.
160 Ich hab' gethan, was ich nicht lassen konnte.

(Er springt in den Kahn.)

Kuoni (zum Fischer).

Ihr seid ein Meister Steuermann. Was sich
Der Tell getraut, das konntet I h r nicht wagen?

Ruodi.

Wohl beßre Männer thun's dem Tell nicht nach,
Es giebt nicht zwei, wie der ist, im Gebirge.

Werni (ist auf den Fels gestiegen).

165 Er stößt schon ab. Gott helf' dir, braver Schwimmer!
Sieh, wie das Schifflein auf den Wellen schwankt!

Kuoni (am Ufer).

Die Flut geht drüber weg — Ich seh's nicht mehr.
Doch, halt, da ist es wieder! Kräftiglich
Arbeitet sich der Wackre durch die Brandung.

Seppi.

170 Des Landvogts Reiter kommen angesprengt.

Kuoni.

Weiß Gott, sie sind's! Das war Hilf' in der Not.

Ein Trupp Landenbergischer Reiter.

Erster Reiter.

Den Mörder gebt heraus, den ihr verborgen!

Zweiter.

Des Wegs kam er, umsonst verhehlt ihr ihn.

Kuoni und Ruodi.

Wen meint ihr, Reiter?

Erster Reiter (entdeckt den Nachen).

Ha, was seh' ich! Teufel!

Werni (oben).

175 Ist's der im Nachen, den ihr sucht? — Reit zu!
Wenn ihr frisch beilegt, holt ihr ihn noch ein.

Zweiter.

Verwünscht! Er ist entwischt.

Erster (zum Hirten und Fischer).

Ihr habt ihm fortgeholfen.

Ihr sollt uns büßen — Fallt in ihre Herde!
Die Hütte reißet ein, brennt und schlagt nieder!

(Eilen fort.)

Seppi (stürzt nach).

180 O meine Lämmer!

Kuoni (folgt).

Weh mir! meine Herde!

Werni.

Die Wütriche!

Ruodi   (ringt die Hände).

Gerechtigkeit des Himmels!
Wann wird der Retter kommen diesem Lande?

(Folgt ihnen.)

Zweite Scene.

Zu Steinen in Schwyz.   Eine Linde vor des Stauffachers Hause an der
Landstraße, nächst der Brücke.

Werner Stauffacher, Pfeifer von Luzern
kommen im Gespräch.

Pfeifer.

Ja, ja, Herr Stauffacher, wie ich Euch sagte.
Schwört nicht zu Östreich, wenn Ihr's könnt vermeiden.
185 Haltet fest am Reich und wacker, wie bisher.
Gott schirme Euch bei Eurer alten Freiheit!

(Drückt ihm herzlich die Hand und will gehen.)

Stauffacher.

Bleibt doch, bis meine Wirtin kommt — Ihr seid
Mein Gast zu Schwyz, ich in Luzern der Eure.

Pfeifer.

Viel Dank! Muß heute Gersau noch erreichen.
190 — Was Ihr auch Schweres mögt zu leiden haben
Von Eurer Vögte Geiz und Übermut,
Tragt's in Geduld! Es kann sich ändern, schnell,
Ein andrer Kaiser kann ans Reich gelangen.
Seid Ihr erst Österreichs, seid Ihr's auf immer.

Er geht ab. Stauffacher setzt sich kummervoll auf eine Bank unter
der Linde. So findet ihn Gertrud, seine Frau, die sich neben
ihn stellt und ihn eine Zeit lang schweigend betrachtet.

Gertrud.

195 So ernst, mein Freund? Ich kenne dich nicht mehr.
Schon viele Tage seh' ich's schweigend an,
Wie finstrer Trübsinn deine Stirne furcht.
Auf deinem Herzen drückt ein still Gebresten;
Vertrau' es mir; ich bin dein treues Weib,
200 Und meine Hälfte fordr' ich deines Grams.

(Stauffacher reicht ihr die Hand und schweigt.)

Was kann dein Herz beklemmen, sag' es mir.
Gesegnet ist dein Fleiß, dein Glücksstand blüht,
Voll sind die Scheunen, und der Rinder Scharen,
Der glatten Pferde wohlgenährte Zucht
205 Ist von den Bergen glücklich heimgebracht
Zur Winterung in den bequemen Ställen.
— Da steht dein Haus, reich wie ein Edelsitz;
Von schönem Stammholz ist es neu gezimmert
Und nach dem Richtmaß ordentlich gefügt;
210 Von vielen Fenstern glänzt es wohnlich, hell;
Mit bunten Wappenschildern ist's bemalt
Und weisen Sprüchen, die der Wandersmann
Verweilend liest und ihren Sinn bewundert.

Stauffacher.

Wohl steht das Haus gezimmert und gefügt,
215 Doch, ach — es wankt der Grund, auf dem wir bauten.

Gertrud.

Mein Werner, sage, wie verstehst du das?

Stauffacher.

Vor dieser Linde saß ich jüngst wie heut',
Das schön Vollbrachte freudig überdenkend,
Da kam daher von Küßnacht, seiner Burg,
220 Der Vogt mit seinen Reisigen geritten.

Vor diesem Hause hielt er wundernd an;
Doch ich erhob mich schnell, und unterwürfig,
Wie sich's gebührt, trat ich dem Herrn entgegen,
Der uns des Kaisers richterliche Macht
225 Vorstellt im Lande. „Wessen ist dies Haus?"
Fragt' er bösmeinend, denn er wußt' es wohl.
Doch schnell besonnen ich entgegn' ihm so:
„Dies Haus, Herr Vogt, ist meines Herrn des Kaisers,
Und Eures und mein Lehen" — Da versetzt er:
230 „Ich bin Regent im Land an Kaisers Statt
Und will nicht, daß der Bauer Häuser baue
Auf seine eigne Hand und also frei
Hinleb', als ob er Herr wär' in dem Lande;
Ich werd' mich unterstehn, Euch das zu wehren."
235 Dies sagend, ritt er trutziglich von dannen,
Ich aber blieb mit kummervoller Seele,
Das Wort bedenkend, das der Böse sprach.

Gertrud.

Mein lieber Herr und Ehewirt! Magst du
Ein redlich Wort von deinem Weib vernehmen?
240 Des edeln Ibergs Tochter rühm' ich mich,
Des vielerfahrnen Manns. Wir Schwestern saßen,
Die Wolle spinnend, in den langen Nächten,
Wenn bei dem Vater sich des Volkes Häupter
•   Versammelten, die Pergamente lasen
245 Der alten Kaiser, und des Landes Wohl
Bedachten in vernünftigem Gespräch.
Aufmerkend hört' ich da manch kluges Wort,
Was der Verständ'ge denkt, der Gute wünscht,
Und still im Herzen hab' ich mir's bewahrt.
250 So höre denn und acht' auf meine Rede!

Denn, was dich preßte, sieh, das wußt' ich längst.
— Dir grollt der Landvogt, möchte gern dir schaden,
Denn du bist ihm ein Hindernis, daß sich
Der Schwyzer nicht dem neuen Fürstenhaus
255 Will unterwerfen, sondern treu und fest
Beim Reich beharren, wie die würdigen
Altvordern es gehalten und gethan.—
Ist's nicht so, Werner? Sag' es, wenn ich lüge!

Stauffacher.

So ist's, das ist des Geßlers Groll auf mich.

Gertrud.

260 Er ist dir neidisch, weil du glücklich wohnst,
Ein freier Mann auf deinem eignen Erb'
— Denn er hat keins. Vom Kaiser selbst und Reich
Trägst du dies Haus zu Lehn; du darfst es zeigen,
So gut der Reichsfürst seine Länder zeigt;
265 Denn über dir erkennst du keinen Herrn
Als nur den Höchsten in der Christenheit —
Er ist ein jüngrer Sohn nur seines Hauses,
Nichts nennt er sein als seinen Rittermantel;
Drum sieht er jedes Biedermannes Glück
270 Mit scheelen Augen gift'ger Mißgunst an.
Dir hat er längst den Untergang geschworen —
Noch stehst du unversehrt — Willst du erwarten,
Bis er die böse Lust an dir gebüßt?
Der kluge Mann baut vor.

Stauffacher.

Was ist zu thun?

Gertrud (tritt näher).

275 So höre meinen Rat! Du weißt, wie hier
Zu Schwyz sich alle Redlichen beklagen

Ob dieses Landvogts Geiz und Wüterei.
So zweifle nicht, daß sie dort drüben auch
In Unterwalden und im Urner Land
280 Des Dranges müd' sind und des harten Jochs —
Denn wie der Geßler hier, so schafft es frech
Der Landenberger drüben überm See —
Es kommt kein Fischerkahn zu uns herüber,
Der nicht ein neues Unheil und Gewalt=
285 Beginnen von den Vögten uns verkündet.
Drum thät' es gut, daß euer etliche,
Die's redlich meinen, still zu Rate gingen,
Wie man des Drucks sich möcht' erledigen;
So acht' ich wohl, Gott würd' euch nicht verlassen
290 Und der gerechten Sache gnädig sein —
Hast du in Uri keinen Gastfreund, sprich,
Dem du dein Herz magst redlich offenbaren?

Stauffacher.

Der wackern Männer kenn' ich viele dort
Und angesehen große Herrenleute,
295 Die mir geheim sind und gar wohl vertraut.

(Er steht auf.)

Frau, welchen Sturm gefährlicher Gedanken
Weckst du mir in der stillen Brust! Mein Innerstes
Kehrst du ans Licht des Tages mir entgegen,
Und was ich mir zu denken still verbot,
300 Du sprichst's mit leichter Zunge kecklich aus.
— Hast du auch wohl bedacht, was du mir rätst?
Die wilde Zwietracht und den Klang der Waffen
Rufst du in dieses friedgewohnte Thal —
Wir wagten es, ein schwaches Volk der Hirten,
305 In Kampf zu gehen mit dem Herrn der Welt?

Der gute Schein nur ist's, worauf sie warten,
Um loszulassen auf dies arme Land
Die wilden Horden ihrer Kriegesmacht,
Darin zu schalten mit des Siegers Rechten
310 Und unterm Schein gerechter Züchtigung
Die alten Freiheitsbriefe zu vertilgen.

Gertrud.

Ihr seid a u c h Männer, wisset eure Art
Zu führen, und dem Mutigen hilft Gott!

Stauffacher.

O Weib! Ein furchtbar wütend Schrecknis ist
315 Der Krieg; die Herde schlägt er und den Hirten.

Gertrud.

Ertragen muß man, was der Himmel sendet;
Unbilliges erträgt kein edles Herz.

Stauffacher.

Dies Haus erfreut dich, das wir neu erbauten.
Der Krieg, der ungeheure, brennt es nieder.

Gertrud.

320 Wüßt' ich mein Herz an zeitlich Gut gefesselt,
Den Brand wärf' ich hinein mit eigner Hand.

Stauffacher.

Du glaubst an Menschlichkeit! Es schont der Krieg
Auch nicht das zarte Kindlein in der Wiege.

Gertrud.

Die Unschuld hat im Himmel einen Freund!
325 — Sieh vorwärts, Werner, und nicht hinter dich!

Stauffacher.

Wir Männer können tapfer fechtend sterben;

Welch Schicksal aber wird das eure sein?

Gertrud.

Die letzte Wahl steht auch dem Schwächsten offen,
Ein Sprung von dieser Brücke macht mich frei.

Stauffacher (stürzt in ihre Arme).

330 Wer solch ein Herz an seinen Busen drückt,
Der kann für Herd und Hof mit Freuden fechten,
Und keines Königs Heermacht fürchtet er —
Nach Uri fahr' ich stehnden Fußes gleich,
Dort lebt ein Gastfreund mir, Herr Walther Fürst,
335 Der über diese Zeiten denkt wie ich.
Auch find' ich dort den edeln Bannerherrn
Von Attinghaus — obgleich von hohem Stamm,
Liebt er das Volk und ehrt die alten Sitten.
Mit ihnen beiden pfleg' ich Rats, wie man
340 Der Landesfeinde mutig sich erwehrt —
Leb wohl — und, weil ich fern bin, führe du
Mit klugem Sinn das Regiment des Hauses —
Dem Pilger, der zum Gotteshause wallt,
Dem frommen Mönch, der für sein Kloster sammelt,
345 Gieb reichlich und entlaß ihn wohlgepflegt.
Stauffachers Haus verbirgt sich nicht. Zu äußerst
Am offnen Heerweg steht's, ein wirtlich Dach
Für alle Wandrer, die des Weges fahren.

Indem sie nach dem Hintergrund abgehen, tritt Wilhelm Tell mit
Baumgarten vorn auf die Scene.

Tell (zu Baumgarten).

Ihr habt jetzt meiner weiter nicht vonnöten.
350 Zu jenem Hause gehet ein; dort wohnt

Der Stauffacher, ein Vater der Bedrängten.
— Doch sieh, da ist er selber — Folgt mir, kommt!

(Gehen auf ihn zu; die Scene verwandelt sich.)

Dritte Scene.

Öffentlicher Platz bei Altorf.

Auf einer Anhöhe im Hintergrund sieht man eine Feste bauen, welche
schon so weit gediehen, daß sich die Form des Ganzen darstellt. Die
hintere Seite ist fertig, an der vordern wird eben gebaut, das Gerüste
steht noch, an welchem die Werkleute auf und nieder steigen; auf
dem höchsten Dach hängt der Schieferdecker — Alles ist in Bewegung
und Arbeit.

Fronvogt. Meister Steinmetz. Gesellen und
Handlanger.

Fronvogt
(mit dem Stabe, treibt die Arbeiter).

Nicht lang' gefeiert, frisch! Die Mauersteine
Herbei, den Kalk, den Mörtel zugefahren!
355 Wenn der Herr Landvogt kommt, daß er das Werk
Gewachsen sieht — Das schlendert wie die Schnecken.

(Zu zwei Handlangern, welche tragen.)

Heißt das geladen? Gleich das Doppelte!
Wie die Tagdiebe ihre Pflicht bestehlen!

Erster Gesell.

Das ist doch hart, daß wir die Steine selbst
360 Zu unserm Twing und Kerker sollen fahren!

Fronvogt.

Was murret ihr? Das ist ein schlechtes Volk,

Zu nichts anstellig, als das Vieh zu melken
Und faul herum zu schlendern auf den Bergen.

Alter Mann (ruht aus).

Ich kann nicht mehr.

Fronvogt (schüttelt ihn).

　　　　　　　　　Frisch, Alter, an die Arbeit!

Erster Gesell.

365　Habt Ihr denn gar kein Eingeweid', daß Ihr
Den Greis, der kaum sich selber schleppen kann,
Zum harten Frondienst treibt?

Meister Steinmetz und **Gesellen.**

　　　　　　　　　's ist himmelschreiend!

Fronvogt.

Sorgt ihr für euch; ich thu', was meines Amts.

Zweiter Gesell.

Fronvogt, wie wird die Feste denn sich nennen,
370　Die wir da baun?

Fronvogt.

　　　　　　Zwing Uri soll sie heißen;
Denn unter dieses Joch wird man euch beugen.

Gesellen.

Zwing Uri!

Fronvogt.

　　　　　　Nun, was giebt's dabei zu lachen?

Zweiter Gesell.

Mit diesem Häuslein wollt Ihr Uri zwingen?

Erster Gesell.

Laß sehn, wie viel man solcher Maulwurfshaufen
375　Muß über 'nander setzen, bis ein Berg

Draus wird, wie der geringste nur in Uri!
(Fronvogt geht nach dem Hintergrund.)

Meister Steinmetz.

Den Hammer werf' ich in den tiefsten See,
Der mir gedient bei diesem Fluchgebäude!
Tell und Stauffacher kommen.

Stauffacher.

O, hätt' ich nie gelebt, um das zu schauen!

Tell.

380 Hier ist nicht gut sein. Laßt uns weiter gehn.

Stauffacher.

Bin ich zu Uri, in der Freiheit Land?

Meister Steinmetz.

O Herr, wenn Ihr die Keller erst gesehn
Unter den Türmen! Ja, wer die bewohnt,
Der wird den Hahn nicht fürder krähen hören.

Stauffacher.

385 O Gott!

Steinmetz.

Seht diese Flanken, diese Strebepfeiler,
Die stehn, wie für die Ewigkeit gebaut!

Tell.

Was Hände bauten, können Hände stürzen.
(Nach den Bergen zeigend.)
Das Haus der Freiheit hat uns Gott gegründet.

Man hört eine Trommel, es kommen Leute, die einen Hut auf einer Stange
tragen, ein Ausrufer folgt ihnen. Weiber und Kinder dringen tumul-
tuarisch nach.

Erster Gesell.

390 Was will die Trommel? Gebet acht!

Meister Steinmetz.

Was für
Ein Fastnachtsaufzug, und was soll der Hut?

Ausrufer.

In des Kaisers Namen! Höret!

Gesellen.

Still doch! Höret!

Ausrufer.

Ihr sehet diesen Hut, Männer von Uri!
Aufrichten wird man ihn auf hoher Säule,
395 Mitten in Altorf, an dem höchsten Ort,
Und dieses ist des Landvogts Will' und Meinung:
Dem Hut soll gleiche Ehre wie ihm selbst geschehn.
Man soll ihn mit gebognem Knie und mit
Entblößtem Haupt verehren — Daran will
400 Der König die Gehorsamen erkennen.
Verfallen ist mit seinem Leib und Gut
Dem Könige, wer das Gebot verachtet.

(Das Volk lacht laut auf, die Trommel wird gerührt, sie gehen
vorüber.)

Erster Gesell.

Welch neues Unerhörtes hat der Vogt
Sich ausgesonnen!   Wir 'nen Hut verehren!
405 Sagt! Hat man je vernommen von dergleichen?

Meister Steinmetz.

Wir unsre Kniee beugen einem Hut!
Treibt er sein Spiel mit ernsthaft würd'gen Leuten?

Erster Gesell.

Wär's noch die kaiserliche Kron'! So ist's
Der Hut von Österreich; ich sah ihn hangen
410 Über dem Thron, wo man die Lehen giebt!

Meister Steinmetz.

Der Hut von Österreich! Gebt acht, es ist
Ein Fallstrick, uns an Östreich zu verraten!

Gesellen.

Kein Ehrenmann wird sich der Schmach bequemen.

Meister Steinmetz.

Kommt, laßt uns mit den andern Abred' nehmen.

(Sie gehen nach der Tiefe.)

Tell (zum Stauffacher).

415 Ihr wisset nun Bescheid. Lebt wohl, Herr Werner!

Stauffacher.

Wo wollt Ihr hin? O, eilt nicht so von dannen!

Tell.

Mein Haus entbehrt des Vaters. Lebet wohl!

Stauffacher.

Mir ist das Herz so voll, mit Euch zu reden.

Tell.

Das schwere Herz wird nicht durch Worte leicht.

Stauffacher.

420 Doch könnten Worte uns zu Thaten führen.

Tell.

Die einz'ge That ist jetzt Geduld und Schweigen.

Stauffacher.

Soll man ertragen, was unleidlich ist?

Tell.

Die schnellen Herrscher sind's, die kurz regieren.
— Wenn sich der Föhn erhebt aus seinen Schlünden,
125 Löscht man die Feuer aus, die Schiffe suchen
Eilends den Hafen, und der mächt'ge Geist
Geht ohne Schaden spurlos über die Erde.
Ein jeder lebe still bei sich daheim;
Dem Friedlichen gewährt man gern den Frieden.

Stauffacher.

430 Meint Ihr?

Tell.

Die Schlange sticht nicht ungereizt.
Sie werden endlich doch von selbst ermüden,
Wenn sie die Lande ruhig bleiben sehn.

Stauffacher.

Wir könnten viel, wenn wir zusammen stünden.

Tell.

Beim Schiffbruch hilft der Einzelne sich leichter.

Stauffacher.

435 So kalt verlaßt Ihr die gemeine Sache?

Tell.

Ein jeder zählt nur sicher auf sich selbst.

Stauffacher.

Verbunden werden auch die Schwachen mächtig.

Tell.

Der Starke ist am mächtigsten allein.

Stauffacher.

So kann das Vaterland auf Euch nicht zählen,
440 Wenn es verzweiflungsvoll zur Notwehr greift?

Tell (giebt ihm die Hand).

Der Tell holt ein verlornes Lamm vom Abgrund
Und sollte seinen Freunden sich entziehen?
Doch, was ihr thut, laßt mich aus eurem Rat,
Ich kann nicht lange prüfen oder wählen;
445 Bedürft ihr meiner zu bestimmter That,
Dann ruft den Tell, es soll an mir nicht fehlen.

(Gehen ab zu verschiedenen Seiten. Ein plötzlicher Auflauf entsteht um
das Gerüste.)

Meister Steinmetz (eilt hin).

Was giebt's?

Erster Gesell (kommt vor, rufend).

Der Schieferdecker ist vom Dach gestürzt.

Bertha mit Gefolge.

Bertha (stürzt herein).

Ist er zerschmettert? Rennet, rettet, helft —
450 Wenn Hilfe möglich, rettet, hier ist Gold —

(Wirft ihr Geschmeide unter das Volk.)

Meister.

Mit Eurem Golde — Alles ist Euch feil
Um Gold; wenn Ihr den Vater von den Kindern
Gerissen und den Mann von seinem Weibe,
Und Jammer habt gebracht über die Welt,
455 Denkt Ihr's mit Golde zu vergüten — Geht!
Wir waren frohe Menschen, eh' Ihr kamt;
Mit Euch ist die Verzweiflung eingezogen.

Bertha (zu dem Fronvogt, der zurückkommt).

Lebt er?

(Fronvogt giebt ein Zeichen des Gegenteils.)

O unglückſel'ges Schloß, mit Flüchen
Erbaut, und Flüche werden dich bewohnen!

(Geht ab.)

Vierte Scene.

Walther Fürſts Wohnung.

Walther Fürſt und Arnold vom Melchthal treten zugleich
ein von verſchiedenen Seiten.

Melchthal.

460 Herr Walther Fürſt —

Walther Fürſt.

Wenn man uns überraſchte!
Bleibt, wo Ihr ſeid.   Wir ſind umringt von Spähern.

Melchthal.

Bringt Ihr mir nichts von Unterwalden? nichts
Von meinem Vater? Nicht ertrag' ich's länger,
Als ein Gefangner müßig hier zu liegen.
465 Was hab' ich denn ſo Sträfliches gethan,
Um mich gleich einem Mörder zu verbergen?
Dem frechen Buben, der die Ochſen mir,
Das trefflichſte Geſpann, vor meinen Augen
Weg wollte treiben auf des Vogts Geheiß,
470 Hab' ich den Finger mit dem Stab gebrochen.

Walther Fürſt.

Ihr ſeid zu raſch.   Der Bube war des Vogts;
Von Eurer Obrigkeit war er geſendet.
Ihr wart in Straf' gefallen, mußtet Euch,
Wie ſchwer ſie war, der Buße ſchweigend fügen.

Melchthal.

475 Ertragen sollt' ich die leichtfert'ge Rede
Des Unverschämten: „Wenn der Bauer Brod
Wollt' essen, mög' er selbst am Pfluge ziehn!"
In die Seele schnitt mir's, als der Bub die Ochsen,
Die schönen Tiere, von dem Pfluge spannte;
480 Dumpf brüllten sie, als hätten sie Gefühl
Der Ungebühr, und stießen mit den Hörnern;
Da übernahm mich der gerechte Zorn,
Und meiner selbst nicht Herr, schlug ich den Boten.

Walther Fürst.

O, kaum bezwingen wir das eigne Herz;
485 Wie soll die rasche Jugend sich bezähmen!

Melchthal.

Mich jammert nur der Vater — Er bedarf
So sehr der Pflege, und sein Sohn ist fern.
Der Vogt ist ihm gehässig, weil er stets
Für Recht und Freiheit redlich hat gestritten.
490 Drum werden sie den alten Mann bedrängen,
Und niemand ist, der ihn vor Unglimpf schütze.
— Werde mit mir, was will, ich muß hinüber.

Walther Fürst.

Erwartet nur und faßt Euch in Geduld,
Bis Nachricht uns herüberkommt vom Walde.
195 — Ich höre klopfen, geht — Vielleicht ein Bote
Vom Landvogt — Geht hinein — Ihr seid in Uri
Nicht sicher vor des Landenbergers Arm;
Denn die Tyrannen reichen sich die Hände.

Melchthal.

Sie lehren uns, was wir thun sollten.

Walther Fürst.

Geht!

500 Ich ruf' Euch wieder, wenn's hier sicher ist.

(Melchthal geht hinein.)

Der Unglückselige, ich darf ihm nicht
Gestehen, was mir Böses schwant — Wer klopft?
So oft die Thüre rauscht, erwart' ich Unglück.
Verrat und Argwohn lauscht in allen Ecken;
505 Bis in das Innerste der Häuser dringen
Die Boten der Gewalt; bald thät' es not,
Wir hätten Schloß und Riegel an den Thüren.

(Er öffnet und tritt erstaunt zurück, da Werner Stauffacher
hereintritt.)

Was seh' ich? Ihr, Herr Werner! Nun, bei Gott!
Ein werter, teurer Gast — Kein beßrer Mann
510 Ist über diese Schwelle noch gegangen.
Seid hoch willkommen unter meinem Dach!
Was führt Euch her? Was sucht Ihr hier in Uri?

Stauffacher (ihm die Hand reichend).

Die alten Zeiten und die alte Schweiz.

Walther Fürst.

Die bringt Ihr mit Euch — Sieh, mir wird so wohl,
515 Warm geht das Herz mir auf bei Eurem Anblick.
— Setzt Euch, Herr Werner — Wie verließet Ihr
Frau Gertrud, Eure angenehme Wirtin,
Des weisen Ibergs hochverständ'ge Tochter?
Von allen Wandrern aus dem deutschen Land,
520 Die über Meinrads Zell nach Welschland fahren,
Rühmt jeder Euer gastlich Haus — Doch sagt,
Kommt Ihr so eben frisch von Flüelen her

Und habt Euch nirgend sonst noch umgesehn,
Eh' Ihr den Fuß gesetzt auf diese Schwelle?

Stauffacher (setzt sich).

525 Wohl ein erstaunlich neues Werk hab' ich
Bereiten sehen, das mich nicht erfreute.

Walther Fürst.

O Freund, da habt Ihr's gleich mit einem Blicke!

Stauffacher.

Ein solches ist in Uri nie gewesen —
Seit Menschendenken war kein Twinghof hier,
530 Und fest war keine Wohnung als das Grab.

Walther Fürst.

Ein Grab der Freiheit ist's. Ihr nennt's mit Namen.

Stauffacher.

Herr Walther Fürst, ich will Euch nicht verhalten,
Nicht eine müß'ge Neugier führt mich her;
Mich drücken schwere Sorgen — Drangsal hab' ich
535 Zu Haus verlassen, Drangsal find' ich hier.
Denn ganz unleidlich ist's, was wir erdulden,
Und dieses Dranges ist kein Ziel zu sehn.
Frei war der Schweizer von uralters her,
Wir sind's gewohnt, daß man uns gut begegnet.
540 Ein solches war im Lande nie erlebt,
Solang' ein Hirte trieb auf diesen Bergen.

Walther Fürst.

Ja, es ist ohne Beispiel, wie sie's treiben!
Auch unser edler Herr von Attinghausen,
Der noch die alten Zeiten hat gesehn,
545 Meint selber, es sei nicht mehr zu ertragen.

Stauffacher.

Auch drüben unterm Wald geht Schweres vor,
Und blutig wird's gebüßt — Der Wolfenschießen,
Des Kaisers Vogt, der auf dem Roßberg hauste,
Gelüsten trug er nach verbotner Frucht;
550 Baumgartens Weib, der haushält zu Alzellen,
Wollt' er zu frecher Ungebühr mißbrauchen,
Und mit der Axt hat ihn der Mann erschlagen.

Walther Fürst.

O, die Gerichte Gottes sind gerecht!
— Baumgarten, sagt Ihr? Ein bescheidner Mann!
555 Er ist gerettet doch und wohl geborgen?

Stauffacher.

Euer Eidam hat ihn übern See geflüchtet;
Bei mir zu Steinen halt' ich ihn verborgen —
— Noch Greulichers hat mir derselbe Mann
Berichtet, was zu Sarnen ist geschehn;
560 Das Herz muß jedem Biedermanne bluten.

Walther Fürst (aufmerksam).

Sagt an, was ist's?

Stauffacher.

          Im Melchthal, da, wo man
Eintritt bei Kerns, wohnt ein gerechter Mann,
Sie nennen ihn den Heinrich von der Halden,
Und seine Stimm' gilt was in der Gemeinde.

Walther Fürst.

565 Wer kennt ihn nicht! Was ist's mit ihm? Vollendet!

Stauffacher.

Der Landenberger büßte seinen Sohn

Um kleinen Fehlers willen, ließ die Ochsen,
Das beste Paar, ihm aus dem Pfluge spannen;
Da schlug der Knab' den Knecht und wurde flüchtig.

Walther Fürst (in höchster Spannung).

570 Der Vater aber — sagt, wie steht's um den?

Stauffacher.

Den Vater läßt der Landenberger fordern,
Zur Stelle schaffen soll er ihm den Sohn,
Und da der alte Mann mit Wahrheit schwört,
Er habe von dem Flüchtling keine Kunde,
575 Da läßt der Vogt die Folterknechte kommen —

Walther Fürst
(springt auf und will ihn auf die andere Seite führen).

O, still, nichts mehr!

Stauffacher (mit steigendem Ton).

„Ist mir der Sohn entgangen,
So hab' ich d i ch!" — Läßt ihn zu Boden werfen,
Den spitz'gen Stahl ihm in die Augen bohren —

Walther Fürst.

Barmherz'ger Himmel!

Melchthal (stürzt heraus).

In die Augen, sagt Ihr?

Stauffacher (erstaunt zu Walther Fürst).

580 Wer ist der Jüngling?

Melchthal
(faßt ihn mit krampfhafter Heftigkeit).

In die Augen? Redet!

Walther Fürst.

O der Bejammernswürdige!

Stauffacher.

Wer ist's?

(Da Walther Fürst ihm ein Zeichen giebt.)

Der Sohn ist's? Allgerechter Gott!

Melchthal.

Und ich

Muß ferne sein! — In seine beiden Augen?

Walther Fürst.

Bezwinget Euch! Ertragt es wie ein Mann!

Melchthal.

585 Um meiner Schuld, um meines Frevels willen!
— Blind also? Wirklich blind, und ganz geblendet?

Stauffacher.

Ich sagt's. Der Quell des Sehns ist ausgeflossen,
Das Licht der Sonne schaut er niemals wieder.

Walther Fürst.

Schont seines Schmerzens!

Melchthal.

Niemals! niemals wieder!

(Er drückt die Hand vor die Augen und schweigt einige Momente,
dann wendet er sich von dem einen zu dem andern und spricht mit
sanfter, von Thränen erstickter Stimme.)

590 O, eine edle Himmelsgabe ist
Das Licht des Auges — Alle Wesen leben
Vom Lichte, jedes glückliche Geschöpf —
Die Pflanze selbst kehrt freudig sich zum Lichte.
Und er muß sitzen, fühlend, in der Nacht,

595 Im ewig Finstern — ihn erquickt nicht mehr
Der Matten warmes Grün, der Blumen Schmelz;
Die roten Firnen kann er nicht mehr schauen —
Sterben ist nichts — doch l e b e n und nicht s e h e n,
Das ist ein Unglück — Warum seht ihr mich
600 So jammernd an? Ich hab' zwei frische Augen
Und kann dem blinden Vater keines geben,
Nicht einen Schimmer von dem Meer des Lichts,
Das glanzvoll, blendend mir ins Auge dringt.

Stauffacher.

Ach, ich muß Euren Jammer noch vergrößern,
605 Statt ihn zu heilen — Er bedarf noch mehr!
Denn alles hat der Landvogt ihm geraubt;
Nichts hat er ihm gelassen als den Stab,
Um nackt und blind von Thür zu Thür zu wandern.

Melchthal.

Nichts als den Stab dem augenlosen Greis!
610 Alles geraubt und auch das Licht der Sonne,
Des Ärmsten allgemeines Gut — Jetzt rede
Mir keiner mehr von Bleiben, von Verbergen!
Was für ein feiger Elender bin ich,
Daß ich auf m e i n e Sicherheit gedacht
615 Und nicht auf deine! — Dein geliebtes Haupt
Als Pfand gelassen in des Wütrichs Händen!
Feigherz'ge Vorsicht, fahre hin — Auf nichts
Als blutige Vergeltung will ich denken.
Hinüber will ich — Keiner soll mich halten —
620 Des Vaters Auge von dem Landvogt fordern —
Aus allen seinen Reisigen heraus
Will ich ihn finden — Nichts liegt mir am Leben,

Wenn ich den heißen, ungeheuren Schmerz
In seinem Lebensblute kühle.

(Er will gehen.)

Walther Fürst.

Bleibt!

625 Was könnt Ihr gegen ihn? Er sitzt zu Sarnen
Auf seiner hohen Herrenburg und spottet
Ohnmächt'gen Zorns in seiner sichern Feste.

Melchthal.

Und wohnt' er droben auf dem Eispalast
Des Schreckhorns oder höher, wo die Jungfrau
630 Seit Ewigkeit verschleiert sitzt — ich mache
Mir Bahn zu ihm; mit zwanzig Jünglingen,
Gesinnt wie ich, zerbrech' ich seine Feste.
Und wenn mir niemand folgt, und wenn ihr alle,
Für eure Hütten bang und eure Herden,
635 Euch dem Tyrannenjoche beugt — die Hirten
Will ich zusammenrufen im Gebirg,
Dort, unterm freien Himmelsdache, wo
Der Sinn noch frisch ist und das Herz gesund,
Das ungeheuer Gräßliche erzählen.

Stauffacher (zu Walther Fürst).

640 Es ist auf seinem Gipfel — Wollen wir
Erwarten, bis das Äußerste —

Melchthal.

Welch Äußerstes

Ist noch zu fürchten, wenn der Stern des Auges
In seiner Höhle nicht mehr sicher ist?
— Sind wir denn wehrlos? Wozu lernten wir
645 Die Armbrust spannen und die schwere Wucht

Der Streitaxt schwingen? Jedem Wesen ward
Ein Notgewehr in der Verzweiflungsangst.
Es stellt sich der erschöpfte Hirsch und zeigt
Der Meute sein gefürchtetes Geweih,
650 Die Gemse reißt den Jäger in den Abgrund —
Der Pflugstier selbst, der sanfte Hausgenoß
Des Menschen, der die ungeheure Kraft
Des Halses duldsam unters Joch gebogen,
Springt auf, gereizt, wetzt sein gewaltig Horn
655 Und schleudert seinen Feind den Wolken zu.

Walther Fürst.

Wenn die drei Lande dächten wie wir drei,
So möchten wir vielleicht etwas vermögen.

Stauffacher.

Wenn Uri ruft, wenn Unterwalden hilft,
Der Schwyzer wird die alten Bünde ehren.

Melchthal.

660 Groß ist in Unterwalden meine Freundschaft,
Und jeder wagt mit Freuden Leib und Blut,
Wenn er am andern einen Rücken hat
Und Schirm — O fromme Väter dieses Landes!
Ich stehe nur ein Jüngling zwischen euch,
665 Den Vielerfahrnen — meine Stimme muß
Bescheiden schweigen in der Landsgemeinde.
Nicht, weil ich jung bin und nicht viel erlebte,
Verachtet meinen Rat und meine Rede;
Nicht lüstern jugendliches Blut, mich treibt
670 Des höchsten Jammers schmerzliche Gewalt,
Was auch den Stein des Felsen muß erbarmen.
Ihr selbst seid Väter, Häupter eines Hauses,

Und wünscht euch einen tugendhaften Sohn,
Der eures Hauptes heil'ge Locken ehre

675 Und euch den Stern des Auges fromm bewache.
O, weil ihr selbst an eurem Leib und Gut
Noch nichts erlitten, eure Augen sich
Noch frisch und hell in ihren Kreisen regen,
So sei euch darum unsre Not nicht fremd.

680 Auch über euch hängt das Tyrannenschwert,
Ihr habt das Land von Östreich abgewendet;
Kein anderes war meines Vaters Unrecht,
Ihr seid in gleicher Mitschuld und Verdammnis.

Stauffacher (zu Walther Fürst).

Beschließet Ihr! Ich bin bereit, zu folgen.

Walther Fürst.

685 Wir wollen hören, was die edeln Herrn
Von Sillinen, von Attinghausen raten —
Ihr Name, denk' ich, wird uns Freunde werben.

Melchthal.

Wo ist ein Name in dem Waldgebirg
Ehrwürdiger als Eurer und der Eure?

690 An solcher Namen echte Währung glaubt
Das Volk, sie haben guten Klang im Lande.
Ihr habt ein reiches Erb' von Vätertugend
Und habt es selber reich vermehrt — Was braucht's
Des Edelmanns? Laßt's uns allein vollenden!

695 Wären wir doch allein im Land! Ich meine,
Wir wollten uns schon selbst zu schirmen wissen.

Stauffacher.

Die Edeln drängt nicht gleiche Not mit uns;
Der Strom, der in den Niederungen wütet,

Bis jetzt hat er die Höhn noch nicht erreicht —
700 Doch ihre Hilfe wird uns nicht entstehn,
Wenn sie das Land in Waffen erst erblicken.

Walther Fürst.

Wäre ein Obmann zwischen uns und Östreich,
So möchte Recht entscheiden und Gesetz.
Doch der uns unterdrückt, ist unser Kaiser
705 Und höchster Richter — so muß Gott uns helfen
Durch unsern Arm — Erforschet Ihr die Männer
Von Schwyz, ich will in Uri Freunde werben;
Wen aber senden wir nach Unterwalden? —

Melchthal.

Mich sendet hin — Wem läg' es näher an —

Walther Fürst.

710 Ich geb's nicht zu; Ihr seid mein Gast, ich muß
Für Eure Sicherheit gewähren!

Melchthal.

Laßt mich!
Die Schliche kenn' ich und die Felsensteige;
Auch Freunde find' ich gnug, die mich dem Feind
Verhehlen und ein Obdach gern gewähren.

Stauffacher

715 Laßt ihn mit Gott hinüber gehn! Dort drüben
Ist kein Verräter — So verabscheut ist
Die Tyrannei, daß sie kein Werkzeug findet.
Auch der Alzeller soll uns nid dem Wald
Genossen werben und das Land erregen.

Melchthal.

720 Wie bringen wir uns sichre Kunde zu,
Daß wir den Argwohn der Tyrannen täuschen?

Stauffacher.

Wir könnten uns zu Brunnen oder Treib
Versammeln, wo die Kaufmannsschiffe landen.

Walther Fürst.

So offen dürfen wir das Werk nicht treiben.
725 — Hört meine Meinung: Links am See, wenn man
Nach Brunnen fährt, dem Mythenstein grad' über,
Liegt eine Matte heimlich im Gehölz,
Das Rütli heißt sie bei dem Volk der Hirten,
Weil dort die Waldung ausgereutet ward.
730 Dort ist's, wo unsre Landmark und die Eure

(Zu Melchthal)

Zusammengrenzen, und in kurzer Fahrt

(Zu Stauffacher)

Trägt Euch der leichte Kahn von Schwyz herüber.
Auf öden Pfaden können wir dahin
Bei Nachtzeit wandern und uns still beraten.
735 Dahin mag jeder zehn vertraute Männer
Mitbringen, die herzeinig sind mit uns,
So können wir gemeinsam das Gemeine
Besprechen und mit Gott es frisch beschließen.

Stauffacher.

So sei's! Jetzt reicht mir Eure biedre Rechte,
740 Reicht Ihr die Eure her, und so wie wir
Drei Männer jetzo unter uns die Hände
Zusammenflechten, redlich, ohne Falsch,
So wollen wir drei Länder auch zu Schutz
Und Trutz zusammenstehn auf Tod und Leben!

Walther Fürst und **Melchthal.**

745 Auf Tod und Leben!

(Sie halten die Hände noch einige Pausen lang zusammengeflochten
und schweigen.)

Melchthal.

Blinder, alter Vater!
Du kannst den Tag der Freiheit nicht mehr s ch a u e n;
Du sollst ihn h ö r e n — Wenn von Alp zu Alp
Die Feuerzeichen flammend sich erheben,
Die festen Schlösser der Tyrannen fallen,
750 In deine Hütte soll der Schweizer wallen,
Zu deinem Ohr die Freudenkunde tragen,
Und hell in deiner Nacht soll es dir tagen!

(Sie gehen auseinander.)

Zweiter Aufzug.

Erste Scene.

Edelhof des Freiherrn von Attinghausen.

Ein gotischer Saal, mit Wappenschildern und Helmen verziert. Der Freiherr, ein Greis von fünfundachtzig Jahren, von hoher, edler Statur, an einem Stabe, worauf ein Gemsenhorn, und in ein Pelzwams gekleidet. Kuoni und noch sechs Knechte stehen um ihn her mit Rechen und Sensen. — Ulrich von Rudenz tritt ein in Ritterkleidung.

Rudenz.

Hier bin ich, Oheim — Was ist Euer Wille?

Attinghausen.

Erlaubt, daß ich nach altem Hausgebrauch
755 Den Frühtrunk erst mit meinen Knechten teile.
(Er trinkt aus einem Becher, der dann in der Reihe herumgeht.)
Sonst war ich selber mit in Feld und Wald,
Mit meinem Auge ihren Fleiß regierend,
Wie sie mein Banner führte in der Schlacht;
Jetzt kann ich nichts mehr, als den Schaffner machen,
760 Und kommt die warme Sonne nicht zu mir,
Ich kann sie nicht mehr suchen auf den Bergen.
Und so in enger stets und engerm Kreis,
Beweg' ich mich dem engesten und letzten,
Wo alles Leben still steht, langsam zu.
765 Mein Schatten bin ich nur, bald nur mein Name.

44

Kuoni (zu Rudenz mit dem Becher).

Ich bring's Euch, Junker.

(Da Rudenz zaudert, den Becher zu nehmen.)

Trinket frisch! Es geht
Aus einem Becher und aus einem Herzen.

Attinghausen.

Geht, Kinder, und wenn's Feierabend ist,
Dann reden wir auch von des Lands Geschäften.

(Knechte gehen **ab.**)

Attinghausen und Rudenz.

Attinghausen.

770 Ich sehe dich gegürtet und gerüstet,
Du willst nach Altorf in die Herrenburg?

Rudenz.

Ja, Oheim, und ich darf nicht länger säumen —

Attinghausen (setzt sich).

Hast du's so eilig? Wie? Ist deiner Jugend
Die Zeit so karg gemessen, daß du sie
775 An deinem alten Oheim mußt ersparen?

Rudenz.

Ich sehe, daß Ihr meiner nicht bedürft,
Ich bin ein Fremdling nur in diesem Hause.

Attinghausen

(hat ihn lange mit den Augen gemustert).

Ja, leider bist du's. Leider ist die Heimat
Zur Fremde dir geworden! — Uli! Uli!
780 Ich kenne dich nicht mehr. In Seide prangst du,

Die Pfauenfeder trägst du stolz zur Schau
Und schlägst den Purpurmantel um die Schultern;
Den Landmann blickst du mit Verachtung an
Und schämst dich seiner traulichen Begrüßung.

Rudenz.

785 Die Ehr', die ihm gebührt, geb' ich ihm gern;
Das Recht, das er sich nimmt, verweigr' ich ihm.

Attinghausen.

Das ganze Land liegt unterm schweren Zorn
Des Königs — Jedes Biedermannes Herz
Ist kummervoll ob der tyrannischen Gewalt,
790 Die wir erdulden — Dich allein rührt nicht
Der allgemeine Schmerz — Dich siehet man
Abtrünnig von den Deinen auf der Seite
Des Landesfeindes stehen, unsrer Not
Hohnsprechend, nach der leichten Freude jagen
795 Und buhlen um die Fürstengunst, indes
Dein Vaterland von schwerer Geißel blutet.

Rudenz.

Das Land ist schwer bedrängt — Warum, mein Oheim?
Wer ist's, der es gestürzt in diese Not?
Es kostete ein einzig leichtes Wort,
800 Um augenblicks des Dranges los zu sein
Und einen gnäd'gen Kaiser zu gewinnen.
Weh ihnen, die dem Volk die Augen halten,
Daß es dem wahren Besten widerstrebt!
Um eignen Vorteils willen hindern sie,
805 Daß die Waldstätte nicht zu Östreich schwören,
Wie ringsum alle Lande doch gethan.
Wohl thut es ihnen, auf der Herrenbank

Zu sitzen mit dem Edelmann — den Kaiser
Will man zum Herrn, um keinen Herrn zu haben.

Attinghausen.

810 Muß ich das hören und aus deinem Munde!

Rudenz.

Ihr habt mich aufgefordert, laßt mich enden!
— Welche Person ist's, Oheim, die Ihr selbst
Hier spielt? Habt Ihr nicht höhern Stolz, als hier
Landammann oder Bannerherr zu sein
815 Und neben diesen Hirten zu regieren?
Wie? Ist's nicht eine rühmlichere Wahl,
Zu huldigen dem königlichen Herrn,
Sich an sein glänzend Lager anzuschließen,
Als Eurer eignen Knechte Pair zu sein
820 Und zu Gericht zu sitzen mit dem Bauer?

Attinghausen.

Ach, Uli! Uli! Ich erkenne sie,
Die Stimme der Verführung! Sie ergriff
Dein offnes Ohr, sie hat dein Herz vergiftet.

Rudenz.

Ja, ich verberg' es nicht — in tiefer Seele
825 Schmerzt mich der Spott der Fremdlinge, die uns
Den Bauernadel schelten — Nicht ertrag' ich's,
Indes die edle Jugend rings umher
Sich Ehre sammelt unter Habsburgs Fahnen,
Auf meinem Erb' hier müßig still zu liegen,
830 Und bei gemeinem Tagewerk den Lenz
Des Lebens zu verlieren — Anderswo
Geschehen Thaten, eine Welt des Ruhms
Bewegt sich glänzend jenseits dieser Berge —

Mir rosten in der Halle Helm und Schild;
835 Der Kriegsdrommete mutiges Getön,
Der Heroldsruf, der zum Turniere ladet,
Er dringt in diese Thäler nicht herein;
Nichts als den Kuhreihn und der Herdeglocken
Einförmiges Geläut vernehm' ich hier.

Attinghausen.

840 Verblendeter, vom eiteln Glanz verführt!
Verachte dein Geburtsland! Schäme dich
Der uralt frommen Sitte deiner Väter!
Mit heißen Thränen wirst du dich dereinst
Heim sehnen nach den väterlichen Bergen,
845 Und dieses Herdenreihens Melodie,
Die du in stolzem Überdruß verschmähst,
Mit Schmerzenssehnsucht wird sie dich ergreifen,
Wenn sie dir anklingt auf der fremden Erde.
O, mächtig ist der Trieb des Vaterlands!
850 Die fremde, falsche Welt ist nicht für dich;
Dort an dem stolzen Kaiserhof bleibst du
Dir ewig fremd mit deinem treuen Herzen!
Die Welt, sie fordert andre Tugenden,
Als du in diesen Thälern dir erworben.
855 — Geh hin, verkaufe deine freie Seele,
Nimm Land zu Lehen, werd' ein Fürstenknecht,
Da du ein Selbstherr sein kannst und ein Fürst
Auf deinem eignen Erb' und freien Boden.
Ach, Uli! Uli! Bleibe bei den Deinen!
860 Geh nicht nach Altorf — O, verlaß sie nicht,
Die heil'ge Sache deines Vaterlands!
— Ich bin der Letzte meines Stamms — Mein Name
Endet mit mir. Da hängen Helm und Schild;

Die werden sie mir in das Grab mitgeben.

865 Und muß ich denken bei dem letzten Hauch,
Daß du mein brechend Auge nur erwartest,
Um hinzugehn vor diesen neuen Lehenhof
Und meine edeln Güter, die ich frei
Von Gott empfing, von Östreich zu empfangen!

Rudenz.

870 Vergebens widerstreben wir dem König,
Die Welt gehört ihm; wollen wir allein
Uns eigensinnig steifen und verstocken,
Die Länderkette ihm zu unterbrechen,
Die er gewaltig rings um uns gezogen?

875 Sein sind die Märkte, die Gerichte, sein
Die Kaufmannsstraßen, und das Saumroß selbst,
Das auf dem Gotthard zieht, muß ihm zollen.
Von seinen Ländern wie mit einem Netz
Sind wir umgarnet rings und eingeschlossen.

880 — Wird uns das Reich beschützen? Kann es selbst
Sich schützen gegen Östreichs wachsende Gewalt?
Hilft Gott uns nicht, kein Kaiser kann uns helfen.
Was ist zu geben auf der Kaiser Wort,
Wenn sie in Geld= und Kriegesnot die Städte,

885 Die untern Schirm des Adlers sich geflüchtet,
Verpfänden dürfen und dem Reich veräußern?
— Nein, Oheim! Wohlthat ist's und weise Vorsicht,
In diesen schweren Zeiten der Parteiung,
Sich anzuschließen an ein mächtig Haupt.

890 Die Kaiserkrone geht von Stamm zu Stamm,
Die hat für treue Dienste kein Gedächtnis;
Doch um den mächt'gen Erbherrn wohl verdienen,
Heißt Saaten in die Zukunft streun.

Attinghausen.

Bist du so weise?
Willst heller sehn als deine edeln Väter,
895 Die um der Freiheit kostbarn Edelstein
Mit Gut und Blut und Heldenkraft gestritten?
— Schiff' nach Luzern hinunter, frage dort,
Wie Östreichs Herrschaft lastet auf den Ländern!
Sie werden kommen, unsre Schaf' und Rinder
900 Zu zählen, unsre Alpen abzumessen,
Den Hochflug und das Hochgewilde bannen
In unsern freien Wäldern, ihren Schlagbaum
An unsre Brücken, unsre Thore setzen,
Mit unsrer Armut ihre Länderkäufe,
905 Mit unserm Blute ihre Kriege zahlen —
— Nein, wenn wir unser Blut dran setzen sollen,
So sei's für uns — wohlfeiler kaufen wir
Die Freiheit als die Knechtschaft ein!

Rudenz.

Was können wir,
Ein Volk der Hirten, gegen Albrechts Heere!

Attinghausen.

910 Lern' dieses Volk der Hirten kennen, Knabe!
Ich kenn's, ich hab' es angeführt in Schlachten,
Ich hab' es fechten sehen bei Favenz.
Sie sollen kommen, uns ein Joch aufzwingen,
Das wir entschlossen sind nicht zu ertragen!
915 — O, lerne fühlen, welches Stamms du bist!
Wirf nicht für eiteln Glanz und Flitterschein
Die echte Perle deines Wertes hin —
Das Haupt zu heißen eines freien Volks,
Das dir aus Liebe nur sich herzlich weiht,

920 Das treulich zu dir steht in Kampf und Tod —
    Das sei dein Stolz, des Adels rühme dich —
    Die angebornen Bande knüpfe fest,
    Ans Vaterland, ans teure, schließ dich an,
    Das halte fest mit deinem ganzen Herzen!
925 Hier sind die starken Wurzeln deiner Kraft;
    Dort in der fremden Welt stehst du allein,
    Ein schwankes Rohr, das jeder Sturm zerknickt.
    O, komm, du hast uns lang' nicht mehr gesehn,
    Versuch's mit uns nur einen Tag — nur heute
930 Geh nicht nach Altorf — Hörst du? Heute nicht;
    Den einen Tag nur schenke dich den Deinen!
           (Er faßt seine Hand.)

Rudenz.

Ich gab mein Wort — Laßt mich — Ich bin gebunden.

Attinghausen

         (läßt seine Hand los, mit Ernst).

    Du bist gebunden — Ja, Unglücklicher!
    Du bist's, doch nicht durch Wort und Schwur,
935 Gebunden bist du durch der Liebe Seile!
           (Rudenz wendet sich weg.)

    — Verbirg dich, wie du willst. Das Fräulein ist's,
    Bertha von Bruneck, die zur Herrenburg
    Dich zieht, dich fesselt an des Kaisers Dienst.
    Das Ritterfräulein willst du dir erwerben
940 Mit deinem Abfall von dem Land — Betrüg dich nicht!
    Dich anzulocken, zeigt man dir die Braut;
    Doch deiner Unschuld ist sie nicht beschieden.

Rudenz.

Genug hab' ich gehört. Gehabt Euch wohl! (Er geht ab.)

Attinghausen.

Wahnsinn'ger Jüngling, bleib! — Er geht dahin!
945 Ich kann ihn nicht erhalten, nicht erretten —
So ist der Wolfenschießen abgefallen
Von seinem Land — so werden andre folgen;
Der fremde Zauber reißt die Jugend fort,
Gewaltsam strebend über unsre Berge.
950 — O unglücksel'ge Stunde, da das Fremde
In diese still beglückten Thäler kam,
Der Sitten fromme Unschuld zu zerstören!
    Das Neue dringt herein mit Macht, das Alte,
Das Würd'ge scheidet, andre Zeiten kommen,
955 Es lebt ein andersdenkendes Geschlecht!
Was thu' ich hier? Sie sind begraben alle,
Mit denen ich gewaltet und gelebt.
Unter der Erde schon liegt m e i n e Zeit;
Wohl dem, der mit der n e u e n nicht mehr braucht zu leben!

(Geht ab.)

Zweite Scene.

Eine Wiese, von hohen Felsen und Wald umgeben.

Auf den Felsen sind Steige mit Geländern, auch Leitern, von denen
man nachher die Landleute herabsteigen sieht. Im Hintergrunde zeigt
sich der See, über welchem anfangs ein Mondregenbogen zu sehen ist.
Den Prospect schließen hohe Berge, hinter welchen noch höhere Eisgebirge ragen. Es ist völlig Nacht auf der Scene, nur der See und
die weißen Gletscher leuchten im Mondlicht.

Melchthal, Baumgarten, Winkelried, Meier von
  Sarnen, Burkhart am Bühel, Arnold von Sewa,

Klaus von der Flüe und noch vier andere Landleute,
alle bewaffnet.

Melchthal (noch hinter der Scene).

960 Der Bergweg öffnet sich, nur frisch mir nach!
Den Fels erkenn' ich und das Kreuzlein drauf;
Wir sind am Ziel, hier ist das Rütli.

(Treten auf mit Windlichtern.)

Winkelried.

Horch!

Sewa.

Ganz leer.

Meier.

's ist noch kein Landmann da. Wir sind
Die Ersten auf dem Platz, wir Unterwaldner.

Melchthal.

965 Wie weit ist's in der Nacht?

Baumgarten.

Der Feuerwächter
Vom Selisberg hat eben Zwei gerufen.

(Man hört in der Ferne läuten.)

Meier.

Still! Horch!

Am Bühel.

Das Mettenglöcklein in der Waldkapelle
Klingt hell herüber aus dem Schwyzerland.

Von der Flüe.

Die Luft ist rein und trägt den Schall so weit.

Melchthal.

970 Gehn einige und zünden Reisholz an,
Daß es loh brenne, wenn die Männer kommen!

(Zwei Landleute gehen.)

Sewa.

’s ist eine schöne Mondennacht.   Der See
Liegt ruhig da als wie ein ebner Spiegel.

Am Bühel.

Sie haben eine leichte Fahrt.

Winkelried (zeigt nach dem See).

Ha, seht!

975　Seht dorthin!   Seht ihr nichts?

Meier.

Was denn? — Ja, wahrlich!
Ein Regenbogen mitten in der Nacht!

Melchthal.

Es ist das Licht des Mondes, das ihn bildet.

Von der Flüe.

Das ist ein seltsam wunderbares Zeichen!
Es leben viele, die das nicht gesehn.

Sewa.

980　Er ist doppelt; seht, ein blässerer steht drüber.

Baumgarten.

Ein Nachen fährt soeben drunter weg.

Melchthal.

Das ist der Stauffacher mit seinem Kahn,
Der Biedermann läßt sich nicht lang’ erwarten.

(Geht mit Baumgarten nach dem Ufer.)

Meier.

Die Urner sind es, die am längsten säumen.

Am Bühel.

985　Sie müssen weit umgehen durchs Gebirg,

Daß sie des Landvogts Kundschaft hintergehen.

(Unterdessen haben die zwei Landleute in der Mitte des Platzes ein Feuer
angezündet.)

Melchthal (am Ufer).

Wer ist da? Gebt das Wort!

Stauffacher (von unten).

Freunde des Landes.

Alle gehen nach der Tiefe, den Kommenden entgegen. Aus dem
Kahn steigen Stauffacher, Itel Reding, Hans auf der
Mauer, Jörg im Hofe, Konrad Hunn, Ulrich der
Schmid, Jost von Weiler und noch drei andere Landleute,
gleichfalls bewaffnet.

Alle (rufen).

Willkommen!

(Indem die Übrigen in der Tiefe verweilen und sich begrüßen, kommt
Melchthal mit Stauffacher vorwärts.)

Melchthal.

O Herr Stauffacher! Ich hab' ihn
Gesehn, der mich nicht wiedersehen konnte!
990 Die Hand hab' ich gelegt auf seine Augen,
Und glühend Rachgefühl hab' ich gesogen
Aus der erloschnen Sonne seines Blicks.

Stauffacher.

Sprecht nicht von Rache. Nicht Geschehnes rächen,
Gedrohtem Übel wollen wir begegnen.
995 — Jetzt sagt, was Ihr im Unterwaldner Land
Geschafft und für gemeine Sach' geworben,
Wie die Landleute denken, wie Ihr selbst
Den Stricken des Verrats entgangen seid.

Melchthal.

Durch der Surennen furchtbares Gebirg,
1000 Auf weit verbreitet öden Eisesfeldern,
Wo nur der heisre Lämmergeier krächzt,
Gelangt' ich zu der Alpentrift, wo sich
Aus Uri und vom Engelberg die Hirten
Anrufend grüßen und gemeinsam weiden,
1005 Den Durst mir stillend mit der Gletscher Milch,
Die in den Runsen schäumend niederquillt.
In den einsamen Sennhütten kehrt' ich ein,
Mein eigner Wirt und Gast, bis daß ich kam
Zu Wohnungen gesellig lebender Menschen.
1010 — Erschollen war in diesen Thälern schon
Der Ruf des neuen Greuels, der geschehn,
Und fromme Ehrfurcht schaffte mir mein Unglück
Vor jeder Pforte, wo ich wandernd klopfte.
Entrüstet fand ich diese graden Seelen
1015 Ob dem gewaltsam neuen Regiment;
Denn so wie ihre Alpen fort und fort
Dieselben Kräuter nähren, ihre Brunnen
Gleichförmig fließen, Wolken selbst und Winde
Den gleichen Strich unwandelbar befolgen,
1020 So hat die alte Sitte hier vom Ahn
Zum Enkel unverändert fort bestanden.
Nicht tragen sie verwegne Neuerung
Im altgewohnten gleichen Gang des Lebens.
— Die harten Hände reichten sie mir dar,
1025 Von den Wänden langten sie die rost'gen Schwerter,
Und aus den Augen blitzte freudiges
Gefühl des Muts, als ich die Namen nannte,
Die im Gebirg dem Landmann heilig sind,

Den Eurigen und Walther Fürsts — Was Euch
1030 Recht würde dünken, schwuren sie zu thun,
Euch schwuren sie bis in den Tod zu folgen.
— So eilt’ ich sicher unterm heil’gen Schirm
Des Gastrechts von Gehöfte zu Gehöfte —
Und als ich kam ins heimatliche Thal,
1035 Wo mir die Vettern viel verbreitet wohnen —
Als ich den Vater fand, beraubt und blind,
Auf fremdem Stroh, von der Barmherzigkeit
Mildthät’ger Menschen lebend —

Stauffacher.

Herr im Himmel!

Melchthal.

Da weint’ ich nicht! Nicht in ohnmächt’gen Thränen
1040 Goß ich die Kraft des heißen Schmerzens aus;
In tiefer Brust, wie einen teuren Schatz,
Verschloß ich ihn und dachte nur auf Thaten.
Ich kroch durch alle Krümmen des Gebirgs,
Kein Thal war so versteckt, ich späht’ es aus;
1045 Bis an der Gletscher eisbedeckten Fuß
Erwartet’ ich und fand bewohnte Hütten,
Und überall, wohin mein Fuß mich trug,
Fand ich den gleichen Haß der Tyrannei;
Denn bis an diese letzte Grenze selbst
1050 Belebter Schöpfung, wo der starre Boden
Aufhört zu geben, raubt der Vögte Geiz —
Die Herzen alle dieses biedern Volks
Erregt’ ich mit dem Stachel meiner Worte,
Und unser sind sie all’ mit Herz und Mund.

Stauffacher.

1055 Großes habt Ihr in kurzer Frist geleistet.

Melchthal.

Ich that noch mehr. Die beiden Festen sind's,
Roßberg und Sarnen, die der Landmann fürchtet;
Denn hinter ihren Felsenwällen schirmt
Der Feind sich leicht und schädiget das Land.
1060 Mit eignen Augen wollt' ich es erkunden,
Ich war zu Sarnen und besah die Burg.

Stauffacher.

Ihr wagtet Euch bis in des Tigers Höhle?

Melchthal.

Ich war verkleidet dort in Pilgerstracht,
Ich sah den Landvogt an der Tafel schwelgen —
1065 Urteilt, ob ich mein Herz bezwingen kann;
Ich sah den Feind, und ich erschlug ihn nicht.

Stauffacher.

Fürwahr, das Glück war Eurer Kühnheit hold.

(Unterdessen sind die andern Landleute vorwärts gekommen und nähern
sich den beiden.)

Doch jetzo sagt mir, wer die Freunde sind
Und die gerechten Männer, die Euch folgten?
1070 Macht mich bekannt mit ihnen, daß wir uns
Zutraulich nahen und die Herzen öffnen.

Meier.

Wer kennte Euch nicht, Herr, in den drei Landen?
Ich bin der Mei'r von Sarnen; dies hier ist
Mein Schwestersohn, der Struth von Winkelried.

Stauffacher.

1075 Ihr nennt mir keinen unbekannten Namen.
Ein Winkelried war's, der den Drachen schlug

Im Sumpf bei Weiler und sein Leben ließ
In diesem Strauß.

Winkelried.

Das war mein Ahn, Herr Werner.

Melchthal (zeigt auf zwei Landleute).

Die wohnen hinterm Wald, sind Klosterleute
1080 Vom Engelberg — Ihr werdet sie drum nicht
Verachten, weil sie eigne Leute sind,
Und nicht wie wir frei sitzen auf dem Erbe —
Sie lieben's Land, sind sonst auch wohl berufen.

Stauffacher (zu den beiden).

Gebt mir die Hand! Es preise sich, wer keinem
1085 Mit seinem Leibe pflichtig ist auf Erden;
Doch Redlichkeit gedeiht in jedem Stande.

Konrad Hunn.

Das ist Herr Reding, unser Altlandammann.

Meier.

Ich kenn' ihn wohl. Er ist mein Widerpart,
Der um ein altes Erbstück mit mir rechtet.
1090 — Herr Reding, wir sind Feinde vor Gericht;
Hier sind wir einig.

(Schüttelt ihm die Hand.)

Stauffacher.

Das ist brav gesprochen.

Winkelried.

Hört ihr? Sie kommen. Hört das Horn von Uri!

Rechts und links sieht man bewaffnete Männer mit Windlichtern die Felsen
herabsteigen.)

Auf der Mauer.

Seht! Steigt nicht selbst der fromme Diener Gottes,
Der würd'ge Pfarrer mit herab? Nicht scheut er

1095 Des Weges Mühen und das Graun der Nacht,
Ein treuer Hirte für das Volk zu sorgen.

Baumgarten.

Der Sigrist folgt ihm und Herr Walther Fürst;
Doch nicht den Tell erblick' ich in der Menge.

Walther Fürst, Rösselmann der Pfarrer, Petermann
der Sigrist, Kuoni der Hirt, Werni der Jäger,
Ruodi der Fischer und noch fünf andere Landleute.
Alle zusammen, dreiunddreißig an der Zahl, treten vorwärts und
stellen sich um das Feuer.

Walther Fürst.

So müssen wir auf unserm eignen Erb'
1100 Und väterlichen Boden uns verstohlen
Zusammen schleichen, wie die Mörder thun,
Und bei der Nacht, die ihren schwarzen Mantel
Nur dem Verbrechen und der sonnenscheuen
Verschwörung leihet, unser gutes Recht
1105 Uns holen, das doch lauter ist und klar
Gleichwie der glanzvoll offne Schoß des Tages.

Melchthal.

Laßt's gut sein! Was die dunkle Nacht gesponnen,
Soll frei und fröhlich an das Licht der Sonnen.

Rösselmann.

Hört, was mir Gott ins Herz giebt, Eidgenossen!
1110 Wir stehen hier statt einer Landsgemeinde
Und können gelten für ein ganzes Volk.
So laßt uns tagen nach den alten Bräuchen
Des Lands, wie wir's in ruhigen Zeiten pflegen;
Was ungesetzlich ist in der Versammlung,
1115 Entschuldige die Not der Zeit. Doch Gott

Ist überall, wo man das Recht verwaltet,
Und unter seinem Himmel stehen wir.

Stauffacher.

Wohl, laßt uns tagen nach der alten Sitte!
Ist es gleich Nacht, so leuchtet unser Recht.

Melchthal.

1120 Ist gleich die Zahl nicht voll, das H e r z ist hier
Des ganzen Volks, die B e s t e n sind zugegen.

Konrad Hunn.

Sind auch die alten Bücher nicht zur Hand,
Sie sind in unsre Herzen eingeschrieben.

Rösselmann.

Wohlan, so sei der Ring sogleich gebildet!
1125 Man pflanze a u f die Schwerter der Gewalt!

Auf der Mauer.

Der Landesammann nehme seinen Platz,
Und seine Waibel stehen ihm zur Seite!

Sigrist.

Es sind der Völker dreie. Welchem nun
Gebührt's, das Haupt zu geben der Gemeinde?

Meier.

1130 Um diese Ehr' mag Schwyz mit Uri streiten;
Wir Unterwaldner stehen frei zurück.

Melchthal.

Wir stehn zurück; wir sind die Flehenden,
Die Hilfe heischen von den mächt'gen Freunden.

Stauffacher.

So nehme Uri denn das Schwert; sein Banner
1135 Zieht bei den Römerzügen uns voran.

Walther Fürst.

Des Schwertes Ehre werde Schwyz zu teil;
Denn seines Stammes rühmen wir uns alle.

Rösselmann.

Den edeln Wettstreit laßt mich freundlich schlichten;
Schwyz soll im Rat, Uri im Felde führen.

Walther Fürst
(reicht dem Stauffacher die Schwerter).

1140 So nehmt!

Stauffacher.

Nicht mir, dem Alter sei die Ehre.

Im Hofe.

Die meisten Jahre zählt Ulrich der Schmid.

Auf der Mauer.

Der Mann ist wacker, doch nicht freien Stands;
Kein eigner Mann kann Richter sein in Schwyz.

Stauffacher.

Steht nicht Herr Reding hier, der Altlandammann?
1145 Was suchen wir noch einen Würdigern?

Walther Fürst.

Er sei der Ammann und des Tages Haupt!
Wer dazu stimmt, erhebe seine Hände!
(Alle heben die rechte Hand auf.)

Reding (tritt in die Mitte).

Ich kann die Hand nicht auf die Bücher legen,
So schwör' ich droben bei den ew'gen Sternen,

1150 Daß ich mich nimmer will vom Recht entfernen.

Man richtet die zwei Schwerter vor ihm auf, der Ring bildet sich um ihn her, Schwyz hält die Mitte, rechts stellt sich Uri und links Unterwalden. Er steht auf sein Schlachtschwert gestützt.)

Was ist's, das die drei Völker des Gebirgs
Hier an des Sees unwirtlichem Gestade
Zusammenführte in der Geisterstunde?
Was soll der Inhalt sein des neuen Bunds,
1155 Den wir hier unterm Sternenhimmel stiften?

Stauffacher (tritt in den Ring).

Wir stiften keinen neuen Bund; es ist
Ein uralt Bündnis nur von Väter Zeit,
Das wir erneuern! Wisset, Eidgenossen!
Ob uns der See, ob uns die Berge scheiden,
1160 Und jedes Volk sich für sich selbst regiert,
So sind wir eines Stammes doch und Bluts,
Und eine Heimat ist's, aus der wir zogen.

Winkelried.

So ist es wahr, wie's in den Liedern lautet,
Daß wir von fern her in das Land gewallt?
1165 O, teilt's uns mit, was Euch davon bekannt,
Daß sich der neue Bund am alten stärke.

Stauffacher.

Hört, was die alten Hirten sich erzählen.
— Es war ein großes Volk, hinten im Lande
Nach Mitternacht, das litt von schwerer Teurung.
1170 In dieser Not beschloß die Landsgemeinde,
Daß je der zehnte Bürger nach dem Los
Der Väter Land verlasse — Das geschah!
Und zogen aus, wehklagend, Männer und Weiber,

Ein großer Heerzug, nach der Mittagsonne,
1175 Mit dem Schwert sich schlagend durch das deutsche Land,
Bis an das Hochland dieser Waldgebirge.
Und eher nicht ermüdete der Zug,
Bis daß sie kamen in das wilde Thal,
Wo jetzt die Muotta zwischen Wiesen rinnt —
1180 Nicht Menschenspuren waren hier zu sehen,
Nur eine Hütte stand am Ufer einsam.
Da saß ein Mann und wartete der Fähre —
Doch heftig wogete der See und war
Nicht fahrbar; da besahen sie das Land
1185 Sich näher und gewahrten schöne Fülle
Des Holzes und entdeckten gute Brunnen
Und meinten, sich im lieben Vaterland
Zu finden — Da beschlossen sie zu bleiben,
Erbaueten den alten Flecken S ch w y z
1190 Und hatten manchen sauren Tag, den Wald
Mit weit verschlungnen Wurzeln auszuroden —
Drauf als der Boden nicht mehr Gnügen that
Der Zahl des Volks, da zogen sie hinüber
Zum schwarzen Berg, ja bis ans Weißland hin,
1195 Wo, hinter ew'gem Eiseswall verborgen,
Ein andres Volk in andern Zungen spricht.
Den Flecken S t a n z erbauten sie am Kernwald,
Den Flecken A l t o r f in dem Thal der Reuß —
Doch blieben sie des Ursprungs stets gedenk;
1200 Aus all den fremden Stämmen, die seitdem
In Mitte ihres Lands sich angesiedelt,
Finden die Schwyzer Männer sich heraus;
Es giebt das Herz, das Blut sich zu erkennen.

(Reicht rechts und links die Hand hin.)

Auf der Mauer.

Ja, wir sind eines Herzens, eines Bluts!

Alle (sich die Hände reichend).

1205 Wir sind ein Volk, und einig wollen wir handeln.

Stauffacher.

Die andern Völker tragen fremdes Joch,
Sie haben sich dem Sieger unterworfen.
Es leben selbst in unsern Landesmarken
Der Sassen viel, die fremde Pflichten tragen,
1210 Und ihre Knechtschaft erbt auf ihre Kinder.
Doch wir, der alten Schweizer echter Stgmm,
Wir haben stets die Freiheit uns bewahrt.
Nicht unter Fürsten bogen wir das Knie,
Freiwillig wählten wir den Schirm der Kaiser.

Rösselmann.

1215 Frei wählten wir des Reiches Schutz und Schirm;
So steht's bemerkt in Kaiser Friedrichs Brief.

Stauffacher.

Denn herrenlos ist auch der Freiste nicht.
Ein Oberhaupt muß sein, ein höchster Richter,
Wo man das Recht mag schöpfen in dem Streit.
1220 Drum haben unsre Väter für den Boden,
Den sie der alten Wildnis abgewonnen,
Die Ehr' gegönnt dem Kaiser, der den Herrn
Sich nennt der deutschen und der welschen Erde,
Und, wie die andern Freien seines Reichs,
1225 Sich ihm zu edelm Waffendienst gelobt;
Denn dieses ist der Freien einz'ge Pflicht,
Das Reich zu schirmen, das sie selbst beschirmt.

Melchthal.

Was drüber ist, ist Merkmal eines Knechts.

Stauffacher.

Sie folgten, wenn der Heribann erging,
1230 Dem Reichspanier und schlugen seine Schlachten.
Nach Welschland zogen sie gewappnet mit,
Die Römerkron' ihm auf das Haupt zu setzen.
Daheim regierten sie sich fröhlich selbst
Nach altem Brauch und eigenem Gesetz;
1235 Der höchste Blutbann war allein des Kaisers.
Und dazu ward bestellt ein großer Graf,
Der hatte seinen Sitz nicht in dem Lande.
Wenn Blutschuld kam, so rief man ihn herein,
Und unter offnem Himmel, schlicht und klar,
1240 Sprach er das Recht und ohne Furcht der Menschen.
Wo sind hier Spuren, daß wir Knechte sind?
Ist einer, der es anders weiß, der rede!

Im Hofe.

Nein, so verhält sich alles, wie Ihr sprecht,
Gewaltherrschaft ward nie bei uns geduldet.

Stauffacher.

1245 Dem Kaiser selbst versagten wir Gehorsam,
Da er das Recht zu Gunst der Pfaffen bog.
Denn als die Leute von dem Gotteshaus
Einsiedeln uns die Alp in Anspruch nahmen,
Die wir beweidet seit der Väter Zeit,
1250 Der Abt herfürzog einen alten Brief,
Der ihm die herrenlose Wüste schenkte —
Denn unser Dasein hatte man verhehlt —
Da sprachen wir: „Erschlichen ist der Brief!

Kein Kaiser kann, was unser ist, verschenken;
1255 Und wird uns Recht versagt vom Reich, wir können
In unsern Bergen auch des Reichs entbehren."
— So sprachen unsre Väter! Sollen wir
Des neuen Joches Schändlichkeit erdulden,
Erleiden von dem fremden Knecht, was uns
1260 In seiner Macht kein Kaiser durfte bieten?
— Wir haben diesen Boden uns erschaffen
Durch unsrer Hände Fleiß, den alten Wald,
Der sonst der Bären wilde Wohnung war,
Zu einem Sitz für Menschen umgewandelt;
1265 Die Brut des Drachen haben wir getötet,
Der aus den Sümpfen giftgeschwollen stieg;
Die Nebeldecke haben wir zerrissen,
Die ewig grau um diese Wildnis hing,
Den harten Fels gesprengt, über den Abgrund
1270 Dem Wandersmann den sichern Steg geleitet;
Unser ist durch tausendjährigen Besitz
Der Boden — und der fremde Herrenknecht
Soll kommen dürfen und uns Ketten schmieden
Und Schmach anthun auf unsrer eignen Erde?
1275 Ist keine Hilfe gegen solchen Drang?

(Eine große Bewegung unter den Landleuten.)

Nein, eine Grenze hat Tyrannenmacht.
Wenn der Gedrückte nirgends Recht kann finden,
Wenn unerträglich wird die Last — greift er
Hinauf getrosten Mutes in den Himmel
1280 Und holt herunter seine ew'gen Rechte,
Die droben hangen unveräußerlich
Und unzerbrechlich wie die Sterne selbst —
Der alte Urstand der Natur kehrt wieder,

Wo Mensch dem Menschen gegenüber steht —
1285 Zum letzten Mittel, wenn kein andres mehr
Verfangen will, ist ihm das Schwert gegeben — —
Der Güter höchstes dürfen wir verteid'gen
Gegen Gewalt. — Wir stehn für unser Land,
Wir stehn für unsre Weiber, unsre Kinder!

Alle (an ihre Schwerter schlagend).

1290 Wir stehn für unsre Weiber, unsre Kinder!

Rösselmann (tritt in den Ring).

Eh' ihr zum Schwerte greift, bedenkt es wohl!
Ihr könnt es friedlich mit dem Kaiser schlichten.
Es kostet euch ein Wort, und die Tyrannen,
Die euch jetzt schwer bedrängen, schmeicheln euch.
1295 — Ergreift, was man euch oft geboten hat,
Trennt euch vom Reich, erkennet Östreichs Hoheit —

Auf der Mauer.

Was sagt der Pfarrer? Wir zu Östreich schwören!

Am Bühel.

Hört ihn nicht an!

Winkelried.

   Das rät uns ein Verräter,
Ein Feind des Landes!

Reding.

   Ruhig, Eidgenossen!

Sewa.

1300 Wir Östreich huldigen, nach solcher Schmach!

Von der Flüe.

Wir uns abtrotzen lassen durch Gewalt,
Was wir der Güte weigerten!

Meier.

Dann wären
Wir Sklaven und verdienten, es zu sein!

Auf der Mauer.

Der sei gestoßen aus dem Recht der Schweizer,
1305 Wer von Ergebung spricht an Österreich!
— Landammann, ich bestehe drauf; dies sei
Das erste Landsgesetz, das wir hier geben.

Melchthal.

So sei's! Wer von Ergebung spricht an Östreich,
Soll rechtlos sein und aller Ehren bar.
1310 Kein Landmann nehm' ihn auf an seinem Feuer.

Alle (heben die rechte Hand auf).

Wir wollen es, das sei Gesetz!

Reding (nach einer Pause).

Es ist's.

Rösselmann.

Jetzt seid ihr frei, ihr seid's durch dies Gesetz.
Nicht durch Gewalt soll Österreich ertrotzen,
Was es durch freundlich Werben nicht erhielt —

Jost von Weiler.

1315 Zur Tagesordnung, weiter!

Reding.

Eidgenossen!
Sind alle sanften Mittel auch versucht?
Vielleicht weiß es der König nicht; es ist
Wohl gar sein Wille nicht, was wir erdulden.
Auch dieses Letzte sollten wir versuchen,
1320 Erst unsre Klage bringen vor sein Ohr,

Eh' wir zum Schwerte greifen. Schrecklich immer,
Auch in gerechter Sache, ist Gewalt.
Gott hilft nur dann, wenn Menschen nicht mehr helfen

Stauffacher (zu Konrad Hunn).

Nun ist's an Euch, Bericht zu geben. Redet!

Konrad Hunn.

1325 Ich war zu Rheinfeld an des Kaisers Pfalz,
Wider der Vögte harten Druck zu klagen,
Den Brief zu holen unsrer alten Freiheit,
Den jeder neue König sonst bestätigt.
Die Boten vieler Städte fand ich dort,

1330 Vom schwäb'schen Lande und vom Lauf des Rheins,
Die all' erhielten ihre Pergamente
Und kehrten freudig wieder in ihr Land.
Mich, euren Boten, wies man an die Räte,
Und die entließen mich mit leerem Trost:

1335 „Der Kaiser habe diesmal keine Zeit;
Er würde sonst einmal wohl an uns denken."
— Und als ich traurig durch die Säle ging
Der Königsburg, da sah ich Herzog Hansen
In einem Erker weinend stehn, um ihn

1340 Die edeln Herrn von Wart und Tegerfeld,
Die riefen mir und sagten: „Helft euch selbst!
Gerechtigkeit erwartet nicht vom König.
Beraubt er nicht des eignen Bruders Kind
Und hinterhält ihm sein gerechtes Erbe?

1345 Der Herzog fleht ihn um sein Mütterliches,
Er habe seine Jahre voll, es wäre
Nun Zeit, auch Land und Leute zu regieren.
Was ward ihm zum Bescheid? Ein Kränzlein setzt' ihm
Der Kaiser auf: das sei die Zier der Jugend."

Auf der Mauer.

1350 Ihr habt's gehört. Recht und Gerechtigkeit
Erwartet nicht vom Kaiser! Helft euch selbst!

Reding.

Nichts andres bleibt uns übrig. Nun gebt Rat,
Wie wir es klug zum frohen Ende leiten.

Walther Fürst (tritt in den Ring).

Abtreiben wollen wir verhaßten Zwang;
1355 Die alten Rechte, wie wir sie ererbt
Von unsern Vätern, wollen wir bewahren,
Nicht ungezügelt nach dem Neuen greifen.
Dem Kaiser bleibe, was des Kaisers ist;
Wer einen Herrn hat, dien' ihm pflichtgemäß.

Meier.

1360 Ich trage Gut von Österreich zu Lehen.

Walther Fürst.

Ihr fahret fort, Östreich die Pflicht zu leisten.

Jost von Weiler.

Ich steure an die Herrn von Rapperswil.

Walther Fürst.

Ihr fahret fort, zu zinsen und zu steuern.

Rösselmann.

Der großen Frau zu Zürch bin ich vereidet.

Walther Fürst.

1365 Ihr gebt dem Kloster, was des Klosters ist.

Stauffacher.

Ich trage keine Lehen als des Reichs.

Walther Fürst.

Was sein muß, das geschehe, doch nicht drüber!
Die Vögte wollen wir mit ihren Knechten
Verjagen und die festen Schlösser brechen;
1370 Doch, wenn es sein mag, ohne Blut. Es sehe
Der Kaiser, daß wir notgedrungen nur
Der Ehrfurcht fromme Pflichten abgeworfen.
Und sieht er uns in unsern Schranken bleiben,
Vielleicht besiegt er staatsklug seinen Zorn;
1375 Denn bill'ge Furcht erwecket sich ein Volk,
Das mit dem Schwerte in der Faust sich mäßigt.

Reding.

Doch lasset hören! Wie vollenden wir's?
Es hat der Feind die Waffen in der Hand,
Und nicht, fürwahr! in Frieden wird er weichen.

Stauffacher.

1380 Er wird's, wenn er in Waffen uns erblickt;
Wir überraschen ihn, eh' er sich rüstet.

Meier.

Ist bald gesprochen, aber schwer gethan.
Uns ragen in dem Land zwei feste Schlösser,
Die geben Schirm dem Feind und werden furchtbar,
1385 Wenn uns der König in das Land sollt' fallen.
Roßberg und Sarnen muß bezwungen sein,
Eh' man ein Schwert erhebt in den drei Landen

Stauffacher.

Säumt man so lang', so wird der Feind gewarnt;
Zu Viele sind's, die das Geheimnis teilen.

Meier.

1390 In den Waldstätten find't sich kein Verräter.

Rösselmann.

Der Eifer auch, der gute, kann verraten.

Walther Fürst.

Schiebt man es auf, so wird der Twing vollendet
In Altorf, und der Vogt befestigt sich.

Meier.

Ihr denkt an euch.

Sigrist.

Und ihr seid ungerecht.

Meier (auffahrend).

1395 Wir ungerecht! Das darf uns Uri bieten!

Reding.

Bei eurem Eide! Ruh'!

Meier.

Ja, wenn sich Schwyz
Versteht mit Uri, müssen w i r wohl schweigen.

Reding.

Ich muß Euch weisen vor der Landsgemeinde,
Daß Ihr mit heft'gem Sinn den Frieden stört!
1400 Stehn wir nicht alle für dieselbe Sache?

Winkelried.

Wenn wir's verschieben bis zum Fest des Herrn,
Dann bringt's die Sitte mit, daß alle Sassen
Dem Vogt Geschenke bringen auf das Schloß;
So können zehen Männer oder zwölf

1405 Sich unverdächtig in der Burg versammeln,
Die führen heimlich spitz'ge Eisen mit,
Die man geschwind kann an die Stäbe stecken;
Denn niemand kommt mit Waffen in die Burg.
Zunächst im Wald hält dann der große Haufe.
1410 Und wenn die andern glücklich sich des Thors
Ermächtiget, so wird ein Horn geblasen,
Und jene brechen aus dem Hinterhalt.
So wird das Schloß mit leichter Arbeit unser.

Melchthal.

Den Roßberg übernehm' ich zu ersteigen,
1415 Denn eine Dirn' des Schlosses ist mir hold,
Und leicht bethör' ich sie, zum nächtlichen
Besuch die schwanke Leiter mir zu reichen;
Bin ich droben erst, zieh' ich die Freunde nach.

Reding.

Ist's aller Wille, daß verschoben werde?

(Die Mehrheit erhebt die Hand.)

Stauffacher (zählt die Stimmen).

1420 Es ist ein Mehr von Zwanzig gegen Zwölf!

Walther Fürst.

Wenn am bestimmten Tag die Burgen fallen,
So geben wir von einem Berg zum andern
Das Zeichen mit dem Rauch; der Landsturm wird
Aufgeboten, schnell, im Hauptort jedes Landes.
1425 Wenn dann die Vögte sehn der Waffen Ernst,
Glaubt mir, sie werden sich des Streits begeben
Und gern ergreifen friedliches Geleit,
Aus unsern Landesmarken zu entweichen.

Stauffacher.

Nur mit dem Geßler fürcht' ich schweren Stand,
1430 Furchtbar ist er mit Reisigen umgeben;
Nicht ohne Blut räumt er das Feld; ja selbst
Vertrieben, bleibt er furchtbar noch dem Land.
Schwer ist's und fast gefährlich, ihn zu schonen.

Baumgarten.

Wo's halsgefährlich ist, da stellt mich hin!
1435 Dem Tell verdank' ich mein gerettet Leben,
Gern schlag' ich's in die Schanze für das Land,
Mein' Ehr' hab' ich beschützt, mein Herz befriedigt.

Reding.

Die Zeit bringt Rat. Erwartet's in Geduld!
Man muß dem Augenblick auch was vertrauen.
1440 — Doch seht, indes wir nächtlich hier noch tagen,
Stellt auf den höchsten Bergen schon der Morgen
Die glühnde Hochwacht aus — Kommt, laßt uns scheiden,
Eh' uns des Tages Leuchten überrascht.

Walther Fürst.

Sorgt nicht, die Nacht weicht langsam aus den Thälern.

(Alle haben unwillkürlich die Hüte abgenommen und betrachten mit stiller
Sammlung die Morgenröte.

Rösselmann.

1445 Bei diesem Licht, das uns zuerst begrüßt
Von allen Völkern, die tief unter uns
Schwer atmend wohnen in dem Qualm der Städte,
Laßt uns den Eid des neuen Bundes schwören.
— Wir wollen sein ein einzig Volk von Brüdern,
1450 In keiner Not uns trennen und Gefahr.

(Alle sprechen es nach mit erhobenen drei Fingern.)

— Wir wollen frei sein, wie die Väter waren,
Eher den Tod, als in der Knechtschaft leben.

(Wie oben.)

— Wir wollen trauen auf den höchsten Gott
Und uns nicht fürchten vor der Macht der Menschen.

(Wie oben. Die Landleute umarmen einander.)

Stauffacher.

1455 Jetzt gehe jeder seines Weges still
Zu seiner Freundschaft und Genoßame!
Wer Hirt ist, wintre ruhig seine Herde
Und werb' im Stillen Freunde für den Bund!
— Was noch bis dahin muß erduldet werden,
1460 Erduldet's! Laßt die Rechnung der Tyrannen
Anwachsen, bis ein Tag die allgemeine
Und die besondre Schuld auf einmal zahlt.
Bezähme jeder die gerechte Wut
Und spare für das Ganze seine Rache;
1465 Denn Raub begeht am allgemeinen Gut,
Wer selbst sich hilft in seiner eignen Sache.

[Indem sie zu drei verschiedenen Seiten in größter Ruhe abgehen, fällt das Orchester mit einem prachtvollen Schwung ein; die leere Scene bleibt noch eine Zeit lang offen und zeigt das Schauspiel der aufgehenden Sonne über den Eisgebirgen.)

Dritter Aufzug.

Erste Scene.

Hof vor Tells Hause.

Tell ist mit der Zimmeraxt, Hedwig mit einer häuslichen Arbeit beschäftigt. Walther und Wilhelm in der Tiefe spielen mit einer kleinen Armbrust.

Walther (singt).

Mit dem Pfeil, dem Bogen
Durch Gebirg und Thal
Kommt der Schütz gezogen
1470 Früh am Morgenstrahl.

Wie im Reich der Lüfte
König ist der Weih —
Durch Gebirg und Klüfte
Herrscht der Schütze frei.

1475 Ihm gehört das Weite,
Was sein Pfeil erreicht,
Das ist seine Beute,
Was da kreucht und fleugt.

(Kommt gesprungen.)

Der Strang ist mir entzwei. Mach' mir ihn, Vater.

Tell.

1480 Ich nicht. Ein rechter Schütze hilft sich selbst.

(Knaben entfernen sich.)

77

Hedwig.

Die Knaben fangen zeitig an zu schießen.

Tell.

Früh übt sich, was ein Meister werden will.

Hedwig.

Ach, wollte Gott, sie lernten's nie!

Tell.

Sie sollen alles lernen. Wer durch's Leben
1485 Sich frisch will schlagen, muß zu Schutz und Trutz
Gerüstet sein.

Hedwig.

            Ach, es wird keiner seine Ruh'
Zu Hause finden.

Tell.

            Mutter, ich kann's auch nicht.
Zum Hirten hat Natur mich nicht gebildet;
Rastlos muß ich ein flüchtig Ziel verfolgen.
1490 Dann erst genieß' ich meines Lebens recht,
Wenn ich mir's jeden Tag aufs neu' erbeute.

Hedwig.

Und an die Angst der Hausfrau denkst du nicht,
Die sich indessen, deiner wartend, härmt.
Denn mich erfüllt's mit Grausen, was die Knechte
1495 Von euren Wagefahrten sich erzählen;
Bei jedem Abschied zittert mir das Herz,
Daß du mir nimmer werdest wiederkehren.
Ich sehe dich, im wilden Eisgebirg
Verirrt, von einer Klippe zu der andern
1500 Den Fehlsprung thun, seh', wie die Gemse dich

Rückspringend mit sich in den Abgrund reißt,
Wie eine Windlawine dich verschüttet,
Wie unter dir der trügerische Firn
Einbricht, und du hinabsinkst, ein lebendig
1505 Begrabner, in die schauerliche Gruft —
Ach, den verwegnen Alpenjäger hascht
Der Tod in hundert wechselnden Gestalten!
Das ist ein unglückseliges Gewerb',
Das halsgefährlich führt am Abgrund hin!

Tell.

1510 Wer frisch umherspäht mit gesunden Sinnen,
Auf Gott vertraut und die gelenke Kraft,
Der ringt sich leicht aus jeder Fahr und Not;
Den schreckt der Berg nicht, der darauf geboren.

(Er hat seine Arbeit vollendet, legt das Gerät hinweg.)

Jetzt, mein' ich, hält das Thor auf Jahr und Tag.
1515 Die Axt im Haus erspart den Zimmermann.

(Nimmt den Hut.)

Hedwig.

Wo gehst du hin?

Tell.

Nach Altorf, zu dem Vater.

Hedwig.

Sinnst du auch nichts Gefährliches? Gesteh mir's!

Tell.

Wie kommst du darauf, Frau?

Hedwig.

Es spinnt sich etwas
Gegen die Vögte — Auf dem Rütli ward
1520 Getagt, ich weiß, und du bist auch im Bunde.

Tell.

Ich war nicht mit dabei — doch werd' ich mich
Dem Lande nicht entziehen, wenn es ruft.

Hedwig.

Sie werden dich hinstellen, wo Gefahr ist;
Das Schwerste wird dein Anteil sein, wie immer.

Tell.

1525 Ein jeder wird besteuert nach Vermögen.

Hedwig.

Den Unterwaldner hast du auch im Sturme
Über den See geschafft — Ein Wunder war's,
Daß ihr entkommen — Dachtest du denn gar nicht
An Kind und Weib?

Tell.

     Lieb Weib, ich dacht' an euch!
1530 Drum rettet' ich den Vater seinen Kindern.

Hedwig.

Zu schiffen in dem wüt'gen See! Das heißt
Nicht Gott vertrauen! Das heißt Gott versuchen!

Tell.

Wer gar zu viel bedenkt, wird wenig leisten.

Hedwig.

Ja, du bist gut und hilfreich, dienest allen,
1535 Und wenn du selbst in Not kommst, hilft dir keiner.

Tell.

Verhüt' es Gott, daß ich nicht Hilfe brauche!

(Er nimmt die Armbrust und Pfeile.)

Hedwig.

Was willst du mit der Armbrust? Laß sie hier!

Tell.

Mir fehlt der Arm, wenn mir die Waffe fehlt.

<small>(Die Knaben kommen zurück.)</small>

Walther.

Vater, wo gehst du hin?

Tell.

Nach Altorf, Knabe,
1540 Zum Ehni — Willst du mit?

Walther.

Ja, freilich will ich.

Hedwig.

Der Landvogt ist jetzt dort. Bleib' weg von Altorf!

Tell.

Er geht, noch heute.

Hedwig.

Drum laß ihn erst fort sein!
Gemahn' ihn nicht an dich; du weißt, er grollt uns.

Tell.

Mir soll sein böser Wille nicht viel schaden,
1545 Ich thue recht und scheue keinen Feind.

Hedwig.

Die recht thun, eben die haßt er am meisten.

Tell.

Weil er nicht an sie kommen kann — Mich wird
Der Ritter wohl in Frieden lassen, mein' ich.

Hedwig.

So, weißt du das?

Tell.

Es ist nicht lange her,

1550 Da ging ich jagen durch die wilden Gründe
Des Schächenthals auf menschenleerer Spur,
Und da ich einsam einen Felsensteig
Verfolgte, wo nicht auszuweichen war,
Denn über mir hing schroff die Felswand her,

1555 Und unten rauschte fürchterlich der Schächen,

(Die Knaben drängen sich rechts und links an ihn und sehen mit gespannter
Neugier zu ihm hinauf.)

Da kam der Landvogt gegen mich daher,
Er ganz allein mit mir, der auch allein war,
Bloß Mensch zu Mensch, und neben uns der Abgrund.
Und als der Herre mein ansichtig ward

1560 Und mich erkannte, den er kurz zuvor
Um kleiner Ursach' willen schwer gebüßt,
Und sah mich mit dem stattlichen Gewehr
Daher geschritten kommen, da verblaßt' er,
Die Knie' versagten ihm, ich sah es kommen,

1565 Daß er jetzt an die Felswand würde sinken.
— Da jammerte mich sein, ich trat zu ihm
Bescheidentlich und sprach: Ich bin's, Herr Landvogt.
Er aber konnte keinen armen Laut
Aus seinem Munde geben — Mit der Hand nur

1570 Winkt' er mir schweigend, meines Wegs zu gehn;
Da ging ich fort und sandt' ihm sein Gefolge.

Hedwig.

Er hat vor dir gezittert — Wehe dir!
Daß du ihn schwach gesehn, vergiebt er nie.

Tell.

Drum meid' ich ihn, und er wird mich nicht suchen.

Hedwig.

1575 Bleib heute nur dort weg. Geh lieber jagen!

Tell.

Was fällt dir ein?

Hedwig.

　　　　Mich ängstigt's. Bleibe weg!

Tell.

Wie kannst du dich so ohne Ursach' quälen?

Hedwig.

Weil's keine Ursach' hat — Tell, bleibe hier!

Tell.

Ich hab's versprochen, liebes Weib, zu kommen.

Hedwig.

1580 Mußt du, so geh — nur lasse mir den Knaben!

Walther.

Nein, Mütterchen. Ich gehe mit dem Vater.

Hedwig.

Wälti, verlassen willst du deine Mutter?

Walther.

Ich bring' dir auch was Hübsches mit vom Ehni.

(Geht mit dem Vater.)

Wilhelm.

Mutter, ich bleibe bei dir!

Hedwig (umarmt ihn).

Ja, du bist
1585 Mein liebes Kind, du bleibst mir noch allein!
(Sie geht an das Hofthor und folgt den Abgehenden lange mit den Augen.)

––––––

Zweite Scene.

Eine eingeschlossene wilde Waldgegend.   Staubbäche stürzen von den Felsen.

Bertha im Jagdkleid.   Gleich darauf Rudenz.

Bertha.

Er folgt mir.   Endlich kann ich mich erklären.

Rudenz (tritt rasch ein).

Fräulein, jetzt endlich find' ich Euch allein,
Abgründe schließen rings umher uns ein;
In dieser Wildnis fürcht' ich keinen Zeugen,
1590 Vom Herzen wälz' ich dieses lange Schweigen —

Bertha.

Seid Ihr gewiß, daß uns die Jagd nicht folgt?

Rudenz.

Die Jagd ist dort hinaus — Jetzt oder nie!
Ich muß den teuren Augenblick ergreifen —
Entschieden sehen muß ich mein Geschick,
1595 Und sollt' es mich auf ewig von Euch scheiden.
    — O, waffnet Eure güt'gen Blicke nicht
Mit dieser finstern Strenge — Wer bin ich,
Daß ich den kühnen Wunsch zu Euch erhebe?
Mich hat der Ruhm noch nicht genannt; ich darf

1600 Mich in die Reih' nicht stellen mit den Rittern,
Die siegberühmt und glänzend Euch umwerben.
Nichts hab' ich als mein Herz voll Treu' und Liebe —

Bertha (ernst und streng).

Dürft Ihr von Liebe reden und von Treue,
Der treulos wird an seinen nächsten Pflichten?

(Rudenz tritt zurück.)

1605 Der Sklave Österreichs, der sich dem Fremdling
Verkauft, dem Unterdrücker seines Volks?

Rudenz.

Von Euch, mein Fräulein, hör' ich diesen Vorwurf?
Wen such' ich denn als Euch auf jener Seite?

Bertha.

Mich denkt Ihr auf der Seite des Verrats
1610 Zu finden? Eher wollt' ich meine Hand
Dem Geßler selbst, dem Unterdrücker, schenken,
Als dem naturvergeßnen Sohn der Schweiz,
Der sich zu seinem Werkzeug machen kann!

Rudenz.

O Gott, was muß ich hören!

Bertha.

Wie? Was liegt
1615 Dem guten Menschen näher als die Seinen?
Giebt's schönre Pflichten für ein edles Herz,
Als ein Verteidiger der Unschuld sein,
Das Recht des Unterdrückten zu beschirmen?
— Die Seele blutet mir um Euer Volk;
1620 Ich leide mit ihm, denn ich muß es lieben,
Das so bescheiden ist und doch voll Kraft;

Es zieht mein ganzes Herz mich zu ihm hin,
Mit jedem Tage lern' ich's mehr verehren.
— Ihr aber, den Natur und Ritterpflicht
1625 Ihm zum geborenen Beschützer gaben,
Und der's verläßt, der treulos übertritt
Zum Feind und Ketten schmiedet seinem Land,
Ihr seid's, der mich verletzt und kränkt; ich muß
Mein Herz bezwingen, daß ich Euch nicht hasse.

Rudenz.

1630 Will ich denn nicht das Beste meines Volks?
Ihm unter Östreichs mächt'gem Scepter nicht
Den Frieden —

Bertha.

          Knechtschaft wollt Ihr ihm bereiten!
Die Freiheit wollt Ihr aus dem letzten Schloß,
Das ihr noch auf der Erde blieb, verjagen.
1635 Das Volk versteht sich besser auf sein Glück;
Kein Schein verführt sein sicheres Gefühl.
Euch haben sie das Netz ums Haupt geworfen —

Rudenz.

Bertha! Ihr haßt mich, Ihr verachtet mich!

Bertha.

Thät' ich's, mir wäre besser — Aber den
1640 Verachtet sehen und verachtungswert,
Den man gern lieben möchte —

Rudenz.

          Bertha! Bertha!
Ihr zeiget mir das höchste Himmelsglück
Und stürzt mich tief in einem Augenblick.

Bertha.

Nein, nein, das Edle ist nicht ganz erstickt
1645 In Euch! Es schlummert nur, ich will es wecken:
Ihr müßt Gewalt ausüben an Euch selbst,
Die angestammte Tugend zu ertöten;
Doch wohl Euch, sie ist mächtiger als Ihr,
Und trotz Euch selber seid Ihr gut und edel!

Rudenz.

1650 Ihr glaubt an mich! O Bertha, alles läßt
Mich Eure Liebe sein und werden!

Bertha.

Seid,
Wozu die herrliche Natur Euch machte!
Erfüllt den Platz, wohin sie Euch gestellt,
Zu Eurem Volke steht und Eurem Lande,
1655 Und kämpft für Euer heilig Recht!

Rudenz.

Weh mir!
Wie kann ich Euch erringen, Euch besitzen,
Wenn ich der Macht des Kaisers widerstrebe?
Ist's der Verwandten mächt'ger Wille nicht,
Der über Eure Hand tyrannisch waltet?

Bertha.

1660 In den Waldstätten liegen meine Güter,
Und ist der Schweizer frei, so bin auch ich's.

Rudenz.

Bertha! welch einen Blick thut Ihr mir auf!

Bertha.

Hofft nicht durch Östreichs Gunst mich zu erringen;
Nach meinem Erbe strecken sie die Hand,

1665 Das will man mit dem großen Erb' vereinen.
Dieselbe Ländergier, die Eure Freiheit
Verschlingen will, sie drohet auch der meinen!
— O Freund, zum Opfer bin ich ausersehn,
Vielleicht, um einen Günstling zu belohnen —
1670 Dort, wo die Falschheit und die Ränke wohnen,
Hin an den Kaiserhof will man mich ziehn,
Dort harren mein verhaßter Ehe Ketten;
Die Liebe nur — die Eure kann mich retten!

Rudenz.

Ihr könntet Euch entschließen, hier zu leben,
1675 In meinem Vaterlande mein zu sein?
O Bertha, all mein Sehnen in das Weite,
Was war es, als ein Streben nur nach Euch?
Euch sucht' ich einzig auf dem Weg des Ruhms,
Und all mein Ehrgeiz war nur meine Liebe.
1680 Könnt Ihr mit mir Euch in dies stille Thal
Einschließen und der Erde Glanz entsagen —
O, dann ist meines Strebens Ziel gefunden;
Dann mag der Strom der wildbewegten Welt
Ans sichre Ufer dieser Berge schlagen —
1685 Kein flüchtiges Verlangen hab' ich mehr
Hinauszusenden in des Lebens Weiten —
Dann mögen diese Felsen um uns her
Die undurchdringlich feste Mauer breiten,
Und dies verschloßne sel'ge Thal allein
1690 Zum Himmel offen und gelichtet sein!

Bertha.

Jetzt bist du ganz, wie dich mein ahnend Herz
Geträumt, mich hat mein Glaube nicht betrogen!

Rudenz.

Fahr' hin, du eitler Wahn, der mich bethört!
Ich soll das Glück in meiner Heimat finden.
1695 Hier, wo der Knabe fröhlich aufgeblüht,
Wo tausend Freudespuren mich umgeben,
Wo alle Quellen mir und Bäume leben,
Im Vaterland willst du die Meine werden!
Ach, wohl hab' ich es stets geliebt! Ich fühl's,
1700 Es fehlte mir zu jedem Glück der Erden.

Bertha.

Wo wär' die sel'ge Insel aufzufinden,
Wenn sie nicht hier ist in der Unschuld Land?
Hier, wo die alte Treue heimisch wohnt,
Wo sich die Falschheit noch nicht hingefunden,
1705 Da trübt kein Neid die Quelle unsers Glücks,
Und ewig hell entfliehen uns die Stunden.
— Da seh' ich d i c h im echten Männerwert,
Den Ersten von den Freien und den Gleichen,
Mit reiner, freier Huldigung verehrt,
1710 Groß, wie ein König wirkt in seinen Reichen.

Rudenz.

Da seh' ich dich, die Krone aller Frauen,
In weiblich reizender Geschäftigkeit,
In meinem Haus den Himmel mir erbauen
Und, wie der Frühling seine Blumen streut,
1715 Mit schöner Anmut mir das Leben schmücken
Und alles rings beleben und beglücken!

Bertha.

Sieh, teurer Freund, warum ich trauerte,
Als ich dies höchste Lebensglück dich selbst

Zerstören sah — Weh mir!   Wie stünd's um mich,
1720 Wenn ich dem stolzen Ritter müßte folgen,
Dem Landbedrücker, auf sein finstres Schloß!
— Hier ist kein Schloß.   Mich scheiden keine Mauern
Von einem Volk, das ich beglücken kann!

Rudenz.

Doch wie mich retten — wie die Schlinge lösen,
1725 Die ich mir thöricht selbst ums Haupt gelegt?

Bertha.

Zerreiße sie mit männlichem Entschluß!
Was auch draus werde — steh zu deinem Volk!
Es ist dein angeborner Platz.

(Jagdhörner in der Ferne.)

Die Jagd

Kommt näher — Fort, wir müssen scheiden — Kämpfe
1730 Fürs Vaterland, du kämpfst für deine Liebe!
Es ist ein Feind, vor dem wir alle zittern,
Und eine Freiheit macht uns alle frei!

(Gehen ab.)

———

Dritte Scene.

Wiese bei Altorf.

Im Vordergrund Bäume, in der Tiefe der Hut auf einer Stange. Der Prospect wird begrenzt durch den Bannberg, über welchem ein Schneegebirg emporragt.

Frießhardt und Leuthold halten Wache.

Frießhardt.

Wir passen auf umsonst.   Es will sich niemand
Heran begeben und dem Hut sein' Reverenz

1735 Erzeigen. 's war doch sonst wie Jahrmarkt hier;
Jetzt ist der ganze Anger wie verödet,
Seitdem der Popanz auf der Stange hängt.

Leuthold.

Nur schlecht Gesindel läßt sich sehn und schwingt
Uns zum Verdrieße die zerlumpten Mützen.
1740 Was rechte Leute sind, die machen lieber
Den langen Umweg um den halben Flecken,
Eh' sie den Rücken beugten vor dem Hut.

Frießhardt.

Sie müssen über diesen Platz, wenn sie
Vom Rathaus kommen um die Mittagsstunde.
1745 Da meint' ich schon, 'nen guten Fang zu thun,
Denn keiner dachte dran, den Hut zu grüßen.
Da sieht's der Pfaff, der Rösselmann — kam just
Von einem Kranken her — und stellt sich hin
Mit dem Hochwürdigen, grad vor die Stange —
1750 Der Sigrist mußte mit dem Glöcklein schellen:
Da fielen all' aufs Knie, ich selber mit,
Und grüßten die Monstranz, doch nicht den Hut. —

Leuthold.

Höre, Gesell, es fängt mir an zu deuchten,
Wir stehen hier am Pranger vor dem Hut;
1755 's ist doch ein Schimpf für einen Reitersmann,
Schildwach' zu stehn vor einem leeren Hut —
Und jeder rechte Kerl muß uns verachten.
— Die Reverenz zu machen einem Hut,
Es ist doch, traun! ein närrischer Befehl!

Frießhardt.

1760 Warum nicht einem leeren, hohlen Hut?

Bückst du dich doch vor manchem hohlen Schädel.

Hildegard, Mechthild und Elsbeth treten auf mit Kindern
und stellen sich um die Stange.

Leuthold.

Und du bist auch so ein dienstfert'ger Schurke
Und brächtest wackre Leute gern ins Unglück.
Mag, wer da will, am Hut vorübergehn,
1765 Ich drück' die Augen zu und seh' nicht hin.

Mechthild.

Da hängt der Landvogt — Habt Respekt, ihr Buben!

Elsbeth.

Wollt's Gott, er ging' und ließ' uns seinen Hut;
Es sollte drum nicht schlechter stehn ums Land!

Frießhardt (verscheucht sie).

Wollt ihr vom Platz! Verwünschtes Volk der Weiber!
1770 Wer fragt nach euch? Schickt eure Männer her,
Wenn sie der Mut sticht, dem Befehl zu trotzen.

(Weiber gehen.)

Tell mit der Armbrust tritt auf, den Knaben an der Hand führend.
Sie gehen an dem Hut vorbei gegen die vordere Scene, ohne daraus
zu achten.

Walther (zeigt nach dem Bannberg).

Vater, ist's wahr, daß auf dem Berge dort
Die Bäume bluten, wenn man einen Streich
Drauf führte mit der Axt?

Tell.

Wer sagt das, Knabe?

Walther.

1775 Der Meister Hirt erzählt's — Die Bäume seien

Gebannt, sagt er, und wer sie schädige,
Dem wachse seine Hand heraus zum Grabe.

Tell.

Die Bäume sind gebannt, das ist die Wahrheit.
— Siehst du die Firnen dort, die weißen Hörner,
1780 Die hoch bis in den Himmel sich verlieren?

Walther.

Das sind die Gletscher, die des Nachts so donnern
Und uns die Schlaglawinen niedersenden.

Tell.

So ist's, und die Lawinen hätten längst
Den Flecken Altorf unter ihrer Last
1785 Verschüttet, wenn der Wald dort oben nicht
Als eine Landwehr sich dagegen stellte.

Walther (nach einigem Besinnen).

Giebt's Länder, Vater, wo nicht Berge sind?

Tell.

Wenn man hinunter steigt von unsern Höhen,
Und immer tiefer steigt, den Strömen nach,
1790 Gelangt man in ein großes, ebnes Land,
Wo die Waldwasser nicht mehr brausend schäumen,
Die Flüsse ruhig und gemächlich ziehn;
Da sieht man frei nach allen Himmelsräumen,
Das Korn wächst dort in langen, schönen Auen,
1795 Und wie ein Garten ist das Land zu schauen.

Walther.

Ei, Vater, warum steigen wir denn nicht
Geschwind hinab in dieses schöne Land,
Statt daß wir uns hier ängstigen und plagen?

Tell.

Das Land ist schön und gütig wie der Himmel;
1800 Doch die's bebauen, sie genießen nicht
Den Segen, den sie pflanzen.

Walther.

                              Wohnen sie
Nicht frei, wie du, auf ihrem eignen Erbe?

Tell.

Das Feld gehört dem Bischof und dem König.

Walther.

So dürfen sie doch frei in Wäldern jagen?

Tell.

1805 Dem Herrn gehört das Wild und das Gefieder.

Walther.

Sie dürfen doch frei fischen in dem Strom?

Tell.

Der Strom, das Meer, das Salz gehört dem König

Walther.

Wer ist der König denn, den alle fürchten?

Tell.

Es ist der Eine, der sie schützt und nährt.

Walther.

1810 Sie können sich nicht mutig selbst beschützen?

Tell.

Dort darf der Nachbar nicht dem Nachbar trauen.

Der Hut auf der Stange

Face p. 95

Walther.

Vater, es wird mir eng im weiten Land;
Da wohn' ich lieber unter den Lawinen.

Tell.

Ja, wohl ist's besser, Kind, die Gletscherberge
1815 Im Rücken haben als die bösen Menschen.

(Sie wollen vorübergehen.)

Walther.

Ei, Vater, sieh den Hut dort auf der Stange!

Tell.

Was kümmert uns der Hut? Komm, laß uns gehen!

(Indem er abgehen will, tritt ihm Frießhardt mit vorgehaltener Pike
entgegen.)

Frießhardt.

In des Kaisers Namen! Haltet an und steht!

Tell (greift in die Pike).

Was wollt Ihr? Warum haltet Ihr mich auf?

Frießhardt.

1820 Ihr habt's Mandat verletzt; Ihr müßt uns folgen.

Leuthold.

Ihr habt dem Hut nicht Reverenz bewiesen.

Tell.

Freund, laß mich gehen!

Frießhardt.

Fort, fort ins Gefängnis!

Walther.

Den Vater ins Gefängnis! Hilfe! Hilfe!

(In die Scene rufend.)

Herbei, ihr Männer, gute Leute, helft!
1825 Gewalt! Gewalt! Sie führen ihn gefangen.

(Rösselmann der Pfarrer und Petermann der Sigrist
kommen herbei mit drei andern Männern.)

Sigrist.

Was giebt's?

Rösselmann.

Was legst du Hand an diesen Mann?

Frießhardt.

Er ist ein Feind des Kaisers, ein Verräter!

Tell (faßt ihn heftig).

Ein Verräter, ich!

Rösselmann.

Du irrst dich, Freund! Das ist
Der Tell, ein Ehrenmann und guter Bürger.

Walther
(erblickt Walther Fürsten und eilt ihm entgegen).

1830 Großvater, hilf! Gewalt geschieht dem Vater.

Frießhardt.

Ins Gefängnis, fort!

Walther Fürst (herbeieilend).

Ich leiste Bürgschaft, haltet!
— Um Gottes willen, Tell, was ist geschehen?

Melchthal und Stauffacher kommen.

Frießhardt.

Des Landvogts oberherrliche Gewalt
Verachtet er und will sie nicht erkennen.

Stauffacher.

1835 Das hätt' der Tell gethan?

Melchthal.

Das lügst du, Bube!

Leuthold.

Er hat dem Hut nicht Reverenz bewiesen.

Walther Fürst.

Und darum soll er ins Gefängnis? Freund,
Nimm meine Bürgschaft an und laß ihn ledig!

Frießhardt.

Bürg' du für dich und deinen eignen Leib!
1840 Wir thun, was unsers Amtes — Fort mit ihm!

Melchthal (zu den Landleuten).

Nein, das ist schreiende Gewalt! Ertragen wir's,
Daß man ihn fortführt, frech, vor unsern Augen?

Sigrist.

Wir sind die Stärkern. Freunde, duldet's nicht!
Wir haben einen Rücken an den andern!

Frießhardt.

1845 Wer widersetzt sich dem Befehl des Vogts?

Noch drei Landleute (herbeieilend).

Wir helfen euch. Was giebt's? Schlagt sie zu Boden!
(Hildegard, Mechthild und Elsbeth kommen zurück.)

Tell.

Ich helfe mir schon selbst. Geht, gute Leute!
Meint ihr, wenn ich die Kraft gebrauchen wollte,
Ich würde mich vor ihren Spießen fürchten?

Melchthal (zu Frießhardt).

1850 Wag's, ihn aus unsrer Mitte wegzuführen!

Walther Fürst und **Stauffacher.**

Gelassen! Ruhig!

Frießhardt (schreit).

Aufruhr und Empörung!

(Man hört Jagdhörner.)

Weiber.

Da kommt der Landvogt!

Frießhardt (erhebt die Stimme).

Meuterei! Empörung!

Stauffacher.

Schrei, bis du berstest, Schurke!

Rösselmann und **Melchthal.**

Willst du schweigen?

Frießhardt (ruft noch lauter).

Zu Hilf', zu Hilf' den Dienern des Gesetzes!

Walther Fürst.

1855 Da ist der Vogt! Weh uns, was wird das werden!

Geßler zu Pferd, den Falken auf der Faust, Rudolph der Harras,
Bertha und Rudenz, ein großes Gefolge von bewaffneten
Knechten, welche einen Kreis von Piken um die ganze Scene
schließen.

Rudolph der Harras.

Platz, Platz dem Landvogt!

Geßler.

Treibt sie auseinander!

Was läuft das Volk zusammen? Wer ruft Hilfe?

(Allgemeine Stille.)

Wer war's? Ich will es wissen.

(Zu Frießhardt.)

Du tritt vor!
Wer bist du, und was hältst du diesen Mann?

(Er giebt den Fallen einem Diener.)

Frießhardt.

1860 Gestrenger Herr, ich bin dein Waffenknecht
Und wohlbestellter Wächter bei dem Hut.
Diesen Mann ergriff ich über frischer That,
Wie er dem Hut den Ehrengruß versagte.
Verhaften wollt' ich ihn, wie du befahlst,
1865 Und mit Gewalt will ihn das Volk entreißen.

Geßler (nach einer Pause).

Verachtest du so deinen Kaiser, Tell,
Und mich, der hier an seiner Statt gebietet,
Daß du die Ehr' versagst dem Hut, den ich
Zur Prüfung des Gehorsams aufgehangen?
1870 Dein böses Trachten hast du mir verraten.

Tell.

Verzeiht mir, lieber Herr! Aus Unbedacht,
Nicht aus Verachtung Eurer ist's geschehn;
Wär' ich besonnen, hieß' ich nicht der Tell.
Ich bitt' um Gnad', es soll nicht mehr begegnen.

Geßler (nach einigem Stillschweigen).

1875 Du bist ein Meister auf der Armbrust, Tell,
Man sagt, du nehmst es auf mit jedem Schützen?

Walther Tell.

Und das muß wahr sein, Herr, 'nen Apfel schießt
Der Vater dir vom Baum auf hundert Schritte.

Geßler.

Ist das dein Knabe, Tell?

Tell.

Ja, lieber Herr.

Geßler.

1880 Hast du der Kinder mehr?

Tell.

Zwei Knaben, Herr.

Geßler.

Und welcher ist's, den du am meisten liebst?

Tell.

Herr, beide sind sie mir gleich liebe Kinder.

Geßler.

Nun, Tell! Weil du den Apfel triffst vom Baume
Auf hundert Schritt, so wirst du deine Kunst
1885 Vor mir bewähren müssen — Nimm die Armbrust —
Du hast sie gleich zur Hand — und mach' dich fertig,
Einen Apfel von des Knaben Kopf zu schießen —
Doch will ich raten, ziele gut, daß du
Den Apfel treffest auf den ersten Schuß;
1890 Denn fehlst du ihn, so ist dein Kopf verloren.

(Alle geben Zeichen des Schreckens.)

Tell.

Herr — Welches Ungeheure sinnet Ihr
Mir an? — Ich soll vom Haupte meines Kindes —
— Nein, nein doch, lieber Herr, das kommt Euch nicht
Zu Sinn — Verhüt's der gnäd'ge Gott — das könnt Ihr
1895 Im Ernst von einem Vater nicht begehren!

Geßler.

Du wirst den Apfel schießen von dem Kopf
Des Knaben — Ich begehr's und will's.

Tell.

Ich soll

Mit meiner Armbruſt auf das liebe Haupt
Des eignen Kindes zielen? — Eher ſterb' ich!

Geßler.

1900 Du ſchießeſt oder ſtirbſt mit deinem Knaben.

Tell.

Ich ſoll der Mörder werden meines Kinds!
Herr, Ihr habt keine Kinder — wiſſet nicht,
Was ſich bewegt in eines Vaters Herzen.

Geßler.

Ei, Tell, du biſt ja plötzlich ſo beſonnen!
1905 Man ſagte mir, daß du ein Träumer ſeiſt
Und dich entfernſt von andrer Menſchen Weiſe.
Du liebſt das Seltſame — drum hab' ich jetzt
Ein eigen Wagſtück für dich ausgeſucht,
Ein andrer wohl bedächte ſich — du drückſt
1910 Die Augen zu und greiffſt es herzhaft an.

Bertha.

Scherzt nicht, o Herr, mit dieſen armen Leuten!
Ihr ſeht ſie bleich und zitternd ſtehn — So wenig
Sind ſie Kurzweils gewohnt aus Eurem Munde.

Geßler.

Wer ſagt Euch, daß ich ſcherze?
(Greift nach einem Baumzweige, der über ihn herhängt.)

Hier iſt der Apfel.

1915 Man mache Raum — Er nehme ſeine Weite,

Wie's Brauch ist — Achtzig Schritte geb' ich ihm —
Nicht weniger noch mehr — Er rühmte sich,
Auf ihrer hundert seinen Mann zu treffen —
Jetzt, Schütze, triff und fehle nicht das Ziel!

Rudolph der Harras.

1920 Gott, das wird ernsthaft — Falle nieder, Knabe,
Es gilt, und fleh' den Landvogt um dein Leben!

Walther Fürst
(beiseite zu Melchthal, der kaum seine Ungeduld bezwingt).

Haltet an Euch, ich fleh' Euch drum, bleibt ruhig!

Bertha (zum Landvogt).

Laßt es genug sein, Herr! Unmenschlich ist's,
Mit eines Vaters Angst also zu spielen.
1925 Wenn dieser arme Mann auch Leib und Leben
Verwirkt durch seine leichte Schuld, bei Gott!
Er hätte jetzt zehnfachen Tod empfunden.
Entlaßt ihn ungekränkt in seine Hütte,
Er hat Euch kennen lernen; dieser Stunde
1930 Wird er und seine Kindeskinder denken.

Geßler.

Öffnet die Gasse — Frisch, was zauderst du?
Dein Leben ist verwirkt, ich kann dich töten;
Und sieh, ich lege gnädig dein Geschick
In deine eigne kunstgeübte Hand.
1935 Der kann nicht klagen über harten Spruch,
Den man zum Meister seines Schicksals macht.
Du rühmst dich deines sichern Blicks. Wohlan!
Hier gilt es, Schütze, deine Kunst zu zeigen;
Das Ziel ist würdig, und der Preis ist groß!
1940 Das Schwarze treffen in der Scheibe, das

Kann auch ein andrer; der ist mir der Meister,
Der seiner Kunst gewiß ist überall,
Dem 's Herz nicht in die Hand tritt, noch ins Auge.

Walther Fürst (wirft sich vor ihm nieder).

Herr Landvogt, wir erkennen Eure Hoheit;
1945 Doch lasset Gnad' vor Recht ergehen! Nehmt
Die Hälfte meiner Habe, nehmt sie ganz!
Nur dieses Gräßliche erlasset einem Vater!

Walther Tell.

Großvater, knie nicht vor dem falschen Mann!
Sagt, wo ich hinstehn soll! Ich fürcht' mich nicht.
1950 Der Vater trifft den Vogel ja im Flug,
Er wird nicht fehlen auf das Herz des Kindes.

Stauffacher.

Herr Landvogt, rührt Euch nicht des Kindes Unschuld?

Rösselmann.

O, denket, daß ein Gott im Himmel ist,
Dem Ihr müßt Rede stehn für Eure Thaten!

Geßler (zeigt auf den Knaben).

1955 Man bind' ihn an die Linde dort!

Walther Tell.

                   Mich binden!
Nein, ich will nicht gebunden sein. Ich will
Still halten wie ein Lamm und auch nicht atmen.
Wenn ihr mich bindet, nein, so kann ich's nicht,
So werd' ich toben gegen meine Bande.

Rudolph der Harras.

1960 Die Augen nur laß dir verbinden, Knabe!

Walther Tell.

Warum die Augen? Denket Ihr, ich fürchte
Den Pfeil von Vaters Hand? — Ich will ihn fest
Erwarten und nicht zucken mit den Wimpern.
— Frisch, Vater, zeig's, daß du ein Schütze bist!
1965 Er glaubt dir's nicht, er denkt uns zu verderben —
Dem Wütrich zum Verdrusse schieß und triff!

(Er geht an die Linde, man legt ihm den Apfel auf.)

Melchthal (zu den Landleuten).

Was? Soll der Frevel sich vor unsern Augen
Vollenden? Wozu haben wir geschworen?

Stauffacher.

Es ist umsonst. Wir haben keine Waffen;
1970 Ihr seht den Wald von Lanzen um uns her.

Melchthal.

O, hätten wir's mit frischer That vollendet!
Verzeih's Gott denen, die zum Aufschub rieten!

Geßler (zum Tell).

Ans Werk! Man führt die Waffen nicht vergebens.
Gefährlich ist's, ein Mordgewehr zu tragen,
1975 Und auf den Schützen springt der Pfeil zurück.
Dies stolze Recht, das sich der Bauer nimmt,
Beleidiget den höchsten Herrn des Landes.
Gewaffnet sei niemand, als wer gebietet.
Freut's euch, den Pfeil zu führen und den Bogen,
1980 Wohl, so will ich das Ziel euch dazu geben.

Tell.

(spannt die Armbrust und legt den Pfeil auf).

Öffnet die Gasse! Platz!

Stauffacher.

Was, Tell? Jhr wolltet — Nimmermehr — Jhr zittert,
Die Hand erbebt Euch, Eure Kniee wanken —

Tell (läßt die Armbrust sinken).

Mir schwimmt es vor den Augen!

Weiber.

Gott im Himmel!

Tell (zum Landvogt).

1985 Erlasset mir den Schuß! Hier ist mein Herz!

(Er reißt die Brust auf.)

Ruft Eure Reisigen und stoßt mich nieder!

Geßler.

Jch will dein Leben nicht, ich will den Schuß.
— Du kannst ja alles, Tell! An nichts verzagst du;
Das Steuerruder führst du wie den Bogen,
1990 Dich schreckt kein Sturm, wenn es zu retten gilt.
Jetzt, Retter, hilf dir selbst — du rettest alle!

(Tell steht in fürchterlichem Kampf, mit den Händen zuckend und die
rollenden Augen bald auf den Landvogt, bald zum Himmel gerichtet. — Plötzlich greift er in seinen Köcher, nimmt einen zweiten Pfeil
heraus und steckt ihn in seinen Goller. Der Landvogt bemerkt alle
diese Bewegungen.)

Walther Tell (unter der Linde).

Vater, schieß zu! Jch fürcht' mich nicht.

Tell.

Es muß!

(Er rafft sich zusammen und legt an.)

Rudenz

(der die ganze Zeit über in der heftigsten Spannung gestanden und
mit Gewalt an sich gehalten, tritt hervor).

Herr Landvogt, weiter werdet Jhr's nicht treiben,

Ihr werdet **nicht** — Es war nur eine Prüfung —
1995 Den Zweck habt Ihr erreicht — Zu weit getrieben,
Verfehlt die Strenge ihres weisen Zwecks,
Und allzustraff gespannt, zerspringt der Bogen.

Geßler.

Ihr schweigt, bis man Euch aufruft!

Rudenz.

Ich will reden!
Ich darf's! Des Königs Ehre ist mir heilig;
2000 Doch solches Regiment muß Haß erwerben.
Das ist des Königs Wille nicht — Ich darf's
Behaupten — Solche Grausamkeit verdient
Mein Volk nicht; dazu habt Ihr keine Vollmacht.

Geßler.

Ha, Ihr erkühnt Euch!

Rudenz.

Ich hab' still geschwiegen
2005 Zu allen schweren Thaten, die ich sah;
Mein sehend Auge hab' ich zugeschlossen,
Mein überschwellend und empörtes Herz
Hab' ich hinabgedrückt in meinen Busen.
Doch länger schweigen wär' Verrat zugleich
2010 An meinem Vaterland und an dem Kaiser.

Bertha
(wirft sich zwischen ihn und den Landvogt).

O Gott, Ihr reizt den Wütenden noch mehr.

Rudenz.

Mein Volk verließ ich, meinen Blutsverwandten

Entsagt' ich, alle Bande der Natur
Zerriß ich, um an Euch mich anzuschließen —
2015 Das Beste aller glaubt' ich zu befördern,
Da ich des Kaisers Macht befestigte —
Die Binde fällt von meinen Augen — Schaudernd
Seh' ich an einen Abgrund mich geführt —
Mein freies Urteil habt Ihr irr geleitet,
2020 Mein redlich Herz verführt — Ich war daran,
Mein Volk in bester Meinung zu verderben.

Geßler.

Verwegner, diese Sprache deinem Herrn?

Rudenz.

Der Kaiser ist mein Herr, nicht Ihr — Frei bin ich
Wie Ihr geboren, und ich messe mich
2025 Mit Euch in jeder ritterlichen Tugend.
Und stündet Ihr nicht hier in Kaisers Namen,
Den ich verehre, selbst wo man ihn schändet,
Den Handschuh wärf' ich vor Euch hin, Ihr solltet
Nach ritterlichem Brauch mir Antwort geben.
2030 — Ja, winkt nur Euren Reisigen — Ich stehe
Nicht wehrlos da, wie die —

(Auf das Volk zeigend.)

Ich hab' ein Schwert,
Und wer mir naht —

Stauffacher (ruft).

Der Apfel ist gefallen!

(Indem sich alle nach dieser Seite gewendet, und Bertha zwischen
Rudenz und den Landvogt sich geworfen, hat Tell den Pfeil abgedrückt.)

Rösselmann.

Der Knabe lebt!

Viele Stimmen.

Der Apfel ist getroffen!

(Walther Fürst schwankt und droht zu sinken, Bertha hält ihn.)

Geßler (erstaunt).

Er hat geschossen? Wie? Der Rasende!

Bertha.

2035 Der Knabe lebt! Kommt zu Euch, guter Vater!

Walther Tell

(kommt mit dem Apfel gesprungen).

Vater, hier ist der Apfel — Wußt' ich's ja,
Du würdest deinen Knaben nicht verletzen.

Tell

(stand mit vorgebogenem Leib, als wollt' er dem Pfeil folgen — die
Armbrust entsinkt seiner Hand — wie er den Knaben kommen sieht,
eilt er ihm mit ausgebreiteten Armen entgegen und hebt ihn mit
heftiger Inbrunst zu seinem Herzen hinauf; in dieser Stellung sinkt
er kraftlos zusammen. Alle stehen gerührt).

Bertha.

O güt'ger Himmel!

Walther Fürst (zu Vater und Sohn).

Kinder! meine Kinder!

Stauffacher.

Gott sei gelobt!

Leuthold.

Das war ein Schuß! Davon
2040 Wird man noch reden in den spätsten Zeiten.

Rudolph der Harras.

Erzählen wird man von dem Schützen Tell,
Solang' die Berge stehn auf ihrem Grunde.

(Reicht dem Landvogt den Apfel.)

Geßler.

Bei Gott! der Apfel mitten durch geschossen!
Es war ein Meisterschuß, ich muß ihn loben.

Rösselmann.

2045 Der Schuß war gut; doch wehe dem, der ihn
Dazu getrieben, daß er Gott versuchte!

Stauffacher.

Kommt zu Euch, Tell, steht auf, Ihr habt Euch männlich
Gelöst, und frei könnt Ihr nach Hause gehen.

Rösselmann.

Kommt, kommt und bringt der Mutter ihren Sohn!
(Sie wollen ihn wegführen.)

Geßler.

2050 Tell, höre!

Tell (kommt zurück).
Was befehlt Ihr, Herr?

Geßler.

Du stecktest
Noch einen zweiten Pfeil zu dir — Ja, ja,
Ich sah es wohl — Was meintest du damit?

Tell (verlegen).

Herr, das ist also bräuchlich bei den Schützen.

Geßler.

Nein, Tell, die Antwort laß ich dir nicht gelten;
2055 Es wird was anders wohl bedeutet haben.
Sag' mir die Wahrheit frisch und fröhlich, Tell;
Was es auch sei, dein Leben sichr' ich dir.
Wozu der zweite Pfeil?

Tell.

Wohlan, o Herr,
Weil Ihr mich meines Lebens habt gesichert,
2060 So will ich Euch die Wahrheit gründlich sagen.

(Er zieht den Pfeil aus dem Goller und sieht den Landvogt mit einem furchtbaren Blick an.)

Mit diesem zweiten Pfeil durchschoß ich — Euch,
Wenn ich mein liebes Kind getroffen hätte,
Und Eurer — wahrlich! hätt' ich nicht gefehlt.

Geßler.

Wohl, Tell! des Lebens hab' ich dich gesichert,
2065 Ich gab mein Ritterwort, das will ich halten —
Doch weil ich deinen bösen Sinn erkannt,
Will ich dich führen lassen und verwahren,
Wo weder Mond noch Sonne dich bescheint,
Damit ich sicher sei vor deinen Pfeilen.
2070 Ergreift ihn, Knechte! Bindet ihn!

(Tell wird gebunden.)

Stauffacher.

Wie, Herr!
So könntet Ihr an einem Manne handeln,
An dem sich Gottes Hand sichtbar verkündigt?

Geßler.

Laß sehn, ob sie ihn zweimal retten wird.
— Man bring' ihn auf mein Schiff! Ich folge nach
2075 Sogleich, ich selbst will ihn nach Küßnacht führen.

Rösselmann.

Das dürft Ihr nicht, das darf der Kaiser nicht,
Das widerstreitet unsern Freiheitsbriefen!

Geßler.

Wo sind sie? Hat der Kaiser sie bestätigt?
Er hat sie nicht bestätigt — Diese Gunst
2080 Muß erst erworben werden durch Gehorsam.
Rebellen seid ihr alle gegen Kaisers
Gericht und nährt verwegene Empörung.
Ich kenn' euch alle — ich durchschau' euch ganz —
Den nehm' ich jetzt heraus aus eurer Mitte;
2085 Doch alle seid ihr teilhaft seiner Schuld.
Wer klug ist, lerne schweigen und gehorchen.

(Er entfernt sich, Bertha, Rudenz, Harras und Knechte folgen, Frießhardt und Leuthold bleiben zurück.)

Walther Fürst (in heftigem Schmerz).

Es ist vorbei; er hat's beschlossen, mich
Mit meinem ganzen Hause zu verderben!

Stauffacher (zum Tell).

O, warum mußtet Ihr den Wütrich reizen!

Tell.

2090 Bezwinge sich, wer meinen Schmerz gefühlt!

Stauffacher.

O, nun ist alles, alles hin! Mit Euch
Sind wir gefesselt alle und gebunden!

Landleute (umringen den Tell).

Mit Euch geht unser letzter Trost dahin!

Leuthold (nähert sich).

Tell, es erbarmt mich — doch ich muß gehorchen.

Tell.

2095 Lebt wohl!

Walther Tell
(sich mit heftigem Schmerz an ihn schmiegend).

O Vater! Vater! Lieber Vater!

Tell
(hebt die Arme zum Himmel).

Dort droben ist dein Vater! Den ruf' an!

Stauffacher.

Tell, sag' ich Eurem Weibe nichts von Euch?

Tell
(hebt den Knaben mit Inbrunst an seine Brust).

Der Knab' ist unverletzt; mir wird Gott helfen.

(Reißt sich schnell los und folgt den Waffenknechten.)

Vierter Aufzug.

Erste Scene.

Östliches Ufer des Vierwaldstättersees.

Die seltsam gestalteten schroffen Felsen im Westen schließen den Prospect. Der See ist bewegt, heftiges Rauschen und Tosen, dazwischen
Blitze und Donnerschläge.

Kunz von Gersau. Fischer und Fischerknabe.

Kunz.

Ich sah's mit Augen an, Ihr könnt mir's glauben;
2100 's ist alles so geschehn, wie ich Euch sagte.

Fischer.

Der Tell gefangen abgeführt nach Küßnacht,
Der beste Mann im Land, der bravste Arm,
Wenn's einmal gelten sollte für die Freiheit.

Kunz.

Der Landvogt führt ihn selbst den See herauf;
2105 Sie waren eben dran, sich einzuschiffen,
Als ich von Flüelen abfuhr; doch der Sturm,
Der eben jetzt im Anzug ist, und der
Auch mich gezwungen, eilends hier zu landen,
Mag ihre Abfahrt wohl verhindert haben.

Fischer.

2110 Der Tell in Fesseln, in des Vogts Gewalt!
O, glaubt, er wird ihn tief genug vergraben,

(113)

Daß er des Tages Licht nicht wieder sieht!
Denn fürchten muß er die gerechte Rache
Des freien Mannes, den er schwer gereizt!

Kunz.

2115 Der Altlandamman auch, der edle Herr
Von Attinghausen, sagt man, lieg' am Tode.

Fischer.

So bricht der letzte Anker unsrer Hoffnung!
Der war es noch allein, der seine Stimme
Erheben durfte für des Volkes Rechte!

Kunz.

2120 Der Sturm nimmt überhand. Gehabt Euch wohl!
Ich nehme Herberg' in dem Dorf; denn heut'
Ist doch an keine Abfahrt mehr zu denken.

(Geht ab.)

Fischer.

Der Tell gefangen, und der Freiherr tot!
Erheb' die freche Stirne, Tyrannei,
2125 Wirf alle Scham hinweg! Der Mund der Wahrheit
Ist stumm, das seh'nde Auge ist geblendet,
Der Arm, der retten sollte, ist gefesselt.

Knabe.

Es hagelt schwer. Kommt in die Hütte, Vater,
Es ist nicht kommlich, hier im Freien hausen.

Fischer.

2130 Raset, ihr Winde! Flammt herab, ihr Blitze!
Ihr Wolken, berstet! Gießt herunter, Ströme
Des Himmels, und ersäuft das Land! Zerstört
Im Keim die ungeborenen Geschlechter!

Ihr wilden Elemente, werdet Herr!
2135 Ihr Bären, kommt, ihr alten Wölfe wieder
Der großen Wüste! Euch gehört das Land.
Wer wird hier leben wollen ohne Freiheit!

Knabe.

Hört, wie der Abgrund tost, der Wirbel brüllt,
So hat's noch nie gerast in diesem Schlunde!

Fischer.

2140 Zu zielen auf des eignen Kindes Haupt,
Solches ward keinem Vater noch geboten!
Und die Natur soll nicht in wildem Grimm
Sich drob empören — O, mich soll's nicht wundern,
Wenn sich die Felsen bücken in den See,
2145 Wenn jene Zacken, jene Eisestürme,
Die nie auftauten seit dem Schöpfungstag,
Von ihren hohen Kulmen niederschmelzen,
Wenn die Berge brechen, wenn die alten Klüfte
Einstürzen, eine zweite Sündflut alle
2150 Wohnstätten der Lebendigen verschlingt!

(Man hört läuten.)

Knabe.

Hört Ihr, sie läuten droben auf dem Berg.
Gewiß hat man ein Schiff in Not gesehn
Und zieht die Glocke, daß gebetet werde.

(Steigt auf eine Anhöhe.)

Fischer.

Wehe dem Fahrzeug, das, jetzt unterwegs,
2155 In dieser furchtbarn Wiege wird gewiegt!
Hier ist das Steuer unnütz und der Steurer;
Der Sturm ist Meister, Wind und Welle spielen

Ball mit dem Menschen — Da ist nah und fern
Kein Busen, der ihm freundlich Schutz gewährte!
2160 Handlos und schroff ansteigend starren ihm
Die Felsen, die unwirtlichen, entgegen
Und weisen ihm nur ihre steinern schroffe Brust.

Knabe (deutet links).

Vater, ein Schiff! es kommt von Flüelen her.

Fischer.

Gott helf' den armen Leuten! Wenn der Sturm
2165 In dieser Wasserkluft sich erst verfangen,
Dann rast er um sich mit des Raubtiers Angst,
Das an des Gitters Eisenstäbe schlägt;
Die Pforte sucht er heulend sich vergebens,
Denn ringsum schränken ihn die Felsen ein,
2170 Die himmelhoch den engen Paß vermauern.

(Er steigt auf die Anhöhe.)

Knabe.

Es ist das Herrenschiff von Uri, Vater,
Ich kenn's am rothen Dach und an der Fahne.

Fischer.

Gerichte Gottes! Ja, er ist es selbst,
Der Landvogt, der da fährt — Dort schifft er hin
2175 Und führt im Schiffe sein Verbrechen mit!
Schnell hat der Arm des Rächers ihn gefunden;
Jetzt kennt er über sich den stärkern Herrn.
Diese Wellen geben nicht auf seine Stimme,
Diese Felsen bücken ihre Häupter nicht
2180 Vor seinem Hute — Knabe, bete nicht!
Greif' nicht dem Richter in den Arm!

Knabe.

Ich bete für den Landvogt nicht — Ich bete
Für den Tell, der auf dem Schiff sich mit befindet.

Fischer.

O Unvernunft des blinden Elements!
2185 Mußt du, um einen Schuldigen zu treffen,
Das Schiff mit sammt dem Steuermann verderben!

Knabe.

Sieh, sieh, sie waren glücklich schon vorbei
Am Buggisgrat; doch die Gewalt des Sturms,
Der von dem Teufelsmünster widerprallt,
2190 Wirft sie zum großen Axenberg zurück.
— Ich seh' sie nicht mehr.

Fischer.

Dort ist das Hackmesser,
Wo schon der Schiffe mehrere gebrochen.
Wenn sie nicht weislich dort vorüberlenken,
So wird das Schiff zerschmettert an der Fluh,
2195 Die sich gähstotzig absenkt in die Tiefe.
— Sie haben einen guten Steuermann
Am Bord; könnt' einer retten, wär's der Tell;
Doch dem sind Arm' und Hände ja gefesselt.

Wilhelm Tell mit der Armbrust.

(Er kommt mit raschen Schritten, blickt erstaunt umher und zeigt die
heftigste Bewegung. Wenn er mitten auf der Scene ist, wirft er
sich nieder, die Hände zu der Erde und dann zum Himmel aus-
breitend.)

Knabe (bemerkt ihn).

Sieh, Vater, wer der Mann ist, der dort kniet?

Fischer.

2200 Er faßt die Erde an mit seinen Händen
Und scheint wie außer sich zu sein.

Knabe (kommt vorwärts).

Was seh' ich! Vater! Vater, kommt und seht!

Fischer (nähert sich).

Wer ist es? — Gott im Himmel! Was! der Tell?
Wie kommt Ihr hieher? Redet!

Knabe.

                 Wart Ihr nicht
2205 Dort auf dem Schiff gefangen und gebunden?

Fischer.

Ihr wurdet nicht nach Küßnacht abgeführt?

Tell (steht auf).

Ich bin befreit.

Fischer und Knabe.

        Befreit! O Wunder Gottes!

Knabe.

Wo kommt Ihr her?

Tell.

        Dort aus dem Schiffe.

Fischer.

                  Was?

Knabe (zugleich).

Wo ist der Landvogt?

Tell.

        Auf den Wellen treibt er.

Fischer.

2210 Ist's möglich? Aber Ihr? wie seid Ihr hier?
Seid Euren Banden und dem Sturm entkommen?

Tell.

Durch Gottes gnäd'ge Fürsehung — Hört an!

Fischer und Knabe.

O, redet, redet!

Tell.

Was in Altorf sich
Begeben, wißt Ihr's?

Fischer.

Alles weiß ich, redet!

Tell.

2215 Daß mich der Landvogt fahen ließ und binden,
Nach seiner Burg zu Küßnacht wollte führen.

Fischer.

Und sich mit Euch zu Flüelen eingeschifft!
Wir wissen alles. Sprecht, wie Ihr entkommen?

Tell.

Ich lag im Schiff, mit Stricken fest gebunden,
2220 Wehrlos, ein aufgegebner Mann — Nicht hofft' ich,
Das frohe Licht der Sonne mehr zu sehn,
Der Gattin und der Kinder liebes Antlitz,
Und trostlos blickt' ich in die Wasserwüste —

Fischer.

O armer Mann!

Tell.

So fuhren wir dahin,
2225 Der Vogt, Rudolph der Harras und die Knechte.

Mein Köcher aber mit der Armbrust lag
Am hintern Gransen bei dem Steuerruder.
Und als wir an die Ecke jetzt gelangt
Beim kleinen Axen, da verhängt' es Gott,
2230 Daß solch ein grausam mördrisch Ungewitter
Gählings herfürbrach aus des Gotthards Schlünden,
Daß allen Ruderern das Herz entsank,
Und meinten alle, elend zu ertrinken.
Da hört' ich's, wie der Diener einer sich
2235 Zum Landvogt wendet' und die Worte sprach:
„Ihr sehet Eure Not und unsre, Herr,
Und daß wir all' am Rand des Todes schweben —
Die Steuerleute aber wissen sich
Vor großer Furcht nicht Rat und sind des Fahrens
2240 Nicht wohl berichtet — Nun aber ist der Tell
Ein starker Mann und weiß ein Schiff zu steuern.
Wie, wenn wir sein jetzt brauchten in der Not?"
Da sprach der Vogt zu mir: „Tell, wenn du dir's
Getrautest, uns zu helfen aus dem Sturm,
2245 So möcht' ich dich der Bande wohl entled'gen."
Ich aber sprach: „Ja, Herr, mit Gottes Hilfe
Getrau' ich mir's und helf' uns wohl hiedannen."
So ward ich meiner Bande los und stand
Am Steuerruder und fuhr redlich hin;
2250 Doch schielt' ich seitwärts, wo mein Schießzeug lag
Und an dem Ufer merkt' ich scharf umher,
Wo sich ein Vorteil aufthät' zum Entspringen.
Und wie ich eines Felsenriffs gewahre,
Das abgeplattet vorsprang in den See —

Fischer.

2255 Ich kenn's, es ist am Fuß des großen Axen,

Tells Flucht

Face p. 120

Doch nicht für möglich acht' ich's — so gar steil
Geht's an — vom Schiff es springend abzureichen —

Tell.

Schrie ich den Knechten, handlich zuzugehn,
Bis daß wir vor die Felsenplatte kämen,
2260 Dort, rief ich, sei das Ärgste überstanden —
Und als wir sie frisch rudernd bald erreicht,
Fleh' ich die Gnade Gottes an und drücke,
Mit allen Leibeskräften angestemmt,
Den hintern Gransen an die Felswand hin.
2265 Jetzt, schnell mein Schießzeug fassend, schwing' ich selbst
Hochspringend auf die Platte mich hinauf,
Und mit gewalt'gem Fußstoß hinter mich
Schleudr' ich das Schifflein in den Schlund der Wasser —
Dort mag's, wie Gott will, auf den Wellen treiben!
2270 So bin ich hier, gerettet aus des Sturms
Gewalt und aus der schlimmeren der Menschen.

Fischer.

Tell, Tell! ein sichtbar Wunder hat der Herr
An Euch gethan; kaum glaub' ich's meinen Sinnen —
Doch saget! Wo gedenket Ihr jetzt hin?
2275 Denn Sicherheit ist nicht für Euch, wofern
Der Landvogt lebend diesem Sturm entkommt.

Tell.

Ich hört' ihn sagen, da ich noch im Schiff
Gebunden lag, er woll' bei Brunnen landen,
Und über Schwyz nach seiner Burg mich führen.

Fischer.

2280 Will er den Weg dahin zu Lande nehmen?

Tell.

Er denkt's.

Fischer.

O, so verbergt Euch ohne Säumen!
Nicht zweimal hilft Euch Gott aus seiner Hand.

Tell.

Nennt mir den nächsten Weg nach Art und Küßnacht.

Fischer.

Die offne Straße zieht sich über Steinen;
2285 Doch einen kürzern Weg und heimlichern
Kann Euch mein Knabe über Lowerz führen.

Tell (giebt ihm die Hand).

Gott lohn' Euch Eure Gutthat! Lebet wohl!

(Geht und kehrt wieder um.)

— Habt Ihr nicht auch im Rütli mitgeschworen?
Mir deucht, man nannt' Euch mir —

Fischer.

Ich war dabei
2290 Und hab' den Eid des Bundes mit beschworen.

Tell.

So eilt nach Bürglen, thut die Lieb mir an!
Mein Weib verzagt um mich; verkündet ihr,
Daß ich gerettet sei und wohl geborgen.

Fischer.

Doch wohin, sag' ich ihr, daß Ihr geflohn?

Tell.

2295 Ihr werdet meinen Schwäher bei ihr finden
Und andre, die im Rütli mitgeschworen —
Sie sollen wacker sein und gutes Muts.

Der Tell sei frei und seines Armes mächtig;
Bald werden sie ein Weiteres von mir hören.

Fischer.

2300 Was habt Ihr im Gemüt?. Entdeckt mir's frei!

Tell.

Ist es geth an, wird's auch zur Rede kommen.

(Geht ab.)

Fischer.

Zeig' ihm den Weg, Jenni — Gott steh' ihm bei!
Er führt's zum Ziel, was er auch unternommen.

(Geht ab.)

Zweite Scene.

Edelhof zu Attinghausen.

Der Freiherr, in einem Armsessel, sterbend. Walther Fürst,
Stauffacher, Melchthal und Baumgarten um ihn beschäftigt. Walther Tell, knieend vor dem Sterbenden.

Walther Fürst.

Es ist vorbei mit ihm, er ist hinüber.

Stauffacher.

2305 Er liegt nicht wie ein Toter — Seht, die Feder
Auf seinen Lippen regt sich! Ruhig ist
Sein Schlaf, und friedlich lächeln seine Züge.

(Baumgarten geht an die Thüre und spricht mit jemand.)

Walther Fürst (zu Baumgarten).

Wer ist's?

Baumgarten (kommt zurück).

Es ist Frau Hedwig, Eure Tochter;
Sie will Euch sprechen, will den Knaben sehn.

(Walther Tell richtet sich auf.)

Walther Fürst.

2310 Kann ich sie trösten? Hab' ich selber Trost?
Häuft alles Leiden sich auf meinem Haupt?

Hedwig (hereindringend).

Wo ist mein Kind? Laßt mich, ich muß es sehn —

Stauffacher.

Faßt Euch! Bedenkt, daß Ihr im Haus des Todes —

Hedwig (stürzt auf den Knaben).

Mein Wälti! O, er lebt mir!

Walther Tell (hängt an ihr).

Arme Mutter!

Hedwig.

2315 Ist's auch gewiß? Bist du mir unverletzt?

(Betrachtet ihn mit ängstlicher Sorgfalt.)

Und ist es möglich? Konnt' er auf dich zielen?
Wie konnt' er's? O, er hat kein Herz — Er konnte
Den Pfeil abdrücken auf sein eignes Kind!

Walther Fürst.

Er that's mit Angst, mit schmerzzerrißner Seele;
2320 Gezwungen that er's, denn es galt das Leben.

Hedwig.

O, hätt' er eines Vaters Herz, eh' er's
Gethan, er wäre tausendmal gestorben!

Stauffacher.

Ihr solltet Gottes gnäd'ge Schickung preisen,
Die es so gut gelenkt —

Hedwig.

Kann ich vergessen,

2325 Wie's hätte kommen können? — Gott des Himmels!
Und lebt' ich achtzig Jahr' — Ich seh' den Knaben ewig
Gebunden stehn, den Vater auf ihn zielen,
Und ewig fliegt der Pfeil mir in das Herz.

Melchthal.

Frau, wüßtet Ihr, wie ihn der Vogt gereizt!

Hedwig.

2330 O rohes Herz der Männer! Wenn ihr Stolz
Beleidigt wird, dann achten sie nichts mehr;
Sie setzen in der blinden Wut des Spiels
Das Haupt des Kindes und das Herz der Mutter!

Baumgarten.

Ist Eures Mannes Los nicht hart genug,

2335 Daß Ihr mit schwerem Tadel ihn noch kränkt?
Für seine Leiden habt Ihr kein Gefühl?

Hedwig

(kehrt sich nach ihm um und sieht ihn mit einem großen Blicke an).

Hast du nur Thränen für des Freundes Unglück?
— Wo waret ihr, da man den Trefflichen
In Bande schlug? Wo war da eure Hilfe?

2340 Ihr sahet zu, ihr ließt das Gräßliche geschehn;
Geduldig littet ihr's, daß man den Freund
Aus eurer Mitte führte — Hat der Tell
Auch so an euch gehandelt? Stand er auch

Bedauernd da, als hinter dir die Reiter
2345 Des Landvogts drangen, als der wüt'ge See
Vor dir erbrauste? Nicht mit müß'gen Thränen
Beklagt' er dich, in den Nachen sprang er, Weib
Und Kind vergaß er und befreite dich —

Walther Fürst.

Was konnten wir zu seiner Rettung wagen,
2350 Die kleine Zahl, die unbewaffnet war!

Hedwig (wirft sich an seine Brust).

O Vater! Und auch du hast ihn verloren!
Das Land, wir alle haben ihn verloren!
Uns allen fehlt er, ach! wir fehlen ihm!
Gott rette seine Seele vor Verzweiflung.
2355 Zu ihm hinab ins öde Burgverließ
Dringt keines Freundes Trost — Wenn er erkrankte!
Ach, in des Kerkers feuchter Finsternis
Muß er erkranken — Wie die Alpenrose
Bleicht und verkümmert in der Sumpfesluft,
2360 So ist für ihn kein Leben als im Licht
Der Sonne, in dem Balsamstrom der Lüfte.
Gefangen! Er! Sein Atem ist die Freiheit;
Er kann nicht leben in dem Hauch der Grüfte.

Stauffacher.

Beruhigt Euch! Wir alle wollen handeln,
2365 Um seinen Kerker aufzuthun.

Hedwig.

Was könnt i h r schaffen ohne ihn? — Solang'
Der Tell noch frei war, ja, d a war noch Hoffnung,
Da hatte noch die Unschuld einen Freund,
Da hatte einen Helfer der Verfolgte,

2370 Euch alle rettete der Tell — Ihr alle
Zusammen könnt nicht s e i n e Fesseln lösen!

(Der Freiherr erwacht.)

Baumgarten.

Er regt sich, still!

Attinghausen (sich aufrichtend).

Wo ist er?

Stauffacher.

Wer?

Attinghausen.

Er fehlt mir,
Verläßt mich in dem letzten Augenblick!

Stauffacher.

Er meint den Junker — Schickte man nach ihm?

Walther Fürst.

2375 Es ist nach ihm gesendet — Tröstet Euch!
Er hat sein Herz gefunden, er ist unser.

Attinghausen.

Hat er gesprochen für sein Vaterland?

Stauffacher.

Mit Heldenkühnheit.

Attinghausen.

Warum kommt er nicht,
Um meinen letzten Segen zu empfangen?
2380 Ich fühle, daß es schleunig mit mir endet.

Stauffacher.

Nicht also, edler Herr! Der kurze Schlaf
Hat Euch erquickt, und hell ist Euer Blick.

Attinghausen.

Der Schmerz ist Leben, er verließ mich auch;
Das Leiden ist so wie die Hoffnung aus.

(Er bemerkt den Knaben.)

2385 Wer ist der Knabe?

Walther Fürst.

Segnet ihn, o Herr!
Er ist mein Enkel und ist vaterlos.

(Hedwig sinkt mit dem Knaben vor dem Sterbenden nieder.)

Attinghausen.

Und vaterlos laß' ich euch alle, alle
Zurück — Weh mir, daß meine letzten Blicke
Den Untergang des Vaterlands gesehn!
2390 Mußt' ich des Lebens höchstes Maß erreichen,
Um ganz mit allen Hoffnungen zu sterben!

Stauffacher (zu Walther Fürst).

Soll er in diesem finstern Kummer scheiden?
Erhellen wir ihm nicht die letzte Stunde
Mit schönem Strahl der Hoffnung? — Edler Freiherr!
2395 Erhebet Euren Geist! Wir sind nicht ganz
Verlassen, sind nicht rettungslos verloren.

Attinghausen.

Wer soll euch retten?

Walther Fürst.

Wir uns selbst. Vernehmt!
Es haben die drei Lande sich das Wort
Gegeben, die Tyrannen zu verjagen.
2400 Geschlossen ist der Bund; ein heil'ger Schwur
Verbindet uns. Es wird gehandelt werden,

Eh' noch das Jahr den neuen Kreis beginnt.
Euer Staub wird ruhn in einem freien Lande.

Attinghausen.

O, saget mir! Geschlossen ist der Bund?

Melchthal.

2405 Am gleichen Tage werden alle drei
Waldstätte sich erheben. Alles ist
Bereit, und das Geheimnis wohlbewahrt
Bis jetzt, obgleich viel' Hunderte es teilen.
Hohl ist der Boden unter den Tyrannen;
2410 Die Tage ihrer Herrschaft sind gezählt,
Und bald ist ihre Spur nicht mehr zu finden.

Attinghausen.

Die festen Burgen aber in den Landen?

Melchthal.

Sie fallen alle an dem gleichen Tag.

Attinghausen.

Und sind die Edeln dieses Bunds teilhaftig?

Stauffacher.

2415 Wir harren ihres Beistands, wenn es gilt;
Jetzt aber hat der Landmann nur geschworen.

Attinghausen
(richtet sich langsam in die Höhe, mit großem Erstaunen).

Hat sich der Landmann solcher That verwogen,
Aus eignem Mittel, ohne Hilf' der Edeln,
Hat er der eignen Kraft so viel vertraut —
2420 Ja, dann bedarf es unserer nicht mehr;
Getröstet können wir zu Grabe steigen,

Es lebt nach uns — durch andre Kräfte will
Das Herrliche der Menschheit sich erhalten.

(Er legt seine Hand auf das Haupt des Kindes, das vor ihm auf den
Knieen liegt.)

Aus diesem Haupte, wo der Apfel lag,
2425 Wird euch die neue, beßre Freiheit grünen;
Das Alte stürzt, es ändert sich die Zeit,
Und neues Leben blüht aus den Ruinen.

Stauffacher (zu Walther Fürst).

Seht, welcher Glanz sich um sein Aug' ergießt!
Das ist nicht das Erlöschen der Natur,
2430 Das ist der Strahl schon eines neuen Lebens.

Attinghausen.

Der Adel steigt von seinen alten Burgen
Und schwört den Städten seinen Bürgereid;
Im Üchtland schon, im Thurgau hat's begonnen,
Die edle Bern erhebt ihr herrschend Haupt,
2435 Freiburg ist eine sichre Burg der Freien,
Die rege Zürich waffnet ihre Zünfte
Zum kriegerischen Heer — Es bricht die Macht
Der Könige sich an ihren ew'gen Wällen —

(Er spricht das Folgende mit dem Ton eines Sehers — seine Rede steigt
bis zur Begeisterung.)

Die Fürsten seh' ich und die edeln Herrn
2440 In Harnischen herangezogen kommen,
Ein harmlos Volk von Hirten zu bekriegen.
Auf Tod und Leben wird gekämpft, und herrlich
Wird mancher Paß durch blutige Entscheidung.
Der Landmann stürzt sich mit der nackten Brust,
2445 Ein freies Opfer, in die Schar der Lanzen!

Er bricht sie, und des Adels Blüte fällt,
Es hebt die Freiheit siegend ihre Fahne.

(Walther Fürsts und Stauffachers Hände fassend.)

Drum haltet fest zusammen — fest und ewig —
Kein Ort der Freiheit sei dem andern fremd —
2450 Hochwachten stellet aus auf euren Bergen,
Daß sich der Bund zum Bunde rasch versammle —
Seid einig — einig — einig —

(Er fällt in das Kissen zurück — seine Hände halten entseelt noch die
andern gefaßt. Fürst und Stauffacher betrachten ihn noch eine
Zeit lang schweigend; dann treten sie hinweg, jeder seinem Schmerz
überlassen. Unterdessen sind die Knechte still hereingedrungen, sie
nähern sich mit Zeichen eines stillern oder heftigern Schmerzens,
einige knieen bei ihm nieder und weinen auf seine Hand; während
dieser stummen Scene wird die Burgglocke geläutet.)

Rudenz zu den Vorigen.

Rudenz (rasch eintretend).

Lebt er? O, saget, kann er mich noch hören?

Walther Fürst
(deutet hin mit weggewandtem Gesicht).

Ihr seid jetzt unser Lehensherr und Schirmer,
2455 Und dieses Schloß hat einen andern Namen.

Rudenz
(erblickt den Leichnam und steht von heftigem Schmerz ergriffen).

O güt'ger Gott! — Kommt meine Reu' zu spät?
Konnt' er nicht wen'ge Pulse länger leben,
Um mein geändert Herz zu sehn?
Verachtet hab' ich seine treue Stimme,
2460 Da er noch wandelte im Licht — Er ist
Dahin, ist fort auf immerdar und läßt mir

Die schwere, unbezahlte Schuld! — O, saget!
Schied er dahin im Unmut gegen mich?

Stauffacher.

Er hörte sterbend noch, was Ihr gethan,
2465 Und segnete den Mut, mit dem Ihr spracht!

Rudenz (kniet an dem Toten nieder).

Ja, heil'ge Reste eines teuren Mannes!
Entseelter Leichnam! Hier gelob' ich dir's
In deine kalte Totenhand — Zerrissen
Hab' ich auf ewig alle fremden Bande;
2470 Zurückgegeben bin ich meinem Volk;
Ein Schweizer bin ich, und ich will es sein
Von ganzer Seele — —

          (Aufstehend.)

                    Trauert um den Freund,
Den Vater aller, doch verzaget nicht!
Nicht bloß sein Erbe ist mir zugefallen,
2475 Es steigt sein Herz, sein Geist auf mich herab,
Und leisten soll euch meine frische Jugend,
Was euch sein greises Alter schuldig blieb.
— Ehrwürd'ger Vater, gebt mir Eure Hand!
Gebt mir die Eurige! Melchthal, auch Ihr!
2480 Bedenkt Euch nicht! O, wendet Euch nicht weg!
Empfanget meinen Schwur und mein Gelübde!

Walther Fürst.

Gebt ihm die Hand! Sein wiederkehrend Herz
Verdient Vertraun.

Melchthal.

                Ihr habt den Landmann nichts geachtet.
Sprecht, wessen soll man sich zu Euch versehn?

Rudenz.

2485 O, denket nicht des Irrtums meiner Jugend!

Stauffacher (zu Melchthal).

Seid einig! war das letzte Wort des Vaters.
Gedenket dessen!

Melchthal.

Hier ist meine Hand!
Des Bauern Handschlag, edler Herr, ist auch
Ein Manneswort! Was ist der Ritter ohne uns?
2490 Und unser Stand ist älter als der Eure.

Rudenz.

Ich ehr' ihn, und mein Schwert soll ihn beschützen.

Melchthal.

Der Arm, Herr Freiherr, der die harte Erde
Sich unterwirft und ihren Schoß befruchtet,
Kann auch des Mannes Brust beschützen.

Rudenz.

Ihr
2495 Sollt meine Brust, ich will die Eure schützen,
So sind wir einer durch den andern stark.
— Doch wozu reden, da das Vaterland
Ein Raub noch ist der fremden Tyrannei?
Wenn erst der Boden rein ist von dem Feind,
2500 Dann wollen wir's in Frieden schon vergleichen.

(Nachdem er einen Augenblick inne gehalten.)

Ihr schweigt? Ihr habt mir nichts zu sagen? Wie?
Verdien' ich's noch nicht, daß ihr mir vertraut?
So muß ich wider euren Willen mich
In das Geheimnis eures Bundes drängen.
2505 — Ihr habt getagt — geschworen auf dem Rütli —

Ich weiß — weiß alles, was ihr dort verhandelt,
Und was mir nicht von euch vertrauet ward,
Ich hab's bewahrt gleichwie ein heilig Pfand.
Nie war ich meines Landes Feind, glaubt mir,
2510 Und niemals hätt' ich gegen euch gehandelt.
   — Doch übel thatet ihr, es zu verschieben;
Die Stunde dringt, und rascher That bedarf's —
Der Tell ward schon das Opfer eures Säumens.—

Stauffacher.

Das Christfest abzuwarten, schwuren wir.

Rudenz.

2515 Ich war nicht dort, ich hab' nicht mit geschworen.
Wartet ihr ab, ich handle.

Melchthal.

                  Was?   Ihr wolltet —

Rudenz.

Des Landes Vätern zähl' ich mich jetzt bei,
Und meine erste Pflicht ist, euch zu schützen.

Walther Fürst.

Der Erde diesen teuren Staub zu geben,
2520 Ist Eure nächste Pflicht und heiligste.

Rudenz.

Wenn wir das Land befreit, dann legen wir
Den frischen Kranz des Siegs ihm auf die Bahre.
   — O Freunde! Eure Sache nicht allein,
Ich habe meine eigne auszufechten
2525 Mit dem Tyrannen — Hört und wißt! Verschwunden
Ist meine Bertha, heimlich weggeraubt,
Mit kecker Frevelthat aus unsrer Mitte!

Stauffacher.

Solcher Gewaltthat hätte der Tyrann
Wider die freie Edle sich verwogen?

Rudenz.

2530 O meine Freunde! Euch versprach ich Hilfe,
Und ich zuerst muß sie von euch erflehn.
Geraubt, entrissen ist mir die Geliebte.
Wer weiß, wo sie der Wütende verbirgt,
Welcher Gewalt sie frevelnd sich erkühnen,
2535 Ihr Herz zu zwingen zum verhaßten Band!
Verlaßt mich nicht, o, helft mir sie erretten —
Sie liebt euch, o, sie hat's verdient um's Land,
Daß alle Arme sich für sie bewaffnen —

Walther Fürst.

Was wollt Ihr unternehmen?

Rudenz.

Weiß ich's? Ach!

2540 In dieser Nacht, die ihr Geschick umhüllt,
In dieses Zweifels ungeheurer Angst,
Wo ich nichts Festes zu erfassen weiß,
Ist mir nur dieses in der Seele klar:
Unter den Trümmern der Tyrannenmacht
2545 Allein kann sie hervorgegraben werden;
Die Festen alle müssen wir bezwingen,
Ob wir vielleicht in ihren Kerker dringen.

Melchthal.

Kommt, führt uns an! Wir folgen Euch. Warum
Bis morgen sparen, was wir heut' vermögen?
2550 Frei war der Tell, als wir im Rütli schwuren;
Das Ungeheure war noch nicht geschehen.

Es bringt die Zeit ein anderes Gesetz;
Wer ist so feig, der jetzt noch könnte zagen!

Rudenz (zu Stauffacher und Walther Fürst).

Indes bewaffnet und zum Werk bereit,
2555 Erwartet ihr der Berge Feuerzeichen;
Denn schneller, als ein Botensegel fliegt,
Soll euch die Botschaft unsers Siegs erreichen,
Und seht ihr leuchten die willkommnen Flammen,
Dann auf die Feinde stürzt wie Wetters Strahl
2560 Und brecht den Bau der Tyrannei zusammen!

(Gehen ab.)

Dritte Scene.

Die hohle Gasse bei Küßnacht.

Man steigt von hinten zwischen Felsen herunter, und die Wanderer
werden, ehe sie auf der Scene erscheinen, schon von der Höhe gesehen.
Felsen umschließen die ganze Scene; auf einem der vordersten ist
ein Vorsprung, mit Gesträuch bewachsen.

Tell (tritt auf mit der Armbrust).

Durch diese hohle Gasse muß er kommen;
Es führt kein andrer Weg nach Küßnacht — Hier
Vollend' ich's — Die Gelegenheit ist günstig.
Dort der Hollunderstrauch verbirgt mich ihm,
2565 Von dort herab kann ihn mein Pfeil erlangen;
Des Weges Enge wehret den Verfolgern.
Mach' deine Rechnung mit dem Himmel, Vogt!
Fort mußt du, deine Uhr ist abgelaufen.

Ich lebte still und harmlos — das Geschoß
2570 War auf des Waldes Tiere nur gerichtet,
Meine Gedanken waren rein von Mord —
Du hast aus meinem Frieden mich heraus
Geschreckt; in gärend Drachengift hast du
Die Milch der frommen Denkart mir verwandelt;
2575 Zum Ungeheuren hast du mich gewöhnt —
Wer sich des Kindes Haupt zum Ziele setzte,
Der kann auch treffen in das Herz des Feinds.

Die armen Kindlein, die unschuldigen,
Das treue Weib muß ich vor deiner Wut
2580 Beschützen, Landvogt! — Da, als ich den Bogenstrang
Anzog — als mir die Hand erzitterte —
Als du mit grausam teufelischer Lust
Mich zwangst, aufs Haupt des Kindes anzulegen —
Als ich ohnmächtig flehend rang vor dir,
2585 Damals gelobt' ich mir in meinem Innern
Mit furchtbarm Eidschwur, den nur Gott gehört,
Daß meines nächsten Schusses erstes Ziel
Dein Herz sein sollte — Was ich mir gelobt
In jenes Augenblickes Höllenqualen,
2590 Ist eine heil'ge Schuld — ich will sie zahlen.

Du bist mein Herr und meines Kaisers Vogt;
Doch nicht der Kaiser hätte sich erlaubt,
Was du — Er sandte dich in diese Lande,
Um Recht zu sprechen — strenges, denn er zürnet —
2595 Doch nicht, um mit der mörderischen Lust
Dich jedes Greuels straflos zu erfrechen;
Es lebt ein Gott, zu strafen und zu rächen.

Komm du hervor, du Bringer bittrer Schmerzen,
Mein teures Kleinod jetzt, mein höchster Schatz —

2600 Ein Ziel will ich dir geben, das bis jetzt
     Der frommen Bitte undurchdringlich war —
     Doch dir soll es nicht widerstehn — Und du,
     Vertraute Bogensehne, die so oft
     Mir treu gedient hat in der Freude Spielen,
2605 Verlaß mich nicht im fürchterlichen Ernst!
     Nur jetzt noch halte fest, du treuer Strang,
     Der mir so oft den herben Pfeil beflügelt —
     Enttänn' er jetzo kraftlos meinen Händen,
     Ich habe keinen zweiten zu versenden.

               (Wanderer gehen über die Scene.)

2610   Auf dieser Bank von Stein will ich mich setzen,
     Dem Wanderer zur kurzen Ruh' bereitet —
     Denn hier ist keine Heimat — Jeder treibt
     Sich an dem andern rasch und fremd vorüber
     Und fraget nicht nach seinem Schmerz — Hier geht
2615 Der sorgenvolle Kaufmann und der leicht
     Geschürzte Pilger — der andächt'ge Mönch,
     Der düstre Räuber und der heitre Spielmann,
     Der Säumer mit dem schwer beladnen Roß,
     Der ferne herkommt von der Menschen Ländern,
2620 Denn jede Straße führt ans End' der Welt.
     Sie alle ziehen ihres Weges fort
     An ihr Geschäft — und meines ist der Mord!

               (Setzt sich.)

     Sonst, wenn der Vater auszog, liebe Kinder,
     Da war ein Freuen, wenn er wieder kam;
2625 Denn niemals kehrt' er heim, er bracht' euch etwas,
     War's eine schöne Alpenblume, war's
     Ein seltner Vogel oder Ammonshorn,
     Wie es der Wandrer findet auf den Bergen —

Jetzt geht er einem andern Weidwerk nach,
2630 Am wilden Weg sitzt er mit Mordgedanken;
Des Feindes Leben ist's, worauf er lauert.
— Und doch an euch nur denkt er, liebe Kinder,
Auch jetzt — euch zu verteid'gen, eure holde Unschuld
Zu schützen vor der Rache des Tyrannen,
2635 Will er zum Morde jetzt den Bogen spannen.

(Steht auf.)

Ich laure auf ein edles Wild — Läßt sich's
Der Jäger nicht verdrießen, Tage lang
Umher zu streifen in des Winters Strenge,
Von Fels zu Fels den Wagesprung zu thun,
2640 Hinan zu klimmen an den glatten Wänden,
Wo er sich anleimt mit dem eignen Blut,
— Um ein armselig Grattier zu erjagen.
Hier gilt es einen köstlicheren Preis,
Das Herz des Todfeinds, der mich will verderben.

(Man hört von ferne eine heitere Musik, welche sich nähert.)

2645 Mein ganzes Leben lang hab' ich den Bogen
Gehandhabt, mich geübt nach Schützenregel;
Ich habe oft geschossen in das Schwarze
Und manchen schönen Preis mir heimgebracht
Vom Freudenschießen — Aber heute will ich
2650 Den Meisterschuß thun und das Beste mir
Im ganzen Umkreis des Gebirgs gewinnen.

Eine Hochzeit zieht über die Scene und durch den Hohlweg hinauf.
Tell betrachtet sie, auf seinen Bogen gelehnt; Stüssi der Flur-
schütz gesellt sich zu ihm.

Stüssi.

Das ist der Klostermei'r von Mörlischachen,
Der hier den Brautlauf hält — ein reicher Mann,

Er hat wohl zehen Senten auf den Alpen.
2655 Die Braut holt er jetzt ab zu Imisee,
Und diese Nacht wird hoch geschwelgt zu Küßnacht.
Kommt mit! 's ist jeder Biedermann geladen.

Tell.

Ein ernster Gast stimmt nicht zum Hochzeitshaus.

Stüssi.

Drückt Euch ein Kummer, werft ihn frisch vom Herzen!
2660 Nehmt mit, was kommt; die Zeiten sind jetzt schwer;
Drum muß der Mensch die Freude leicht ergreifen.
Hier wird gefreit und anderswo begraben.

Tell.

Und oft kommt gar das eine zu dem andern.

Stüssi.

So geht die Welt nun. Es giebt allerwegen
2665 Unglücks genug — Ein Russi ist gegangen
Im Glarner Land, und eine ganze Seite
Vom Glärnisch eingesunken.

Tell.

                    Wanken auch
Die Berge selbst? Es steht nichts fest auf Erden.

Stüssi.

Auch anderswo vernimmt man Wunderdinge.
2670 Da sprach ich einen, der von Baden kam.
Ein Ritter wollte zu dem König reiten,
Und unterwegs begegnet ihm ein Schwarm
Von Hornissen; die fallen auf sein Roß,
Daß es vor Marter tot zu Boden sinkt,
2675 Und er zu Fuße ankommt bei dem König.

Tell.

Dem Schwachen ist sein Stachel auch gegeben.

Armgard kommt mit mehreren Kindern und stellt sich an den Eingang des Hohlwegs.

Stüſſi.

Man deutet's auf ein großes Landesunglück,
Auf schwere Thaten wider die Natur.

Tell.

Dergleichen Thaten bringet jeder Tag;
2680 Kein Wunderzeichen braucht sie zu verkünden.

Stüſſi.

Ja, wohl dem, der sein Feld bestellt in Ruh'
Und ungekränkt daheim sitzt bei den Seinen.

Tell.

Es kann der Frömmste nicht im Frieden bleiben,
Wenn es dem bösen Nachbar nicht gefällt.

(Tell sieht oft mit unruhiger Erwartung nach der Höhe des Weges.)

Stüſſi.

2685 Gehabt Euch wohl — Ihr wartet hier auf jemand?

Tell.

Das thu' ich.

Stüſſi.

Frohe Heimkehr zu den Euren!
— Ihr seid aus Uri? Unser gnäd'ger Herr,
Der Landvogt, wird noch heut' von dort erwartet.

Wandrer (kommt).

Den Vogt erwartet heut' nicht mehr. Die Wasser
2690 Sind ausgetreten von dem großen Regen,
Und alle Brücken hat der Strom zerrissen.

(Tell steht auf.)

Armgard (kommt vorwärts).

Der Landvogt kommt nicht!

Stüssi.

Sucht Ihr was an ihn?

Armgard.

Ach, freilich!

Stüssi.

Warum stellet Ihr Euch denn
In dieser hohlen Gass' ihm in den Weg?

Armgard.

2695 Hier weicht er mir nicht aus, er muß mich hören.

Frießhardt

(kommt eilfertig den Hohlweg herab und ruft in die Scene).

Man fahre aus dem Weg — Mein gnäd'ger Herr,
Der Landvogt, kommt dicht hinter mir geritten.

(Tell geht ab.)

Armgard (lebhaft).

Der Landvogt kommt!

(Sie geht mit ihren Kindern nach der vordern Scene. Geßler und
Rudolph der Harras zeigen sich zu Pferd auf der Höhe des
Wegs.)

Stüssi (zu Frießhardt).

Wie kamt Ihr durch das Wasser.
Da doch der Strom die Brücken fortgeführt?

Frießhardt.

2700 Wir haben mit dem See gefochten, Freund,
Und fürchten uns vor keinem Alpenwasser.

Stüssi.

Ihr wart zu Schiff in dem gewalt'gen Sturm?

Frießhardt.

Das waren wir. Mein Lebtag denk' ich dran —

Stüssi.

O, bleibt, erzählt!

Frießhardt.

Laßt mich, ich muß voraus,
2705 Den Landvogt muß ich in der Burg verkünden.

(Ab.)

Stüssi.

Wär'n gute Leute auf dem Schiff gewesen,
In Grund gesunken wär's mit Mann und Maus;
Dem Volk kann weder Wasser bei noch Feuer.

(Er sieht sich um.)

Wo kam der Weidmann hin, mit dem ich sprach?

(Geht ab.)

Geßler und Rudolph der Harras zu Pferd.

Geßler.

2710 Sagt, was Ihr wollt, ich bin des Kaisers Diener
Und muß drauf denken, wie ich ihm gefalle.
Er hat mich nicht ins Land geschickt, dem Volk
Zu schmeicheln und ihm sanft zu thun — Gehorsam
Erwartet er; der Streit ist, ob der Bauer
2715 Soll Herr sein in dem Lande oder der Kaiser.

Armgard.

Jetzt ist der Augenblick! Jetzt bring' ich's an!

(Nähert sich furchtsam.)

Geßler.

Ich hab' den Hut nicht aufgesteckt zu Altorf
Des Scherzes wegen, oder um die Herzen
Des Volks zu prüfen; diese kenn' ich längst.
2720 Ich hab' ihn aufgesteckt, daß sie den Nacken

Mir lernen beugen, den sie aufrecht tragen —
Das Unbequeme hab' ich hingepflanzt
Auf ihren Weg, wo sie vorbeigehn müssen,
Daß sie drauf stoßen mit dem Aug' und sich
2725 Erinnern ihres Herrn, den sie vergessen.

Rudolph.

Das Volk hat aber doch gewisse Rechte —

Geßler.

Die abzuwägen, ist jetzt keine Zeit!
— Weitschicht'ge Dinge sind im Werk und Werden;
Das Kaiserhaus will wachsen; was der Vater
2730 Glorreich begonnen, will der Sohn vollenden.
Dies kleine Volk ist uns ein Stein im Weg —
So oder so — Es muß sich unterwerfen.

(Sie wollen vorüber. Die Frau wirft sich vor dem Landvogt nieder.)

Armgard.

Barmherzigkeit, Herr Landvogt! Gnade! Gnade!

Geßler.

Was bringt Ihr Euch auf offner Straße mir
2735 In Weg? — Zurück!

Armgard.

    Mein Mann liegt im Gefängnis;
Die armen Waisen schrei'n nach Brod — Habt Mitleid
Gestrenger Herr, mit unserm großen Elend!

Rudolph.

Wer seid Ihr? Wer ist Euer Mann?

Armgard.

    Ein armer
Wildheuer, guter Herr, vom Rigiberge,

2740 Der überm Abgrund weg das freie Gras
     Abmähet von den schroffen Felsenwänden,
     Wohin das Vieh sich nicht getraut zu steigen —

Rudolph (zum Landvogt).

Bei Gott, ein elend und erbärmlich Leben!
Ich bitt' Euch, gebt ihn los, den armen Mann!
2745 Was er auch Schweres mag verschuldet haben,
     Strafe genug ist sein entsetzlich Handwerk.

(Zu der Frau.)

Euch soll Recht werden — Drinnen auf der Burg
Nennt Eure Bitte — Hier ist nicht der Ort.

Armgard.

Nein, nein, ich weiche nicht von diesem Platz,
2750 Bis mir der Vogt den Mann zurückgegeben!
     Schon in den sechsten Mond liegt er im Turm
     Und harret auf den Richterspruch vergebens.

Geßler.

Weib, wollt Ihr mir Gewalt anthun? Hinweg!

Armgard.

Gerechtigkeit, Landvogt! Du bist der Richter
2755 Im Lande an des Kaisers Statt und Gottes.
     Thu' deine Pflicht! So du Gerechtigkeit
     Vom Himmel hoffest, so erzeig' sie uns!

Geßler.

Fort! Schafft das freche Volk mir aus den Augen!

Armgard (greift in die Zügel des Pferdes).

Nein, nein, ich habe nichts mehr zu verlieren.
2760 — Du kommst nicht von der Stelle, Vogt, bis du
     Mir Recht gesprochen — Falte deine Stirne,

Rolle die Augen, wie du willst — Wir sind
So grenzenlos unglücklich, daß wir nichts
Nach deinem Zorn mehr fragen —

Geßler.

                Weib, mach' Platz,
2765 Oder mein Roß geht über dich hinweg.

Armgard.

Laß es über mich dahin gehn — Da —

(Sie reißt ihre Kinder zu Boden und wirft sich mit ihnen ihm in den Weg.

                   Hier lieg' ich
Mit meinen Kindern — Laß die armen Waisen
Von deines Pferdes Huf zertreten werden!
Es ist das Ärgste nicht, was du gethan —

Rudolph.

2770 Weib, seid Ihr rasend?

Armgard (heftiger fortfahrend).

                Tratest du doch längst
Das Land des Kaisers unter deine Füße!
— O, ich bin nur ein Weib! Wär' ich ein Mann,
Ich wüßte wohl was Besseres, als hier
Im Staub zu liegen —

(Man hört die vorige Musik wieder auf der Höhe des Wegs, aber gedämpft

Geßler.

            Wo sind meine Knechte?
2775 Man reiße sie von hinnen, oder ich
Vergesse mich und thue, was mich reuet.

Rudolph.

Die Knechte können nicht hindurch, o Herr!
Der Hohlweg ist gesperrt durch eine Hochzeit.

Geßlers Tod

Face p. 147

Geßler.

Ein allzu milder Herrscher bin ich noch
2780 Gegen dies Volk — die Zungen sind noch frei,
Es ist noch nicht ganz, wie es soll, gebändigt —
Doch es soll anders werden, ich gelob' es:
Ich will ihn brechen, diesen starren Sinn,
Den kecken Geist der Freiheit will ich beugen.
2785 Ein neu Gesetz will ich in diesen Landen
Verkündigen — ich will —

(Ein Pfeil durchbohrt ihn; er fährt mit der Hand ans Herz und will sinken.
Mit matter Stimme:)
　　　　　Gott sei mir gnädig!

Rudolph.

Herr Landvogt — Gott! Was ist das? Woher kam das?

Armgard (auffahrend).

Mord! Mord! Er taumelt, sinkt! Er ist getroffen!
Mitten ins Herz hat ihn der Pfeil getroffen!

Rudolph (springt vom Pferde).

2790 Welch gräßliches Ereignis — Gott — Herr Ritter —
Ruft die Erbarmung Gottes an! — Ihr seid
Ein Mann des Todes!

Geßler.
　　　　　Das ist Tell's Geschoß!

(Ist vom Pferde herab dem Rudolph Harras in den Arm gegleitet und wird
auf der Bank niedergelassen.)

Tell
(erscheint oben auf der Höhe des Felsen).

Du kennst den Schützen, suche keinen andern!
Frei sind die Hütten, sicher ist die Unschuld
2795 Vor dir, du wirst dem Lande nicht mehr schaden.

(Verschwindet von der Höhe. Volk stürzt herein.)

Stüssi (voran).

Was giebt es hier? Was hat sich zugetragen?

Armgard.

Der Landvogt ist von einem Pfeil durchschossen.

Volk (im Hereinstürzen).

Wer ist erschossen?

(Indem die Vordersten von dem Brautzug auf die Scene kommen, sind die Hintersten noch auf der Höhe, und die Musik geht fort.)

Rudolph der Harras.

Er verblutet sich.

Fort, schaffet Hilfe! Setzt dem Mörder nach!
2800 — Verlorner Mann, so muß es mit dir enden;
Doch meine Warnung wolltest du nicht hören!

Stüssi.

Bei Gott! Da liegt er bleich und ohne Leben!

Viele Stimmen.

Wer hat die That gethan?

Rudolph der Harras.

Rast dieses Volk,
Daß es dem Mord Musik macht? Laßt sie schweigen!

(Musik bricht plötzlich ab, es kommt noch mehr Volk nach.)

2805 Herr Landvogt, redet, wenn Ihr könnt — Habt Ihr
Mir nichts mehr zu vertrauen?

(Geßler giebt Zeichen mit der Hand, die er mit Heftigkeit wiederholt, da sie nicht gleich verstanden werden.)

Wo soll ich hin?

— Nach Küßnacht? — Ich versteh' Euch nicht — O werdet
Nicht ungeduldig — Laßt das Irdische,

Denkt jetzt Euch mit dem Himmel zu versöhnen!

(Die ganze Hochzeitgesellschaft umsteht den Sterbenden mit einem fühllosen Grausen.)

Stüssi.

2810 Sieh, wie er bleich wird — Jetzt, jetzt tritt der Tod
Ihm an das Herz — die Augen sind gebrochen.

Armgard (hebt ein Kind empor).

Seht, Kinder, wie ein Wüterich verscheidet!

Rudolph der Harras.

Wahnsinn'ge Weiber, habt ihr kein Gefühl,
Daß ihr den Blick an diesem Schrecknis weidet?
2815 Helft — Leget Hand an — Steht mir niemand bei,
Den Schmerzenspfeil ihm aus der Brust zu ziehn?

Weiber (treten zurück).

Wir ihn berühren, welchen Gott geschlagen!

Rudolph der Harras.

Fluch treff' euch und Verdammnis!

(Zieht das Schwert.)

Stüssi (fällt ihm in den Arm).

Wagt es, Herr!
Eu'r Walten hat ein Ende.   Der Tyrann
2820 Des Landes ist gefallen.   Wir erdulden
Keine Gewalt mehr.   Wir sind freie Menschen.

Alle (tumultuarisch).

Das Land ist frei!

Rudolph der Harras.

Ist es dahin gekommen?
Endet die Furcht so schnell und der Gehorsam?

(Zu den Waffenknechten, die hereindringen.)

Ihr seht die grausenvolle That des Mords,
2825 Die hier geschehen — Hilfe ist umsonst —
Vergeblich ist's, dem Mörder nachzusetzen.
Uns drängen andre Sorgen — Auf, nach Küßnacht,
Daß wir dem Kaiser seine Feste retten!
Denn aufgelöst in diesem Augenblick
2830 Sind aller Ordnung, aller Pflichten Bande,
Und keines Mannes Treu' ist zu vertrauen.

Indem er mit den Waffenknechten abgeht, erscheinen sechs barmherzige Brüder.

Armgard.

Platz! Platz! da kommen die barmherz'gen Brüder.

Stüssi.

Das Opfer liegt — Die Raben steigen nieder.

Barmherzige Brüder

(schließen einen Halbkreis um den Toten und singen in tiefem Ton)

Rasch tritt der Tod den Menschen an,
2835　　Es ist ihm keine Frist gegeben;
Es stürzt ihn mitten in der Bahn,
Es reißt ihn fort vom vollen Leben.
Bereitet oder nicht, zu gehen,
Er muß vor seinen Richter stehen!

(Indem die letzten Zeilen wiederholt werden, fällt der Vorhang.)

Fünfter Aufzug.

Erste Scene.

Öffentlicher Platz bei Altorf.

Im Hintergrunde rechts die Feste Zwing Uri mit dem noch stehenden Baugerüste, wie in der dritten Scene des ersten Aufzugs; links eine Aussicht in viele Berge hinein, auf welchen allen Signalfeuer brennen. Es ist eben Tagesanbruch, Glocken ertönen aus verschiedenen Fernen.

Ruodi, Kuoni, Werni, Meister Steinmetz und viele andere Landleute, auch Weiber und Kinder.

Ruodi.

2840 Seht ihr die Feu'rsignale auf den Bergen?

Steinmetz.

Hört ihr die Glocken drüben überm Wald?

Ruodi.

Die Feinde sind verjagt.

Steinmetz.

Die Burgen sind erobert.

Ruodi.

Und wir im Lande Uri dulden noch
Auf unserm Boden das Tyrannenschloß?
2845 Sind wir die Letzten, die sich frei erklären?

Steinmetz.

Das Joch soll stehen, das uns zwingen wollte?
Auf, reißt es nieder!

Alle.

Nieder! nieder! nieder!

Ruodi.

Wo ist der Stier von Uri?

Stier von Uri.

Hier.   Was soll ich?

Ruodi.

Steigt auf die Hochwacht, blast in Euer Horn,
2850 Daß es weitschmetternd in die Berge schalle
Und, jedes Echo in den Felsenklüften
Aufweckend, schnell die Männer des Gebirgs
Zusammenrufe!

Stier von Uri geht ab.   Walther Fürst kommt.

Walther Fürst.

Haltet, Freunde!   Haltet!
Noch fehlt uns Kunde, was in Unterwalden
2855 Und Schwyz geschehen.   Laßt uns Boten erst
Erwarten!

Ruodi.

Was erwarten?   Der Tyrann
Ist tot, der Tag der Freiheit ist erschienen.

Steinmetz.

Ist's nicht genug an diesen flammenden Boten,
Die rings herum auf allen Bergen leuchten?

Ruodi.

2860 Kommt alle, kommt, legt Hand an, Männer und Weiber!

Brecht das Gerüste! Sprengt die Bogen! Reißt
Die Mauern ein! Kein Stein bleib' auf dem andern!

Steinmetz.

Gesellen, kommt! Wir haben's aufgebaut,
Wir wissen's zu zerstören.

Alle.

Kommt, reißt nieder!

(Sie stürzen sich von allen Seiten auf den Bau.)

Walther Fürst.

2865 Es ist im Lauf. Ich kann sie nicht mehr halten.

Melchthal und Baumgarten kommen.

Melchthal.

Was? Steht die Burg noch, und Schloß Sarnen liegt
In Asche, und der Roßberg ist gebrochen?

Walther Fürst.

Seid Ihr es, Melchthal? Bringt Ihr uns die Freiheit?
Sagt! Sind die Lande alle rein vom Feind?

Melchthal (umarmt ihn).

2870 Rein ist der Boden. Freut Euch, alter Vater!
In diesem Augenblicke, da wir reden,
Ist kein Tyrann mehr in der Schweizer Land.

Walther Fürst.

O, sprecht, wie wurdet Ihr der Burgen mächtig?

Melchthal.

Der Rudenz war es, der das Sarner Schloß
2875 Mit mannlich kühner Wagethat gewann.
Den Roßberg hatt' ich nachts zuvor erstiegen.
— Doch höret, was geschah. Als wir das Schloß,
Vom Feind geleert, nun freudig angezündet,

Die Flamme prasselnd schon zum Himmel schlug,
2880 Da stürzt der Diethelm, Geßlers Bub, hervor
Und ruft, daß die Bruneckerin verbrenne.

Walther Fürst.

Gerechter Gott!

(Man hört die Balken des Gerüstes stürzen.)

Melchthal.

Sie war es selbst, war heimlich
Hier eingeschlossen auf des Vogts Geheiß.
Rasend erhub sich Rudenz — denn wir hörten
2885 Die Balken schon, die festen Pfosten stürzen,
Und aus dem Rauch hervor den Jammerruf
Der Unglückseligen.

Walther Fürst.

Sie ist gerettet?

Melchthal.

Da galt Geschwindsein und Entschlossenheit!
— Wär' er nur unser Edelmann gewesen,
2890 Wir hätten unser Leben wohl geliebt;
Doch er war unser Eidgenoß, und Bertha
Ehrte das Volk — So setzten wir getrost
Das Leben dran und stürzten in das Feuer.

Walther Fürst.

Sie ist gerettet?

Melchthal.

Sie ist's. Rudenz und ich,
2895 Wir trugen sie selbander aus den Flammen,
Und hinter uns fiel krachend das Gebälk.
— Und jetzt, als sie gerettet sich erkannte,
Die Augen aufschlug zu dem Himmelslicht,

Jetzt stürzte mir der Freiherr an das Herz,
2900 Und schweigend ward ein Bündnis jetzt beschworen,
Das, fest gehärtet in des Feuers Glut,
Bestehen wird in allen Schicksalsproben —

Walther Fürst.

Wo ist der Landenberg?

Melchthal.

Über den Brünig.

Nicht lag's an mir, daß er das Licht der Augen
2905 Davontrug, der den Vater mir geblendet.
Nach jagt' ich ihm, erreicht' ihn auf der Flucht
Und riß ihn zu den Füßen meines Vaters.
Geschwungen über ihn war schon das Schwert;
Von der Barmherzigkeit des blinden Greises
2910 Erhielt er flehend das Geschenk des Lebens.
Urfehde schwur er, nie zurück zu kehren;
Er wird sie halten; unsern Arm hat er
Gefühlt.

Walther Fürst.

Wohl Euch, daß Ihr den reinen Sieg
Mit Blute nicht geschändet!

Kinder
(eilen mit Trümmern des Gerüstes über die Scene).

Freiheit! Freiheit!
(Das Horn von Uri wird mit Macht geblasen.)

Walther Fürst.

2915 Seht, welch ein Fest! Des Tages werden sich
Die Kinder spät als Greise noch erinnern.

(Mädchen bringen den Hut auf einer Stange getragen; die ganze Scene
füllt sich mit Volk an.)

Ruodi.

Hier ist der Hut, dem wir uns beugen mußten.

Baumgarten.

Gebt uns Bescheid, was damit werden soll.

Walther Fürst.

Gott! Unter diesem Hute stand mein Enkel!

Mehrere Stimmen.

2920 Zerstört das Denkmal der Tyrannenmacht!
Ins Feuer mit ihm!

Walther Fürst.

           Nein, laßt ihn aufbewahren!
Der Tyrannei mußt' er zum Werkzeug dienen,
Er soll der Freiheit ewig Zeichen sein!

(Die Landleute, Männer, Weiber und Kinder stehen und sitzen auf den
Balken des zerbrochenen Gerüstes malerisch gruppiert in einem großen
Halbkreis umher.)

Melchthal.

So stehen wir nun fröhlich auf den Trümmern
2925 Der Tyrannei, und herrlich ist's erfüllt,
Was wir im Rütli schwuren, Eidgenossen.

Walther Fürst.

Das Werk ist angefangen, nicht vollendet.
Jetzt ist uns Mut und feste Eintracht not;
Denn, seid gewiß, nicht säumen wird der König,
2930 Den Tod zu rächen seines Vogts und den
Vertriebnen mit Gewalt zurückzuführen.

Melchthal.

Er zieh' heran mit seiner Heeresmacht!

Ist aus dem Innern doch der Feind verjagt;
Dem Feind von außen wollen wir begegnen.

Ruodi.

2935 Nur wen'ge Päſſe öffnen ihm das Land,
Die wollen wir mit unſern Leibern decken.

Baumgarten.

Wir ſind vereinigt durch ein ewig Band,
Und ſeine Heere ſollen uns nicht ſchrecken!

Röſſelmann und Stauffacher kommen.

Röſſelmann (im Eintreten).

Das ſind des Himmels furchtbare Gerichte.

Landleute.

2940 Was giebt's?

Röſſelmann.

In welchen Zeiten leben wir!

Walther Fürſt.

Sagt an, was iſt es? — Ha, ſeid Ihr's, Herr Werner?
Was bringt Ihr uns?

Landleute.

Was giebt's?

Röſſelmann.

Hört und erſtaunet!

Stauffacher.

Von einer großen Furcht ſind wir befreit —

Röſſelmann.

Der Kaiſer iſt ermordet.

Walther Fürſt.

Gnäd'ger Gott!

(Landleute machen einen Aufſtand und umdrängen den Stauffacher.)

Alle.

2945 Ermordet! Was! Der Kaiser! Hört! Der Kaiser!

Melchthal.

Nicht möglich! Woher kam Euch diese Kunde?

Stauffacher.

Es ist gewiß. Bei Bruck fiel König Albrecht
Durch Mörders Hand — ein glaubenswerter Mann,
Johannes Müller, bracht' es von Schaffhausen.

Walther Fürst.

2950 Wer wagte solche grauenvolle That?

Stauffacher.

Sie wird noch grauenvoller durch den Thäter.
Es war sein Neffe, seines Bruders Kind,
Herzog Johann von Schwaben, der's vollbrachte.

Melchthal.

Was trieb ihn zu der That des Vatermords?

Stauffacher.

2955 Der Kaiser hielt das väterliche Erbe
Dem ungeduldig Mahnenden zurück;
Es hieß, er denk' ihn ganz darum zu kürzen,
Mit einem Bischofshut ihn abzufinden.
Wie dem auch sei — der Jüngling öffnete
2960 Der Waffenfreunde bösem Rat sein Ohr,
Und mit den edeln Herrn von Eschenbach,
Von Tegerfelden, von der Wart und Palm
Beschloß er, da er Recht nicht konnte finden,
Sich Rach' zu holen mit der eignen Hand.

Walther Fürst.

2965 O, sprecht, wie ward das Gräßliche vollendet?

Stauffacher.

Der König ritt herab vom Stein zu Baden,
Gen Rheinfeld, wo die Hofstatt war, zu ziehn,
Mit ihm die Fürsten H a n s und L e o p o l d
Und ein Gefolge hochgeborner Herren.
2970 Und als sie kamen an die R e u ß, wo man
Auf einer Fähre sich läßt übersetzen,
Da drängten sich die Mörder in das Schiff,
Daß sie den Kaiser vom Gefolge trennten.
Drauf, als der Fürst durch ein geackert Feld
2975 Hinreitet, — eine alte große Stadt
Soll drunter liegen aus der Heiden Zeit —
Die alte Feste Habsburg im Gesicht,
Wo seines Stammes Hoheit ausgegangen —
Stößt Herzog Hans den Dolch ihm in die Kehle,
2980 Rudolph von Palm durchrennt ihn mit dem Speer,
Und Eschenbach zerspaltet ihm das Haupt,
Daß er heruntersinkt in seinem Blut,
Gemordet von den Seinen, a u f dem Seinen.
Am andern Ufer sahen sie die That;
2985 Doch durch den Strom geschieden, konnten sie
Nur ein ohnmächtig Wehgeschrei erheben;
Am Wege aber saß ein armes Weib,
In ihrem Schoß verblutete der Kaiser.

Melchthal.

So hat er nur sein frühes Grab gegraben,
2990 Der unersättlich alles wollte haben!

Stauffacher.

Ein ungeheurer Schrecken ist im Land umher;
Gesperrt sind alle Pässe des Gebirgs,
Jedweder Stand verwahret seine Grenzen;

Die alte Zürich selbst schloß ihre Thore,
2995 Die dreißig Jahr' lang offen standen, zu,
Die Mörder fürchtend und noch mehr — die Rächer.
Denn, mit des Bannes Fluch bewaffnet, kommt
Der Ungarn Königin, die strenge Agnes,
Die nicht die Milde kennet ihres zarten
3000 Geschlechts, des Vaters königliches Blut
Zu rächen an der Mörder ganzem Stamm,
An ihren Knechten, Kindern, Kindeskindern,
Ja, an den Steinen ihrer Schlösser selbst.
Geschworen hat sie, ganze Zeugungen
3005 Hinabzusenden in des Vaters Grab,
In Blut sich wie in Maientau zu baden.

Melchthal.

Weiß man, wo sich die Mörder hingeflüchtet?

Stauffacher.

Sie flohen alsbald nach vollbrachter That
Auf fünf verschiednen Straßen auseinander
3010 Und trennten sich, um nie sich mehr zu sehn —
Herzog Johann soll irren im Gebirge.

Walther Fürst.

So trägt die Unthat ihnen keine Frucht!
Rache trägt keine Frucht! Sich selbst ist sie
Die fürchterliche Nahrung, ihr Genuß
3015 Ist Mord, und ihre Sättigung das Grausen.

Stauffacher.

Den Mördern bringt die Unthat nicht Gewinn;
Wir aber brechen mit der reinen Hand
Des blut'gen Frevels segenvolle Frucht.
Denn einer großen Furcht sind wir entledigt;

3020 Gefallen ist der Freiheit größter Feind,
Und wie verlautet, wird das Scepter gehn
Aus Habsburgs Haus zu einem andern Stamm,
Das Reich will seine Wahlfreiheit behaupten.

Walther Fürst und Mehrere.

Vernahmt Ihr was?

Stauffacher.

Der Graf von Luxemburg
3025 Ist von den mehrsten Stimmen schon bezeichnet.

Walther Fürst.

Wohl uns, daß wir beim Reiche treu gehalten;
Jetzt ist zu hoffen auf Gerechtigkeit!

Stauffacher.

Dem neuen Herrn thun tapfre Freunde not;
Er wird uns schirmen gegen Östreichs Rache.

(Die Landleute umarmen einander.)

Sigrist mit einem Reichsboten.

Sigrist.

3030 Hier sind des Landes würd'ge Oberhäupter.

Rösselmann und Mehrere.

Sigrist, was giebt's?

Sigrist.

Ein Reichsbot' bringt dies Schreiben

Alle (zu Walther Fürst).

Erbrecht und leset!

Walther Fürst (liest).

„Den bescheidnen Männern
Von Uri, Schwyz und Unterwalden bietet
Die Königin Elsbeth Gnad' und alles Gutes."

Viele Stimmen.

3035 Was will die Königin?   Ihr Reich ist aus.

Walther Fürst (liest).

„In ihrem großen Schmerz und Witwenleid,
Worein der blut'ge Hinscheid ihres Herrn
Die Königin versetzt, gedenkt sie noch
Der alten Treu' und Lieb' der Schwyzerlande."

Melchthal.

3040 In ihrem Glück hat sie das nie gethan.

Rösselmann.

Still! Lasset hören!

Walther Fürst (liest).

„Und sie versieht sich zu dem treuen Volk.
Daß es gerechten Abscheu werde tragen
Vor den verfluchten Thätern dieser That.
3045 Darum erwartet sie von den drei Landen,
Daß sie den Mördern nimmer Vorschub thun,
Vielmehr getreulich dazu helfen werden,
Sie auszuliefern in des Rächers Hand,
Der Lieb' gedenkend und der alten Gunst,
3050 Die sie von Rudolphs Fürstenhaus empfangen."
(Zeichen des Unwillens unter den Landleuten.)

Viele Stimmen.

Der Lieb' und Gunst!

Stauffacher.

Wir haben Gunst empfangen von dem Vater;
Doch wessen rühmen wir uns von dem Sohn?
Hat er den Brief der Freiheit uns bestätigt,
3055 Wie vor ihm alle Kaiser doch gethan?

Hat er gerichtet nach gerechtem Spruch
Und der bedrängten Unschuld Schutz verliehn?
Hat er auch nur die Boten wollen hören,
Die wir in unsrer Angst zu ihm gesendet?
3060 Nicht eins von diesem allen hat der König
An uns gethan, und hätten wir nicht selbst
Uns Recht verschafft mit eigner mut'ger Hand,
Ihn rührte unsre Not nicht an — Ihm Dank?
Nicht Dank hat er gesät in diesen Thälern.
3065 Er stand auf einem hohen Platz, er konnte
Ein Vater seiner Völker sein; doch ihm
Gefiel es, nur zu sorgen für die Seinen;
Die er gemehrt hat, mögen um ihn weinen!

Walther Fürst.

Wir wollen nicht frohlocken seines Falls,
3070 Nicht des empfangnen Bösen j e t z t gedenken,
Fern sei's von uns! Doch daß wir r ä c h e n sollten
Des Königs Tod, der nie uns Gutes that,
Und die verfolgen, die uns nie betrübten,
Das ziemt uns nicht und will uns nicht gebühren.
3075 Die Liebe will ein freies Opfer sein;
Der Tod entbindet von erzwungnen Pflichten,
— Ihm haben wir nichts weiter zu entrichten.

Melchthal.

Und weint die Königin in ihrer Kammer,
Und klagt ihr wilder Schmerz den Himmel an,
3080 So seht Ihr hier ein angstbefreites Volk
Zu eben diesem Himmel dankend flehen —
Wer Thränen ernten will, muß Liebe säen.

(Reichsbote geht ab.)

Stauffacher (zu dem Volk).

Wo ist der Tell? Soll er allein uns fehlen,
Der unsrer Freiheit Stifter ist? Das Größte
3085 Hat er gethan, das Härteste erduldet,
Kommt alle, kommt, nach seinem Haus zu wallen,
Und rufet Heil dem Retter von uns allen!

(Alle gehen ab.)

Zweite Scene.

Tells Hausflur.

Ein Feuer brennt auf dem Herd. Die offenstehende Thüre zeigt
ins Freie.

Hedwig. Walther und Wilhelm.

Hedwig.

Heut' kommt der Vater. Kinder, liebe Kinder!
Er lebt, ist frei, und wir sind frei und alles!
3090 Und euer Vater ist's, der's Land gerettet.

Walther.

Und ich bin auch dabei gewesen, Mutter!
Mich muß man auch mit nennen. Vaters Pfeil
Ging mir am Leben hart vorbei, und ich
Hab' nicht gezittert.

Hedwig (umarmt ihn).

Ja, du bist mir wieder
3095 Gegeben! Zweimal hab' ich dich geboren!
Zweimal litt ich den Mutterschmerz um dich!

Es ist vorbei — Ich hab' euch beide, beide!
Und heute kommt der liebe Vater wieder!

Ein Mönch erscheint an der Hausthüre.

Wilhelm.

Sieh, Mutter, sieh — dort steht ein frommer Bruder;
3100 Gewiß wird er um eine Gabe flehn.

Hedwig.

Führ' ihn herein, damit wir ihn erquicken;
Er fühl's, daß er ins Freudenhaus gekommen.

(Geht hinein und kommt bald mit einem Becher wieder.)

Wilhelm (zum Mönch).

Kommt, guter Mann! Die Mutter will Euch laben.

Walther.

Kommt, ruht Euch aus und geht gestärkt von dannen!

Mönch
(scheu umherblickend, mit zerstörten Zügen).

3105 Wo bin ich? Saget an, in welchem Lande?

Walther.

Seid Ihr verirret, daß Ihr nicht wißt?
Ihr seid zu Bürglen, Herr, im Lande Uri,
Wo man hineingeht in das Schächenthal.

Mönch
(zur Hedwig, welche zurückkommt).

Seid Ihr allein? Ist Euer Herr zu Hause?

Hedwig.

3110 Ich erwart' ihn eben — doch was ist Euch, Mann?
Ihr seht nicht aus, als ob Ihr Gutes brächtet.
— Wer Ihr auch seid, Ihr seid bedürftig, nehmt!

(Reicht ihm den Becher.)

Mönch.

Wie auch mein lechzend Herz nach Labung schmachtet,
Nichts rühr' ich an, bis Ihr mir zugesagt —

Hedwig.

3115 Berührt mein Kleid nicht, tretet mir nicht nah,
Bleibt ferne stehn, wenn ich Euch hören soll.

Mönch.

Bei diesem Feuer, das hier gastlich lodert,
Bei Eurer Kinder teurem Haupt, das ich
Umfasse —

(Ergreift die Knaben.)

Hedwig.

Mann, was sinnet Ihr?　Zurück
3120 Von meinen Kindern! — Ihr seid kein Mönch! Ihr seid
Es nicht!　Der Friede wohnt in diesem Kleide;
In Euren Zügen wohnt der Friede nicht.

Mönch.

Ich bin der unglückseligste der Menschen.

Hedwig.

Das Unglück spricht gewaltig zu dem Herzen;
3125 Doch Euer Blick schnürt mir das Innre zu.

Walther (aufspringend).

Mutter, der Vater!

(Eilt hinaus.)

Hedwig.

O mein Gott!

(Will nach, zittert und hält sich an.)

Wilhelm (eilt nach).

Der Vater!

Walther (draußen).

Da bist du wieder!

Wilhelm (draußen).

Vater, lieber Vater!

Tell (draußen).

Da bin ich wieder — Wo ist eure Mutter?

(Treten herein.)

Walther.

Da steht sie an der Thür' und kann nicht weiter;
3130 So zittert sie vor Schrecken und vor Freude.

Tell.

O Hedwig! Hedwig! Mutter meiner Kinder!
Gott hat geholfen — Uns trennt kein Tyrann mehr.

Hedwig (an seinem Halse).

O Tell! Tell! Welche Angst litt ich um dich!

(Mönch wird aufmerksam.)

Tell.

Vergiß sie jetzt und lebe nur der Freude!
3135 Da bin ich wieder! Das ist meine Hütte!
Ich stehe wieder auf dem Meinigen!

Wilhelm.

Wo aber hast du deine Armbrust, Vater?
Ich seh' sie nicht.

Tell.

Du wirst sie nie mehr sehn.
An heil'ger Stätte ist sie aufbewahrt;
3140 Sie wird hinfort zu keiner Jagd mehr dienen.

Hedwig.

O Tell! Tell!

(Tritt zurück, läßt seine Hand los.)

Tell.

Was erschreckt dich, liebes Weib?

Hedwig.

Wie — wie kommst du mir wieder? — Diese Hand
— Darf ich sie fassen? — Diese Hand — O Gott!

Tell (herzlich und mutig).

Hat euch verteidigt und das Land gerettet;
3145 Ich darf sie frei hinauf zum Himmel heben.

(Mönch macht eine rasche Bewegung, er erblickt ihn.)

Wer ist der Bruder hier?

Hedwig.

Ach, ich vergaß ihn!
Sprich du mit ihm; mir graut in seiner Nähe.

Mönch (tritt näher).

Seid Ihr der Tell, durch den der Landvogt fiel?

Tell.

Der bin ich, ich verberg' es keinem Menschen.

Mönch.

3150 Ihr seid der Tell! Ach, es ist Gottes Hand,
Die unter Euer Dach mich hat geführt.

Tell (mißt ihn mit den Augen).

Ihr seid kein Mönch! Wer seid Ihr?

Mönch.

Ihr erschlugt
Den Landvogt, der Euch Böses that — Auch ich
Hab' einen Feind erschlagen, der mir Recht
3155 Versagte — Er war Euer Feind wie meiner —
Ich hab' das Land von ihm befreit.

Tell (zurückfahrend).

> Ihr seid —
Entsetzen! — Kinder! Kinder, geht hinein!
Geh, liebes Weib! Geh, geh! — Unglücklicher,
Ihr wäret —

Hedwig.

> Gott, wer ist es?

Tell.

> Frage nicht!
3160 Fort! fort! Die Kinder dürfen es nicht hören.
Geh aus dem Hause — weit hinweg — Du darfst
Nicht unter einem Dach mit diesem wohnen.

Hedwig.

Weh mir, was ist das? Kommt!

> (Geht mit den Kindern.)

Tell (zu dem Mönch).

> Ihr seid der Herzog
Von Österreich — Ihr seid's! Ihr habt den Kaiser
3165 Erschlagen, Euern Ohm und Herrn.

Johannes Parricida.

> Er war
Der Räuber meines Erbes.

Tell.

> Euern Ohm
Erschlagen, Euern Kaiser! Und Euch trägt
Die Erde noch! Euch leuchtet noch die Sonne!

Parricida.

Tell, hört mich, eh' Ihr —

Tell.

> Von dem Blute triefend
3170 Des Vatermordes und des Kaisermords,

Wagst du zu treten in mein reines Haus?
Du wagst's, dein Antlitz einem guten Menschen
Zu zeigen und das Gastrecht zu begehren?

Parricida.

Bei Euch hofft' ich Barmherzigkeit zu finden;
3175 Auch Ihr nahmt Rach' an Eurem Feind.

Tell.

Unglücklicher!
Darfst du der Ehrsucht blut'ge Schuld vermengen
Mit der gerechten Notwehr eines Vaters?
Hast du der Kinder liebes Haupt verteidigt?
Des Herdes Heiligtum beschützt? das Schrecklichste,
3180 Das Letzte von den Deinen abgewehrt?
— Zum Himmel heb' ich meine reinen Hände,
Verfluche dich und deine That — Gerächt
Hab' ich die heilige Natur, die d u
Geschändet — Nichts teil' ich mit dir — Gemordet
3185 Hast d u, i ch hab' mein Teuerstes verteidigt.

Parricida.

Ihr stoßt mich von Euch, trostlos, in Verzweiflung?

Tell.

Mich faßt ein Grausen, da ich mit dir rede.
Fort! Wandle deine fürchterliche Straße!
Laß rein die Hütte, wo die Unschuld wohnt!

Parricida (wendet sich, zu gehen).

3190 So kann ich, und so will ich nicht mehr leben!

Tell.

Und doch erbarmt mich deiner — Gott des Himmels!
So jung, von solchem adeligen Stamm,

Der Enkel Rudolphs, meines Herrn und Kaisers,
Als Mörder flüchtig, hier an meiner Schwelle,
3195 Des armen Mannes, flehend und verzweifelnd —

(Verhüllt sich das Gesicht.)

Parricida.

O, wenn Ihr weinen könnt, laßt mein Geschick
Euch jammern; es ist fürchterlich — Ich bin
Ein Fürst — ich war's — ich konnte glücklich werden,
Wenn ich der Wünsche Ungeduld bezwang.
3200 Der Neid zernagte mir das Herz — Ich sah
Die Jugend meines Vetters Leopold
Gekrönt mit Ehre und mit Land belohnt,
Und mich, der gleiches Alters mit ihm war,
In sklavischer Unmündigkeit gehalten —

Tell.

3205 Unglücklicher, wohl kannte dich dein Ohm,
Da er dir Land und Leute weigerte!
Du selbst mit rascher, wilder Wahnsinnsthat
Rechtfertigst furchtbar seinen weisen Schluß.
— Wo sind die blut'gen Helfer deines Mords?

Parricida.

3210 Wohin die Rachegeister sie geführt;
Ich sah sie seit der Unglücksthat nicht wieder.

Tell.

Weißt du, daß dich die Acht verfolgt, daß du
Dem Freund verboten und dem Feind erlaubt?

Parricida.

Darum vermeid' ich alle offne Straßen;
3215 An keine Hütte wag' ich anzupochen —
Der Wüste kehr' ich meine Schritte zu;

Mein eignes Schrecknis irr' ich durch die Berge
Und fahre schaudernd vor mir selbst zurück,
Zeigt mir ein Bach mein unglückselig Bild.
3220 O, wenn Ihr Mitleid fühlt und Menschlichkeit —

(Fällt vor ihm nieder.)

Tell (abgewendet).

Steht auf! Steht auf!

Parricida.

Nicht bis Ihr mir die Hand gereicht zur Hilfe.

Tell.

Kann ich Euch helfen? Kann's ein Mensch der Sünde?
Doch stehet auf — Was Ihr auch Gräßliches
3225 Verübt — Ihr seid ein Mensch — Ich bin es auch;
Vom Tell soll keiner ungetröstet scheiden —
Was ich vermag, das will ich thun.

Parricida

(aufspringend und seine Hand mit Heftigkeit ergreifend).

O Tell!

Ihr rettet meine Seele von Verzweiflung.

Tell.

Laßt meine Hand los — Ihr müßt fort. Hier könnt
3230 Ihr unentdeckt nicht bleiben, könnt entdeckt
Auf Schutz nicht rechnen — Wo gedenkt Ihr hin?
Wo hofft Ihr Ruh' zu finden?

Parricida.

Weiß ich's? Ach!

Tell.

Hört, was mir Gott ins Herz giebt — Ihr müßt fort
Ins Land Italien, nach Sankt Peters Stadt!

3235 Dort werft Ihr Euch dem Papst zu Füßen, beichtet
Ihm Eure Schuld und löset Eure Seele.

Parricida.

Wird er mich nicht dem Rächer überliefern?

Tell.

Was er Euch thut, das nehmet an von Gott!

Parricida.

Wie komm' ich in das unbekannte Land?
3240 Ich bin des Wegs nicht kundig, wage nicht,
Zu Wanderern die Schritte zu gesellen.

Tell.

Den Weg will ich Euch nennen, merket wohl!
Ihr steigt hinauf, dem Strom der Reuß entgegen,
Die wildes Laufes von dem Berge stürzt —

Parricida (erschrickt).

3245 Seh' ich die Reuß? Sie floß bei meiner That.

Tell.

Am Abgrund geht der Weg, und viele Kreuze
Bezeichnen ihn, errichtet zum Gedächtnis
Der Wanderer, die die Lawine begraben.

Parricida.

Ich fürchte nicht die Schrecken der Natur,
3250 Wenn ich des Herzens wilde Qualen zähme.

Tell.

Vor jedem Kreuze fallet hin und büßet
Mit heißen Reuethränen Eure Schuld —
Und seid Ihr glücklich durch die Schreckensstraße,
Sendet der Berg nicht seine Windeswehen

3255 Auf Euch herab von dem beeisten Joch,
　　So kommt Ihr auf die **Brücke**, welche **stäubet**.
　　Wenn sie nicht einbricht unter Eurer Schuld,
　　Wenn Ihr sie glücklich hinter Euch gelassen,
　　So reißt ein schwarzes **Felsenthor** sich auf —
3260 Kein Tag hat's noch erhellt — da geht Ihr durch,
　　Es führt Euch in ein heitres **Thal** der Freude —
　　Doch schnellen Schritts müßt Ihr vorüber eilen;
　　Ihr dürft nicht weilen, wo die Ruhe wohnt.

Parricida.

　　O Rudolph! Rudolph! Königlicher Ahn!
3265 So zieht dein Enkel ein auf deines Reiches Boden!

Tell.

　　So immer steigend kommt Ihr auf die Höhen
　　Des **Gotthards**, wo die ew'gen Seen sind,
　　Die von des Himmels Strömen selbst sich füllen.
　　Dort nehmt Ihr Abschied von der deutschen Erde,
3270 Und muntern Laufs führt Euch ein andrer Strom
　　Ins Land Italien hinab, Euch das gelobte —

　　　(Man hört den Kuhreihen, von vielen Alphörnern geblasen.)

　　Ich höre Stimmen. Fort!

Hedwig (eilt herein).

　　　　　　Wo bist du, Tell?
　　Der Vater kommt! Es nahn in frohem Zug
　　Die Eidgenossen alle —

Parricida (verhüllt sich).

　　　　　　Wehe mir!
3275 Ich darf nicht weilen bei den Glücklichen.

Tell.

　　Geh, liebes Weib! Erfrische diesen Mann,

Belad' ihn reich mit Gaben; denn sein Weg
Ist weit, und keine Herberg' findet er.
Eile! Sie nahn.

Hedwig.
Wer ist es?

Tell.
Forsche nicht!
3280 Und wenn er geht, so wende deine Augen,
Daß sie nicht sehen, welchen Weg er wandelt!

Parricida geht auf den Tell zu mit einer raschen Bewegung; dieser aber
bedeutet ihn mit der Hand und geht. Wenn beide zu verschiedenen
Seiten abgegangen, verändert sich der Schauplatz, und man sieht
in der

Letzten Scene

den ganzen Thalgrund vor Tells Wohnung, nebst den Anhöhen, welche
ihn einschließen, mit Landleuten besetzt, welche sich zu einem
malerischen Ganzen gruppieren. Andere kommen über einen hohen
Steg, der über den Schächen führt, gezogen. Walther Fürst mit
den beiden Knaben, Melchthal und Stauffacher kommen vorwärts; andere drängen nach; wie Tell heraustritt, empfangen ihn
alle mit lautem Frohlocken.

Alle.
Es lebe Tell, der Schütz und der Erretter!

Indem sich die Vordersten um den Tell drängen und ihn umarmen,
erscheinen noch Rudenz und Bertha, jener die Landleute, diese
die Hedwig umarmend. Die Musik vom Berge begleitet diese stumme
Scene. Wenn sie geendigt, tritt Bertha in die Mitte des Volks.

Bertha.
Landleute! Eidgenossen! Nehmt mich auf
In euern Bund, die erste Glückliche,

3285 Die Schutz gefunden in der Freiheit Land.
In eure tapfre Hand leg' ich mein Recht,
Wollt ihr als eure Bürgerin mich schützen?

Landleute.

Das wollen wir mit Gut und Blut.

Bertha.

Wohlan!
So reich' ich diesem Jüngling meine Rechte,
3290 Die freie Schweizerin dem freien Mann!

Rudenz.

Und frei erklär' ich alle meine Knechte.

(Indem die Musik von neuem rasch einfällt, fällt der Vorhang.)

NOTES.

(177)

NOTES.

ACT I. SCENE 1.

* 𝕬𝖚𝖋𝖟𝖚𝖌 (from 𝖆𝖚𝖋-𝖟𝖎𝖊𝖍𝖊𝖓, 'to draw up'), at first the raising of the curtain at the beginning of an act, was soon taken to mean *act*.

* For no apparent reason 𝕾𝖈𝖊𝖓𝖊 (French *scène;* pronounce two syllables in German) is used in 𝕿𝖊𝖑𝖑 instead of the German equivalent 𝕬𝖚𝖋-𝖙𝖗𝖎𝖙𝖙 (from 𝖆𝖚𝖋-𝖙𝖗𝖊𝖙𝖊𝖓, 'to step up,' 'to appear'), which is now the term most used to indicate the entrance of the actors.

* 𝖁𝖎𝖊𝖗-𝖜𝖆𝖑𝖉-𝖘𝖙ä𝖙𝖙𝖊𝖗-𝖘𝖊𝖊, lit. 'Four-wood-steads' (districts) -lake,' i.e. *Lake of the Four Forest Cantons*, so named from the four cantons (𝖂𝖆𝖑𝖉-𝖘𝖙ä𝖙𝖙𝖊) Uri, Schwyz, Unterwalden and Luzern, lying around it; in English Lake Lucerne.

* 𝕾𝖈𝖍𝖜𝖞𝖟 (pronounce 𝕾𝖈𝖍𝖜𝖎𝖊𝖟), the canton of Schwyz, just across the lake. The scene is laid on the western shore of Lake Lucerne, in Canton Uri, not far from Treib, and directly opposite Brunnen, at a point where the lake is only about half a mile wide. See map.

* 𝖚𝖓𝖜𝖊𝖎𝖙, now generally with genitive.

* 𝖘𝖎𝖊𝖍𝖙 𝖒𝖆𝖓 ... 𝖑𝖎𝖊𝖌𝖊𝖓, *one sees (are seen) ... lying.* Note this infinitive idiom with 𝖘𝖎𝖊𝖍𝖙; it is common with such verbs as 𝖘𝖊𝖍𝖊𝖓, 𝖋𝖎𝖓𝖉𝖊𝖓, 𝖋ü𝖍𝖑𝖊𝖓, 𝖍𝖊𝖎ß𝖊𝖓, 𝖍ö𝖗𝖊𝖓, 𝖍𝖊𝖑𝖋𝖊𝖓, 𝖓𝖊𝖓𝖓𝖊𝖓, and is often best translated by the present participle.

* 𝕳𝖆𝖋𝖊𝖓. The 𝕳𝖆𝖋𝖊𝖓 (also 𝕳𝖆𝖈𝖐𝖊𝖓 or 𝕳𝖆𝖌𝖌𝖊𝖓, lit. 'Hook') of to-day is a peak, rising from a pass of the same name, just N. E. of the village of Schwyz; Schiller identifies it with the two peaks (𝕾𝖕𝖎𝖙𝖟𝖊𝖓), der große 𝕸𝖞𝖙𝖍𝖊𝖓 and der kleine 𝕸𝖞𝖙𝖍𝖊𝖓, near by. The

---

* Shows that the note is on a word occurring in the stage directions.

(179)

Eisgebirge, really not visible, are those of Canton Glarus, directly
east.

* **noch ehe,** emphatic; *even before.*

* **Kuh=reihen** (also **Kuh=reigen**), lit. 'cow-dance'; *the Kuhreihen.*
It is the Swiss herdman's call to his cows, especially at milking-
time.   Sometimes merely a call, it is usually a simple, plain-
tive melody, a "yodel," without words and consisting of long-
drawn-out notes.   These are generally sung, but often played on
the Alphorn (cf. 3271 *), and have many variations, three of
which are given below in the songs of the **Fischerknabe, Hirt,** and
Jäger.

1. **Es lächelt der See** = der See lächelt.   This expletive **es,** as
grammatical subject, introducing the real, logical subject (here **der
See),** is very common in both prose and verse. — **ladet,** old and
poetic for modern prose **ladet . . . ein.**   The poetic personification
here is very effective.

4. In prose **so süß wie Flöten.**

9. **es ruft,** *something calls.*   **Es,** as indefinite logical subject, is
quite common; very different, however, from **es** in 1.   Schiller often
uses it with fine poetic effect to lend an air of mystery to the statement.

10. **Lieb** (for **Lieber**) **Knabe.**   A neuter adjective, nom. or acc.,
often loses its ending in poetry and familiar style; in masc. and
fem. such omission is poetic and rare. — **bist.**   The omission of the
subject lends a familiar, colloquial tone.

11–12. Such superstitions about the charms of the water are very
old; thus, legend says, Hylas, one of the Argonauts, was drawn into
the water by the Naïads.   Swiss tradition ascribes to Lake Calan-
dari (now **der Schwellisee),** near Chur, the mysterious power of
drawing into its waters all who fall asleep near it.   Goethe's ballad
Der Fischer has the same idea.

17. The cattle are driven up to the high mountain pastures (**zu
Berg fahren**) late in spring, spend the summer grazing, and are then
gradually driven down to the valleys (**zu Thal fahren, heimtreiben,**
62) for the winter (203–206). — **kommen** (present for future) **wieder,**
repeats and explains the first half of the line.   Notice the very unusual and highly poetic word order in 17–20.

20. **Brünnlein,** intermittent springs, fed by melting snows, and active only from May to September; also called Mai=Brunnen.

25. **Es donnern** (cf. 1, note), i.e. with the noise of avalanches and cracking ice. — **Steg,** probably *path,* possibly *foot-bridge* of tree-trunks.

26. For prose (Es) grauet dem Schützen nicht. Impersonal construction with logical subj. in dat. and the grammatical subj., es, omitted.

31. **Meer.** Here acc. absolute, used adverbially; not the object of some preposition or participle understood. The construction is idiomatic, both in English and German, though in English *with* is very commonly used. Cf. 'He stood hat in hand' and 'He stood with his hat in his hand.'

35. **Wassern,** i.e. figuratively the *waters* of the **neblichtes Meer** (the clouds).

As yet these three singers have no individual names; so far they are merely types of the three chief classes of Swiss people. Each song, too, is characteristic, in metre and spirit, of the class the singer represents. This is a quiet, harmless, even dreamy people; they love their lakes and mountains; though gentle, they are strong, brave and daring, and fear neither nature nor man. This lyric introduction is skilfully used to put us at once in the midst of the idyllic scenes and characters among which the play is to be laid. Cf. in this connection the opening scenes in Shakespeare's *Macbeth.*

* **Schatten . . . laufen.** A storm darkens the sunny landscape, at the same time anticipating the conflict between people and rulers, and typifying the tyrannical oppression so soon to blight the lives of these happy people.

Ruodi (pronounce Rŭō'di), **Werni, Kuoni** (pronounce Kŭō'ni, almost Kwónee), **Seppi** are Swiss diminutives from Rudolph (older Ruodolph), Werner, Konrad (older Kuon=rat), and Jo=seph respectively. The endings -i and -li are South German and Swiss diminutives for -chen, -lein; thus Madli = Mädchen, Mägdelein, Kindli = Kindlein, etc.

37. **Jenni,** dim. of Johann; cf. Eng. *Johnny.* — **Naue** is primarily a freight-barge or ferry-boat; sometimes a small *boat;* here Jenni's Kahn.

38. Der graue Thal=vogt (lit. 'the gray dale-governor'), the wind, driving the dark storm-clouds, is thus personified. — **Firn** was originally an adj. (akin to fern and, like it, implying distance in time), meaning 'old,' 'last year's.' It is the old snow of previous years, turned more or less to ice; successive layers of it gradually form the glaciers.

39. The **Mythenstein** of to-day is a rock rising some eighty feet out of the lake near Treib. Ruodi means, no doubt, the **Mythenstock,** one of the peaks of the **Hafen,** mentioned in the introductory stage directions as surrounded by clouds, the *hood* in question here. Schiller was never in Switzerland, and such a mistake is very natural.

40. Wetter=loch (also **Wind=loch**), some mountain cleft from which the wind blows fresher on the approach of a storm. In 38–40 we have the fisherman's weather-signs, in 42–45 follow those of the herdsman and hunter.

41. 's (= es) **kommt,** pronounce skommt. — **Wächter,** lit. 'watcher, is Kuoni's dog; cf. Eng. *Watch.*

46. Lug . . . ob, South German and Swiss for sehen, nachsehen. Cf. colloquial Eng. 'look and see if (whether).' — **sich verlaufen** (hat). Note once for all this very common omission of the tense auxiliary after a past participle.

47. Lisel (or **Liseli** for **Liselein**), dim. of **Lise,** from **Elisabeth**; here the cow's name. — **Am Geläut**(e), i.e. by the sound of her bells.

48. die, demonst. with personal force, *she;* a very common construction.

49. ein schön(es) **Geläut** (cf. 10, note), *a fine set of bells.* Each herdsman has a number of different-toned bells, harmonizing with each other and with the **Kuhreihen.** — **Meister (Hirt),** term of politeness here; has force also of **Ober=hirt,** 'chief herdsman.'

50. Euer. In this text **Ihr** (you) and its forms have capitals when singular, a small letter when plural; usage varies, however.

52. Des Attinghäusers, *Baron Attinghausen's.* Cf. Act II, Scene I. Note the use of =er (old gen. pl. ending, or analogy with it) in forming adj. from names of places. Cf. **Wiener Wurst,** 'Vienna sausage.' — **mir zugezählt,** lit. 'counted to me,' i.e. *in my charge.*

53. ber Kuh (dat.) . . . zu Halſe ſteht, *looks on that cows neck.* ſtehen, with dat. + adverb means 'to suit,' 'to be becoming.'

55 f. nähm' ich ihr (dat. of separation; *from her*), condensed form of conditional subjunct., for wenn ich nähm' (nehmen ſollte). — nicht klug, *foolish*, *crazy*.

57. Das Tier, i.e. animals in general. Cf. Eng. 'the horse' = horses as a class.

59. Die, emphatic demonst., *They.*—wo, like Eng. 'where' often with force of *when;* e.g. 'where (= when, if) conditions are favorable.'

60. 'ne = Eine. What is said here of the chamois, and in 55 of the cows, is literally true. — die, cf. 48, note.

61. mit heller Pfeife (for mit hellem Pfeifen), a sharp, hoarse call, which serves the others as a danger signal.

62. See 17, note. Die Alp is the high mountain *pasture*, never mowed, but left for grazing.

63. Glück=ſelig, for glücklich. — Die, demonst. 'that'; *the same.*

64. kehrt ſich's = kehrt man.

65. gelaufen. Note once for all that in German a verb of motion takes the *past*, in Eng. the *present* part. to express the mode of motion.

66. ber Baumgart, familiar for Baumgarten. — Alzellen, see map. This use of the def. art. implies that the person is well known, hence often adds a tinge of familiarity or contempt.

68. was giebt's (lit. 'what is there') ſo eilig, *what's the hurry?* — Bindet (den Kahn) los.

70. was habt Ihr, *what's the matter with you?* — denn, cf. Eng. introductory *well!*

72. Beringer von Landenberg (the Landenberger of 282), imperial bailiff in Unterwalden, is meant. — Vogt, lit. 'advocate,' 'guardian,' and applied to various offices, is in Tell the representative of the Emperor, governing in his stead (cf. 224, 2026); in this sense of 'governor,' 'bailiff,' the word occurs in several compounds in the play; thus in the *dramatis personæ* Gessler is Reichs=vogt, in 77 Wolfenschiessen is Burg=vogt, cf. also Thal=vogt, 38, and Fron= vogt, * 353.

73. Mann des Todes, *a dead man.*

75. ſteh' (for werde ſtehen) ... Rede, *I'll answer* (or *talk to*) *you.*
This use of pres. indic. for fut. is very common, especially in
emphatic expression; cf. 69, 79. — Euch Rede ſtehen = Euch zur
Rede ſtehen, lit. 'stand for answer (account) to you.'

76. was ... gegeben, 'what has there been,' *what has happened?*

78. Wolfenſchießen (also Wolfenſchieß), one of the younger Swiss
nobles, who, attracted by the splendor of the Austrian court, took
sides against their own country (cf. Act II, Scene 1, especially 946).
He *had his seat in* (82) castle Roßberg, near Stanz. See map. —
der, *he;* cf. 48, note. — läßt etc., *is he having you pursued?*

82. Haus=recht. It was his legal (*household*) right.

89. er, Ruodi, who has gone (after 75) to untie his boat.

91. Angſt des Todes, prose Todesangſt, *in mortal terror.*

92. Schiller omits the ſie ſagte, upon which the subjunctives (of
indirect statement) lieg', hab', ſei depend and thus intensifies the
dramatic effect by indicating Baumgarten's great excitement.

94. Ungebührliches ... verlangt, *made insulting demands.*

96. lief friſch (here, as often = ſchnell) hinzu, *ran up quickly.*

97. hab' ich ihm's Bad geſegnet, *I blessed his bath for him*, ironical for 'I made him suffer for it.' The axe-blow here takes the
place of the pious wish: "God bless your bath" always spoken by
the attendant of the mediaeval bather.

100. ums, *from* (*at the hands of*). Shows Unterwalden's feeling
toward her ruler as the storm of oppression, typified in 41 ff.,
breaks upon her.

101. mir, *I am*, etc. Cf. 26, note.

103. Strong feeling justifies the change to the familiar form of
address.

104. (Es) geht nicht (cf. Eng. slang, 'it's no go'), (*I*) *can't do it.*
After a look at the water and his boat, Ruodi returns.

108. ja, *you know;* or Eng. Why! introducing a sentence.

109. Der Föhn iſt los (lit. 'loose'), *the Föhn is up.* It is a violent
southerly wind, blowing warm and dry over the Alps, useful in
melting the snow, but dangerous to boats on the narrow arm of the
lake.

111. mein, frequent in poetry for meiner (genit.).

112. Es geht ums (prose gilt das) Leben, *His life is at stake.*

115. **Kind,** not sing. but an old plural; such are common in poetry. — **Seht hin,** *look there.*

121. **Rettungsufer,** etc., acc. absolute (cf. 31, note), *with the . . . in sight.* It was half a mile away.

123. The word-order is very emphatic and poetic. Cf. 17, note.

124 f. **hinübertrüge,** *might (would) carry across,* condensed potential subjunct.; cf. 55, note. -- (**ich**) **muß.**

126. **Bürglen,** Tell's home and traditional birth-place, a hamlet south of the lake and a mile from Altorf. — **der Tell,** cf. 66, note. Tell's first word suggests at once his character.

130. **Königs,** here and often for **Kaisers**; Albrecht von Habsburg is meant. — **saß,** *had his seat.*

133. **fürcht't** for **fürchtet;** such shortened forms are common in poetry and in dialect.

135. **zeugen,** for prose **bezeugen.** — **zu wagen (ist).**

136. **läßt sich alles wagen,** *anything may be risked.* Schiller often uses these very short speeches to gain vivid dramatic action and to emphasize character; many such lines in **Tell** are almost proverbs now. Cf. the collection at the end of the notes.

139. **brave,** *true, worthy;* **brav** is more than *brave.*

141. **läßt sich's gemächlich raten,** *it is easy to advise.*

143. **Der See kann sich (erbarmen), der Landvogt (aber) nicht.**

145. **und wär's,** *even if it were.* — **und** (*or*) . . . **leiblich(es),** for **eigenes.** Note the emphatic change to indicative: **Es kann** (for **könnte**) **nicht sein.**

146. **Simons und Judä (Tag),** *St. Simon's and St. Jude's day.* **Judä** is Lat. genitive of **Judas.** This fixes the date of the scene, October 28 (1307). The season is also evident from 16, 61. Ruodi takes refuge in the common superstition that the lake demanded a victim on that day.

149. **dem Manne muß Hilfe** (prose adds **zu Teil**) **werden,** *the man must be helped.* **Werden** with dat. (of recipient) means 'to be given to,' cf. 646.

152. Characteristic of Tell, the man of deeds, not words (cf. 127, 148 ff.). Schiller intends the contrast between Tell and Ruodi to be striking. Numerous instances in this play show the poet's skill

in thus using contrast as a means of emphasizing character and
heightening the dramatic effect.

155. Wohl, *true!*

158 f. Als in (die Hand) der Menschen. — was (for etwas)
Menschliches (lit. 'anything human'), *if anything should happen
to me.*

160. lassen, (*let alone*) *leave undone.* Schiller purposely allows
only a glance (125–160) at Tell, but it suffices to show his character
in bold relief. His rescue of Baumgarten hints at what he may do
for the whole Swiss people, whose distress is typified by the wrong
Baumgarten suffers.

161. Meister Steuermann (i.e. has been apprentice and become
master-steersman, cf. Eng. 'master-workman') is here used reproach-
fully. **Meister,** here different from 49, has the accent. Cf. 49, note.

163. Wohl, *even.*

166. d(a)rüber weg, *over it.*

171. Weiß Gott, etc., *Good Heavens! It is they* (*there they are*).

173. Des Wegs. — des has demonstrative force (= dieses), expressed by spaced type and strong accent. This adverbial genitive
is very common, especially with kommen, gehen, fahren.

175 f. Reit (= Reit't = Reitet, cf. fürcht't, 133) **zu,** *ride on.* —
Wenn ihr frisch beilegt, *if you will hurry.* bei-legen (lit. 'lay to')
seems to be a nautical word misunderstood by Schiller for '*lay on.*'
It does not occur elsewhere in this sense.

178. Ihr sollt uns (ethical dat.) **büßen,** *you shall pay for it.*

182. The bright opening of the scene is in powerful contrast with
this cry of despair. Yet in this despair is the vague hope that help
must soon come to suffering no longer to be borne.

This scene is often cited as a fine specimen of skilful dramatic
exposition. In 182 lines the reader becomes acquainted with Swiss
scenery, with the character and daily lives of Swiss people, learns
at once the theme of the play — just resistance by an outraged
people to ruthless oppression — and, in a glance at Tell, the strong,
brave man, the unassuming, unselfish citizen, quick to see and relieve distress, sees the cool and courageous deliverer, who later comes
to the rescue, not of an individual, as here, but of a whole people.
The scene unites, in a way, all three of the plots of the play (cf. In-

troduction, p. xxxvii). We have the People and their wrongs as the beginning of the People's drama; Tell's rescue of Baumgarten belongs to the Tell drama, because Tell acts as a private individual; the mention of Attinghausen (51 f.) suggests the Nobles, whose part in the action is developed later.

ACT I. SCENE 2.

* **Stauffacher,** Tschudi's **Wernherr von Stauffach,** is an historical character; according to the chroniclers, an influential citizen of old burgher family still living in 1341 in **Steinen,** a considerable village some three miles from **Schwyz.** See map.

* **Pfeifer von Luzern,** a fictitious character, used here to embody and express the political views of the town and canton of **Luzern** (Eng. Lucerne), which, by right of purchase, belonged to the Counts of Habsburg (i.e. Austria) since 1291, and which (190 ff.) feels their tyranny as much as the other cantons.

185. **Reich** = **das deutsche Reich.** The Cantons owed direct allegiance to the Empire, because that meant (1) protection against grasping neighbors, notably the Habsburg Dukes of Austria, and (2) a large measure of independence, since the emperor was far away. When Albrecht of Habsburg was elected Emperor, he declined their proffered allegiance to him as Emperor, but demanded their submission to him as Duke of Austria, claiming the cantons as private property of the Habsburgs and thus seeking to secure the Swiss to Habsburg as vassals, even though after his death the imperial throne might pass, by election, to some other House. For the relation of Habsburg-Austria to the German Empire, and of both to the Forest Cantons, see Introduction, pp. xviii–xxii. — * **will,** *is about to.*

187. **Bleibt doch,** *stay, I pray you;* **doch** strengthens the invitation.

189. **Viel(en) Dank** (cf. 10, note), accusative absolute. Cf. Eng. *Many thanks!* — **Gersau,** on the lake just under the Rigi. See map.

190. **Was auch Schweres,** *whatever hardship;* **auch,** often also **nur** or **immer,** generalizes **was.**

193. **auß Reich gelangen,** *come to the throne.* The crown was not hereditary then, as now; since each new emperor was elected, it was easily possible that *a different emperor* (i.e. of some other House than Austria) should come to the throne.

194. **erft,** *once.* — **feid Jhr's,** *you are* (*it* = the first half-line) *hers.*

196. **feh',** *have seen;* note this idiomatic pres. with **fchon** and **feit.**

198. **auf . . . Herzen drückt,** — **drücken auf** usually takes acc., rarely dat. — **Gebreften,** really the obsolete inf. (ge)breften used as a noun, has lost its old meaning, 'want,' 'lack,' and is here figurative; *sorrow.* This interview is quite similar in general tone to that between Brutus and Portia in *Julius Cæsar*, Act II, Scene 1. Gertrud has been called the Swiss Portia; the resemblance is sometimes striking and may be due to the performance of *Julius Cæsar* in Weimar (Oct. 1, 1803), while Schiller was at work on **Tell.** Cf. Introduction, p. xxxi.

203. **Scharen** and **Zucht,** both subjects of **ift** (205), which agrees, as usual, with the one nearest to it.

208. **neu,** not 'newly,' but *recently.*

210. **Von vielen Fenftern,** etc., *its many windows shine bright and homelike.*

212. Even yet the better Swiss houses are often adorned with such *wise sayings.* The gable bears the date, the owner's name and coat-of-arms; below, in two to six lines, follows the **Spruch,** usually religious, sometimes comic, in character.

214. **Wohl** (*yes, I know*) concedes what Gertrud has said.

218. **Vollbrachte,** participle as noun; from **vollbringen.**

220. **Der Vogt,** Hermann Gessler von Bruneck, legendary **Land-vogt** of Schwyz and Uri. See map for his castle, near Küssnacht. The historical Gesslers lived in Aargau in the 14th century, but no Gessler ever ruled in Uri.

229. **Eures,** like **meines,** agrees with **Herrn;** if construed with **Haus** understood, it would mean 'and is your (house) too, as the Emperor's representative, but it is my fief.' This reply shows the attitude of the Swiss toward their rulers — all due respect within proper limits, but distinct opposition to unlawful authority. —

𝕷𝖊𝖍𝖊𝖓, general term for lands or other property, or rights, granted to a vassal by a feudal lord in return for allegiance and service.

232. 𝕬𝖚𝖋 𝖘𝖊𝖎𝖓𝖊 𝖊𝖎𝖌𝖊𝖓𝖊 𝕳𝖆𝖓𝖉 (cf. 𝖆𝖚𝖋 𝖊𝖎𝖌𝖊𝖓𝖊 𝕱𝖆𝖚𝖘𝖙 (fist), 'on one's own hook'), *whenever he pleases;* i.e. without Gessler's permission. Oppression is rife in Schwyz, as well as in Uri (177 ff.) and Unterwalden. (90 ff.) Pfeifer's advice (183 ff.) shows the situation in Luzern.

233. 𝖆𝖑𝖘𝖔, *thus;* never 'also.' — 𝖋𝖗𝖊𝖎, pred. adj., not adverb. — 𝖍𝖎𝖓= 𝖑𝖊𝖇(𝖊) and 𝖇𝖆𝖚𝖊 (231) are optative subjunctives; 𝖜𝖆̈𝖗(𝖊), unreal subjunct.

238. 𝕸𝖆𝖌𝖘𝖙 𝖉𝖚, here for 𝖂𝖎𝖑𝖑𝖘𝖙 𝖉𝖚.

240. 𝖗𝖚̈𝖍𝖒' 𝖎𝖈𝖍 𝖒𝖎𝖈𝖍, lit. 'I boast myself'; *I am proud to be.* Tschudi names her Margaretha Herlobig; Schiller calls her Gertrud, and makes her, as daughter of *the noble Iberg,* a member of a prominent family, thus justifying her heroic nature and ripe political judgment. A Konrad Iberg is mentioned as magistrate in Schwyz in 1311.

241. 𝖘𝖆𝖘𝖘𝖊𝖓, preterite of customary action, *used to sit.*

244. 𝕻𝖊𝖗𝖌𝖆𝖒𝖊𝖓𝖙𝖊 (lit. 'parchments'), the *charters* of rights, granted by former emperors (Friedrich II. and Rudolph of Habsburg).

253. 𝖉𝖆𝖘𝖘 ... 𝖓𝖎𝖈𝖍𝖙, i.e. a hinderance, resulting in his *not* doing so; 𝖓𝖎𝖈𝖍𝖙, once common after 𝖍𝖚̈𝖙𝖊𝖓, 𝖛𝖊𝖗𝖍𝖚̈𝖙𝖊𝖓, 𝖍𝖎𝖓𝖉𝖊𝖗𝖓 and other verbs meaning 'prevent,' 'forbid,' etc., is now pleonastic; the negative idea (prevention) is contained here in 𝕳𝖎𝖓𝖉𝖊𝖗𝖓𝖎𝖘. — 𝕱𝖚̈𝖗𝖘𝖙𝖊𝖓𝖍𝖆𝖚𝖘; the House of Habsburg-Austria. See Introduction, p. xx f., and 185, note.

257. 𝖊𝖘 𝖌𝖊𝖍𝖆𝖑𝖙𝖊𝖓 𝖚𝖓𝖉 𝖌𝖊𝖙𝖍𝖆𝖓 (𝖍𝖆𝖇𝖊𝖓), emphatic form; *always did;* (lit. 'held and did').

264. 𝕾𝖔 𝖌𝖚𝖙, German idiom often omits the expected 𝖆𝖑𝖘 or 𝖜𝖎𝖊 in such comparisons. — He held his property in fief direct from the Emperor, every 𝕽𝖊𝖎𝖈𝖍𝖘𝖋𝖚̈𝖗𝖘𝖙 did the same, hence their equality as imperial vassals.

266. Since the time of Charlemagne, the German Emperor, crowned by the Pope as head of the "Holy Roman Empire of the German Nation," claimed to be *the highest lord* in Christendom.

267. Younger sons got titles, sometimes money, but no lands.

272. 𝕹𝖔𝖈𝖍, *as yet, so far.* — 𝖊𝖗𝖜𝖆𝖗𝖙𝖊𝖓, rare for 𝖜𝖆𝖗𝖙𝖊𝖓 or 𝖆𝖇-𝖜𝖆𝖗𝖙𝖊𝖓.

277. 𝕺𝖇, old and poetical for 𝖜𝖊𝖌𝖊𝖓 (with gen.) or 𝖚̈𝖇𝖊𝖗 (with acc.).

281 f. 𝖘𝖈𝖍𝖆𝖋𝖋𝖙 𝖊𝖘 𝖋𝖗𝖊𝖈𝖍, *is acting outrageously.* — 𝖚̈𝖇𝖊𝖗𝖒 𝕾𝖊𝖊, i.e. in Unterwalden, where Beringer von Landenberg (𝖉𝖊𝖗 𝕷𝖆𝖓𝖉𝖊𝖓-𝖇𝖊𝖗𝖌-𝖊𝖗. Cf. Eng. similar idiom 'New York-er') was 𝖁𝖔𝖌𝖙.

284 f. 𝕲𝖊𝖜𝖆𝖑𝖙-𝖇𝖊𝖌𝖎𝖓𝖓𝖊𝖓, for 𝕲𝖊𝖜𝖆𝖑𝖙-𝖙𝖍𝖆𝖙; note this rare division of a compound at the end of a line. — 𝖛𝖔𝖓, *on the part of.*

286. 𝖙𝖍𝖆̈𝖙, old idiom with the force of 𝖜𝖆̈𝖗𝖊. — 𝖊𝖚𝖊𝖗 𝖊𝖙𝖑𝖎𝖈𝖍𝖊 = 𝖊𝖎𝖓𝖎𝖌𝖊 𝖛𝖔𝖓 𝖊𝖚𝖈𝖍; after numerals the preposition with dat. of the pronoun is very common, but the simple partitive gen. is also used.

288 ff. 𝖊𝖗𝖑𝖊𝖉𝖎𝖌𝖊𝖓, for modern prose 𝖊𝖓𝖙𝖑𝖊𝖉𝖎𝖌𝖊𝖓. — 𝕾𝖔, *for.*—𝖚𝖓𝖉, etc., *but would,* etc. Note this as the first suggestion of united resistance; coming from such a source, it gains our sympathy at once.

294. 𝖆𝖓𝖌𝖊𝖘𝖊𝖍𝖊𝖓(𝖊) 𝖌𝖗𝖔𝖘𝖊 𝕳𝖊𝖗𝖗𝖊𝖓𝖑𝖊𝖚𝖙𝖊, *prominent, influential men,* i.e. of the upper classes of the burghers. One can still hear tourists called 𝖉' 𝕳𝖊𝖊𝖗𝖆𝖑𝖚̈𝖙 (= 𝖉𝖎𝖊 𝕳𝖊𝖗𝖗𝖊𝖓𝖑𝖊𝖚𝖙𝖊, 'gentlefolks') in the Alps.

295. 𝖌𝖊𝖍𝖊𝖎𝖒, lit. 'private,' 'secret' (hence 𝕳𝖊𝖎𝖒, 'home'), here in the old sense of 'intimate'; *who are intimate and trusted friends of mine.*

299. 𝖘𝖙𝖎𝖑𝖑, *even in secret,* goes with 𝖉𝖊𝖓𝖐𝖊𝖓.

304 f. 𝖂𝖎𝖗 𝖜𝖆𝖌𝖙𝖊𝖓 (pret. subj.) 𝖊𝖘, *we should dare!* ('do you mean?'); a rhetorical question. 𝕰𝖘 is explained by line 305. — 𝕳𝖊𝖗𝖗𝖓 𝖉𝖊𝖗 𝖂𝖊𝖑𝖙, cf. 266, note.

312–29. Here again, as in 135 ff., the short speeches animate the dialogue.

314. Cf. 10, note. The omission of *both* inflectional endings is rare and highly poetic.

319. Poetical and emphatic for 𝖉𝖊𝖗 𝖚𝖓𝖌𝖊𝖍𝖊𝖚𝖗𝖊 𝕶𝖗𝖎𝖊𝖌.

328. Like Portia (*Julius Cæsar,* II, 1), she does not shun even *a last resort.*

331. 𝕳𝖊𝖗𝖉 𝖚𝖓𝖉 𝕳𝖔𝖋 (oftener 𝕳𝖆𝖚𝖘 𝖚𝖓𝖉 𝕳𝖔𝖋; cf. Eng. *house and home*) is one of those alliterative phrases, so common in German, especially in conversation. Cf. 𝕲𝖊𝖑𝖉 𝖚𝖓𝖉 𝕲𝖚𝖙, 𝕸𝖆𝖓𝖓 𝖚𝖓𝖉 𝕸𝖆𝖚𝖘, 𝕷𝖊𝖎𝖇 𝖚𝖓𝖉 𝕷𝖊𝖇𝖊𝖓, 𝕾𝖈𝖍𝖚𝖙𝖟 𝖚𝖓𝖉 𝕾𝖈𝖍𝖎𝖗𝖒, 𝕾𝖙𝖔𝖈𝖐 𝖚𝖓𝖉 𝕾𝖙𝖊𝖎𝖓, etc. Cf. Eng. 'life

and limb,' 'kith and kin,' 'hide and hair,' 'stock and stone.' In both English and German such forms are handed down from the old alliterative poetry.

333 f. fahr', *go*, used here, perhaps, because he would naturally go by boat; fahren is also often used in a general sense for gehen, reisen. — **stehnden Fußes** ('with standing foot,' i.e. 'just as I stand') is adverb. gen. Cf. Lat. abl. absolute *stante pede*. Translate *at once*. — **Herr Walther Fürst**, Tell's father-in-law; according to Tschudi he lived in Attinghausen. Schiller makes him a citizen of Altorf (cf. 1539 ff.), a town near the south end of the lake. — **mir,** (dat. of interest), *of mine*.

336. Bannerherrn. The leader of the canton's troops in battle, a nobleman of rank, entitled to carry the principal banner. Der Freiherr (*Baron*) von Attinghausen is an historical character. He was a prominent Swiss nobleman, chief magistrate of Uri, honored for his manliness, his age and wealth, and beloved by the people for his true, unselfish patriotism.

341. weil, here in its old sense of dieweil, während, *while*.

343. Gottes=hause. He means the monastery of St. Meinradszell, at Einsiedeln, not far from Steinen; founded, tradition says, in the ninth century by Meinrad, a Hohenzollern nobleman, who was afterward killed there. In its place Otto the Great built (946 A.D.) the Benedictine monastery of Einsiedeln, which is still, as then, a great pilgrim resort. Cf. 520.

346. Zu äußerst (lit. 'on the outside') **am**, *right out on*.

348. Des Weges, cf. 173, note. **fahren**, here, as in 17, 333 and often, in the general sense of *go*.

* tritt Wilhelm Tell, etc. While Tell and Baumgarten have been coming from the lake, two hours distant, the reader has learned the situation at Steinen, the end of their journey; their reappearance shows their escape and skilfully weaves the two scenes together.

349. habt ... vonnöten (= von + Nöten, dat. pl. of Not, 'need'), *have no further need of me;* usually nötig haben + acc.

351. Vater der Bedrängten. In all such hints at Stauffacher's qualities, Schiller gradually develops the character, which is to be so prominent later on.

The exposition begun in Scene 1 is continued. Types of other and higher classes of Swiss people in other cantons appear. These, too, feel the tyrant's hand; men and women alike resent it, and, though calmer and more patient under it, are no less determined to resist. The idea of united resistance is first suggested — not by some lawless rabble, but by a high-minded, peace-loving woman, the type of her class. It is accepted and will be spread by one of the most conservative of the responsible, law-abiding citizens. There is trouble ahead for the tyrants; for such people, though slow to anger, are stoutly resolute, when convinced they are right. The idea of resistance marks the first positive step forward in the 'People's drama.'

ACT I.   SCENE 3.

Scenes 1 and 2 testify to the tyranny of the governors in two of the Forest Cantons, Unterwalden and Schwyz; Scene 3 takes us to a third canton, Uri, and gives us still further and stronger evidence of it there.

* **fid̄ barſtellt** (lit. 'presents (shows) itself'), *can be seen.*

353. **nidt̄ lang gefeiert,** *don't stop so long;* impatient commands, such as these of the rough overseer, are often thus expressed by the past part. (cf. **zugefaȟren,** 354) or by the infinitive. — **Herbei,** compounds of **her** and **ḣin** often express emphatic command, without any verb. Cf. **Hierȟer,** '(come) here!' **Hinaus,** 'get out!' 'out with you!'

356–8. **Das,** *These fellows,* contemptuous. — **Heißt das geladen,** *do you call* (or *is*) *that loaded* (*a load*)? — **Pflicht beſteḣlen** (lit. 'rob duty'), *shirk work.*

360 f. **Twing** (same as **Zwing,** 370), akin to **zwingen,** 'to force,' 'to compel'; *dungeon, keep.* — **was,** for **warum.**

368. **was meines Amtes,** lit. 'what belongs to my office,' i.e. *my duty;* an idiomatic possessive genitive used as predicate. As Gessler's servant and a foreigner, the overseer had no sympathy with the Swiss.

373. **wollt Iȟr,** *do you mean to* (or *think you can*). — **zwingen,** *keep down.* Note the play on words between this and *Zwing Uri* in 372; *Keep*(= dungeon)*Uri,* the castle, is to *keep down* Uri, the

canton. The tyranny grows worse; every man's liberty is in danger.

375. 'nander = einander. — bis . . . draus wird, *until it become a* . . .

* **Tell und Stauffacher** (connecting links between Scenes 1, 2, and 3.) Tell, having rescued Baumgarten (349 ff.), is on his way home to Bürglen; Stauffacher goes with him as far as Altorf, where he expects to see Walther Fürst (cf. 333 f.). The scene passes, therefore, in the afternoon of the same day as Scenes 1 and 2.

377. **tiefsten See,** *depths of the lake.*

379 f. **hätt',** optative subjunct., expressing strong wish. **sein,** simple inf. without zu, is here the real subject.

386. **Flanken,** the sharp-cornered, often V-shaped, projections, which strengthen the corners of a fort or castle; *bastions* or *walls.* — **Strebe=pfeiler** are sloping buttresses supporting the side walls.

390 f. **will, soll,** translate both by *means*, and note the idiomatic use of each without a complementary infinitive. — **der Hut.** In Swiss judicial meetings, a hat was put on a pole, as a symbol of authority. This old custom is no doubt the basis of the fictitious reference here. The hat has here become the archducal hat of Austria (i.e. the Habsburgs) and symbol of Gessler's authority.

394. **Aufrichten . . . Säule** (for Stange); the unusual word-order adds great emphasis.

401. **Verfallen ist,** etc., *forfeited with life and goods to the king is he*, etc. — **Wer** includes its antecedent. Note the highly poetic word-order.

405. **der=gleichen,** really an old genitive, now an adj. Cf. the same change in Eng. 'of that kind' which becomes adj. in 'that kind of.'

408. **noch,** *only.* — **so,** *but.* — **Kron',** they are ready to acknowledge imperial authority, but not that of Austria as such.

410. When in Switzerland, Kaiser Albrecht resided at Stein zu Baden (cf. 2966) in Aargau; it was here that the Swiss fiefs were granted and that the Gesell had seen the archducal hat.

412. Obeisance to the hat would have meant allegiance to the Habsburgs (Austria), whereas Uri was dependent directly and only on the Empire.

415. i.e. you know what I think (how matters stand). The last part of a conversation on political affairs on the way hither from Steinen.

416. 𝔚𝔬 𝔴𝔬𝔩𝔩𝔱 . (lit. 'mean to,' 'intend to') . 𝔥𝔦𝔫, *where are you going?* Again idiomatic use of 𝔴𝔬𝔩𝔩𝔢𝔫 without the infin. necessary in Eng.; 390 note. — 𝔥𝔦𝔫 implies direction.

421. The only thing to do is to be patient and silent. These terse one-line speeches, in striking contrast to each other, for which Schiller found his model in Greek and French drama, greatly increase the dramatic intensity of the passage. Cf. also 433 ff. and 136, 312, notes.

423. 𝔰𝔠𝔥𝔫𝔢𝔩𝔩 has here its original meaning *bold, rash*. Cf. the common proverb, 𝔊𝔢𝔰𝔱𝔯𝔢𝔫𝔤𝔢 ℌ𝔢𝔯𝔯𝔢𝔫 𝔯𝔢𝔤𝔦𝔢𝔯𝔢𝔫 𝔫𝔦𝔠𝔥𝔱 𝔩𝔞𝔫𝔤𝔢.

425. This is still custom, indeed law, in many parts of Switzerland, especially in Uri.

431 f. 𝔡𝔬𝔠𝔥, emphasizes the opinion; *surely*. — 𝔏𝔞𝔫𝔡𝔢, i.e. the Forest Cantons. — 𝔨𝔬𝔫𝔫𝔱𝔢𝔫, *might do;* idiomatic use of the auxiliary without any infinitive. — 𝔰𝔱ü𝔫𝔡𝔢𝔫, old form for 𝔰𝔱ä𝔫𝔡𝔢𝔫.

437. A remarkable line. Note the very emphatic position of 𝔙𝔢𝔯𝔟𝔲𝔫𝔡𝔢𝔫, and the strong contrasts 𝔙𝔢𝔯𝔟𝔲𝔫𝔡𝔢𝔫 — 𝔞𝔩𝔩𝔢𝔦𝔫, 𝔖𝔠𝔥𝔴𝔞𝔠𝔥𝔢𝔫 — 𝔪ä𝔠𝔥𝔱𝔦𝔤. This whole passage is extremely effective; it is a good example of Schiller's power of expressing truth in terse, vigorous, yet beautiful form and figure; he is the most quotable poet in German; of the ten lines 429–438 at least seven have become 'winged words,' and virtually proverbs, among his people. Cf. the list at the end of the notes.

442. 𝔰𝔬𝔩𝔩𝔱𝔢, rhetorical question; past subj., implying here emphatic denial, *and would* (do you think), etc.

443. 𝔴𝔞𝔰, for 𝔴𝔞𝔰 ... 𝔞𝔲𝔠𝔥, cf. 190, note. Here, and often, Schiller takes pains to make Tell a private individual, having no part in the concerted, hence political, action of the People's drama.

446. 𝔢𝔰 𝔰𝔬𝔩𝔩 𝔞𝔫 𝔪𝔦𝔯 𝔫𝔦𝔠𝔥𝔱 𝔣𝔢𝔥𝔩𝔢𝔫, *I shall not be found wanting.* The rhyme in this passage adds great dramatic force; Schiller uses it here, and often in this and other plays, to show a rise of emotion and, as an element of lyric expression, to add further emphasis to an already important passage, often at the end of an act or scene.

* **Bertha** (von **Bruneck**, a castle in Aargau) is a fictitious character, represented as a relative of Gessler, and under his guardianship, though by birth herself a Swiss.

451. **Mit Eurem Golde,** expresses angry contempt of the idea that money could help in such a case. — **Euch** (ethical dat.), *you think*. However natural the mistake, the reproach is unjust. Her heart is Swiss.

458 f. Eloquent testimony from one who had many reasons for siding with the tyrants.

Along with renewed evidences of Habsburg's tyranny (371, 393 ff.), the scene shows the attitude towards it of still other and larger classes of people (artisans, town-people). Even the daughter of nobility takes sides against her kinsman, Gessler. Leading citizens begin to talk of united resistance. Tell's brief reappearance develops further his character as a man slow to speak, but ready to act, to help in time of need. The scene again unites all three of the plots of the play and prepares the way for their later development.

ACT I. SCENE 4.

* **Fürst's Wohnung,** cf. 333, note. — **Arnold** (called **vom Melchthal** from his home in the Melch valley, in Unterwalden near Kerns; see map) was the son of Heinrich *von* der Halden (cf. 562) or better *an* der Halden.

466. **Um . . . zu,** *that I should*, etc.

467. **Dem frechen Buben,** dat. of possession with **Finger** (470). — **mir,** poss. dat. with **Ochsen.** Note the highly poetic order of **mir** (467), **weg wollte treiben** (469), **nicht** (463).

471. **des Vogts** (pred. gen.), not Gessler's, but Landenberg's, cf. 72, 281, notes.

474. **wie,** for **wie . . . auch,** *however.* Cf. 190, note.

484. **Wir, Jugend.** Note the contrast.

490. Prose: (**Es**) **ist niemand** (**da**). — **schütze,** note the subjunct. implying probability.

492. (**Es**) **werde.** — **muß** (without infin.) **hinüber** (to Unter-walden).

494. vom Walde, i.e. the Kernwald (1197), near which he lived; it divided Unterwalden into two parts: ob (above) dem Wald and nid ('neath) dem Wald (cf. 546, 718). See map.

502. Was mir Böses schwant, *what evil I fear* (*anticipate*). schwanen (late word for more usual ahnen) is derived from Schwan, the bird of prophecy.

506. thät' . . . hätten, the subj. of softened assertion; *it would almost seem necessary.*

508*. da, *as.* Stauffacher has reached the end of his journey; this fixes the date of Scene 4, afternoon of same day as in Scenes 1, 2, 3. Cf. 333, 375*, note. — **Nun, bei Gott!** *Well, I declare!* Such expressions are much more common in German than in English, but rarely have their literal English force; they are emphatic, but not irreverent.

514 f. Sieh (interjectional force), **mir wird,** etc., *Ah! It does me good.* — **warm geht . . . auf** (lit. 'expands'), *warms.*

520. Cf. 343, note. **Welsch** (or Wälsch=)land is *Italy;* welsch is also a generic term for anything not German.

522 f. frisch, a favorite word in Tell, here *direct.* — **nirgend sonst noch,** very emphatic, *nowhere else besides.* — **Flüelen,** landing-place for Altorf. See map.

525. erstaunlich (es, cf. 10, 314, notes) **neues Werk,** i.e. the Zwing Uri (370).

530. fest, *secure,* against attack or escape.

532. Euch verhalten (for vorenthalten or verschweigen), *keep from you.*

538. von ur=alters her, *from the earliest times on down;* **her,** shows motion towards speaker; ur=alters is adverbial gen., cf. Eng. *from of old.* The phrase, usually von alters her, is strengthened by the prefix ur–, which denotes original (early) source.

541–2. trieb. treiben, here in different senses. **trieb,** cf. 62, 17, note. **'s treiben,** *to act, carry on.*

544. noch, i.e. who was there while the 'old times' were *still* present; omit in translation. The passage indicates the attitude of the older nobility.

550 ff. der (i.e. Baumgarten) **haus=hält** ('lives'), *the wife of B. who lives . . . he tried to wrong most shamefully.* The order is very poetic. — **der Mann,** *her husband.*

555 f. doch implies affirmative answer, *is he not?* — **Eidam,** Tell is meant. — **übern** = über den. Cf. 349 ff.

564. gilt was (= etwas), *is worth something* (*has weight*).

570. wie steht's um den, *what about him?*

573. Zur Stelle schaffen (for **bringen**), i.e. bring the son before him.

575*. will, *starts to* (*tries to*). — **Ist mir,** etc. Note the strong ellipsis (*he said*) marking Stauffacher's rising emotion.

585. um meiner Schuld (willen). Cf. 465. Notice the now changed feeling, and especially the climax **Schuld — Frevel;** also the "eloquent tautology" **blind — geblendet.**

587. aus=geflossen, i.e. has run dry; a bold figure.

594. fühlend, *feeling his way*. The literal meaning is best.

596. warmes Grün, *rich green*. — **Schmelz,** lit. 'enamel,' refers to the fine glossy appearance of Alpine flowers. — **die roten Firnen,** i.e. *red* from the 'Alpine Glow.' The reflected rays of the sun, below the horizon, morning and evening, often color the snow peaks a deep, rich red, while the valleys are quite dark.

600. frische, *good*. This whole passage is famous for its lofty poetic tone, rendered more effective by the very unusual and poetic word-order of **sich** (593), **der Matten, der Blumen** (596), **Die Firnen** (597).

605. mehr, i.e. is in greater distress than simple blindness.

610. geraubt (**gelassen,** 616). Note the strong emphasis of these exclamatory participles.

614. denken with **auf** refers to the future, with **an** to the present or past (cf. 618).

623. wenn, etc., *if I can only*, etc.

626 f. Auf . . . Herrenburg, *in his lordly castle;* in Sarnen, the chief town in **Ob dem Wald.** — **Zorns,** poetic use of gen. with **spotten.** Notice the remarkably poetic order **und wohnt' . . . ich mache** (pres. for fut.), and the change from subj. to ind., emphasizing the impassioned climax to which his feeling has gradually risen.

629 f. Schreckhorn, Jungfrau, two of the highest peaks in the Bernese Oberland, S. E. of Luzern, in Schiller's time considered inaccessible. — **verschleiert,** i.e. by clouds; the figure does not apply literally. Perhaps the veiled virgin suggests simple inaccessibility;

if so, **ſeit Ewigkeit** is literally true for Schiller, because this veil of mystery was not torn from the face of the mountain till 1811, six years after his death, when it was first ascended.

640. **Es,** i.e. this tyranny.—**Wollen wir,** not *let us,* but *shall we?*

646. **Jedem Weſen,** dat. of recipient, cf. 149, note.

654 f. **gereizt,** *when aroused,* elliptical condition; a common idiom in both English and German. — **wetzt,** refers to the bull's tearing the earth with his horns. — **zu,** *towards.*

659 f. **die alten Bünde,** *the ancient compacts* which united Uri, Schwyz and Unterwalden in a league, renewed in 1291. Stauffacher speaks for himself and his canton, Schwyz. Melchthal speaks for Unterwalden, while Fürst represents Uri. — **Freundſchaft** (in old sense of *kindred, connections*), i.e. he has many relatives.

662. **am andern,** i.e. each in the other (his neighbor).

666 f. **Landsgemeinde** is the assembly or canton council, a general open-air meeting of all the voters of a canton to decide important questions. Such meetings are still held once a year in several of the cantons. — **Nicht,** construe with **verachtet.** — **erlebte** = erlebt habe.

669. Prose would supply **ſondern,** *but,* after **Blut.**

671. **was** has no antecedent. The sense is: such as must (would) move even a stony cliff to pity.

675. **euch,** dat. of interest. — **ehre . . . bewache,** subj. influenced by **wünſcht,** implying purpose, *who shall,* etc., or probability, *who would.*

682. His father, a wealthy, influential man, firm in his allegiance to the empire as against the grasping House of Habsburg (Austria), (cf. 184 f.), had embittered Landenberg and called down the tyrant's vengeance upon his head. Fürst and Stauffacher, having done the same, were equally 'guilty' and liable to punishment.

686. **Herrn von Sillinen** (pronounce **Si'l-linen**) lived near a village of the same name, below Altorf on the Gotthard road, see map; a tower of the old castle still remains.

689. **Eurer — der Eure,** he turns first to one, then to the other.

693. **Was** (= warum, 360, note) **braucht's,** etc., lit. 'why is there need'; *what need is there of the nobles;* his distrust is due to the

fact that the younger nobility, represented by Rudenz, sided with
Austria. Cf. Act II, Scene 1.

695 f. **Wären** (opt. subj. expressing strong wish) **wir doch** (emphatic, *only*) **allein,** i.e. would there were no nobles! — **Schon,** not
already; its force lies rather in the strong emphasis it adds — to be
reproduced by proper intonation.

702. **Ob=mann,** i.e. one standing (ob, über) above the contending
parties.

704. **der,** *he, who;* poetic omission of the antecedent.

706. Even the over-cautious Fürst is aroused.

709. **wem läg . . . an,** *whom could it concern,* etc.; potential
subj.

711. **gewähren,** note the two senses: here *answer for;* in 714,
give.

718. **der Alzeller** (218, note) is Baumgarten. — **nid,** cf. 494, note.

722. See map and introductory note to Act I, Scene 1.

726. **Mythenstein,** cf. 39, note. — **grad über,** may mean *just above*
the rock, Mythenstein, or = gerade gegenüber, *just opposite* the two
peaks, the Mythen.

728. **Rütli** (long ü), a small meadow-clearing, below Selisberg,
100 feet above the lake.

737. **gemeinsam** (*in common*) **das Gemeine** (*common good*) is very
emphatic.

739. **Eure** (Fürst), **die Eure** (Melchthal).

741. It is significant that Schiller selects just these three for this
personal compact, which typifies the union of the **drei Lande;** not
only does each represent a different canton (Fürst, Uri; Stauffacher,
Schwyz; Melchthal, Unterwalden), but each is also a type of different age and character; Melchthal is young and hot-headed,
Stauffacher mature and deliberate, Fürst old and over-cautious. All
three have, directly or indirectly, felt the tyrant's hand.

748. This use of signal fires on mountain tops is very old, and
common everywhere. — **Erheben und fallen,** both go with **wenn.**

752. **und hell,** etc., *and bright shall day dawn in thy darkness.*
Here, as often, the rhyme is used with fine effect in closing the
scene (cf. 446, note) and marking the climax in Melchthal's determination.   Note the dramatic skill with which Melchthal's

changing mood — melancholy grief, 590 ff., giving way to ever more violent and passionate wrath, 615 ff., and then to calm, grim resolve, 745 ff. — is portrayed, and also the dramatic progress of the scene from the expression of opinion and feeling (460–655) to calm discussion (645–738) and at last to definite action, resulting, at the climax, in the alliance formed (738 ff.).

The scene, still a part of the exposition of the play, further develops the People's drama and shows that, along with the increasing cruelty of the governors, the love of liberty is also growing. The distress of individuals has spread over every district and class. Typical efforts of individual defense and well grounded fears of further oppression have led to plans for resistance which shall unite all three cantons. The whole people is the hero and their struggle for liberty is to be the theme of the play. The conflict involves great ódds; the uncertain issue excites keen interest.

ACT II. SCENE 1.

Several days of necessary preparation for the Rütli meeting pass between Acts I and II. Both Scenes of II fall on the same day, the first in the forenoon, the second after midnight. Tschudi gives the date as Nov. 8, ten days after Act I.

* **Freiherr** (same as **Baron**, *Baron*, a rank of nobility just below **Graf**, *Count*) **von Attinghausen.** Cf. 336, note. Ruins of his castle, near Attinghausen, are still shown to tourists. In 1240, while still a boy, he fought, Schiller says, at Faenza (cf. 912, note); in 1301, as Landammann of Uri, he was cantonal ambassador to Emperor Albrecht. His extreme age here (85 years) is fictitious; Schiller makes him old enough to have been at Faenza in order to have him contemporary with the charters of Friedrich II., the basis of Swiss liberty. — **Kuoni,** cf. 37. — **Rechen und Sensen.** Though the grass in the Swiss valleys is often cut quite late, November is too late for hay-making in the Alps; the point escaped the poet's attention. Cf. also 1914. — **Ulrich von Rudenz,** a fictitious character invented to embody and express the opinions of the younger Swiss nobility.

755. **Früh=trunk** (lit. 'early drink'), an unusual word, after the

analogy of Früh=ſtück ('breakfast'), meaning a *morning draught* of
wine or cider, prepared from the juice of fruits or berries. The passage aptly illustrates the patriarchal relation existing between the
old master and servant, which contrasts strongly with the ideas of
Rudenz, the *young* nobleman.

762 f. in enger . . . engerm, etc., *in ever narrowing circle.* Notice that only the second of these comparatives has the ending
which really belongs to both.

766. Ich bring's (the draught) **Euch,** *I pledge you* (*drink your
health*). — **Es geht** (*comes*), etc., i.e. we drink from one cup and feel
with one heart. — **friſch,** i.e. without any hesitation or misgiving.

771. Herrenburg, Schiller seems to assume either that Zwing
Uri is finished or that Gessler had another castle in Altorf.

773. Haſt du's ſo eilig = Haſt du ſolche Eile; a confusion of eilig
ſein and Eile haben. — **Jugend,** dat. with **gemeſſen.**

779. zur Fremde, *a strange place;* with werden the pred. noun is
often in dat. after zu. — **Uli,** Swiss dimin. from Ulrich. Cf. 35*,
note.

781. trägſt . . . zur Schau, *make proud show of.* — **ſchlägſt,** here
throw. The silk costume, the peacock's feather and the purple
mantle all indicate attachment to the Austrian court. Attinghausen,
a type of the older nobility, prefers the Swiss Pelzwamms.

787 ff. Albrecht (called both **König** and **Kaiſer**) was angry because the Swiss resisted his private Habsburg claims to the cantons. Cf. 185, note, and Introduction, pp. xix, xxi.

799. koſtete = würde koſten. — **einzig(es) . . . Wort.** Namely, to
acknowledge Habsburg-Austria's claims. Cf. 787, note.

802 f. Augen halten (for zuhalten), *keep closed;* cf. older Eng.
'eyes are holden.' — **Daß es,** *so that they.* — **dem,** *their own.* The
reproach is, of course, intended for his uncle.

804. On the use of nicht after hindern, cf. 253, note. — **ſie,** the
older nobles.

807 ff. Wohl thut es, *it flatters.* — **Herrenbank,** *the nobles' bench*
in public meetings, to which, however, chosen citizens then had
equal rights with noblemen. The Waldstätte thus in large measure ruled themselves, since the Emperor was too far away to make
his authority much felt (809).

812. **Perſon,** here in old sense, *personage, rôle, part.*

814. The **Land=ammann** (from **Amt=mann,** 'official,' 'magistrate') was the *chief magistrate* in a canton, chosen once a year by all the citizens. — **Bannerherrn,** cf. 336, note.

825. **Fremdlinge,** the Austrians with Gessler.

826 ff. Note the contrast, emphasized here, between the patriarchal simplicity of the older nobles, now passing away, and the impatient ambition which leads the inexperienced young men of the new era to despise the "peasant nobility" and rustic ways of their fathers, to forget their country and to yearn for the splendors of the court and the great opportunities for distinction afforded by the frequent wars of the Emperor. — **müſſig ſtill,** *idle and silent.* — **bei gemeinem,** *in degrading.*

841. Notice the remarkable force of these imperatives (so also in 855) and the deep emotion in the contrast: **Geh hin** (855) and **Geh nicht** (860).

845. **Herden=reihen** (*herd-song*), etc.; a loving reference to the same **Kuh=reihen,** of which Rudenz speaks with such contempt in 838. The Switzer's home-sickness (cf. **Schmerzens=ſehnſucht,** 847), on hearing the **Kuhreihen** in a foreign land, is proverbial.

849. **Trieb** ('natural impulse for'), *love of.*

853. **Die,** (emphatic) *that.*

862. **der Letzte,** by poetic license only; historians say that the family lived on for several generations. Schiller made him the last of his race here, in order to heighten the dramatic effect.

866. **brechend**(es), lit. 'breaking,' as in older Eng.; our modern idiom demands 'closing' (i.e. in death).

868. That is, having given the estates to Austria, to receive them again, in feudal tenure, as an Austrian subject. **frei,** *as a freeman.*

871 ff. **Die Welt gehört ihm.** In accordance with their title as Roman Emperors they claimed the whole world; cf. 266, note. — **Länderkette,** i.e. the surrounding Swiss districts over which the Habsburgs had gained control.

875 ff. The chroniclers say that Albrecht had control of the *markets* of Luzern and Zug, and that he gave the tolls, collected on the Gotthard, to his sons. The Gotthard is the watershed dividing Switzerland from northern Italy.

878. **feinen Ländern,** i.e. belonging to him, not as Emperor, but as Count of Habsburg and Duke of Austria.

880-2. i.e. can the other Estates of the Empire (by whom every emperor was elected) protect us or themselves against Habsburg? — **fein Kaifer,** i.e. any one not a Habsburg.

883. **Was . . . geben auf,** *what faith is to be put in.*

885. **Adlers,** i.e. **Reichsadler,** *imperial eagle.* — **veräußern,** *alienate from.* All this was only too true; it happened repeatedly that important rights and privileges, towns, estates, even whole provinces, were thus *mortgaged and alienated from the Empire.*

890. i.e. by election. Cf. 193, note.

892 f. **wohl verdienen um** (prose prefers **fich verdient machen um**), cf. English idiom 'to deserve well of'; *to gain the favor of.* — **heißt,** *means, is.* — **in** (*for*) **die Zukunft,** i.e. to be reaped in future.

894. **willft,** *do you claim to* (*think you can*).

897 f. Cf. Pfeifer von Luzern's opinion, 184 ff., note.

901. **bannen** ('put under the ban'), i.e. forbid all except the nobility to hunt them.

904 f. **mit unfrer Armut,** resulting from this taxation. — **Mit unferm Blute,** etc., i.e. fight their battles with (the help of) Swiss troops, which was really often done. Cf. 911 f., 1229 ff.

912. **Favenz** (German form of **Faenza**), in North Italy, near Ravenna. In 1240, in his war with the Pope, Friedrich II. was besieging the town. Seeing their opportunity, the Swiss sent him a detachment of 600 men, on condition that he grant them a charter attesting their dependence only on the Empire; this he did in return for the service rendered (see Introduction, p. **xx**). Attinghausen's presence is not authentic. Cf. introductory note to this scene.

913. **Sie follen kommen,** *let them come!*

920 f. **zu dir fteht,** *stands by you.* — **Das, des,** emphatic, *that.*

922. **Die angebornen Bande,** i.e. those natural ties binding him to his own country and people.

928. i.e. *not* for a long time now.

939. **Das Fräulein,** originally applied *only* to young ladies of rank, is a term of great respect here; same as **Ritterfräulein** (939).

940 ff. Bertha also tells him this, cf. 1663-73. **Braut,** not bride,

but *betrothed*. — **Deiner Unschuld,** i.e. for you, unsuspecting, simple-hearted fellow.

943. **Gehabt** (imper. of gehaben) **Euch wohl** (old for **Lebt wohl),** *Farewell.*

945. **erhalten,** for zurück=halten, *restrain.*

949. **Gewaltsam strebend,** construe with **Jugend.**

The scene introduces two new and important characters, strongly contrasted and intended as types of the older and younger native Swiss nobility in their attitude towards the Waldstätte and towards Habsburg-Austria. As part of the exposition, it really belongs in Act I. (Cf. Introduction, p. xxxv f.) It brings out also the contrast between the united people (Act I.) and the divided nobles, between the pomp of Austria and the patriarchal simplicity of old Swiss life. In the conflict between **Volk** and **Vögte,** as presented in Act I, this scene develops a new element of danger to the cause of the people — the adherence of the younger nobility to Austria — and renders the already uncertain issue even more doubtful. The scene belongs to the Rudenz or Nobles Plot, so far only hinted at, and begins the development of the part they are to take.

ACT II.   SCENE 2.

* **Eine Wiese,** the Rütli; cf. 728, note. For the time, see introductory note to the preceding scene.

* **Mond=regen=bogen,** a very rare phenomenon (978 f.).

* **Prospekt,** here *background*, shut in by the mountains (across the lake) mentioned in introductory note to I, 1. — **Winkelried,** etc. For these invented characters Schiller has chosen such names as occur in the chronicles or other Swiss documents; so also below, 987 f.

960 f. **mir nach,** has imperative force. — **Den Fels,** etc., the Selisberg, rising above the Rütli.

965. **Selisberg,** village high up on the mountain just mentioned.

967. Signal for early morning prayer in the hermit's **Wald= kapelle** on the *Schwyz* shore.

970. **Gehn . . . zünden,** etc., subjunct. as softened imperative.

972. **Monden=nacht,** also Mond=nacht. **Monden** is the old weak

gen. sg. for 𝕸𝖔𝖓𝖉𝖊𝖘 (977); such old sing. forms are common in compounds and some set phrases. Cf. 𝕾𝖔𝖓𝖓𝖊𝖓-𝖘𝖈𝖍𝖊𝖎𝖓, and 1085, 1108.

973. 𝖆𝖑𝖘 𝖜𝖎𝖊, the use of *both* these words is distinctly colloquial. Usually one, either one, is enough.

983. 𝖊𝖗𝖜𝖆𝖗𝖙𝖊𝖓 (here in passive sense), *be long waited for*, i.e. *does not delay;* prose would have 𝖆𝖚𝖋 𝖘𝖎𝖈𝖍 𝖜𝖆𝖗𝖙𝖊𝖓.

985 f. 𝖜𝖊𝖎𝖙 𝖚𝖒-𝖌𝖊𝖍𝖊𝖓 (here the separable 𝖚𝖒′-𝖌𝖊𝖍𝖊𝖓), *go away round.* — 𝖍𝖎𝖓𝖙𝖊𝖗𝖌𝖊𝖍𝖊𝖓, the insep. 𝖍𝖎𝖓𝖙𝖊𝖗𝖌𝖊′𝖍𝖊𝖓, *elude.*

987*. 𝖉𝖗𝖊𝖎, evidently a mistake for 𝖛𝖎𝖊𝖗; as each of the three leaders was to bring ten (cf. 735) men, and the total is given as 33 (cf. 1098*).

991. 𝖌𝖊𝖘𝖔𝖌𝖊𝖓 (from 𝖘𝖆𝖚𝖌𝖊𝖓), the metaphor is much confused; he means the sight of his blind father has filled him with thoughts of vengeance.

993. 𝕲𝖊𝖘𝖈𝖍𝖊𝖍(𝖊)𝖓𝖊𝖘 does not refer to 𝖀𝖻𝖊𝖑, but is abstract; *what has been done.* This is no time for personal vengeance. — 𝖜𝖔𝖑𝖑𝖊𝖓, softened imperative.

996 ff. 𝖋𝖚̈𝖗 (𝖉𝖎𝖊) 𝖌𝖊𝖒𝖊𝖎𝖓𝖊 𝕾𝖆𝖈𝖍(𝖊). The two friends who parted 752* meet again; their interview, naturally apart from the others, is skilfully used to show us Melchthal's preparations for the Rütli conference.

999. 𝕾𝖚𝖗𝖊′𝖓𝖓𝖊𝖓 (elsewhere, and better, 𝕾𝖚′𝖗𝖊𝖓𝖊𝖓), a lofty ridge between Uri and Unterwalden; the Surenen pass leads from Altorf to Engelberg.

1001 f. 𝕷𝖆̈𝖒𝖒𝖊𝖗-𝖌𝖊𝖎𝖊𝖗 (lit. *lambs-vulture*, Eng. also has same word), the largest of European birds of prey.

1003. 𝕰𝖓𝖌𝖊𝖑𝖇𝖊𝖗𝖌, a mountain — also village, with a monastery (cf. 1079) in Unterwalden. See map.

1005 f. 𝕲𝖑𝖊𝖙𝖘𝖈𝖍𝖊𝖗 𝕸𝖎𝖑𝖈𝖍, dirty-white water from the glaciers.

1007. 𝖊𝖎𝖓𝖘𝖆𝖒𝖊𝖓, because the herdsmen had gone down into the valleys for the winter; cf. 15 ff., 62 ff.

1012. 𝕰𝖍𝖗-𝖋𝖚𝖗𝖈𝖍𝖙 is object of 𝖘𝖈𝖍𝖆𝖋𝖋𝖙𝖊 (for 𝖛𝖊𝖗𝖘𝖈𝖍𝖆𝖋𝖋𝖙𝖊). The order in the whole passage is poetic.

1014. 𝖊𝖓𝖙𝖗𝖚̈𝖘𝖙𝖊𝖙, construe as predicate with 𝕾𝖊𝖊𝖑𝖊𝖓. — 𝕺𝖇 (here with dat., cf. 277, note). — 𝕽𝖊𝖌𝖎𝖒𝖊𝖓𝖙, i.e. the tyranny of Landenberg and others.

1022. tragen (for ertragen), *tolerate;* note the emphatic and poetic word-order, so also 1029, **Was Euch,** etc.

1035. mir die (= meine) **Vettern** (lit. 'cousins'), *relatives, kinsmen.* Cf. 659 f., note.

1043 f. Krümme, for metrical reason instead of prose **Krümmung.** Cf. 712. — **ich späht' es aus,** for **daß ich es nicht ausspähte.** Two constructions confused: **Jedes Thal, auch so versteckt, ich späht' es aus;** and **kein Thal war so versteckt, daß ich es nicht ausspähte.** Such confusion is not uncommon both in Eng. and German. Cf. coll. Eng. 'no valley was so hidden, *but what* (that) I searched it out.'

1051. geben, *yield, produce.*

1057. Roßberg und Sarnen, cf. 78, 626, notes.

1072. kennte, past subj. interrogative form, with exclamatory force, *who wouldn't know you!* (i.e. 'would say he *did* not'); it is akin to subj. of indirect discourse. Cf. 442, note.

1073 f. Mei'r, lit. *overseer* (in charge of rents and other business of farm or monastery). The office being often hereditary, the title became, in time, the name of the family. — **Struth von Winkel-ried.** Schiller makes him a descendent of the famous Winkelried, who, the chroniclers say, was knighted for bravery before Favenz (1240); afterwards banished for murder, he expiated his guilt by killing a dragon at **Öd-weiler** (lit. 'deserted village'), near **Roßberg,** but was himself killed by the dragon's poisonous blood, which touched him.

1079. hinterm Wald, beyond the Kernwald, in **Ob dem Wald.** Others come up, the private interview (its purpose accomplished, 996 ff., note) gives place to general conversation, introductions, greetings, etc.

1081. eigne Leute, (people, who are another's *own*) *bondmen,* cf. **Leib-eigne** and **mit dem Leibe pflichtig** (*subject to*), 1085.

1084. Es ... wer, *let him ... who,* etc. — **preisen,** for **glücklich preisen,** 'count oneself fortunate.' — **Erden,** not pl. but weak dat. sg. Cf. 972, note.

1087. History mentions an Itel (Ital) Reding, Landammann of Schwyz about 1428. — **Alt** (= **der alte,** *former, Ex-*) **Landammann** (814, note).

1091 f. It is a fine dramatic touch to thus make them bury *per-*

sonal hostility for the sake of the common cause. — **brav,** (not 'brave'), *well* (*nobly*).

1092. The battle horn, made of the horn of the auerox (**Ur-ochs**), whence the name, **Uri.** The seal of Uri shows the head of the animal.

1097 ff. The impetuous Melchthal is the first to arrive, then Stauffacher, while the old and over-cautious Fürst comes last; their character is indicated by the order of their coming.

The ever grateful Baumgarten looks in vain for his deliverer, Tell. He is absent for good reason, cf. 441–446. Schiller had dramatic reasons, also, for his absence. Cf. 443, note, and the character-sketch of Tell in the Introduction, p. xxxiii f. — **dreiunddreißig,** the correct total, though really only 32 are mentioned; cf. note on 987*, where the mistake occurs.

1106 f. Gleichwie ... Schoß des Tages, lit. 'as the radiant, open bosom,' etc. (note the contrast with 1102), *as bright, open day-light.* — **Laßt's gut sein** (lit. 'let it be well'; Eng. 'let that do'), *never mind.* — **Soll** (Eng. supplies *come*). Cf. the well-known proverb:

> **Es ist nichts so fein gesponnen,**
> **'s kommt doch ans Licht der Sonnen.**

1109. Eid=genossen. Though the confederacy has not yet been formed, the term applies; they have been confederates before (1156 ff.). "The Swiss Confederacy" is still called **die Schweizerische Eidgenossen=schaft.** After the necessary greetings, introductions, etc., here begins the real business of the meeting. Contrast this solemn, ghostly moonlight scenery with the smiling sunshine of Act I, Scene 1, the grim earnestness of this with the cheerfulness of the opening lines.

1112 f. tagen, unlike **tagen** ('dawn') in 752, means here to hold a meeting, *deliberate.* Cf. **Reichs=tag,** the German Parliament, English *Diet;* also the terms, 'adjourn' (French *jour,* 'day') and 'sine die.' — **wie wir's** ('s = **tagen**), etc., *as we are accustomed to do* (it).

1114. It was *unconstitutional* in three points; they numbered only 33 (1120) and were not duly elected, they met at night (1119), they had no statute-books (1122). Cf. 666, **Landsgemeinde,** note. — **Ent= schuldige,** imperative subjunct. pred. of **Not.**

1119. **Wohl,** *well then!* **Ist . . . gleich** = ob=gleich (es) ist.   Inversion; so also 1120, 1122.

1124 ff. In such meetings the Landammann sat on a low platform, two swords, symbols of his authority (**Schwerter der Gewalt,** 1125), were stuck in the ground before him, two officials (**Waibel**) stood near (1127) to announce his decisions to the people, gathered around the **Ring** within which he sat (1124).   Note position of **auf.**

1131. **frei,** *voluntarily.*   Self is forgotten for the common cause.

1135 ff. **Römerzügen,** state-journeys to Rome, made by the newly elected German emperors, to be crowned by the Pope as head of the Holy Roman Empire (cf. 266, note).   The Swiss, as the emperor's vassals, furnished their part of the great procession; cf. 1229 ff. — **uns,** dat. — **des Schwertes** (cf. 1125) **Ehre,** i.e. let Schwyz have the president. — **seines Stammes,** Schwyz, traditionally the canton first settled (cf. 1167–1203, especially 1188 ff.), gave her name (in the later forms **Schweiz** and **Schweizer**) to the whole country and people.

1145 f. **was** = warum. — **Tages** (cf. 1112, note) **Haupt,** i.e. President of the meeting.

1148 ff. Note the exalted and poetic solemnity of Reding's address. — **droben** (1149) in prose order follows **Sternen.** — **zusammen= führte** (1153) = zusammengeführt hat.

1156 f. Each speaker stepped into the ring and faced the president or judge; cf. 1124, note. — **uralt Bündnis** may mean the league of 1291, or, perhaps, an older one (A.D. 1246–7).   The organization complete, business is taken up; in the first main division of the scene (1156–1204) Stauffacher, the real leader, seeks to show the unity of the Swiss people.

1159 f. **Ob** = obgleich. — **und,** *and though.*

1163. **in den Liedern,** i.e. current popular songs.   Especially the well-known **Ostfriesen=lied** (17th century) is meant, which is authority for the purely traditional Swedish and Frisian origin of the Swiss (see Introduction, p. xvi f.).

1169 ff. **hinten** (*far up, away back*) **im Lande** (Sweden is meant) **nach Mitter=nacht** (for **Norden,** *to the north.*   Cf. also **Mit=tag= sonne,** *south,* 1174) **je der** ('ever the') **zehnte,** *every tenth.*

1173. **Und (es) zogen.** Note the very unusual and poetic word-order.

1179. **Muotta** (uo, pron. as one syllable, almost **Mwotta**); see map.

1182 f. **wartete der Fähre,** rare use of **warten** with gen., *tend*, etc. Note the very poetic form **wogete,** for prose **wogte.**

1192. **Gnügen** (the inf. genügen, from genug, used as noun) **that,** *sufficed;* thun has here a semi-auxiliary sense, hence **Gnügen thun** = genügen; used with dat. **der Zahl.**

1194. **Zum schwarzen Berg,** i.e. across the lake to the Brünig (= **Braun-eck(e),** so-called from its thick woods), on the south-west corner of Unterwalden. — **Weiß-land,** the snow-covered peaks of the Bernese Oberland in **Ober-Hasli,** south of the Brünig.

1196. In the cantons Tessin and Wallis Italian and French are spoken.

1200. He means the Alamanni, Burgundians, Franks. See Introduction, p. xvii f.

1203. **Es,** expletive; **Herz** (and **Blut**) is the real subject.

1205. Sums up the theme (union) of the first part of their deliberations (1155 ff., note) and ushers in that (namely liberty) of the second (1206–1314).

1206. **Völker,** of other cantons. Stauffacher is still the leading spirit.

1209. **Sassen** (from sitzen), partitive gen., lit. 'settlers,' here for **Hintersassen,** *vassals,* without citizen-rights, *owing allegiance to others* **(fremde Pflichten tragen).**

1215 f. i.e. voluntarily they sought **Reichs-unmittelbar-keit,** i.e. dependence directly upon the empire, and not upon any feudal lord (cf. 912, note), which was granted in the charter of Friedrich II., in 1240. — **Schutz und Schirm,** emphatic alliterative synonyms (cf. 331, note).

1219. **Recht schöpfen** (lit. 'draw,' as water), old legal term, *get iustice.* — **wo,** *from whom.* Noble sentiment, nobly expressed by a law-abiding people.

1222. **die** (= diese) **Ehr',** i.e. to be **Oberhaupt** over their land **(für den Boden).**

1223. **Erde,** i.e. of Germany and Italy. Cf. 871, 266, 520, notes.

1225. gelobt (from geloben) depends on haben (1220).

1229 f. Heri=bann, for Heer=bann, lit. 'army summons,' i.e. imperial summons to vassals to take the field. — feine, the emperor's.

1231. gewappnet (from Wappen, 'coat-of-arms'); prose requires gewaffnet, from Waffe, 'weapon.' Cf. 1135, note.

1235. Der höchste Blut=bann allein, *only the highest criminal jurisdiction*, i.e. cases involving capital punishment.

1237. So that he would not be influenced by any partisan feeling or fear of any one. — bestellt, *delegated* by the emperor.

1243. verhält sich alles, *it is all*, etc.

1247 ff. This quarrel with Einsiedeln (343, note) is historical. In 1018, Heinrich II., ignorant of the peasants' existence and ownership (1251 f.), had given the pasture to Einsiedeln; in time quarrels naturally arose; in 1114 the abbot appealed in behalf of the monastery to Heinrich V., who decided in his favor (cf. 1246). The peasants refused compliance (cf. 1245), and when Konrad III. tried to force them (in 1144), they withdrew from the Empire (cf. 1255 f.).

1259. fremden Knecht, contemptuous reference to Gessler and the other Habsburg bailiffs.

1261. erschaffen, *created* (cleared and made it fertile), is splendidly emphatic.

1265 ff. One of the many Swiss dragon stories. Cf. the Winkelried legend, 1073, note. Here, as in most such cases, the dragon is a personification of treacherous disease rising from the swamps in fogs and noxious vapors. He is "killed" by clearing and draining the swamps (1267 f.).

1270 f. tausend=jährig, round number for a very long time, though it had really been nearly 1000 years since the first Alamannic migrations. — Herrenknecht, 1259, note.

1279 ff. greift . . . getrosten Mutes (adverb. gen.) in . . . Him=mel, *with confidence reaches up to heaven.* The lofty poetic tone is eminently in keeping with the situation here.

1283. Urstand (on Ur-, cf. 538, note), *primitive state* (in which each defends his own rights), as indicated in 1284.

1285. Zum (lit. 'for the'), *as the.*

1287. i.e. their freedom; note the poetic word-order.

1295 f. Rösselmann is, of course, not in earnest, though wishing.

as a man of peace (1316), to avoid open rupture; doubtless (cf. 1312–14), he intends merely to test the confederates.   Perhaps he shrewdly suggests this most distasteful proposition in order to make them do the opposite.

1297. **Wir . . . schwören,** *What! we swear*, etc.   This simple exclamatory inf. strongly emphasizes the indignation felt.   Cf. also **huldigen** (1300), **lassen** (1301).

1302. **Güte,** Austria's first overtures.   Cf. 185, note, and 1314.

1312. **'s,** i.e. **frei.**   Cf. the same **es** in 1303.   Thus ends the second part of their deliberations.   Not only are they a united people (1156–1205), but they are and mean to remain a free people (1206–1314).   Cf. 1205, note.   The third part of the scene shows how they propose to maintain their liberty.

1318. **wohl gar . . . nicht,** *probably not at all his.* — **es = was wir erdulden.**

1324 f. **Nun . . . Euch** (cf. **die Reihe ist an Euch**), *now it's your turn.* — **Rheinfeld**(en), a once strongly fortified town on the Rhine near Bâle (Basel).

1327. The old charter of liberties granted by Friedrich II., and confirmed by every emperor before Albrecht.   Cf. 912, note.

1330 f. **vom schwäbischen Lande** (**Schwaben**), Swabia, a large South German province. — **vom Lauf** (lit. 'course'), etc., *from along the Rhine.* — **die,** demonst. for personal; so also 1334, 1341.

1336 ff. **sonst einmal wohl,** *some other time, no doubt.* — **Hansen,** obsol. acc. of **Hans** (dim. of **Johannes**).   Duke John of Swabia, Albrecht's nephew, the **Johannes Parricida** of Act V, Scene 2, is meant. — **Herrn,** for usual pl. **Herren.**

1344. **hinter=hält,** here for **vorenthält,** *withholds from.* — **sein . . . Erbe** was the dukedom of Swabia, from his father, and lands in Switzerland, from his mother, i.e. **sein Mütterliches** (**Erbe**).

1346. **Er habe** (subj. of indirect statement with principal verb omitted; so also **wäre** [and **sei,** 1349] — note the irregular change of tense.   Cf. 92, note) **seine Jahre voll,** *he was* (*he said*) *of age.*

1348. **Was . . . Bescheid,** *what answer did he get?*   Cf. 149, 646, note.

1350 ff. Here begins the third chapter of their deliberations —

armed resistance is the only way to maintain their liberty; and self-defense, not conquest, is their purpose (1354–57).

1358 ff. Dem Kaiser, etc., sound Biblical (Matt. xxii, 21 ; Mark xii, 17) advice, from a law-abiding citizen. — **Herrn,** feudal lord, from whom they *held land in fief* (1360). — **fahret fort,** pres. indic. with imperative force (cf. also 1363, 1365).

1362. steure an, *pay taxes to.* — **Rappersweil,** now written and pronounced Rapperschwyl, a town on the north shore of Lake Zürich.

1364. Frau zu Zür(i)ch, the Frau-Münster, i.e. Nunnery of *Our Lady* (Virgin Mary, — cf. Fr. Notre Dame) *in Zürich*, founded 833 by Ludwig the German, and richly endowed with property and privileges. Cf. Introduction, p. xviii.

1366. als (die). — **geschehe,** subj., as imperative; so also **sehe** (1370).

1372. in unsern Schranken, i.e. within our legal rights.

1374. staats-klug, *with shrewd statesmanship.* The next lines are a very poetic and noble tribute to the Swiss. — **Furcht,** *respect.*

1383. uns, construed with **ragen** as dat. of interest, has the force of gegen **uns.** The **Schlösser** were Rossberg and Sarnen (cf. 78, 626, notes), *each* of which (hence **muß** in 1386) had to be captured.

1391. Note the emphasis of the poetic order **Eifer . . . der gute.**

1395 f. uns das bieten, *offer us that affront.* — **Eide,** their oath, as citizens, to the constitution, whereby they obtained political rights and swore to do nothing hurtful to the common weal. The strongest possible appeal, since refusal to obey was treason.

1401 f. Fest des Herrn, *till Christmas;* other chroniclers say till New Year's day (A.D. 1308). — **bringt's die Sitte mit** (sich), i.e. *it is customary.* — **Sassen,** here for In-sassen, *tenants.* The castle is Sarnen.

1406. Die führen, (i.e. in accordance with my plan) 'they will carry,' *let them carry.* Cf. 1359, note, and same idiom in **hält** (1409), **wird geblasen** (1411), **brechen** (1412).

1415 ff. Dirn(e), *girl.* — **ist mir hold** (lit. 'gracious'), *is in love with me.* — **leicht bethör'** (lit. 'deceive') **ich sie** (cf. Eng. coll. "I fooled him into doing that"), *I can easily induce her to.* — **ſchwanke Leiter,** *swaying rope-ladder.*

1418 f. **Bin ich droben erſt,** *once up there, I,* etc. — **aller,** gen. pl. — **daß (es) verſchoben werde,** *that we postpone.*

1423. **Zeichen . . . Rauch,** cf. 748, note. — **Land=ſturm,** more than **Land=wehr** ('militia'), is every man able to bear arms. **Land=ſturm aufbieten,** *to call the country to arms,* say *call to arms will be read at once in,* etc.

1429 f. **ſchweren Stand,** shows his character and prepares the way for later events. — **furchtbar,** i.e. has a terrible retinue.

1436. **ſchlag' . . . Schanze,** *will . . . risk.* **Schanze** (Fr. *chance*) different here from **Schanze,** *fortification.* Cf. Eng. *take the chances.*

1438. **Zeit,** cf. the proverb **Kommt Zeit, kommt Rat.** — **'s,** the result.

1442. **Hochwacht,** the rosy tints of the dawn falling on the highest summits are compared with **Feuer=zeichen,** 748, 596, notes.

1444 *. **mit ſtiller Sammlung,** from **ſammeln,** 'to collect' (one's thoughts), *in silent meditation.*

1450 *. **mit erhobenen drei Fingern,** symbolic of the Trinity. That Rösselmann, the pastor, administers the oath gives it a kind of consecration.

1452. **den Tod,** absol. acc. — * **wie oben,** i.e. stage direction after 1450.

1456. **Genoſſame** (cf. **Genoſſenſchaft,** 1109, note), 'community,' i.e. all belonging to a village, castle, monastery, etc., also later, a political *district;* Uri is still divided into **Genoſſenſchaften;** *to his own village and people* (cf. 659 f., note).

1464. **das Ganze,** i.e. the common cause.

1465. **Raub begehen** an + dat. ('comit theft on'), 'steals from' (*injures*). It is Stauffacher, ever the leader, who gives this advice. The rhyme is effective.

* **fällt . . . mit Schwung ein,** *comes in with* (begins) *a splendid flourish,* which, with the slowly rising sun, the sun of Swiss freedom, never fails of fine dramatic effect.

One of the most important and carefully wrought scenes in the play (cf. the detailed order of the meeting — arrival, general discussion, organization and election of president, deliberation, result, oath—), affording still deeper insight into Swiss character and into conditions prevailing. The action advances a long step; plans for united resistance, suggested before, have been definitely formed; hope is awakened for the cause of freedom, and the outcome is anxiously looked for. The scene belongs wholly to the People's Plot, which, begun in I, 2, and developed in I, 4, here reaches a climax. The strong contrast between the divided Nobles in II, 1. and the united People here is self-evident.

ACT III. SCENE 1.

Acts III and IV fall on Nov. 19 (Tschudi says 18), 1307. Scene 1 passes about noon at that day, since, immediately afterward, Tell goes to Altorf (1516), a mile distant, where he arrives in the early afternoon, cf. 1744.

* **Hedwig,** Schiller gives her this name; chroniclers say simply that she was Walther Fürst's daughter. Cf. 556.

1470. am Morgenstrahl, unusual for **beim Morgenstrahl,** probably confused with **am Morgen.** This little poem is called the **Schützen-lied** and is such a favorite in Germany that it has almost become a folk-song.

1472. Der Weih (also **die Weihe,** generic dialect name for large birds of prey); *eagle* is doubtless meant here.

1474 f. frei (adv.), i.e. unrestrained. — **das Weite** (adj. as noun), *all space.*

1478. was da (= **was auch**), *whatever.* — **kreucht und fleugt,** old forms for **kriecht, fliegt.**

1479. mir ent=zwei, *broken.* — **Mach' mir** (in both cases **mir,** dat. of interest) **ihn,** *fix it for me ;* a good example of **machen** in general sense.

1482. was (for **wer** ; neuter generalizes the statement), *whoever.* The line has almost become a proverb in Germany.

1485. frisch . . . schlagen, *vigorously make his way.*

1486. keiner, neither of the boys. — **zu Hause,** i.e. as a shepherd or herdsman, rather than as a hunter. — **Ruh' . . . finden,** i.e. be satisfied.

1490 f. erst, *only.* — **auf's neu' erbeute** (lit. 'capture'), *win anew,* i.e. by saving it from some danger.

1494 f. **Knechte,** either Tell's own, indicating that he had considerable property, or those of the village. — **sich,** each other; omit in translation.

1497. Note the very expressive use of the subjunctive **werdest** with **zittert,** i.e. for fear *that* (or *lest*) *you may not,* etc.

1500. **den Fehl**(from **fehlen,** 'miss')**sprung** (*false leap*) **thun,** *making a false leap.* Cf. **Fehl=tritt,** 'mis-step.' — **Rück=springend** goes with **Gemse,** cf. 650.

1502 f. **Wind=lawine,** or **Staub-**('dust')**lawine,** is an avalanche of dry, freshly fallen snow, driven down from high altitudes by heavy winds; they occur in fall and winter, and differ greatly from the **Schlag=lawinen** (1782), which are masses of snow, mixed with blocks of ice, and which, loosened by the summer sun, rush down with terrible force, and strike (**Schlag=**) with loud noise in the valleys. — **Firn,** cf. 38, note. Snow often covers the mouth of a crevasse, concealing the abyss below.

1510. **frisch,** *alertly, sharply.*

1514 f. **auf Jahr und Tag** (cf. Eng. coll. 'forever and a day,' 'for a year and a day'), an old legal term for a full year, now an idiom meaning *a good, long time.* — **erspart,** *saves,* i.e. makes unnecessary.

1516. **Vater,** i.e. Hedwig's father, Walther Fürst.

1517. **auch** (introductory), *now aren't you,* etc.

1518 ff. **wie kommst,** etc., *what makes you think that?* — **es spinnt,** etc. (lit. 'something is spinning'), *some scheme is on foot.* Some time must have elapsed since Act II, Scene 2. Tschudi says ten days. He also says Tell was present at the Rütli; Schiller prefers to leave him out of the meeting. Cf. 1097, note. — (**es**) **ward getagt,** *there was a meeting.*

1526. **Den Unterwaldner,** Baumgarten. Cf. 151 ff.

1531. **heißt,** *is,* cf. 356, note. Note the exclamatory infin. **schiffen,** with (more commonly without, cf. 1297, 1300) **zu.** We would expect **in den See.** — **Gott versuchen,** *tempting Providence.*

1536. **Verhüt'** . . . **nicht.** Cf. 253, note; 805.

1540. **willst** (without infin.) **mit,** cf. Eng. *go along* (*go too*).

1542. **laß,** etc., *let him* (*get*) *away first.*

1545 ff. Cf. the well-known proverb **Thue Recht und scheue nie=**

manb. **Die recht thun,** *those who,* etc. Note the poetic word-order. — **eben die,** *just those.* — **an sie kommen,** *get at them.*

1550 f. This meeting with Gessler is Schiller's invention, and shows Gessler's reason for hating Tell (cf. 1572 f.). — **Schächenthal,** see map.

1553. (**Es**) **nicht aus=zu=weichen war,** *where there was no escaping* (a meeting), i.e. the narrow path made it impossible for Gessler to avoid him in passing.

1556. gegen . . . daher, *along toward.*

1559. Herre, old for **Herr.** — **mein ansichtig ward,** *saw me.* **mein,** for **meiner,** is genit. with **ansichtig.** Cf. Eng. 'catch sight *of.*'

1561. This previous punishment is invented to help explain the personal relation between the two men.

1562 f. sah . . . daher . . . kommen, *saw me come striding along.* — **verblaßt(e),** now generally applied to things, **erblassen** applies to persons.

1566. (**Es**) **jammerte mich sein** (for **seiner,** gen.), *I pitied him.* Cf. also 486; the log. subj. is here acc., the log. obj. gen. Shows Tell's generous, forgiving nature.

1568. keinen armen (i.e. **geringen, kleinen,** 'little,' 'poor') **Laut,** i.e. *not a single word.*

1575. dort weg = **von dort weg.**

1578. Weil's, *just because;* i.e. she can give no reason, but her intuitive fear of evil is ground enough for her. A skilful touch of woman's nature, as is also her yielding as soon as she learns that Tell has promised to go.

1583. bring . . . auch (et)**was,** *Oh, but I'll bring,* etc.

1585 *. den Ab=gehenden, dat. pl. (not acc. sg.) with **folgt.** Simple but effective means of showing her deep feeling of anxiety.

A charming and typical picture of Swiss home-life, developing further the character of Tell, the man, the husband and father, and showing what the *mothers* in Swiss homes feel in such trying times. While the **Eidgenossen** have planned resistance, Tell's chief desire is to be let alone. Hedwig's anxiety hints that he may not have his wish, and is a foreboding of evil, serving to further enliven and intensify the interest. The scene develops the Tell Plot, only hinted at before. It emphasizes the purely personal and individual (not

political) relation of Tell to Gessler (as man to man), explains
Gessler's hatred of him and later cruelty to him; these personal
relations, not any political motives, are the basis of Tell's later
action.

ACT III.   SCENE 2.

The time is about the same as in III, 1.   This scene gives Tell
opportunity to go from Bürglen to Altorf.

* **Staub-bäche,** lit. 'dust (i.e. fine spray) brooks,' are little streams,
rushing over high cliffs and dashed into fine spray by the force of
the fall. — **im Jagd-kleid,** Schiller's mistake; November is too late
for hunting in the Alps.

1587 ff. One of several passages in the scene where the intended
lyric effect is heightened by rhyme.   Cf. 1682 f., 1686 ff., 1696 ff.,
1707 ff.

1594 f. Note the poetic word-order.   **und,** i.e. even if, etc.

1600. in . . . Reih' . . . stellen, i.e. take my place among, compare myself with.

1604. Der . . . wird, *who are faithless in.*   In such cases the pronoun antecedent is usually repeated and the verb agrees with it in
person (as **der Ihr . . . seid**), but if the antecedent is not repeated,
the verb takes third person.   So also in 1626, 1628. — **treulos . . . an,** treulos usually has simple dat. without the preposition.

1612 f. natur-vergeß(e)nen (past part. with active force), i.e. forgetting the place and duty by nature devolving upon him; *degen-
erate.*   Cf. **Gott-vergessen,** 'god-less.' — **seinem,** Gessler's.

1917 f. sein . . . zu beschirmen.   Note these subject infinitives,
with and without **zu.**

1631. (will ich) **Ihm . . . nicht . . . Frieden** (bereiten).

1633. This *last stronghold* of liberty is the Forest Cantons.

1635. versteht sich . . . auf (lit. ' in regard to'), *understand better
their own happiness.*

1639. Thät, condensed condit. subjunct. (wenn ich . . . thät); (es)
wäre, etc. — **den,** etc. *To see him despised . . . whom,* etc.; despised,
no doubt, by his own people, perhaps, too, by the Austrians, whose
dupe he was.

1651 f. läßt (causative *makes*) **mich alles sein,** etc., *will enable me to be and become (anything) all.* — **Seid (das) wozu.**

1653. Note **wohin** with the verb of motion **gestellt.**

1658 f. Verwandten, i.e. of Gessler especially; as **Geßler von Bruneck** he is made a relative of hers, to whose care she is entrusted and who seems anxious to marry her himself. Cf. 1611, 1720 f. — **Wille,** i.e. 'that I should side with Austria.'

1660 f. In Aargau, cf. 446. * note. She makes common cause with the Swiss. — **'s,** i.e. **frei.**

1665 f. dem großen Erb', i.e. not the imperial possessions, but those of Habsburg. This scene is only imaginary, but Albrecht's greed is historical. Cf. 1343 ff.

1670. Dort goes with **hin** (1671) implying direction.

1672. Prose would have **(die) Ketten verhaßter Ehe harren mein** (for **meiner,** gen. of **ich**).

1676 f. Sehnen in das Weite, *longing* (to get out) *into the wide world.* — **als,** *but.*

1680. könnt, conditional, *if you can.*

1686. des Lebens Weiten, *larger spheres of life.*

1688. Die . . . Mauer breiten, *extend around us* (a) *their firm, impenetrable wall.*

1690. Construe: **Zum Himmel allein. — gelichtet** (lit. 'lightened'; from **lichten,** 'to cut away undergrowth or branches to let light through.' Cf. **Lichtung,** 'clearing') **sein,** *be clear and open.* Notice the **du** in 1691, as compared with more formal **Ihr** above.

1693. bethört (hat), not pres. ind., but past part.

1697. Familiar to him from boyhood, they live in his memory as old friends.

1700. Es fehlte, pret. subj. (not indic.), conclusion of conditional sentence, *would be lacking;* no happiness would be complete without it. — **der Erden,** old gen. sg. Cf. 972, note.

1701. The reference is to the fabled **Inseln der Seligen,** *Isles of the Blessed.*

1703 f. heimisch wohnt, emphatic fusion of **heimisch ist,** 'is at home,' and simple **wohnt,** 'dwells.' — **sich . . . hinfinden,** *find one's way.*

1705 f. trübt, entfliehen, poetical presents with future sense.

1710. **wie ... König wirkt,** *like a king ruling.* — **Reichen,** pl. for sake of rhyme.

1712 f. **weiblich reizender,** *in charming womanly,* etc. — **erbauen, schmücken, beleben, beglücken,** infinitives with **seh'** (1711).

1719. **Wie stünd's um mich,** *how would it be with me?* — **Ritter,** probably Gessler. Cf. 1658, note.

1727. **Was auch d(a)raus werde,** *whatever may come of it.*

The scene is a bright chapter in the sad story of the Swiss, just such a love scene as Schiller delighted to paint — with a fitting background of grand romantic scenery. It is full of poetic beauty and lyric passion, expressed by unusual word-order and frequent use of rhyme. Cf. 1697 ff., 1704 ff., 1711 ff., etc. The action takes a long step forward when Bertha wins Rudenz back to his own people. Bertha, the young girl of noble family, is thus the companion-piece to Gertrud (I, 2), the mature matron of humbler birth; each inspires the man she loves to open resistance of the tyrants. The Swiss cause seems more hopeful; with the sympathy and help of the younger nobility, the cantons can better cope with Austria. The scene belongs wholly to the Rudenz (or Nobles') drama.

ACT III. SCENE 3.

The scene connects directly with III, 1, and takes place soon after; scene 2 gives Tell time to come from Bürglen.

* **Wiese bei** (*near*) **Altorf,** 395 says mitten in Altorf; cf. also l. 1743.

* **Bann**[from bannen, 'to forbid' (access to), hence, 'protect by law']**berg,** *the Bannberg.* It is a high hill overlooking Altorf and covered with woods, which protect the village from falling stones and avalanches; even yet it is forbidden to cut the trees on it, hence **die Bäume sind gebannt** (1778).

1737. **Popanz** (pronounce Pŏ′panz), *bugbear.* The reference here is to the hat. They had been standing guard for some three weeks, cf. 393 ff.

1739 f. **uns zum Verdrieße** (old for Verdrusse), 'for our vexation,' *to annoy us.* — **Was** (indefinite neuter collective for alle welche) **rechte Leute sind,** *all* (who are) *decent people.* **recht** here in sense of *respectable, of better class.*

1741 f. **den halben,** *half the.* — **beugten,** pret. subj. *would bend.*

1744. **Mittagsstunde,** taken with what follows, gives the time of this scene, i.e. not long after noon.

1749. **Hochwürdigen.** The 'Host' or sacramental wafer is meant.

1752. **Monstranz,** *monstrance* (cf. Lat. *monstrare*), the richly ornamented glass box containing the Eucharist. The **Glöcklein** carried by the sacristan called attention to its presence.

1753 f. **Es fängt . . . deuchten,** *I begin to feel as if we were.*

1755. **doch,** *after all,* here, as in 1759, merely adds emphasis to the statement.

1761. Inversion common in exclamation, especially when followed by **doch** (*you know,* implying that contradiction is impossible).

* **Mechthild** (cf. **Mathilde**), **Elsbeth,** for **Elisabeth.**

1764. **wer da** (= **wer auch**), *whoever,* cf. 1478, note. — **Mag,** *let.*

1767 ff. **Wollt's** = **wollte es,** optat. subjunc. — **und ließ' . . . Hut,** i.e. leave us *only* his hat. — **sollte drum . . . ums Land,** 'it would not on that account be (lit. 'stand') worse for the country.' *The country would not be worse off for it.* — **Volk der Weiber,** cf. Eng. *women-folks.* — **Wollt,** cf. 492, note.

1771. **Wenn . . . Mut** (cf. 'mood') **sticht,** lit. 'if desire impels ('pricks') them,' i.e. *if they would like to.*

* **Tell . . . tritt auf,** Tell and Walther have had time (while Act III, Scene 2, is passing) to come from Bürglen to Altorf (cf. 1539), a distance of about a mile. — **vordere Scene,** *front of stage.*

1773 f. **Die Bäume bluten,** old, wide-spread superstition. — **Streich führte,** condit. subjunct., *should deal a blow.*

1776. **Gebannt,** here *charmed,* in 1778 *protected* by law; cf. note on **Bannberg,** at opening of this scene.

1777. **Dem** (poss. dat.) **seine,** colloquial for **dem die.**

1779. **Hörner,** i.e. sharp snow-peaks, cf. **Schreck-horn,** 629.

1782. **Schlag-lawinen,** cf. note on 1502.

1786. **Land-wehr** (cf. **wehren,** 'to defend'), lit. 'defence of the land'; now usually means militia, for defense only; here in older sense of *bulwark.*

1790. **großes, ebnes Land.** May mean Germany or Italy; it makes no difference and may have been purposely left in doubt.

1793. **nach allen Himmels-räumen,** i.e. in all directions. Here, as often, the rhyme accompanies a very poetic description.

1798 f. **Statt daß** (= Statt + zu with inf.), *instead of* + Eng. pres. part. — **der Himmel,** here *the climate*.

1803. i.e. to the Church and the State, to clerical and princely owners.

1807. **das Salz,** etc., i.e. the sale of salt was a state monopoly.

1812 f. *I feel oppressed in that broad land,* i.e. when I think of how things are there; **eng** and **weit** form effective contrast. — **Da,** *then* (in that case). — **unter,** here, as often, *among*.

1815.* **wollen,** *are about to* ('start to').

1817. Tell knows what the hat means and wishes to avoid it.

1818.* **greift** (lit. 'seizes,' cf. Eng. 'grips') **in,** *lays hold of*.

1823.* **In die Scene,** i.e. towards the back-ground.

1824. **Herbei,** with imperative force. *Here!*

1826. the second **was** = **warum,** so also 1857, 1859, and often.

1830 f. **geschieht** (geschehen, lit. 'happen'), *is being done to,* etc.

1834 f. **erkennen,** for anerkennen. — **hätt',** exclamatory interrogative subj. *What!* (do you mean that) *Tell has,* etc.? Cf. 1072, note. — **Das lügst du, Bube,** *that's a lie, you scoundrel*.

1840. **unsers Amtes,** cf. p. 368, note.

1847. **schon,** merely for emphasis and to express Tell's self-assurance, *never mind, I'll,* etc.

1855. **was wird das** (daraus) **werden,** *what will come of this?* Expresses his grave fears for the result, for he knows Gessler's character.

* **den Falken,** etc., adverbial acc., *with a falcon,* etc. They are returning from the hunt mentioned 1592, **Bertha** and **Rudenz** having joined them. — **Rudolph der Harras,** a fictitious character here, though the name occurs in accounts of the battle of Sempach (A.D. 1386). This, **Geßler's** first appearance (and he is the only **Vogt** who does appear), is very impressive; on horseback and splendidly attended, he is an imposing figure; his first harsh words show his whole character; at once judge and tyrant, he quiets the tumult and overawes the people in a moment.

1860 ff. **Gestrenger Herr** (cf. Eng. 'dread sovereign') lost its original force and became a term of politeness; *Your Lordship.* — über frischer That, wie, *in the very act, as,* etc.

1866. Gessler calls him by name at once; he knows Tell already. Cf. 1556 ff. — Kaiser, the hat meant Habsburg (not imperial) authority. Cf. 409.

1872. Verachtung Eurer (for Euer gen. of Ihr), *contempt of you.*

1873. The meaning of the name, Tell, has been much discussed. Some connect it with *telum,* arrow, making der Tell = 'archer.' Others derive it from dalen or talen, 'to talk foolishly,' or from toll, originally = Eng. 'dull,' though now stronger (= 'mad'); others from Taller, 'peasant.' The name appears in various forms, as Tell, Thall, Täll, Thell. The chronicler, from whom this line was taken, regarded Tell as a nickname meaning 'foolish,' 'simple,' i.e. Wilhelm Tell = William the Simple. Cf. also Introduction, p. xxviii.

1874. nicht mehr begegnen, in prose nicht wieder geschehen. The pause following here heightens the dramatic effect; so also after 1857, 1865.

1876. du nehmst es auf mit, *you are ready to take it up* (*contest*).

1878. dir, ethical dat., *shoot you an apple.* Schiller puts this boast in the mouth of the boy, that it may suggest to Gessler the cruel idea of making the father shoot the apple from the son's head. The two lines were put in in response to a hint from Goethe. — Schritte (also 1916), commonly sg. Schritt, as in 1884.

1893. nein doch (very emphatic), *Oh! no.* — kommt . . . zu (for more usual in den) Sinn, *you cannot mean that.* The grim earnestness of what follows is in effective contrast with the easy-going humor of the opening of the scene.

1896. This fut. (and 1900 pres.) indic. with imperative force is very effective.

1908. eigen, *special;* bitter taunt added to already inhuman cruelty.

1909. wohl, *no doubt.* — sich bedächte, *would* (bethink himself) *hesitate.*

1914. The vivid dramatic action makes us forget that November is too late for apples on the trees in Switzerland.

1918. **ihrer** (part. gen. with **hundert**; cf. 286, note; 293) refers to **Schritte.** Tell had made no such boast.

1921. **Es gilt** (from **gelten,** 'to pass for,' 'be a question of,' 'concern,' which is used in many idioms), for the common **es gilt das Leben,** 'life is at stake'; or, taken in perfectly general sense, **es gilt,** 'the crisis has come,' *all is at stake.*

1922. i.e. in view of the Rütli decision to postpone any uprising; cf. 1401, 1419, 1455-66. **Haltet an Euch,** *control yourself.*

1924. **also** (never means 'also'), *so, thus.*

1927. **hätte,** subjunct. in softened expression of opinion.

1929 f. **kennen lernen** (for kennen gelernt), this use of the inf. instead of past part. after another inf., common also with **sehen, helfen, hören, heißen, lehren,** is like that of the aux. verbs of mode. Cf. **Er hat . . . thun wollen. — Stunde,** gen. with **denken** (for gedenken, 'remember').

1931 f. **Gasse,** here the narrow space, *lane,* between two lines of people. — The unfeeling torture continues, shows Gessler's true self, and explains Tell's later conduct.

1938. **Hier gilt es** (cf. 1921, note), *here is a chance to,* etc.

1941. **mir,** i.e. in my opinion, *I call him,* etc.

1943. **Dem's** (dem das), *whose;* i.e. whose feelings (*heart*) do not make eye dim or hand unsteady.

1945. **lasset Gnad' . . . ergehen,** lit. 'let mercy go out for right,' i.e. show mercy instead of enforcing justice.

1949. **hin=stehen** (for sich hinstellen), *go stand.*

1951. **fehlen auf,** i.e. miss (the apple) and strike the heart, etc.

1954. **Rede stehen,** *give account.* Note how the words of each speaker bring out his character.

1964. **Frisch** (lit. 'fresh,' 'brisk,' 'quick'), here a simple exclamation, *Come!* Cf. Eng. *Quick, now!* — **'s** = the rest of the line.

1966. **Dem Wütrich zum Verdrusse** (lit. 'for vexation to the tyrant'), *to vex the tyrant.* Cf. 1739, note.

1971 f. **mit frischer That** (*with prompt action*), without the delay agreed on in 1401 ff.

1979. **Freut's** (conditional) **euch** (you people); he lashes the others over Tell's shoulders.

1988. **Kannst ja,** *Why! you can do,* etc. Gessler wants neither his life nor the shot, but seeks to humble the archer and torture the father and thus wreak cowardly vengeance for 1559-1571.

1990 f. Gessler has evidently heard of Tell's having saved Baumgarten (151 ff.). **zu retten gilt,** *when it means (is a question of) saving somebody;* cf. also 1921, note. — **Du retteſt alle** is another cruelly ironical reference to his rescue of Baumgarten.

* The strong contrast between the beginning (III, 1) and the end of Tell's journey, between the quiet happiness of 1772 ff. and the present agony of Tell, greatly intensifies the dramatic effect. (Cf. beginning and end of I, 1.) It is just this **fürchterlicher Kampf** (between the father-heart and the independent manhood Gessler was trying to crush) that dictates all his later conduct.

1992 f. ſchieß zu, *shoot on!* — **Es muß,** *it must be done.*

* **mit Gewalt . . . gehalten,** cf. 1922. Rudenz, now knowing Bertha's attitude (1726 ff.) and brought to see his duty by this inhuman tyranny, at last takes his people's part.

1999. darf's (= **darf reden**), *have the right to* — the nobleman's right to speak at any time.

2004 ff. ſtill, apparently unnecessary, but idiomatic with **ſchweigen.** Rudenz, without intending deception, and now in his true character, gives himself rather more credit than he deserves; his attitude, 770 ff., towards his uncle's entreaties was not especially patriotic, but experience has taught him much already. — **ſehend Auge,** he might have seen, but would not.

2016. Da ich . . . befeſtigte, lit. 'in that I,' etc., *by strengthening.*

2020. daran ('on the point of'), *I was about to.*

2029. Antwort, *satisfaction,* i.e. in the duel he would have to fight.

2031. die, demonst. *these,* i.e. the peasants.

2032. Und wer mir naht. This skilfully developed crisis attracts attention to Rudenz and Gessler, and spares the spectator the pain of seeing Tell shoot at the boy. It also gives time for an apple, with an arrow through it, to be thrown from behind the scenes.

2036. Wußt' ich's ja, *Why, I knew;* the inversion is emphatic.

2037.* ſtand, Eng. uses *has been standing.*

2039 ff. Even in these exclamations of natural surprise does

Schiller portray character. Thus Leuthold and Harras admire the
wonderful *shot* (2039–42), Bertha and Fürst rejoice (2035, 2038) that
the *father's anguish* is relieved; the boy, knowing nothing of such
suffering, is proud of his father's *skill* (2036 f.); Rösselmann, incensed at Gessler (2045 f.), calls down Heaven's wrath upon him;
Stauffacher rejoices that Tell is *free* (3047 f.); Gessler is surprised
and angry that Tell has shot (2034) and, failing in one plan to destroy his enemy, seeks another (2050 ff.).

2048. **männlich gelöft** (lit. 'redeemed'), *quit yourself like a man.*

2050. **Du ſtecktest . . . zu dir,** i.e. *You* ('put in your doublet')
concealed about you. Cf. stage direction after 1991.

2054. **laß gelten,** *let pass, accept.*

2055. **wird . . . wohl,** fut. shows confident opinion; *no doubt it
meant.*

2056. **friſch und fröhlich,** *freely and frankly.*

2057. **ſich(e)r'(e),** *assure,* note the acc. + dat. which is the usual
construction of the simple verb; 2059 and 2064 use acc. + gen.,
where prose would have **mich (dich) verſichert.**

2061. **durch-ſchoß . . . Euch,** *would have shot you.* The past
indic. (instead of pluperfect subj. or conditional) lends Tell's words
a terrible emphasis, further strengthened by the contrast with his
previous humble attitude (1985 f.), and places the result (2063)
beyond doubt. This whole passage, 2058(**wohlan**)–2063, forms the
inscription on the pedestal of a life-size statue of Tell, erected
some years ago in Altorf on the traditional scene of the famous
shot.

2063. **Eurer** (for **Euer**), gen. (cf. 1919 acc.), with **fehlen,** cf. 1996.

2077 f. **Freiheits-briefen,** etc. A characteristic remark of
Rösselmann, who knows all about the old charters; according to
them it was unlawful to imprison or try a man outside of his own
canton. Tell lived in Uri, but Küssnacht was in the canton of
Schwyz. Gessler feels free to ignore privileges not confirmed by
the present Kaiser. Cf. 1325–1336.

2086.* Bertha follows, not from choice, but because, as her
guardian, Gessler has authority over her; another manuscript
makes him seize her by the hand and lead her away. Rudenz is
of course unwilling to leave her.

2089 f. **warum mußtet Jhr**, *what made you*, etc.　Cf. Eng. coll. 'why did you have to.' — **Bezwinge sich**, etc., *Let him control himself who*, etc.

2091-3. In spite of the oath of the Rütli confederates (1448 ff.), in which Tell had no part! Shows the regard in which he was held; even Stauffacher, leader of the Rütli meeting, loses heart.

2097. sag' ich, etc., i.e. *shall I* take no message to your wife?

This is aptly called the **Meisterscene** of the whole play.　First it shows careful dramatic structure; each part easily and naturally leads up to and into the next — an introduction describes the guards (1733-55), the father and son (1772-1817), and the arrest (1818-55); the main action (1855-2050) shows the coming and the cruelty of Gessler (1855-1910), the resulting conflict in Tell (1910-92), the interference of Rudenz (1993-2031), the shot (2031-50); the conclusion is Gessler's new plan of destroying his enemy (2050-98). Again the scene shows greater dramatic intensity than any other, and it brings the action to a *crisis* in Tell's fearful struggle and his terrible oath; the confederates, too, are incensed almost beyond control.　It has been too much.　Revenge must come — though the catastrophe is delayed by Tell's being taken prisoner.　All three of the plots are brought together and further development of the action is thus held in suspense.

ACT IV.　SCENE 1.

* **Östliches Ufer**, etc., i.e. of the lower arm (called **Urner See**) of the lake, about half way from Brunnen to Flüelen.　The scene passes, very soon after III, 3, late in the afternoon of the same day.　Cf. introductory note to III, 1.

* **Kunz** (for **Konrad**) **von Gersau** (see map) is a fictitious character, introduced here to connect this scene with what precedes and follows.　Just from Flüelen (2106), he tells what has happened since the close of the last scene, while the news he brings of Attinghausen's illness (2116) prepares us for the next scene.

* **Fischer**, no doubt the Ruodi of I, 1.　He is here essentially the same as in I, 1, a man of words, not deeds; his boy's name is Jenni (cf. 2302), just as in I, 1; no other fisherman is mentioned among the **Personen** (cf. p. 3); he was at the Rütli (2290), so was Ruodi (stage direction after 1098); one MS. of the play gives here the *name*, Ruodi, instead of **Fischer**. We are evidently to suppose simply that, after I, 1, Ruodi and Jenni moved into another hut across the lake.

2103. gelten ... für, unusual for simple gelten. *If there ever should be a fight for liberty.* Cf. 1990, note.

2105. eben d(a)ran, cf. 2020, note.

2114. Des freien Mannes, i.e. of Tell, if he should get free again.

2116. am Tode, for im Sterben, *at the point of death.*

2121. Dorf, Sissigen or Sisikon, at the foot of the Axenberg, three miles from Flüelen.

2125-27. Mund der Wahrheit refers to Attinghausen, **das seh'nde Auge,** possibly to Attinghausen (Düntzer), possibly to Rudenz, after Attinghausen's death (**Freiherr tot**) their natural protector, who, though *seeing*, was *blind* to their interests. Cf. **Verblendeter,** 840, **mein sehend Auge,** etc., 2006. (Riehemann-Bellermann.) — **Der Arm** refers to Tell. Without these three representative men, all seems to him lost, hence his cry of desperation, 2130 ff.

2133. The inconsistency of such elevated language in the mouth of a peasant fisherman has been often noted; Schiller is thought to have had in mind the famous passage in *King Lear* (III, 2):

"Blow, winds, and crack your cheeks! rage! blow! . . .
Crack Nature's moulds, all germens spill at once."

2136. Wüste (gen., not dat.), cf. the legendary account of the settlement of the country given by Stauffacher, 1261 ff.

2141. geboten, from gebieten.

2149. Klüfte, i.e. the walls of the gorges.

2153. daß (es) gebetet werde (impersonal pass.), *that prayer be offered.* The subj. indicates purpose.

2159. gewährte, potential subj., might, etc.

2160. Handlos, lit. 'hand-less,' i.e. offering no hold, which, like a helping hand, might be grasped; *the cliffs, rising steep and inaccessible, stare him in the face.* Note the highly poetic effect of the alliteration and unusual word-order in these lines.

2165 f. ſich verfangen, *has once been caught.* The lake here is really an immense gorge, full of water. Note the unusual word-order in the next lines. — **er** (and 2168), the storm.

2171 f. Herren=ſchiff, *Governor's boat,* cf. Herren=burg, 771, Herren=bank, 807, note. Gessler's boat showed red (Habsburg-Austrian color) deck and flag.

2178. geben nicht (more commonly nichts, as object) **auf,** *yield not to, heed not.*

2181. Greif (lit. 'seize') **nicht . . . in den Arm,** *Stay not the judge's arm* (i.e. by your prayer). The fisherman knows that Tell is also on the boat (cf. 2104 ff., also 2215–18), but in his excitement forgets it.

2183. mit, i.e. with the others; *also.* Note the skill which shows us (through these fishermen) Tell actually on the journey upon which he started in 2098.

2186. mit ſamt, *together with.* The double preposition is emphatic and poetical. The **Steuermann** is Tell, whom Ruodi had already seen handle a boat (cf. 151 ff., see also 2196 f.).

2188 ff. Buggis=grat, Hack=meſſer, Axen=berg, dangerous, jutting cliffs on the east shore, some two miles north of Flüelen. The **Teufels=münſter** is a similar cliff further up on the west shore.

2194 f. Fluh (also Flüh, Flüe, etc.), a Swiss word for 'bald, steep rock'; found in many compounds; cf. Flüe=len, Klaus von der Flüe (Dramatis Personæ).

2197 f. einer = irgend einer. — **könnt',** unreal condition. — **ja** (explanatory, *you know*) **gefeſſelt,** the contrast between this desperate situation and his appearance soon after is splendidly dramatic.

2215. Daß connects with **wißt,** 2214. — **ſahen,** old form of ſangen.

2220. aufgegebner (lit. 'a given-up'), *despairing* man.

2227. Granſen (lit. 'beak'), the pointed end of a boat; der vordere Granſen is the prow, der hintere Granſen, *the stern.*

2229. kleinen Axen, a lower peak of the Axenberg, nearer Flüelen. — **Gäh**(for jäh, 2194, note)**lings herfür**(for hervor)**brach.** Cf. 109, 875, notes. Schiller uses many of the old forms of the chronicle from which this account was taken. Cf. 2194, 2215, 2247 ff., 2257 ff.

2238 ff. wiſſen ſich . . . nicht Rat (lit. 'know not counsel for themselves '), *know not what to do*. — **vor** (here 'because of ') **Furcht**, gives the reason. Cf. Eng. '*for* very joy.' — **des Fahrens . . . berichtet**, *skilled in steering*.

2242. wie (wäre es), etc. — **ſein . . . brauchten**, *should make use of him*. The gen. (**ſein**) with **brauchen** is poetical.

2244. wenn . . . getrauteſt, pret. subj.; subtle use of unreal condition, *if you* (trusted yourself to) *felt you could*, implying possible (not the usual impossible) fulfillment. — Gessler is feeling his way. — **möchte**, simple *might*, not 'would like to.'

2247 ff. hie=dannen, Tschudi's expression, for modern **von dannen, von hier weg**. — **fuhr redlich** (Tschudi again) **hin**, *rowed* (stoutly) *steadily on*. **redlich** now means *honest(ly)*, cf. 286. This story of Tell's escape follows Tschudi very closely.

2252. Vorteil (lit. 'advantage'), old military expression for 'advantageous point,' (*to see*) *if a chance for escape might present itself*.— **aufthät'**, potential subj.

2257 ff. angehen, here *to ascend*. — **vom Schiff** (ab) **. . . zu** (er=) **reichen**, would be the prose form; *to reach it by a leap from the boat*. — **Schrie**, etc., takes up 2253 and shows Tell's excitement. — **haudlich zuzugehen**, *to pull* (row) *hard*. Tschudi's (**hantlich**) **zugind** (= **zögen**, from **ziehen**) was mistaken for **zugingen** (from **zugehen**, in the sense of 'go at '). — **kämen**, subj. in indirect discourse.

2263. Angeſtemmt. Eng. uses *pres.* part. *bearing on* (the tiller).

2266. Platte (now **Tellsplatte**, see map), a flat jutting rock, now crowned with a little chapel, adorned with frescos illustrating Tell's deeds. The order of words in the whole passage is very unusual and poetic.

2274. hin, indicates direction of motion; no infin. is 'understood' in German, though Eng. requires *go*.

2279. über Schwyz, *by way of Schwyz*.

2281. denkt's, for **gedenkt's**, i.e. *means to* (intends to) *do it*.

2283 ff. Nennt mir. This reply shows Tell's fearless manhood and indicates some awful purpose concerning Gessler. — **Arth,** a considerable village at the southern end of Lake Zug. The fisherman knows a *shorter*, safer route along the west shore of Lake Lowerz,

whereas Gessler intended going along the east shore, via Schwyz,
Steinen to Arth and Küssnacht.   See map.

2295. **Schwäher,** i.e. Walther Fürst.

2301. **zur Rede kommen,** more commonly **zur Sprache kommen,**
be told.   Just like the Tell of 419, 445 f.   Lines 2283, 2299 ff. seem
to indicate that his plan to kill Gessler has already been formed.

The despair of the whole Swiss *people* over Tell's fate is skilfully expressed in the words of the fisherman.   Despite the Rütli
meeting, there seems no hope now.   But this situation is relieved
by Tell's remarkable escape; the purposely retarded action (cf. end
of III, 3) can go on again; the end is awaited with ever increasing
interest and expectancy.

ACT IV.   SCENE 2.

After the scene of the apple-shot, when Tell had been led away,
Fürst, Stauffacher, and Melchthal hasten to near-by Attinghausen
(village, cf. II, 1; see map), we may suppose, in response to the
news that the Freiherr is dying (cf. 2116); Tell's boy naturally
goes with his grandfather; Hedwig has heard the news and her
presence explains itself.   The scene passes at the same time as the
preceding.

2304 f. **vorbei** ('past'), *all over.* — **hinüber** (lit. 'across'), *he is
gone.* — **die Feder,** a down-feather, laid upon the lips to show
whether the breath has ceased.

2314 f. **mir,** (in both lines) good examples of the common ethical
dat. which often admits of no adequate translation.

2320.   Cf. 1921, note.

2326. **ich seh'** (i.e. present for vivid future, *shall see*) ... **gebun=
den,** she either imagines this or has heard an exaggerated report.

2332. **setzen,** for **setzen ... ein,** *to stake.*   She means that Tell *in
his blind excitement* has staked the child's head and the mother's
heart upon his shot, just as in a game of chance all is staked on a
card or a throw of the dice.   So far, the *mother heart* runs away
with her head; her thought is only for her boy and she does Tell
gross injustice, forgetting (if she had heard it) that his own and
the boy's life depended on the shot.

2336.* **großen,** i.e. with a look of surprise and reproach. Reminded of Tell's own suffering (2334 ff.), it is from now on the *wife* that speaks.

2337. **du,** full of effective reproach, thus said to a stranger. It is not strange that she knew what happened in Altorf; such news spreads rapidly.

2354. **vor,** *from.*

2356. **erkrankte,** pret. subj. (exclamatory). *Oh! if he should get sick!*

2358. **die Alpenrose** is really not a rose, but a kind of rhododendron, thriving only in high altitudes, close to the snow line.

2361. **Balsam=strom,** etc., *refreshing breezes.*

2371. **rettete,** pret. subj. (potential), *could have saved.*

2374 f. **den Junker** (cf. Eng. 'younker,' 'youngster'), name given to young noblemen; Rudenz, of course, is meant. — **gesendet (worden),** *he has been sent for.*

2383. He means that ability to feel pain is a sign of life; now that all pain *has left* him, death is near.

2397. He naturally thinks that only the nobles can do this.

2401. **Es wird,** etc., *action will be taken* (impersonal).

2415. **wenn es gilt,** i.e. when the time comes for actual struggle. Cf. 1921, 1990, 2103, notes.

2420. **unserer** (for **unser,** gen. with **bedarf**), i.e. the nobles.

2422 f. **Es,** etc., perfectly general; *there will be life* (new life) *after us.* — **Das Herrliche,** etc., i.e. liberty. — **Andre Kräfte,** i.e. other than the nobles, namely the people.

2424 f. A reference to Walther Tell as type of the younger generation, of the citizen class, that is to free the country. The dying Baron no doubt heard of the apple-shot from those who told him of the changed attitude of Rudenz. Cf. 2464 f. Contrast this passage with the pessimism of 944–59.

2431 ff. The Baron speaks of political and social tendencies already current — the greater importance of the towns and of the citizen class, the removal of the nobility to the cities (2431 f.). — **Ücht** ('morning-gray') **land,** lit. 'twilight (i.e. foggy) land'; the district between the Bernese Alps and the Jura; it was once full of fog-covered swamps, later reclaimed. **Bern** and **Freiburg** were its

chief towns. — **Thur=gau** (lit. 'district of the Thur'), then much
larger than the present canton, included nearly all of northeastern
Switzerland. **Zürich**, its chief town, was very important commer-
cially, hence **die rege. — waffnet** (2436), against Austria in the
years 1345, 1351, 1352. — **Es bricht**, i.e. in several fruitless attacks
by the Habsburgs, especially by Albrecht II., in 1351–52.

2439 ff. After the retrospect comes the prophecy for the future—
results of wars with the Austrians and Burgundians. Important
battles were Morgarten (in 1315), Laupen (in 1339), Sempach (in
1386), Näfels (in 1388).

2443 ff. mancher Paß, Morgarten (see map) and Näfels, directly
east of Morgarten, below Lake Zürich. — **Der Landmann.** Reference to Arnold von Winkelried's heroic death in the battle of
Sempach. Legend says that he made an opening for his comrades
by seizing as many as he could of the enemy's lances and forcing
them into his own breast.

2451. So that the different members may come together
quickly. — **Entseelt,** *in death.*

2453.* **hin,** i.e. towards the body.

2455. i.e. because it has another owner, Rudenz.

2460. Da, *while.*

2462 f. The liberation of the Cantons. — **dahin=scheiden** = *part,*
i.e. *die.*

2478 f. Vater, said to Fürst; **die Eurige,** to Stauffacher.

2483. (als) **nichts geachtet** = *verachtet.*

2484. *what shall we (one) expect of (from) you.* **sich versehen** with
gen. of the thing (**wessen**) means 'to look confidently for,' 'expect,'
sich zu jemandem versehen, 'to look to some one for,' 'expect of.'
Melchthal had good reason to hesitate. Cf. Rudenz's attitude in
his interview with Attinghausen, II, 1.

2485. denket, for prose **gedenket,** or **denket + an + acc.**

2489. Ein Mannes=wort, *a (true) man's pledge.* — **Stand,** i.e.
rank or class in the community.

2500. Dann . . . vergleichen, *then we will adjust* (lit. 'compare')
our differences (**es**).

2513. ward, *has become.*

2528 f. hätte, subj. in rhetorical question implies 'do you mean

to say that,' etc. — **bie freie Ebte,** Bertha was an Ebel-fräulein, also
Ritter-fräulein (936, note, 939). — **ber Tyrann** (also **ber Wütenbe,**
2533) is, of course, Gessler, who, enraged at Bertha's defense of
Tell (1923 ff.), has had her secretly carried away from her home (in
some castle in the Waldstätte, cf. 1660) and imprisoned.

2534. **Welcher Gewalt,** etc., *what criminal force they* (Gessler's
minions) *will make bold to use.* (Cf. 940 ff. 1668–73 explains
Banb.)

2542. **nichts Festes . . . erfassen,** *get hold of nothing definite.*

2544. **Unter,** *from under.*

2547. **Ob,** etc., for (um zu versuchen) ob, *to see if we,* etc.

2552. Under the changed conditions his Rütli oath no longer
binds him to delay.

2553. **ber . . . könnte,** remarkable subj. with relative, expressing
possibility; (*so cowardly*) *that he could,* or *so cowardly as to,* etc.

2555. Cf. 748, note, 1422 f.

2559. A remarkable example of poetic word-order. Fürst and
Stauffacher, not opposing Rudenz and Melchthal, seem to feel that
the Rütli oath would not be violated by immediate action.

The scene gives Tell time for the journey begun 2294, and relates
development among the Eidgenossen meanwhile. If Tell's mind is
made up, Rudenz, too, awakens to his new responsibility after his
uncle's death; he has felt the tyrant's hand and is roused to the
fighting point. Prince and peasant (Melchthal) have joined hands.
From two sides, individual (Tell) and general (Rudenz and confederates), the blow is impending which shall set the Schwitzer
free. The grand old patriarch, Attinghausen, though he has never
suffered as the rest, gives their cause his dying blessing. The
scene again unites all three of the plots.   How?

ACT IV.   SCENE 3.

* This scene connects directly with IV, 1 (2300 ff.); during
Scene 2 Tell has come to the end of his journey from the lake; we
find him later in the afternoon of the same day. The **Hohle Gasse,**
hollow way (sunken road), then a deep, narrow road betwen over-
hanging rocks and trees, has been filled up by a good modern

turn-pike. The place, half a mile from Immensee, is marked by another Tell chapel (see map).

2568. **Uhr** (= Sand-Uhr) . . . **abgelaufen,** reference to the running sand in the hour-glass; *thy hour has come.*

2572 ff. **heraus-geschreckt,** *aroused from.* — **Milch der frommen Denkart** (cf. Eng. 'milk of human kindness'), i.e. Gessler had filled his peaceful nature with rankling poison (of hatred, revenge).

2575. **zum,** for usual an + acc.

2584 f. **ohnmächtig** (lit. 'powerless,' here *vainly*) **flehend,** etc., *as I writhed in vain entreaty before thee.* — **Damals** takes up again the **Da** in 2580.

2590. Tell thus has two grounds for his action — natural and necessary defense of his family, upon which he felt Gessler would soon wreak vengeance for his escape, and the *sacred obligation* of keeping the oath wrung from him in a moment of agony by Gessler's cruelty. He acts as an individual, not from the motives of the confederates.

2595. **der,** etc. Prose would use the strong adjective without any article.

2596. **Dich jedes Greuels** . . . **erfrechen** (cf. frech, 'bold,' 'impudent'), *to dare* (to do) *unpunished every horrible deed.*

2598. Addressed to the arrow, which he now takes out.

2601. **un-durch-dring-lich,** lit. 'impenetrable' (fig. of arrow and target), *inaccessible to.* — **fromme Bitte,** i.e. the requests of Gessler's subjects.

2604. **Freude Spielen,** i.e. **Freuden-schießen** (2649), shooting matches.

2606. **nur jetzt noch** ('only now still'), *only this once more.*

2609. **keinen zweiten,** possibly literal — the arrow mentioned in 2051 — for he may have left his *quiver* in the boat; but probably he means he will have no second chance at Gessler.

2610. **Auf dieser Bank,** etc., this famous line is often quoted as an instance of Schiller's "bad grammar"; auf with verb of motion takes acc., but **sich setzen** has here the force of Platz nehmen, ausruhen (*rest*), hence, very correctly, the dat.

2612. **treibt sich** . . . **rasch** . . . **vorüber,** *each hurries past the other* (*like a stranger*) *carelessly.*

2616 f. leicht geschürzte, 'lightly girt,' i.e. figuratively, *careless, easy-going;* note the contrast with sorgenvoll; also andächtig — düster — heiter.

2620. führt, etc., i.e. by connecting remote points.

2625. In prose (ohne daß) er euch etwas bracht', *without bringing you something.*

2627 f. Ammonshorn, *ammonite,* a kind of fossil shell, so called because it looks like the ram's horns ascribed to Jupiter Ammon. — war's, *either it was ... or.* — Wie es, *such as.*

2637. Läßt sich's (usually with doch) ... verdrießen (lit. 'vex'), *does not let it weary him.* Inverted for emphasis, not conditional.

2641 f. This story that hunters cut open the ball of the foot and *glue themselves* to the steep rocks with the congealing blood is taken from Scheuchzer and not from actual life. — Grat(lit. 'ridge,' 'crag')tier, a kind of chamois, living only on the highest crags; it is red-brown in color and much smaller than the ordinary chamois (Waldtier) which lives on the wooded slopes.

2650. das Beste (name given to the victor's prize in a shooting match), *the best prize* (cf. 2643–44).

Tell's shot must be justified as righteous self-defence, lest it appear as murder. Nor must it be the work of sudden anger, hence in a *monologue* he shows us his inmost heart, as he calmly arraigns his purpose before the bar of his own conscience and deliberately decides that he may and must kill the tyrant to protect his home and his life.

* Hoch=zeit, 'wedding,' here, of course, *wedding party.* The poetic force of the often pointed (2658, 2663, 2804) contrast between the *wedding* and Gessler's *death* is very strong. The wedding-party is also used to secure the necessary separation of Gessler from his retinue (2778) and to explain the very dramatic presence of the people at the tyrant's death. — gelehnt, *leaning,* etc., cf. 2263, note.

2652 ff. Kloster=mei'r, name given to the overseer of monastery farm-work and property; cf. 1073, note. — Mörlischachen, on the lake near Küssnacht. — Braut=lauf hält, *is getting married.* Braut=lauf (lit. 'bridal-race'), because in old German weddings a race for the bride was actually run; the word, outliving the custom, has become synonymous with Hochzeit. — **Senten,** allied with Senne (15), a small *herd* of cattle (generally over 20) tended by a Senn in the high Alps. — **zu Imisee,** *from* (lit. 'at') *Imisee,* same as Immensee (see map). — (Es) **wird . . . geschwelgt** (general), *there will be revelling.*

2660 f. nehmt mit, etc., *take whatever comes,* i.e. whatever *pleasure* comes (along with other things). — **leicht ergreifen,** *be quick to take.*

2662. wird gefreit (impersonal and general, as in 2656), *here they're marrying,* etc.

2663. Stüssi does not understand such mysterious references, the reader does — this serves to heighten the dramatic effect.

2665 ff. Ein Ruffi, etc., *There's been a landslide in Glarus.* **Ruffi** (also Rufi, Rüfi, etc.), Swiss name for the often very dangerous landslides occurring mainly in spring. — **Glärnisch,** a cluster of peaks rising 10,000 feet above Glarus, capital of canton Glarus, east of Schwyz.

2670. Da, etc., *For instance, I met* (*spoke with*) *a man.* — **Baden** (cf. Stein zu Baden, 2966), a small town on the Limmat, northwest of Zürich in Aargau; Emperor Albrecht had a castle there.

2677. Man deutet's auf, etc. (lit. 'point it to'), *they say it means,* etc.; cf. note on denken auf, 614. Very natural among these semi-superstitious peasants.

2684.* Höhe, i.e. the top of the hill over which he is restlessly expecting Gessler to appear.

2685 f. Gehabt, from gehaben (cf. 943, note). — **Das thu' ich** is splendidly dramatic.

2691 f. der Strom, the Muotta (see map). — **Sucht an . . . ihn** (cf. Gesuch an jemanden richten, which explains the unusual **an** + acc. here), i.e. *have you some request to make of him?*

2698.* nach der vordern Scene, *to the front of the stage.*

2703 f. mein Leb-tag (for meinen Lebtag or meine Leb-tage; cf. Eng. coll. 'all the days of my life'), *as long as I live.* — **Muß voraus,** *must go on ahead;* idiom — there is no infinitive 'understood.'

2707 f. Wär'n, condition; wär's, conclusion; *would have gone to the bottom* (**In Grund**) *with all on board* (**mit Mann und Maus**), cf. 331, note. — **Dem** (emphatic) **Volk,** *such people.* — **bei** (**kommen**), 'get at,' i.e. *hurt.*

2709. wo kam . . . hin, *where has . . . gone.*

2713 f. ihm (i.e. **Volk**) **sanft thun,** *deal gently with.* — **der Streit,** *the question.*

2716. bring' . . . an, *bring up,* i.e. state her request.

2721. Mir, ethical dat., not indirect obj.

2727 f. Die (demonst.), *these.* — **im Werk und Werden,** *planned and in progress.*

2730. Vater . . . begonnen, i.e. what Rudolph of Habsburg, Emperor from 1273 to 1291, had done by establishing the supremacy of the House of Austria. — **Sohn,** Albrecht. — **will** (also 2729), *intends to.*

2732. So oder so, 'one way or another,' *whether or no.*

2736. Waisen, now *orphans,* here in older sense of fatherless (as here, since the father was in prison) or motherless children.

2739. Wild=heu=er, *wild hayer;* poor peasants, with no pastures of their own, who cut "free" (unclaimed) grass on almost inaccessible heights, cf. 2740 ff. — **Rigi=berge,** the Rigi near by.

2740. überm . . . weg, *from over.*

2745. Was . . . auch Schweres, *whatever crime.*

2747. Euch . . . werden, cf. 149, note.

2751. den Mann, *my husband.* — **In** (*into*) **den sechsten Mond** (= **Monat**), *going on six months.*

2756. so . . . so, *as . . . so.*

2758. Schafft, etc., *Get this . . . out of my sight.*

2763. nichts (emphatic **nicht**) **nach . . . fragen,** *care nothing for.*

2770. Tratest . . . doch (very emphatic order), *Well! you have long since,* etc.

2775. *Somebody get her away from here.*

2781. wie es (**sein**) **soll.**

2786. Ich will — Gott sei mir gnädig. Gessler's cruelty reaches its climax in terrible threats for the future; with fine dramatic effect the poet chooses this the best of all opportunities to cut him down; just as he has unfolded his tyrannical plans and laid bare his cruel heart, the arrow cuts short his vow to crush this people, if he cannot break their spirit; his last act of cruelty —

riding down a helpless mother and her children (invented for this very purpose) — so vividly recalls his past villainy and so righteously enrages the reader that Tell's deed appears as just retribution, the defense of his home and loved ones, not as murder.

* fährt mit . . . Hand, *puts his hand.*

2794 ff. Tell came to kill the enemy of his own home, but after hearing Gessler's declarations and seeing his treatment of Armgard and her children he realizes that he has struck down not only his own (individual) enemy, but also the enemy of his country, the oppressor of innocence everywhere.

2798.* geht fort, *continues.*

2804. Rast, not in sense of 'rage,' but 'to be mad.'

2810 ff. tritt . . . an, *lays hold of* (lit. 'approaches'). — **gebrochen,** cf. 866, note. — **Seht Kinder.** The manner of the elders and the contrast between these innocent children and the dying tyrant are intensely dramatic; so also the contrast in 2804.

2815. Leget Hand an, *Take hold.* — **Steht . . . bei,** *help.*

2818. Wagt es, *Just dare it!* The moment the tyrant is gone the peasants change their tone.

2831. (Es) ist . . . zu vertrauen, *there is no faith to be put.* — **Treu'** (dat.), *fidelity.*

* Barmherzige Brüder. The order of the Brothers of Mercy was established in 1540 by Juan di Dio (also called Juan Ciudad) in Seville; Schiller probably thought it much older. Their dress was black, hence Stüssi's rude reference to them as *ravens* around a corpse.

2836 ff. Es stürzt ihn (fig. of runner), *he is overthrown;* **es reißt . . . fort,** *he is hurried away.* — **stehen** (for treten, sich stellen), implying motion towards, hence acc. **seinen.** This chorus, after the manner of that in Greek tragedy, which Schiller had imitated the year before in the Braut von Messina, is a very solemn and impressive close to the scene.

The expected catastrophe comes; the individual blow (Scene 2, end) has been struck. Swiss freedom is half achieved (Rudenz' expedition being still in doubt). The scene, one of the finest Schiller ever wrote, is worthy of the events it describes. Not only are the beginning and end, the monologue and the chorus very impressive, but the many striking contrasts — Tell and Stüssi, der ernſte Gaſt — das Hochzeitshaus, 2658, the Mord and Muſif, 2804, the innocent children and the dying tyrant, 2812, etc., are also very effective.

ACT V. SCENE I.

The scene is again laid in Altorf, before Zwing Uri (I, 3); Tschudi gives the time as the morning after Gessler's death, yet it must be a day or two later. After 2086* Bertha is sent to Sarnen; a little later Rudenz and Melchthal start to capture the castles; Rossberg was taken the night before Sarnen fell (2874—76); there must also be time enough for the news of Gessler's death to reach Altorf (2856, 2930), and for Tell, Rudenz, Melchthal, and Bertha to get back.

2841. **Die Burgen,** Rossberg and Sarnen.

2846. **Joch,** i.e. Zwing Uri, cf. 371.

2848. **Stier von Uri,** *Bull of Uri.* The name Uri is thought to be derived from Ur = *auer-ox;* Uri's coat-of-arms showed the bull's head, and in battle her troops carried an enormous bull's horn (1092), which was borne and blown by one called der Stier von Uri.

2849. **Hoch=wacht,** a high *signal-point,* different from 1442.

2853—56. Very characteristic of the old, over-cautious Fürst.

2858. *Have we not enough in these,* etc.

2865. **im Lauf,** (lit. 'on its course'), i.e. *they have begun.*

2867. **gebrochen,** *stormed, destroyed.*

2869. **Lande** (and **Land** 2872), the three Forest Cantons.

2877. **Schloß,** Sarnen.

2880 f. **Geßler's Bub** (= Knappe), i.e. his *servant,* no doubt one of several who had brought Bertha here. Cf. 2528, note; 2883. — **Bruneck=er=in,** lit. 'the lady of Bruneck'; note fem. ending =in and cf. 281 f., note.

2884. **erhub,** for usual erhob, from erheben.

2888 f. **Da galt** (cf. 1921, 1990, notes), *That was the time for.* — **Edelmann,** i.e. feudal lord.

2890 ff. **hätten . . . geliebt,** i.e. would have hesitated and taken no risk. — **ſetzten . . . getroſt . . . dran,** *cheerfully risked.*

2903. **Über den** (acc. of implied motion) **Brünig(=paß),** see map;

it is allied to Bruneck, Bertha's family name. Cf. 1194, note. The chroniclers say he was allowed to go north, towards Luzern.

2906. Nach jagt' (*rushed, flew*), vivid poetic word-order. The passage shows splendid magnanimity and self-control.

2911. Ur-fehbe, an oath not to avenge injury suffered, i.e. oath to keep the peace; *a solemn oath.*

2923. der Freiheit . . . Zeichen, as it always, from ancient times, has been. We still speak of the "cap of Liberty."

2927 ff. Not complete because their ultimate enemy, the Habsburg Emperor, may interfere. Act V must remove this danger and assure us that their independence is complete and permanent.

2947. Bruck (also **Brugg**), a small town on the Aar, near the mouth of the Reuss, some 20 miles from Zürich.

2949. Schiller intends this as a tribute to his friend, the great Swiss historian, Johannes von Müller, a native of Schaffhausen (lived 1752–1809), whose personal letters and "History of Switzerland" were a great assistance in writing the play.

2952 f. Duke Johann was the son of Rudolph, Albrecht's brother, and is the same as Herzog Hans of 1338 ff. The murder was really done on May 1, 1308.

2954 f. des Vater-mords, here for Verwandten-mord. Cf. Lat. *parricidium,* meaning the murder of any near relative; hence the name Johann Parricida (3165). — **das väterliche Erbe,** Konrad Hunn speaks of fein Mütterliches, 1344, note. Tschudi mentions both.

2957 ff. Es hieß, *it was rumored; they said.* — **darum . . . kürzen,** (*cut off from*), *deprive of.* — **abzufinden** (cf. Eng. 'pay off'), *put off with,* etc. — **Wie dem . . . sei,** *Be that as it may.*

2966 ff. Stein zu Baden, name of Albrecht's castle. Cf. 2670, note. Stein is very common in such castle names; cf. Rhein-stein, Königs-stein. — **Gen** (for Gegen, *towards*) **Rheinfeld**(-en), cf. 1324 f., note. — **Hans** (Johann von Schwaben, 2953), Albrecht's nephew; **Leopold,** Albrecht's son.

2975. alte . . . Stadt, the old Roman (hence **Heiden**) town of Vindonissa (modern Windisch), a border fortress against the Germans and one of the capitals of Helvetia, but destroyed in 594 by Childebert II., Emperor of the Franks.

2977 f. $\mathfrak{Habsburg}$, shortened from $\mathfrak{Habichts}$(hawk's)$\mathfrak{burg}$, the old home of the Habsburgs, the Austrian Royal Family. — $\mathfrak{Wo}$ ($= \mathfrak{von\ wo}$), *whence.*

2983. $\mathfrak{den\ Seinen} =$ his own kin. — $\mathfrak{dem\ Seinen}$, his own territory.

2989. $\mathfrak{frühes}$, *untimely;* he was 58 years old.

2993. $\mathfrak{Stand}$ (i.e. $\mathfrak{Reichs\text{-}stand}$, *Estate*, division of the Empire). A $\mathfrak{Stand}$ might be a duchy, bishopric, county, canton, or even a single city (cf. $\mathfrak{Reichs\text{-}stadt}$).

2997 f. $\mathfrak{des\ Bannes}$, i.e. the ban of outlawry. — $\mathfrak{Der\ Ungarn}$ $\mathfrak{Königin}$, Agnes was Albrecht's oldest daughter and, since 1301, widow of Andreas III. of Hungary.

3001 ff. The chroniclers tell many stories of her cruel revenge; that the castles of the murderers were destroyed and hundreds of men, women, and children ($\mathfrak{ganze\ Zeugungen}$, *whole generations*) killed.   Modern history gives her a better character. — $\mathfrak{in\ Maientau}$, Bullinger says that after having had 63 men beheaded, she walked about in their blood, saying she was "bathing in May dew."

3010. $\mathfrak{um\ .\ .\ .\ sehen}$, *to see* (*and never saw*).

3013. $\mathfrak{sich}$ (dat.) $\mathfrak{selbst}$, etc., *it is its own fearful food.*   Cf. Shakespeare's: 'doth make the meat it feeds upon.'

3019. Their liberty is now secure.

3023 f. In Nov. 1308 the Electors did assert their independence of Habsburg by choosing Henry of Luxemburg as Emperor; he reigned, as Henry VII., 1308–1313. — $\mathfrak{was}$, i.e. anything about the probable successor of Albrecht.

3025 ff. $\mathfrak{mehrsten}$ (now vulg.) for $\mathfrak{meisten}$. — $\mathfrak{Ist\ zu\ hoffen\ auf}$ (future, 614, note), *there is hope of.*   Henry did confirm (in 1309) the old (Friedrich II.) charters of Uri and Schwyz and granted one of the same kind to Unterwalden.   This made them the feudal vassals of the Empire, not the private property of any princely House.

3034. $\mathfrak{Elsbeth}$, for $\mathfrak{Elisabeth}$, widow of Albrecht. — $\mathfrak{alles\ Gutes}$, for $\mathfrak{alles\ Gute}$.

3037. $\mathfrak{Worein}$, 'in(to) which,' cf. Eng. *where-in.*

3042 f. Cf. 2484, note.   The usual gen. is replaced by $\mathfrak{Daß\ es}$, etc. — $\mathfrak{Abscheu\ vor}$.   Cf. 'aversion *for*.'

3052. **Bater,** i.e. Rudolf of Habsburg, Emperor 1273–1291.

3058. Cf. 1327 ff. *Did he even deign to.*

3063 ff. **rührte . . . an,** conditional subjunc. for **würde angerührt haben. — konnte sein,** *could have been.* Note the emphatic indic.

3068. **Die** (diejenigen, die) **er gemehrt,** *those whom he has aggrandized.*

3074. **will . . . nicht gebühren,** very emphatic, *is by no means our duty.* (Buchheim.)

3075. **will,** *must.*

3077. **nichts weiter,** i.e. no further obligation.

3078–80. **Und . . . So,** *and if . . . still* (at the same time).

3081 f. **eben diesem,** *this very same.* — **Thränen,** i.e. of sympathy.

The other attack (Rudenz-Melchthal, noble and peasant now united) upon the tyrants has also been successful (cf. IV, 2, end), the triumph of liberty is complete and permanent. All danger is over, now that the tyrants' castles are destroyed; nor is revenge from without to be feared, for their ultimate enemy, the Emperor, is dead, and another, more kindly disposed, will rule in his stead. The three plots are united in Stauffacher's grateful thought of Tell.

ACT V. SCENE 2.

* **Hausflur,** usually 'hall,' 'entry,' here *room,* serving as living-room, dining-room, kitchen combined. Picture, p. 172.

* **zeigt in's Freie,** lit. 'points into the free' (air), i.e. *affords a view out doors.* The scene is the same as in III, 1; time same as in V, 1.

3088. **Und alles** (ist frei), *and everybody is free.*

3093. **Ging . . . hart vorbei** (hart rare for nahe or dicht, cf. Eng. 'hard by'), lit. 'passed hard by my life,' i.e. *came very near hitting me.*

3104.* **mit zer=störten Zügen,** *with haggard, wild look.* **zer=stört,** generally 'ruined,' here for ver=stört, 'troubled.'

3109. **Herr,** for modern **Mann** or **Gatte,** *husband.*

3110. **was ist Euch,** *what is the matter with you.* At once her woman's instinct tells her something is wrong.

3113. **Wie auch,** *however much.*

3117 f. A very ancient and classic invocation of hospitality.

3125. **schnürt** (lit. 'lace up,' hence 'compress') **mir das Innre zu,** *your look* (*oppresses my heart*) *frightens me.* Hedwig's gradually increasing fear, prompted by her intuition alone, is well portrayed.

* **hält sich an,** *takes hold of something to support herself.*

3139. Quite a common custom in classic as well as mediæval times, though there is no basis, not even in legend, for the statement here.

3145. **frei,** i.e. with a clear conscience. Gives Tell's own view of his deed. Compare his consciousness of innocence with Parricida's manner.

3159. **Ihr wäret.** The subj., following indic. **seid** (3156), powerfully expresses Tell's horror; he can hardly believe what he hears; *You are . . .* (*can it be that*) *you are?*

3162 f. **wohnen,** for **weilen,** *stay.* — **Herzog von Österreich,** another name for the same Herzog Johann von Schwaben of 2953, called in history Johannes Parricida (cf. 2954, note).

3171. Tell's angry contempt makes him say **du.**

3176 ff. This passage embodies the real purpose of this scene — to so contrast the deed of Parricida with that of Tell, as to make the one appear murder, the other self-defense, thus fully vindicating Tell.

3184. **Nichts teil',** etc., *I have nothing in common with you.*

3192 f. **so jung,** he was 18 years old. — **Enkel Rudolphs,** i.e. his father, Rudolph, was son of Rudolph of Habsburg, who, unlike Albrecht, was much esteemed in the Forest Cantons.

3195. **Des armen Mannes,** expands **meiner,** *a poor man like me.*

3198 f. **konnte werden,** for **hätte werden können.** — **bezwang,** for **bezwungen hätte.** These indicatives lend intense dramatic emphasis.

3201. **Vetter Leopold,** Albrecht's second son, later defeated at Morgarten.

3210. According to Weiss all were executed but Walther von Eschenbach, who escaped to Würtemberg and became a herdsman, and Parricida himself, who, after having found refuge in a monastery in Pisa, was condemned to life-imprisonment by Henry VII.

3213. Tschudi's expression; *i.e.* his friends were forbidden to shelter him, his enemies allowed to kill him. **erlaubt (bift).**

3217. Eignes Schrecknis, *a terror to myself.*

3218. vor mir felbft ('from myself'), *at the sight of myself.*

3223. Mensch der Sünde, *sinful* (in general sense) *mortal.*

3230. entdeckt, shortened condition, *if*, etc.

3244 f. wildes (generally **wilden**) **Laufes,** adv. gen., *in wild course.* — **Seh',** *Am I to see.* Cf. 2970.

3253 ff. This **Schreckens=ftraße** runs along the steep bank of the Reuss through the wild gorge of Schöllenen, from Göschenen to the Devil's Bridge (**die Brücke, welche ftäubet,** *the spray-covered bridge;* cf. **Staubbach,** III, 2, introductory note); this latter (since 1830 a new granite structure) was once a slight hanging chain-bridge spanning the Reuss, where it dashes over the rocks around the **Teufels=ftein,** covering the bridge with spray. Avalanches (**Win= des=wehen,** lit. *drifts* forced along by wind) from the icy summits above (**Joch,** lit. 'yoke,' 'mountain-ridge') are very common and dangerous along this road.

3259. reißt . . . sich auf ('tears itself open'), *i.e. opens suddenly.* This *rocky gateway* is the so-called **Urner Loch,** once a narrow cleft, since 1707 quite a wide tunnel, over 200 feet long.

3261 f. This *bright vale of joy* is the **Urferenthal;** its open, green pastures are in marked contrast to the gloomy gorges just described. — **schnellen Schrittes,** adv. gen., *with quick steps.*

3265. Deines Reiches Boden, Canton Tessin and Italy, part of the Holy Roman Empire. Cf 266, note.

3267. Seen, seven small lakes of unchanging depth (**ew'gen**) on the Gotthard Pass, fed by the snows on the high Alps.

3270 f. muntern Laufs, cf. the *strong* form of the adj. 3244. — **ein andrer Strom,** the Tessin, or Ticino, which, like the Reuss, has its source in the lakes just mentioned. — **Euch** (dat., *for you*) **das gelobte,** *the Promised Land*, i.e. of rest and peace; cf. Bible term **Das gelobte Land** = the "Holy Land."

The drama closes as it began with fine descriptions of nature; here its rugged grandeur, there (Act I, 1) its exquisite beauty; it is indeed remarkable that Schiller who was never in Switzerland can describe the scenery and localities so vividly and accurately.

3281.* **bedeutet ihn**, *makes a sign to him.* — **kommen ... gezogen**, *come marching.*

3286. **mein Recht**, *my cause.*

3291. **Knechte**, i.e. **Sassen**, 1209, note, **eigne Leute**, 1081, note,
1143. Appropriate ending for this drama of freedom.

The scene has the purpose of still further justifying the deed of
Tell, by comparing it with Parricida's. The murder of the emperor is all the more vivid in the murderer's presence.   Tell vindi-
cates himself to others as he had already done to himself (2561 ff.).
Again the three plots are united — by different roads all three
have led to their goal in this bright picture of liberty, union,
fraternity.

FAMILIAR QUOTATIONS.

1. Das Tier hat auch Vernunft. (Werni, 57.)
2. Greif' an mit Gott! Dem Nächsten muß man helfen.
   Es kann uns allen Gleiches ja begegnen. (Kuoni, 107 f.)
3. Wo's not thut, läßt sich alles wagen. (Tell, 136.)
4. Der brave Mann denkt an sich selbst zuletzt. (Tell, 139.)
5. Vom sichern Port läßt sich's gemächlich raten. (Ruodi, 141.)
6. Mit eitler Rede wird hier nichts geschafft. (Tell, 148.)
7. Ich hab' gethan was ich nicht lassen konnte. (Tell, 160.)
8. Der kluge Mann baut vor. (Gertrud, 274.)
9. Dem Mutigen hilft Gott. (Gertrud, 313.)
10. Ertragen muß man, was der Himmel sendet;
    Unbilliges erträgt kein edles Herz. (Gertrud, 316 f.)
11. Wüßt' ich mein Herz an zeitlich Gut gefesselt,
    Den Brand wärf' ich hinein mit eigner Hand. (Gertrud, 320 f.)
12.   Es schont der Krieg
    Auch nicht das zarte Kindlein in der Wiege. (Stauffacher, 322 f.)
13. Die Unschuld hat im Himmel einen Freund. (Gertrud, 324.)
14. Die letzte Wahl steht auch dem Schwächsten offen. (Gertrud, 328.)
15. Was Hände bauten, können Hände stürzen. (Tell, 388.)
16. Das schwere Herz wird nicht durch Worte leicht. (Tell, 419.)
    Doch können Worte uns zu Thaten führen. (Stauffacher, 420.)
17. Die schnellen Herrscher sind's, die kurz regieren. (Tell, 423.)
18. Ein jeder lebe still bei sich daheim;
    Dem Friedlichen gewährt man gern den Frieden. (Tell, 428 f.)
19. Die Schlange sticht nicht ungereizt. (Tell, 430.)
20. Beim Schiffbruch hilft der Einzelne sich leichter. (Tell, 434.)
21. Ein jeder zählt nur sicher auf sich selbst. (Tell, 436.)
22. Verbunden werden auch die Schwachen mächtig. (Stauffacher, 437.)
23. Der Starke ist am mächtigsten allein. (Tell, 438.)

24. Wie soll die rasche Jugend sich bezähmen! (Fürst, 485.)

25. Die Gerichte Gottes sind gerecht! (Fürst, 553.)

26. O eine edle Himmelsgabe ist
Das Licht des Auges — Alle Wesen leben
Vom Lichte, jedes glückliche Geschöpf —
Die Pflanze selbst kehrt freudig sich zum Lichte. (Melchthal, 590 ff.)

27. O, mächtig ist der Trieb des Vaterlands. (Attinghausen, 849.)

28. O, lerne fühlen, welches Stamms du bist!
Wirf nicht für eitlen Glanz und Flitterschein
Die echte Perle deines Wertes hin. (Attinghausen, 915 ff.)

29. Ans Vaterland, ans teure, schließ' dich an,
Das halte fest mit deinem ganzen Herzen!
Hier sind die starken Wurzeln deiner Kraft;
Dort in der fremden Welt stehst du allein,
Ein schwankes Rohr, das jeder Sturm zerknickt. (Attinghausen, 923 ff.)

30. Das Neue dringt herein mit Macht, das Alte,
Das Würdige scheidet; andre Zeiten kommen,
Es lebt ein anders denkendes Geschlecht. (Attinghausen, 953 ff.)

31.   Es preise sich, wer keinem
Mit seinem Leibe pflichtig ist auf Erden;
Doch Redlichkeit gedeiht in jedem Stande. (Stauffacher, 1084 ff.)

32.   Was die dunkle Nacht gesponnen,
Soll frei und fröhlich an das Licht der Sonnen. (Melchthal, 1107 f.)

33. Gott ist überall, wo man das Recht verwaltet,
Und unter seinem Himmel stehen wir. (Rösselmann, 1115 ff.)

34.   Schrecklich immer,
Auch in gerechter Sache, ist Gewalt.
Gott hilft nur dann, wenn Menschen nicht mehr helfen.
(Reding, 1321 ff.)

35.   Bill'ge Furcht erwecket sich ein Volk,
Das mit dem Schwerte in der Faust sich mäßigt. (Fürst, 1375 f.)

36. Der Eifer auch, der gute, kann verraten. (Rösselmann, 1391.)

37. Man muß dem Augenblick auch was vertrauen. (Reding, 1439.)

38. Wir wollen trauen auf den höchsten Gott
Und uns nicht fürchten vor der Macht der Menschen. (Reding, 1453 f.)

39. Raub begeht am allgemeinen Gut,
Wer selbst sich hilft in seiner eignen Sache. (Stauffacher, 1465 f.)

40. Ein rechter Schütze hilft sich selbst. (Tell, 1480.)

41. Früh übt sich, was ein Meister werden will. (Tell, 1482.)

42.   Wer durch's Leben
Sich frisch will schlagen, muß zu Schutz und Trutz
Gerüstet sein.   (Tell, 1484 ff.)

43. Dann erst genieß' ich meines Lebens recht,
Wenn ich mir's jeden Tag aufs neu' erbeute. (Tell, 1490 f.)

44. Wer frisch umherspäht mit gesunden Sinnen,
Auf Gott vertraut und die gelenke Kraft,
Der ringt sich leicht aus jeder Fahr und Not;
Den schreckt der Berg nicht, der darauf geboren. (Tell, 1510.)

45. Die Axt im Haus erspart den Zimmermann. (Tell, 1515.)

46. Ein jeder wird besteuert nach Vermögen. (Tell, 1525.)

47. Wer gar zu viel bedenkt, wird wenig leisten. (Tell, 1533.)

48. Thue recht und scheue keinen Feind. (Tell, 1545.)

49. Der kann nicht klagen über harten Spruch,
Den man zum Meister seines Schicksals macht. (Geßler, 1935 f.)

50.   Der ist mir der Meister,
Der seiner Kunst gewiß ist überall,
Dem's Herz nicht in die Hand tritt, noch ins Auge. (Geßler, 1941 ff.

51.   Zu weit getrieben,
Verfehlt die Strenge ihres weisen Zwecks,
Und allzustraff gespannt, zerspringt der Bogen. (Rudenz, 1995 ff.)

52.   Man führt die Waffen nicht vergebens.
Gefährlich ist's, ein Mordgewehr zu tragen,
Und auf den Schützen springt der Pfeil zurück. (Geßler, 1973 ff.)

53. Das Alte stürzt, es ändert sich die Zeit,
Und neues Leben blüht aus den Ruinen. (Attinghausen, 2426 f.)

54. Seid einig — einig — einig. (Attinghausen, 2452.)

55. Des Bauern Handschlag ist auch ein Manneswort. (Melchthal, 2488.)

56. Es lebt ein Gott, zu strafen und zu rächen. (Tell, 2597.)

57. Dem Schwachen ist sein Stachel auch gegeben. (Tell, 2676.)

58. Es kann der Frömmste nicht im Frieden bleiben,
Wenn es dem bösen Nachbar nicht gefällt. (Tell, 2683 f.)

59. Das Volk hat aber doch gewisse Rechte. (Rudolph der Harras, 2627.)

60. Rasch tritt der Tod den Menschen an;
Es ist ihm keine Frist gegeben;

Es stürzt ihn mitten in der Bahn,
Es reißt ihn fort vom vollen Leben.
Bereitet oder nicht, zu gehen,
Er muß vor seinen Richter stehen. (Barmherzige Brüder, 2834 ff.)

61. Rache trägt keine Frucht. (Fürst, 3013.)
62. Dem neuen Herrn thun tapfere Freunde not. (Stauffacher, 3028.)
63. Die Liebe will ein freies Opfer sein. (Fürst, 3075.)
64. Wer Thränen ernten will, muß Liebe säen. (Melchthal, 3082.)
65. Das Unglück spricht gewaltig zu dem Herzen. (Hedwig, 3124.)

SUBJECTS FOR SHORT GERMAN PAPERS

1. Das Ufer des Vierwaldstättersees.
2. Die Rettung Konrad Baumgartens.
3. Geßler's Groll auf Stauffacher.
4. Stauffacher und seine Frau.
5. Die Zwingburg in Altorf.
6. Die Blendung des alten Melchthal.
7. Der schweizerische Adel und die Vögte.
8. Attinghausens Liebe zum Vaterlande.
9. Das Rütli.
10. Die Versammlung auf dem Rütli.
11. Arnold vom Melchthal in seiner Heimat (999–1066).
12. Die Einwanderung der Schweizer (1167–1203).
13. Konrad Hunn beim Kaiser (1325–1349).
14. Der Eidschwur auf dem Rütli.
15. Tell in seiner Familie.
16. Die Gefahren einer Gemsenjagd.
17. Tells Zusammentreffen mit Geßler (1549–1571).
18. Bertha von Bruneck, ein schweizerisches Edelfräulein.
19. Der Hut auf der Stange.
20. Tells Gefangennahme.
21. Der Apfelschuß.

2469

VOCABULARY

A

ab, *adv. and sep. pref.,* **off,** down, away.

ab=brechen, brach, gebrochen, bricht, *intr.,* break **off,** stop, cease.

ab=drücken, *tr.* (*lit.* press **off**), let fly (arrow), shoot.

aber, *conj.,* but, however.

ab=fahren, fuhr, gefahren, fährt, *intr.,* ſ., start **off,** set out, leave, set sail.

Ab=fahrt, *f.* -en, departure.

Ab=fall, *m.* -s, "e, defection, desertion.

ab=fallen, fiel, gefallen, fällt, *intr.,* ſ., fall **off,** desert, be faithless to.

ab=finden, fand, gefunden, *tr.,* put **off,** settle with, satisfy.

ab=führen, *tr.,* lead **off** (away), carry away.

ab=gehen, ging, gegangen, *intr.,* ſ., go **off** (away), depart; leave (the stage), exit, exeunt; *pres. part. as noun,* 1585*.

ab=gewinnen, gewann, gewonnen, *tr.,* win from (*dat.*).

Ab=grund, *m.* -s, "e, abyss, gulf, precipice.

ab=holen, *tr.,* fetch, go for, go and get.

ab=laufen, lief, gelaufen, läuft, *intr.,* ſ., run down; Uhr ist abgelaufen, hour has come, 2568.

ab=mähen, *tr.,* mow (cut) **off.**

ab=messen, maß, gemessen, mißt, *tr.,* measure **off,** survey and portion out, 900.

ab=nehmen, nahm, genommen, nimmt, *tr.,* take **off.**

ab=platten, *tr.,* flatten **off** (down); *past part. as adj.,* flat, level, 2254.

Ab=rede, *f.* -n, agreement; — nehmen, take counsel, 414.

ab=reichen, *tr.,* reach.

Ab=scheu, *m.* -s, abhorrence, aversion, detestation.

Ab=schied, *m.* -s, -e, departure, leave; parting, 1496; — nehmen, take leave of, bid farewell to, 3269.

ab=senken, *refl.,* sink, slope, descend.

ab=stoßen, stieß, gestoßen, stößt, (*tr.*) *intr.,* push (shove) **off** (from shore).

Abt, *m.* -es, "e, abbot.

ab=treiben, trieb, getrieben, *tr.,* drive **off;** throw (shake) **off,** 1354.

ab=trotzen, *tr.* (*dat. pers. and acc. thing*), extort from.

251

ab=trünnig, *adj.*, faithless, disloyal (to, von).

ab=wägen, wog, gewogen, *tr.*, weigh, consider well.

ab=warten, *tr.*, wait for, await; *also intr.*, 2516, wait, delay.

ab=wehren, *tr.*, ward off, avert.

ab=weiden, *tr.*, graze over, *past part.* grazed bare, 62.

ab=wenden, *tr.*, *refl.*, turn away, avert (*face*); alienate, 681.

ab=werfen, warf, geworfen, wirft, *tr.*, throw (cast) off.

ach, *interj.*, ah! oh! alas! why!

Acht, *f.* ban of outlawry.

achten, *tr.*, judge, think, consider; esteem, regard, 2483; heed, 2331; *with* auf *intr.*, listen to, heed, 250; pay attention to, 1771 *.

acht=geben, gab, gegeben, giebt, *intr.*, give heed, pay attention to (*with* auf + *acc.*).

acht=zig, *num.*, eighty.

ackern, *tr.*, plough, cultivate.

Adel, *m.* –s, nobility, the nobles.

adel=ig, *adj.*, noble.

Adler, *m.* –s, —, eagle; Imperial Eagle, 885.

Agnes. Oldest daughter of Emperor Albrecht I., widow of Andreas III. of Hungary (died 1301).

Ahn, *m.* –s *or* –en, –en, forefather, ancestor, grandfather.

ahnen, *tr. and intr.* (*impers. with dat.*), forebode, anticipate; *part. as adj.*, prophetic, 1691.

Albrecht, *m.* –s. Albrecht I.

(1250–1308), oldest son of Rudolph of Habsburg; Duke of Austria, Emperor of Germany 1298–1308.

all (–er, –e, –es), *adj. and pron.*, all; each, every, any; alles, everybody, 352 *, 3089, everything, 451.

allein, *adj.*, alone; *adv.*, only; *conj.*, but, however.

aller=wegen, *adv.*, everywhere.

all=gemein, *adj.*, general, common, public.

all=gerecht *adj.*, all righteous, merciful, 582.

all=zu, *adv.*, all too, too.

all=zu=straff, *adv.*, too tight (tense).

Alp, *f.* –en, mountain pasture; peak, 747; *pl.*, the Alps.

Alpen=blume, *f.* –n, Alpine flower.

Alpen=jäger, *m.* –s, —, Alpine hunter.

Alpen=rose, *f.* Alpine rose, 2358, *note.*

Alpen=trift, *f.* –en, Alpine (mountain) pasture.

Alpen=wasser, *n.* –s, —, Alpine stream, torrent.

Alp=horn, *n.* –(e)s, "er, alphorn, herdsman's horn.

als, *conj.*, as, when; (*with comp.*) than; (*with neg.*) but, except, save, cf. 1676; (*in conditional clauses*, als ob), as if. als wie = wie, 973.

als=bald, *adv.*, immediately, directly.

also, *conj.*, so, then, therefore;

adv., so, thus; Nicht —, No indeed! 2381.

alt, *adj.* (älter, ältest), old, ancient; *as m. noun,* old man, 364; *neut.*, the old order of things, 953.

Alter, *n.* -8, —, age, old age.

alt=gewohnt, *part. adj.*, long accustomed.

Alt=land=ammann, *m.* -8, -e *and* ᵘer, old (former, ex-) land-ammann, *i.e.* chief magistrate.

Altorf (also written Alt=dorf = old village). Capital of Uri, south of Lake Lucerne.

Alt=vordern, *m. pl.*, ancestors, forefathers; *for* Vor=fahren.

Alzellen (also Altzellen). Village in Unterwalden.

Alzeller, *indec. adj.* (*of place*) *from* Alzellen, of (from) Alzellen; *as noun, m.* -8, —, man of Alzellen, 718.

Ammann (= Amt=mann), *m.* -(e)8, ᵘer *or* -e, ammann (*Swiss magistrate*).

Ammons=horn, *n.* -(e)8, ᵘer, ammonite (*a fossil shell*).

Amt, *n.* -(e)8, ᵘer, office, duty, business; *idiom.gen.* 368,1840, my (our) duty.

an, *prep.* (*dat. or acc.*), on, by, at, near, to, of, *in many idioms;* an's Reich), to the throne, 193; an + denken = think of; *sep. pref. and adv.*, as to, 446; — Such (*dat.*) = your turn, 1324.

an=befehlen, befahl, befohlen, be=

fiehlt, *tr.* (*dat.* + *acc. or inf.*), direct, command, bid.

An=blick, *m.* -8, -e, sight.

an=blicken, *tr.*, look at, regard.

an=bringen, brachte, gebracht, *tr.*, bring up, mention, 2716.

andächtig, *adj.*, devout, reverent, pious.

ander, *adj.*, another, other, different, next, following.

ändern, *tr.* (*and refl.*), change.

anders, *adv.*, otherwise, differently.

anders=denkend, *part. as adj.*, thinking otherwise, of different opinion.

anders=wo, *adv.*, elsewhere.

An=fang, *m.* -8, ᵘe, beginning.

an=fangen, fing, gefangen, fängt, *intr. and tr.*, begin, commence.

an=fangs, *adv.* (*gen. of* Anfang), at first.

an=fassen, *tr.*, seize, lay hold of.

an=flehen, *tr.*, beseech, entreat, call upon.

an=führen, *tr.*, lead (on), command.

an=füllen, *refl.*, to fill up with, become crowded.

an=geboren, *part. adj.*, inborn, innate, hereditary; natural, 1728.

an=gehen, ging, gegangen, *intr.*, ſ., ascend, rise, 2257.

angenehm, *adj.*, pleasant, agreeable, kind; good, 517.

Anger, *m.* -8, —, field, green, meadow.

an=gesehen, *part. adj.*, reputable, distinguished.

an=geſtammt, *part. adj.*, natural, innate.

an=greifen, griff, gegriffen, *tr.*, lay hold of, grasp; go (set) at (about), undertake, 1910.

Angſt, *f.* ⁔e, anxiety, anguish; — des Todes, mortal terror, 91.

angſt=befreit, *part. adj.*, freed from anxiety.

ängſt=igen, *tr.*, alarm, make uneasy; *refl.*, fret, worry, 1798.

ängſt=lich, *adj.*, anxious.

an=halten, hielt, gehalten, hält, *intr.*, stop; *refl.*, catch hold of something for support, 3126*.

An=höhe, *f.* -n, height, hill.

an=hören, *tr.*, listen to, hear.

Anker, *m.* -s, —, anchor.

an=klagen, *tr.*, accuse; cry to, 3079.

an=klingen, klang, geklungen, *intr.*, sound, strike the ear.

an=kommen, kam, gekommen, *intr.*, ſ., arrive, approach.

an=legen, *tr.*, lay (to) on; Hand —, set to work, 2815, 2860; *intr.*, take aim, 1992*; aim at, 2584.

an=leimen, *refl.*, glue oneself on (fast).

an=liegen, lag, gelegen, *intr.*, lie near, concern, be important to, 709.

an=locken, *tr.*, allure, entice, draw on.

An=mut, *f.*, grace, charm.

an=nehmen, nahm, genommen, nimmt, *tr.*, accept, take.

an=pochen, *intr.*, knock at.

an=rufen, rief, gerufen, *tr.*, call to; call upon, 2096, invoke, 2791.

an=rühren, *tr.*, touch; move (*to sympathy*), 3063.

an=ſagen, *tr.*, speak, say on, tell.

an=ſchließen, ſchloß, geſchloſſen, *refl.*, attach oneself (to, an), join.

an=ſehen, ſah, geſehen, ſieht, *tr.*, look at (on), see, perceive.

an=ſichtig, *adj.* (*with gen.*), with werden, become aware of, catch sight of.

an=ſiedeln, *refl.*, settle.

an=ſinnen, ſann, geſonnen, ask (expect) of, demand of.

an=ſprengen, *intr.*, ſ., ride up, come up at full speed.

An=ſpruch, *m.* -s, ⁔e, claim; in — nehmen, lay claim to.

an=ſteigen, ſtieg, geſtiegen, *intr.*, ſ., rise, ascend.

an=ſtellig, *adj.*, fit, good for (at).

an=ſtemmen, *tr.*, push against; brace oneself, 2263.

An=teil, *m.* -s, -e, part, share, lot.

an=thun, that, gethan, *tr.*, do to, offer; Lieb' —, do kindness (favor), 2291.

Antlitz, *n.* -es, -e, face.

an=treten, trat, getreten, tritt, *tr.*, approach.

Antwort, *f.* -en, answer.

an=wachſen, wuchs, gewachſen, wächſt, *intr.*, ſ., grow on, increase.

an=ziehen, zog, gezogen, *tr.*, draw (put) on; draw, pull, 2581.

An=zug, *m.* -s, *"*e, approach;
im —, approaching, coming,
45, 105, 2107.

an=zünden, *tr.*, set fire to, light,
kindle.

Apfel, *m.* -s, *"*, apple.

Arbeit, *f.* -en, work, labor, task.

arbeiten, *tr. and intr.*, work;
refl. (make) force one's way,
169.

Arbeiter, *m.* -s, —, workman,
laborer.

arg (ärger, ärgst), *adj.*, bad;
superl. as noun, the worst.

Arg=wohn, *m.* -s, suspicion.

arm (ärmer, ärmst), *adj.*, poor;
little, insignificant, 1568; *superl. as noun*, 611.

Arm, *m.* -es, -e, arm.

Armbrust, *f.* *"*e, cross-bow.

arm=selig, *adj.*, poor, wretched,
paltry.

Arm=sessel, *m.* -s, —, arm-chair.

Armut, *f.*, poverty.

Arth. Village on Lake Zug.

Asche, *f.* -n (*very rare*), ashes.

Atem, *m.* -s, breath.

atem=los, *adj.*, breathless, out
of breath.

atmen, *intr.*, breathe.

Attinghaus(en). Village south
of Lake Lucerne, near Altorf.

Attinghäuser, *m.* -s, —, the
Baron of Attinghausen.

auch, *adv. conj.*, also, too, even;
with wer, was, wie, wo, ever;
— nicht, not even, though,
even, 1122; so —, however.

Aue, *f.* -n, grassy plain, field,
meadow.

auf, *prep.* (*dat. or acc.*), upon,
on, to, toward, at, *in many
idioms;* for (title-page); *interj.*,
Up! Away! 2827, 2847; *as
sep. pref. and adv.*, up, up-
ward; open (515).

auf=bauen, *tr.*, build up, erect.

auf=bewahren, *tr.*, keep, preserve, put away.

auf=bieten, bot, geboten, call out,
call to arms.

auf=blühen, *intr.*, s., (begin to)
bloom; *fig.* grow up, 1695.

auf=fahren, fuhr, gefahren, fährt,
intr., s., start up (*in anger or
surprise*).

auf=finden, fand, gefunden, *tr.*,
find out, discover.

auf=fordern, *tr.*, call upon, ask,
summon.

auf=geben, gab, gegeben, giebt,
tr., give up, resign; *part. adj.*,
hopeless, 2220.

auf=gehen, ging, gegangen, *intr.*,
s., go up, rise; open, swell,
515.

auf=halten, hielt, gehalten, hält,
tr., hold up, stop, detain.

auf=hangen, hing, gehangen,
hängt (*pres. now taken from
aufhängen*), *tr.*, hang up, 1869.

auf=heben, hob, gehoben, *tr.*, lift
(take) up, raise.

auf=hören, *intr.*, stop, cease.

auf=lachen, *intr.*, laugh out,
break out laughing.

Auf=lauf, *m.* -s, *"*e, tumult,
uproar.

auf=legen, *tr.*, lay on (upon),
place upon.

auf=löfen, *tr.,* **loosen;** *fig.* dissolve (*bond*), 2829.

auf=merfen, *intr.,* listen (closely), pay attention.

auf=merffam, *adj.,* attentive.

auf=nehmen, nahm, genommen, nimmt, *tr.,* take **up,** receive, harbor; es mit + *dat.* —, cope with, be a match for, 1876.

auf=paffen, *intr.,* watch, look out

auf=pflanzen, *tr.,* set **up.** [for.

auf=raufchen, *intr.,* f., surge **up.**

auf=recht, *adj.,* upright.

auf=reißen, riß, geriffen, *tr.,* tear open; *refl.,* open suddenly, 3259.

auf=richten, *tr.,* raise, set **up;** *refl.,* rise, get **up,** 2309*, 2372*.

auf=rufen, rief, gerufen, *tr.,* call on, summon.

Auf=ruhr, *m.* -s, tumult, riot, rebellion.

auf=rühren, *tr.,* stir **up.**

auf=fchieben, fchob, gefchoben, *tr.,* postpone.

auf=fchlagen, fchlug, gefchlagen, fchlägt, *tr.,* lift **up** (*eyes*), i.e. open.

Auf=fchub, *m.* -s, delay, postponement.

auf=fetzen, *tr.,* (set **up),** lay (put) upon.

auf=fpringen, fprang, gefprungen, *intr.,* f., spring (start) **up.**

Auf=ftand, *m.* -s, "e, (uprising) tumult, commotion.

auf=ftecken, *tr.,* set (put) **up.**

auf=ftehen, ftand, geftanden, *intr.* f., stand (get) **up,** rise.

auf=fteigen, ftieg, geftiegen, *intr.,* f., go **up,** rise, ascend.

auf=tauen, *intr.,* f., thaw.

auf=thun, that, gethan, *tr.,* open; *refl.,* disclose (present) itself, 2252.

auf=treten, trat, getreten, tritt, *intr.,* f., enter, appear (*on stage*).

auf=wecken, *tr.,* wake **up,** rouse.

Auf=zug, *m.* -s, "e, act (*from drawing up curtain*).

auf=zwingen, zwang, gezwungen, *tr., dat.* + *acc.,* force up**on.**

Auge, *n.* -es, -en, eye.

Augen=blick, *m.* -s, -e, moment.

augen=blicks, *gen. as adv.,* at once.

augen=los, *adj.,* (eyeless), sightless.

aus, *prep. with dat.,* out of, of, by, from, through = on account of; *adv. and sep. pref.,* out, over, past.

aus=breiten, *tr.,* spread, (stretch) out.

auseinander=fliehen, floh, geflohen, *intr.,* f., flee apart, separate (*in flight*).

auseinander=gehen, ging, gegangen, *intr.,* f., separate, disperse.

auseinander=treiben, trieb, getrieben, *tr.,* drive apart, scatter.

aus=erfehen, erfah, erfehen, erfieht, *tr.,* select, designate. *Cf.* grammar for the compound (*sep.* + *insep.*) *pref.*

aus=fechten, focht, gefochten, ficht, *tr.,* fight out, settle.

aus-fließen, floß, geflossen, *intr.*, f., flow out, cease to flow, 587.

aus-gehen, ging, gegangen, *intr.*, f., go out (forth), start from.

aus-gießen, goß, gegossen, *tr.*, pour out, empty.

aus-liefern, *tr.*, deliver up (over).

aus-löschen, *tr.*, put out, extinguish.

aus-reuten, *tr.*, root (out) up, clear away (*forest*).

aus-roden, *tr.*, clear away (*forest*), root up (out).

Aus-rufer, *m.* -s, —, crier.

aus-ruhen, *intr. and refl.*, rest, stop to rest, 364.

aus-sehen, sah, gesehen, sieht, *intr.*, look, seem.

außen, *adv.*, out, outside, from without.

außer, *prep.* (*dat.*), out; except, save; — sich, beside oneself, 2201.

äußerst (*superl. of* äußer), *adj.*, utmost, extreme; as noun, the worst, 641; *adv. phrase*, zu —, right out, 346.

Aus-sicht, *f.* -en, view, prospect.

aus-sinnen, sann, gesonnen, *tr.* (*acc.* + *dat.* sich)), think out, devise.

aus-spähen, *tr.*, spy out, search out.

aus-sprechen, sprach, gesprochen, spricht, *tr.*, speak out, say out.

aus-stellen, *tr.*, station, put out, set (*watch, guard*).

aus-suchen, *tr.*, seek out, choose.

aus-treten, trat, getreten, tritt,

intr., f., *lit.* step out; overflow, 2690.

aus-üben, *tr.*, exercise; Gewalt —, do violence, 1646.

aus-weichen, wich, gewichen, *intr.*, f., turn aside, evade, avoid.

aus-ziehen, zog, gezogen, *intr.*, f., set out, go forth, depart.

Axenberg, *m.* -s. Mountain on east shore of Lake Lucerne. See map; *shortened gen.* 2255, *dat.* 2229.

Axt, *f.* ᵘe, axe; battle axe, 312.

B

Bach, *m.* -es, ᵘe, brook.

Bad, *n.* -es, ᵘer, bath.

baden, *refl.*, bathe.

Baden. Town in Aargau, near Zürich; one of Emperor Albrecht's residences.

Bahn, *f.* -en, way, 631; course, career, 2836.

Bahre, *f.* -n, bier.

bald, *adv.*, soon, easily; —...—, now . . . now.

Balken, *m.* -s, —, beam, timber.

Ball, *m.* -(e)s, ᵘe, ball.

Balsam-strom, *m.* -(e)s, ᵘe, balmy stream (*air*), refreshing breeze.

Band, *n.* -es, ᵘer, band.

Band, *n.* -es, -e, tie, 922; bond, (union), 2535; fetter, 1959.

bändigen, *tr.*, tame, break in, subdue.

bang(e), *adj.*, afraid, anxious, alarmed (for).

Bank, *f.* ᵘe, bench, seat.

Bann, *m.* –es, ban of outlawry.

Bann=berg, *m.* –s. A hill overlooking Altorf.

bannen, *tr.*, preserve (*game*),
901, note, 1778; charm, 1776.

Banner, *m.*, –s, —, banner.

Banner=herr, *m.* –n, –en, ban-
neret.

bar, *adj.*, bare, without (*gen.*),

Bär, *m.* –en, –en, bear. [1309.

barm=herzig, *adj.*, merciful,
compassionate; –e Brüder,
Brothers of Mercy.

Barm=herzigkeit, *f.* (–en), mercy,
pity.

Bau, *m.* –(e)s, (–e), Bauten,
building, structure.

bauen, *tr.*, build.

Bauer, *m.* –s *or* –n, –n, peasant.

Bäuer=in, *f.* –nen, peasant-
woman.

Bauern=adel, *m.* –s, peasant-
nobility.

Bau=gerüst(e), *n.* –(e)s, –e, scaffolding.

Baum, *m.* –es, ̈e, tree.

Baum=zweig, *m.* –(e)s, –e,
branch, twig.

bebauen, *tr.*, cultivate.

beben, *intr.*, tremble, shiver,
quake.

Becher, *m.* –s, —, cup, beaker.

bedauern, *tr.*, pity, be sorry for.

bedenken, bedachte, bedacht, *tr.*,
think over, meditate on; discuss, 246; consider, remember,
2313; *refl.*, hesitate, 1909,
2480.

bedeuten, *tr.*, mean, signify;
make a sign to, 3281 *.

bedrängen, *tr.*, oppress, afflict;
past part. as noun, 140, 351.

bedürfen, bedurfte, bedurft, bedarf, *intr.* (*with gen.*) *and tr.*,
need, be in need of.

bedürftig, *adj.*, needy.

beeist, *part. adj.*, ice-covered.

Befehl, *m.* –s, –e, command,
mandate, order.

befehlen, befahl, befohlen, be-
fiehlt, *tr.* (*dat. of pers.*), command, order, bid.

befestigen, *tr.*, strengthen; *refl.*,
fortify.

befinden, befand, befunden, *refl.*,
find oneself, be.

beflecken, *tr.*, stain. spot.

beflügeln, *tr.*, wing, speed.

befolgen, *tr.*, follow.

befördern, *tr.*, further, promote.

befreien, *tr.*, free, rescue.

befriedigen, *tr.*, appease, satisfy.

befruchten, *tr.*, make fertile.

begeben, begab, begeben, begiebt,
refl., *with gen.* give up, 1426;
betake oneself, go, come,
1734; happen, come to pass,
2214.

begegnen, *intr.*, ſ., (*dat.*), meet;
happen to, befall, 108, 159,
1874; treat, 539.

begehen, beging, begangen, *tr.*,
commit.

begehren, *tr.*, demand, ask for,
desire.

Begeisterung, *f.* enthusiasm, inspiration.

Begierde, *f.* –n, eagerness.

beginnen, begann, begonnen,

intr., 2431; *tr.*, 2400, 2730, begin.

begleiten, *tr.*, accompany.

beglücken, *tr.*, bless, make happy; ſtill beglückt, quiet, happy, 951.

begraben, begrub, begraben, begräbt, *tr.*, bury; *past part. as noun*, 1505.

begrenzen, *tr.*, bound, limit, close.

begrüßen, *tr.*, greet; *refl.*, exchange greeting, 988 *.

Begrüßung, *f.* –en, greeting.

beharren, *intr.* (bei, auf + *dat.*), stand by, remain steadfast.

behaupten, *tr.*, maintain, affirm.

bei, *prep. with dat., adv. and sep. pref.*, **by**, with, at, near, among, in, at the house of, on, upon; bei mir, at my house, 557; bei eröffneter Scene, after the scene opens, *1; kann ... bei, get at, hurt, 2708.

beichten, *tr.*, confess.

beide, *adj. pl.*, both.

bei=legen, *intr.*, lay on, hurry, 176, note.

bei=ſeite, *adv.*, aside.

Bei=ſpiel, *n.* –s, –e, example, parallel.

beiſpiel=los, *adj.*, unparalleled.

Bei=ſtand, *m.* –s, "e, help, support.

bei=ſtehen, ſtand, geſtanden, *intr.*, stand by, help.

bei=zählen, *tr.*, count among (as one of).

bejammerns=würdig, *adj.*, pitiable, wretched.

bekannt, *part. adj.*, **known,** acquainted; — machen, introduce.

beklagen, *tr.*, bewail; *refl.*, complain (of).

beklemmen, *tr.*, grieve, distress.

bekriegen, *tr.*, make war upon.

beladen, belud, beladen, *tr.*, **laden.**

beleben, *tr.*, enliven, cheer.

belebt, *part. adj.*, animate, living.

beleidigen, *tr.*, insult, offend.

belohnen, *tr.*, reward.

bemalen, *tr.*, paint.

bemerken, *tr.*, observe, notice; catch sight of, 2198 *; state (*in record*), 1216.

bequem, *adj.*, comfortable, convenient.

bequemen, *refl.*, submit to.

beraten, beriet, beraten, berät, *refl.*, confer with, take counsel.

berauben, *tr.*, rob.

bereit, *adj.*, **ready.**

bereiten, *tr.*, prepare, make ready; —, in progress, 526.

Berg, *m.* –(e)s, –e, mountain.

bergen, barg, geborgen, birgt, *tr.*, hide.

Berg=weg *m.* –s, –e, mountain path.

Bericht, *m.* –(e)s, –e, report.

berichten, *tr.*, report; *past part.*, (informed), skilled, 2240.

Bern. Bern(e), capital of canton Bern.

berſten, barſt, geborſten, *intr.*, ſ., burst.

berufen, *part. adj.*, of repute; wohl —, well spoken of, 1083.

beruhigen, *refl.*, compose one-self.

berühren, *tr.*, touch.

beschäftigen, *tr.*, employ, occupy; *past part.*, busy, 2303 *.

Bescheid, *m.* -s, -e, information, answer; — geben, tell, 2918; — wissen, know definitely; zum — werden, be given (receive) as answer, 1348.

bescheiden, beschied, beschieden, *tr.*, destine for, assign.

bescheiden, *adj.*, *now* = modest; older sense = experienced, prudent, good, 554, 3032.

bescheiden=lich, *adv.*, modestly.

bescheinen, beschien, beschienen, *tr.*, shine on.

beschirmen, *tr.*, defend, protect.

beschließen, beschloß, beschlossen, *tr.*, decide, settle, resolve.

beschützen, *tr.*, protect (vor, from, 2580), defend, 1437.

Beschütz=er, *m.* -s, —, defender, protector.

beschwören, *tr.*, swear (to); seal, 2900.

besehen, besah, besehen, besieht, *tr.*, look at, examine.

besetzen, *tr.*, occupy, fill.

besiegen, *tr.*, conquer.

Besinnen, *inf. as noun*, *n.* -s, reflection, thought.

Besitz, *m.* -es, possession.

besitzen, besaß, besessen, *tr.*, possess.

besonder, *adj.*, individual.

besonnen, *part. adj.*, cautious, prudent, thoughtful; schnell —, with quick presence of mind.

besprechen, besprach, besprochen, bespricht, *tr.*, discuss, confer about.

besser (*comp. of* gut), *adj.*, better; *as noun*, 2773.

best (*superl. of* gut), *adj.*, best; *as noun*, welfare, good, interest; best prize, 2650.

bestätigen, *tr.*, confirm, ratify.

bestehen, bestand, bestanden, *intr.*, last, endure; (*with* auf), insist on, 1306.

bestehlen, bestahl, bestohlen, bestiehlt, *tr.*, steal from, shirk.

bestellen, *tr.*, appoint; send for, 1236; cultivate, 2681.

besteuern, *tr.*, tax.

bestimmt, *part. adj.*, certain, appointed.

Besuch, *m.* -(e)s, -e, visit.

beten, *intr.*, pray, offer prayer.

bethören, *tr.*, fool, beguile, induce.

betrachten, *tr.*, look at, contemplate.

betrüben, *tr.*, trouble, harm.

betrügen, betrog, betrogen, *tr.*, deceive; *refl.*, delude oneself, be mistaken, 940.

beugen, *tr.*, bow, humble, conquer; *refl.*, bow, 635, 2917.

Beute, *f.* booty.

bewachen, *tr.*, watch, guard.

bewachsen, *part. adj.*, overgrown, covered with.

bewaffnen, *tr.*, arm, equip.

bewahren, *tr.*, keep, guard, pro-

bewähren, *tr.*, prove, show. [tect.

bewegen, *refl.*, stir, move; *past part.*, bewegt, stormy, *2099.

Bewegung, *f.* -en, movement, commotion.

beweiden, *tr.*, graze, pasture.

beweisen, bewies, bewiesen, *tr.*, show.

bewohnen, *tr.*, inhabit, occupy.

bewundern, *tr.*, admire, wonder at.

bezähmen, *tr.* (*and refl.*), tame, restrain.

bezeichnen, *tr.*, mark, indicate.

bezwingen, bezwang, bezwungen, *tr. and refl.*, subdue, conquer; control, 484, 584, etc.; force, capture, 2546.

bieder, *adj.*, honest, good, worthy.

Bieder=mann, *m.* -es, "er, good, true man.

biegen, bog, gebogen, *tr.*, bend; pervert, 1246.

bieten, bot, geboten, *tr.*, offer; say to (= offer insult), 1395.

Bild, *n.* -es, -er, form, image.

bilden, *tr. and refl.*, form, make.

billig, *adj.*, just, reasonable.

Binde, *f.* -n, bandage.

binden, band, gebunden, *tr.*, bind.

bis, *prep.* (*acc.*), *adv.*, *conj.*, to, as far as; till, until.

Bischof, *m.* -s, "e, bishop.

Bischofs=hut, *m.* -(e)s, "e, bishop's hat = bishopric, 2958.

bisher, *adv.*, till now, (hitherto), always, 185.

Bitte, *f.* -n, request, entreaty.

bitten, bat, gebeten, *tr.*, ask, beg; *intr. with* um, ask for, 1874.

bitter, *adj.*, bitter.

blasen, blies, geblasen, bläst, *tr. and intr.*, blow.

blaß (blässer, blässest, or blasser, blassest), *adj.*, pale.

bleiben, blieb, geblieben, *intr.*, f., remain, stay; *as noun*, 612.

bleich, *adj.*, pale.

bleichen, blich, geblichen, *intr.*, f., grow pale, fade.

blenden, *tr.*, blind.

Blick, *m.* -(e)s, -e, look, glance; sight, 992; prospect, 1662.

blicken, *intr.*, look.

blind, *adj.*, blind.

Blitz, *m.* -es, -e, lightning.

blitzen, *intr.* (*impers.*), flash, gleam.

bloß, *adj.*, bare, mere; *adv.*, simply, only, just.

blühen, *intr.*, bloom; prosper, 202.

Blume, *f.* -n, flower.

Blut, *n.* -(e)s, blood; race.

Blut=bann, *m.* -(e)s, criminal jurisdiction.

Blüte, *f.* -n, flower.

bluten, *intr.*, bleed.

blutig, *adj.*, bloody, in blood.

Blut=schuld, *f.* blood-guilt = murder.

bluts=verwandt, *part. adj.*, akin by blood; *as noun*, blood-kin, relatives, 2012.

Boden, *m.* -s, —, ground; zu —, down (to the ground).

Bogen, *m.* -s, — or ", bow; arch, 2861.

Bogen=sehne, *f.* -n, bow-string.

Bogen=strang, *m.* -(e)s, "e, bow-string.

bohren, *tr.*, bore, thrust (into).

Bord, *m. and n.* –(e)s, –e, board, shipboard, edge.

bös(e), *adj.*, bad, wicked, evil, ill; *masc. noun,* wicked man; *neut. noun,* evil, wickedness, wrong, harm, 502, 3070, 3153.

bös=meinend (*part. adj.*), *adv.*, maliciously, with evil purpose.

Bote, *m.* –n, –n, messenger.

Boten=segel, *n.* –s, —, messenger-sail(*boat*).

Bot=schaft, *f.* –en, tidings, news.

Brand, *m.* –es, ˮe, brand, firebrand.

branden, *intr.*, break (*waves*), surge, dash.

Brandung, *f.*, breakers, surf.

Brauch, *m.* –es, ˮe, custom, usage.

brauchen, *tr.*, want, need; *with gen.*, use, make use of, 2242; *impers. intr. with gen.*, be need of, 693.

bräuch=lich (old for gebräuchlich), *adj.*, customary.

braun, *adj.*, brown.

brausen, *intr.*, roar; *as noun,* 108 *.

Braut, *f.* ˮe, betrothed, promised bride.

Braut=lauf, *m.* –s, ˮe, wedding.

Braut=zug, *m.* –s, ˮe, weddingparty.

brav, worthy, good, noble; brave, 139, 2102.

brechen, brach, gebrochen, bricht, *tr.*, break, destroy (wreck, 2192); *fig.*, gather, 3017; *intr.*,

1412, 2117, 2148; (*of eye*) close, fail, grow dim, 866, 2811.

breiten, *tr.*, extend, spread.

brennen, brannte, gebrannt, *tr. and intr.*, burn.

Brief, *m.* –es, –e, letter, charter.

bringen, brachte, gebracht, *tr.*, bring; take, 2049; pledge (*in drinking*), 766.

Bringer, *m.* –s, —, bringer, bearer.

Brot, *n.* –es, –e, bread.

Bruck, Bruck (Brugg), a town in Aargau not far from Zürich.

Brücke, *f.* –n, bridge.

Bruder, *m.* –s, ˮ, brother; Barmherzige Brüder, Brothers of Mercy; — = monk, 3099.

brüllen, *intr.*, bellow, roar, low.

Brun=eck. Castle in Aargau, south of Bruck.

Bruneck=erin, *f.* my lady of Bruneck.

Brünig. Mountain-pass between Underwalden and Bern.

Brunnen, *m.* –s, —, spring, well.

Brunnen. Town on the east shore of Lake Lucerne.

Brünnlein, *n.* –s, —, little spring.

Brust, *f.* ˮe, breast.

Brut, *f.* –en, brood.

Bube, *m.* –n, –n, boy, servant, 471; fellow, rascal, 467, 1835.

Buch, *n.* –es, ˮer, book.

Buch=handlung, *f.* –en, (book-) publishing house. Cf. titlepage.

Bucht, *f.* –en, bight, bay, inlet.

bücken, *tr. and refl.,* bend, **bow.**

Buggis=grat, *m.* -8, a dangerous cliff of the Axenberg.

Büh(e)l, *m.* -8, — (*part of proper name*), hill, (*S.G., Swiss*).

buhlen, *intr.* (*with,* um), court, **woo.**

Bund, *m.* -e8, ⁐e, union, league, covenant, confederation.

Bünd=nis, *n.* -ffe8, -ffe, covenant, league.

bunt, *adj.,* bright, gay-colored.

Burg, *f.* -en, castle, fortress.

bürgen, *intr.,* stand (give) security (bail).

Bürger, *m.* -8, —, citizen, burgher.

Bürger=eid, *m.* -(e)8, -e, civic oath (as citizen).

Bürger=in, *f.* -nen, (female) citizen.

Burg=glocke, *f.* -n, castle-bell.

Bürglen. Village near Altorf in the Schächen valley. Tell's home.

Bürg=schaft, *f.* security, bail; — leiften, give (go) bail, 1831.

Burg=verließ, *n.* -e8, -e, keep, dungeon.

Burg=vogt, *m.* -8, ⁐e, bailiff, governor.

Busen, *m.* -8, —, **bosom,** breast; bay, inlet, 2159.

Buße, *f.* punishment, penalty.

büßen, *tr. and intr.,* pay for, atone for, suffer for; punish, 566, 1561; satisfy (desire), böfe Luft gebüßt, vented his malice, 273.

C

Christenheit, *f.* christendom.

Christ=fest, *n.* -e8, -e, Christmas.

Cotta'schen, J. G., *proper adj.,* J. G. Cotta's (*publishers*). Cf. title-page.

D

da, *adv.,* **there,** here, then; *conj.,* when, while; since, as.

da=bei, *adv.,* **thereby,** therein; present, 1521, 2289; in that, 372.

Dach, *n.* -e8, ⁐er, roof; awning, or **deck,** 2172.

da=gegen, *adv.,* **against** (it, that, them).

da=heim, *adv.,* at **home.**

da=her, *adv. and sep. pref.,* hither, from there; along, on.

daher=kommen, kam, gekommen, *intr.,* f., **come** along.

da=hin, *adv. and sep. pref.,* thither, there, away; bi8 —, till then, 1459; —, to this (that), 2822; gone (= dead), 2461.

dahin=fahren, fuhr, gefahren, fährt, *intr.,* f., go (drive, row) along (on).

dahin=gehen, ging, gegangen, *intr.,* f., go away, depart; + über, pass over, 2766.

dahin=scheiden, fchied, gefchieden, *intr.,* f., depart, die.

dahin=wandern, *intr.,* f., **wander** along (thither).

da=mals, *adv.,* then, at that time.

da-mit, *adv.,* **therewith, with** (by) it (that, them); *conj.,* so that, 2069, 3101.

dämpfen, *tr.,* muffle, soften.

Dank, *m.* -es, **thanks,** gratitude.

danken, *intr.* (*dat.*), **thank,** give

dann, *adv.,* **then.**   [thanks.

dannen, *adv.* (*with* von), **thence,** away, from there; hie — (2247), *older for* von —.

dar-an, *adv.,* **thereon,** thereby, on (at, by, in) it (them); — fein, be about to, 2020, 2105.

dar-auf, *adv.,* **thereupon,** upon (to) it (that, them), then, after that, 94, 1192, 1585 *.

darauf-kommen, kam, gekommen, *intr.,* f., **come** to think of, 1518.

d(a)r-aus, *adv.,* from (of, out of) it, (that); — werden, come of it, 376, 1727.

d(a)r-in, *adv.,* **therein,** in it (that).

d(a)r-ob, *adv.,* **thereat,** about it.

dar-reichen, *tr.,* **reach** (stretch) out.

dar-stellen, *refl.,* **show** itself, be seen.

d(a)r-über, *adv.,* **over** (beyond, more than) **that** (it); at (about) that.

dar-um, *adv.,* **thereabout,** for (about) it (that); of it, 2957; therefore, for that reason.

d(a)r-unter, *adv.,* **under** it (that); among them; down there, 981.

Da-fein, *n.* -s, existence.

daß, *conj.,* **that,** so that, in order that (to).

da-von, *adv.,* **thereof,** of it **(that),** therefrom; away.

davon-tragen, trug, getragen, trägt, *tr.,* carry away (off).

da-zu, **thereto,** to *or* for it *or* **that.**

da-zwischen, *adv.,* **between** (among) them; at intervals, now and then.

decken, *tr.,* cover, defend.

dein, *poss. adj. and pron.,* **thy, thine,** your; *pl. as noun,* your people, 792, 859.

Denk-art, *f.* -en, way of **think-** ing, nature, character.

denken, dachte, gedacht, *tr. and intr.* (*with gen. or* an, auf, über *with acc.*), **think** (of, about); (*for* gedenken), remember, 1930, 2485.

Denk-mal, *n.* -s, "er, monument, emblem.

denn, *conj.* (*stands first*), for, because; *adv.,* **then,** therefore.

der (die, das), *def. art.,* **the;** *demonst. adj. and pron., pers. pron.,* this **(that)** one, he, she, it; *rel. pron.,* who, which, that; das (356), these fellows (*in contempt*).

der-einst, *adv.,* some day (time).

der-gleichen, *indec. adj.,* (the) like, such (as), that kind.

der-felbe (diefelbe, dasfelbe), *adj.* (*pron.*), the same.

deuchten, *impers.* (*dat. or acc.*), seem, appear.

deuten, *tr.,* explain, (*with* auf) say it means, 2677; *intr.,* point, make a sign.

deutſch, *adj.*, German.

dicht, *adj.*, dense, close; *adv.*, close (upon), 71, 2697.

dienen, *intr.* (*dat.*), serve.

Diener, *m.* -s, —, servant.

Dienſt, *m.* -es, -e, service.

dienſt=fertig, *adj.*, officious.

dieſer [dieſe, dies(es)], *adj. and pron.*, **this** (one), that (one); the latter.

dies=mal, *adv.*, this time.

Diethelm. Diethelm (*proper name*).

Ding, *n.* -s, -e, thing.

Dirne, *f.* -n, maid, girl.

doch, *adv. and conj.*, yet, but, **though,** notwithstanding; surely; *emphatic as in* Bleibt —, do (pray) stay, 187; *assumes assent, as in* 555; Why! 2770.

Dolch, *m.* -s, -e, dagger.

Donner, *m.* -s, —, thunder.

donnern, *intr.* (*also impers.*), thunder; *inf. also as noun.*

Donner=ſchlag, *m.* -s, "e, peal (clap, roll) of thunder.

doppelt, *adj.*, double; *as noun,* 357.

Dorf, *n.* -es, "er, village.

dort, *adv.*, there, yonder.

dort=hin, *adv.*, there, that way.

Drache, *m.* -n, -n, dragon.

Drachen=gift, *n.* -s, -e, dragon's poison, venom.

dran = daran.

Drang, *m.* -es, oppression, tyranny.

drängen, *tr.*, oppress, distress; *refl.*, press (crowd) upon (*with*

an, 1555*); *with* in, force oneself into, 2504.

Drang=ſal, *n.* -s, -e, oppression.

drauf = darauf.

draus = daraus.

draußen, *adv.*, outside, without.

drei, *num.*, **three;** *old infl. pl.* dreie, 1128.

dreißig, *num.*, **thirty.**

drei=und=dreißig, *num.*, **thirty-three.**

dringen, drang, gedrungen, *intr.*, ſ., press, force way; be urgent, 149, 2512.

drinnen, *adv.*, inside, within.

dritt, *num. adj.*, **third.**

drob = darob.

droben, *adv.*, above, up there, on high.

drohen, *tr. and intr.* (*dat.*), threaten, menace; be about to, 2033*.

drüben, *adv.*, over there (yonder).

drüber (= darüber), more than that, over that, 1228.

Druck, *m.* -(e)s, -e, oppression.

drücken, *tr.*, press, oppress, afflict; *past part. as noun*, 1277; weigh upon, 198.

drum = darum.

drunter = darunter.

du, *pers. pron. 2d pers.*, **thou,** you.

dulden, *tr.*, bear, tolerate, suffer.

duldſam (for geduldig), *adv.*, patiently.

dumpf, *adj.*, dull, heavy; deep, 480.

dunkel, *adj.*, dark, gloomy.

dünken, *intr.* (*dat.*), seem.

durch, *prep., sep. and insep. pref.,* through, by, because (by means) of, during; *adv.,* through.

durchbohr'en, *insep., tr.,* bore through, pierce.

durchdri'ngen, durchbra'ng, durch-dru'ngen, *insep., tr.,* pierce through, penetrate.

durch=gehen, ging, gegangen, *sep., intr.,* go (pass) through.

durchre'nnen, durchra'nnte, durch-ra'nnt, *insep., tr.,* run through, pierce.

durchschau'en, *insep., tr.,* see (look) through, *i.e.* understand.

durchschie'ßen, durchscho'ß, durch-scho'ssen, *insep., tr.,* shoot through.

dürfen, durfte, gedurft, darf, *intr. and modal aux.,* dare, be allowed, may, have right to.

Durst, *m.* -es, thirst.

düster, *adj.,* dark, gloomy, sullen.

E

eben, *adj.,* even, flat, smooth, 973, 1790; *adv.,* even, just, just now.

Echo, *n.* -s, -s, echo.

echt, *adj.,* real, true, genuine,

Ecke, *f.* -n, corner. [sterling.

edel, *adj.,* noble; *often as noun* (*pl.*), nobility; *f. sg.,* noblewoman, 2529; *neut. noun,* nobleness, 1644.

Edel=hof, *m.* -s, "e, nobleman's seat, castle.

Edel=mann, *m.* -(e)s, ("er *or*) —leute, nobleman.

Edel=sitz, *m.* -es, -e, nobleman's seat (castle, house).

Edel=stein, *m.* -s, -e, jewel, precious stone.

eh(e), *conj.,* ere, before.

Ehe, *f.* -n, marriage.

eher, *adv.* (*comp. of* ehe), sooner, rather, before.

Ehe=wirt, *m.* -s, -e, (*old for* Mann, Gatte), husband.

Ehni, *m.* -s, *Swiss dim. of* Ahn, grandfather; zum (vom) —, to (from) grandpa's, 1540, 1583.

Ehre, *f.* -n, honor.

ehren, *tr.,* honor, revere, respect.

Ehren=gruß, *m.* -es, "e, salute of honor, homage.

Ehren=mann, *m.* -(e)s, "er, man of honor, (good) worthy man.

Ehr=furcht, *f.* reverence, respect.

Ehr=geiz, *m.* -es, ambition.

Ehr=sucht, *f.* ambition.

ehr=würdig, *adj.,* venerable, esteemed, worthy.

ei, *interj.,* why! well! oh!

Eid, *m.* -es, -e, oath.

Eidam, *m.* -s, -e (*for modern* Schwieger=sohn), son-in-law.

Eid=genoss(e), *m.* -n, -n, confederate.

Eid=schwur, *m.* -s, "e, oath.

Eifer, *m.* -s, zeal, ardor.

eifrig, *adj.,* zealous, eager.

eigen, *adj.,* own; peculiar, special, 1908; auf —e Hand,

on his own (hook) account,
232; —e Leute, bondmen,
serfs, 1081, *so also* 1143.

eigen=finnig, (*adj.*) *adv.*, will-
fully, stubbornly.

eilen, *intr.*, h. *or* f., hurry, hasten.

eilends, *adv.*, hastily, hurriedly.

eil=fertig, (*adj.*) *adv.*, in haste.

eilig, *adj.*, hasty; was giebt's fo
—, what's the hurry? 68;
Haft du's fo —, are you in
such haste? 773.

ein, *indef. art. num.*, a, an, one;
fo —, folch —, — folcher, such
a (an); welch —, what a (an);
was für —, what kind of a

ein, *as sep. pref.*, in, into. [(an).

ein=ander, *indec. recip. pron.*
(*dat. or acc.*), one another,
each other; 'nander = ein=
ander.

ein=brechen, brach, gebrochen,
bricht, *intr.*, f., break (in,
down), give way.

ein=fallen, fiel, gefallen, fällt,
intr., f., fall in; begin (of
music); occur to, 1576.

ein=förmig, *adj.*, monotonous.

Ein=gang, *m.* -s, "e, entrance.

ein=gehen, ging, gegangen, *intr.*,
f., go in, enter.

Ein=geweide, *n.* -s, –, bowels (of
mercy) = heart, feeling.

ein=holen, *tr.*, overtake, catch.

einig, *adj.*, one, united; some
(*generally pl.*), a few.

ein=kaufen, *tr.*, buy, purchase.

ein=kehren, *intr.*, f., turn in, stop
(at an inn), lodge.

ein=mal, *adv.*, once, some day;
auf —, all at once, suddenly,
1462; fonft —, some other
time, 1336.

ein=reißen, riß, geriffen, *tr.*, pull
(tear) down.

Eins, *f.* one.

ein=fam, *adj.*, lonely, solitary;
alone, 1181.

ein=fchiffen, *refl.*, take ship, em-
bark.

ein=fchlafen, fchlief, gefchlafen,
fchläft, *intr.*, f., fall asleep.

ein=fchließen, fchloß, gefchloffen,
tr., shut in, confine, surround.

ein=fchränken, *tr.*, confine, restrain.

ein=fchreiben, fchrieb, gefchrieben,
tr., write in, engrave.

Einfiedeln. Town and monastery
in Schwyz, near Lake Zurich.

ein=finken, fank, gefunken, *intr.*,
f., sink in, give way, fall
down.

ein=ftürzen, *intr.*, f., fall in
(down).

Ein=tracht, *f.* union, harmony.

ein=treten, trat, getreten, tritt,
intr., f., enter; *inf. as noun*,
2938*.

einzeln, *adj.*, single, individual.

ein=ziehen, zog, gezogen, *tr.*, draw
in; *intr.*, f., enter, come in.

einzig, *adj.*, only, single, alone
for einig, united, 1449.

Eis, *n.* -es, ice.

eis=bedeckt, *part. adj.*, icy, ice-
covered.

Eifen, *n.* -s, –, iron, = spear-
head, 1406.

Eisen=stab, *m.* -s, ⁻e, iron rod.

Eises=feld, *n.*-(e)s, -er, ice-field.

Eises=turm, *m.* -(e)s, ⁻e, ice-tower.

Eises=wall, *m.*-(e)s, ⁻e, ice-wall.

Eis=gebirge, *n.* -s, -, ice-mountains.

Eis=palast, *m.* -(e)s, ⁻e, ice-palace.

eitel, *adj.*, vain, empty, idle.

Element, *n.* -s, -e, element.

Elend, *n.* -s, misery, wretchedness.

elend, *adj.*, wretched, miserable; *as noun*, wretch, 613.

Elsbeth. *Dim. of* Elisabeth, Emperor Albrecht's widow.

empfangen, empfing, empfangen, empfängt, *tr.*, receive.

empfinden, empfand, empfunden, *tr.*, feel, experience.

empor=heben, hob, gehoben, *tr.*, lift (up).

empor=ragen, *intr.*, rise (tower) above.

empören, *tr.*, stir up; *past part.*, indignant, 2007; *refl.*, rebel, revolt, 2143.

Empörung, *f.* -en, revolt, rebellion.

Ende, *n.* -s, -n, end, issue, close.

enden, *intr.*, end.

endigen, *intr.*, end, stop.

endlich, *adj.*, final; *adv.*, at last, finally.

eng(e), *adj.*, narrow; — werden, to feel oppressed, 1812.

Enge, *f.* -n, narrowness.

Engel, *m.* -s, -, angel.

Engel=berg. Village and monastery in Unterwalden.

Enkel, *m.* -s, -, grand(son)child, descendant.

entbehren, *intr.* (*gen.*), be (do) without.

entbinden, entband, entbunden, *tr.*, release.

entblößen, *tr.*, bare, uncover.

entdecken, *tr.*, discover, catch sight of; tell, disclose, 2300.

entfernen, *refl.*, retire, withdraw; depart (differ, deviate) from, 1150, 1906.

entfliehen, entfloh, entflohen, *intr.*, f., flee, fly, pass (*of time*).

entgegen, *prep.* (*after dat.*) *and sep. pref.*, toward, against, to meet; up, 3243.

entgegen=eilen, *intr.*, f., run to meet.

entgegen=gehen, ging, gegangen, *intr.*, f., go to meet (towards).

entgegen=kehren, *tr.*, turn towards (against).

entgegen=starren, *intr.*, stare at (in the face).

entgegen=treten, trat, getreten, tritt, *intr.*, f., step towards, go to meet.

entgegnen, *tr.*, answer, reply.

entgehen, entging, entgangen, *intr.*, f., escape.

entkommen, entkam, entkommen, *intr.*, f., escape.

entlassen, entließ, entlassen, entläßt, *tr.*, dismiss, let go.

entledigen, *tr.* (*acc. and gen.*), free, release from, relieve of.

entreißen, entriß, entrissen, *tr.*, tear away, wrest from.

entrichten, *tr.*, pay, discharge (*a duty*).

entrinnen, entrann, entronnen, *intr.*, f., escape, leave.

entrüsten, *tr.*, provoke, enrage; *past part.*, indignant, 1014.

entsagen, *intr.* (*dat.*), give up, renounce.

entscheiden, entschied, entschieden, *tr. and intr.*, decide, settle.

Entscheidung, *f.* -en, decision (= battle), 2443.

entschließen, entschloß, entschlossen, *refl.*, determine, resolve.

entschlossen, *part. adj.*, determined, resolved.

Entschlossenheit, *f.*, promptness, resoluteness.

Entschluß, *m.* -sses, "sse, resolve, determination.

entschuldigen, *tr.*, excuse, justify.

entseelt, *part. adj.*, dead, lifeless.

Entsetzen, *n.* -s, horror.

entsetz=lich, *adj.*, wretched, dreadful.

entsinken, entsank, entsunken, *intr.*, f., drop (fall) from; fail, 2232.

entspringen, entsprang, entsprungen, *intr.*, f., escape; *as noun*, 2252.

entstehen, entstand, entstanden, *intr.*, f., arise; *old sense*, fail, be wanting, 700.

entweichen, entwich, entwichen, *intr.*, f., withdraw from.

entwischen, *intr.*, f., escape, get (slip) away.

entziehen, entzog, entzogen, *refl.* (*with dat.*), forsake, desert.

entzwei, *adv.*, in two, broken.

er, *pers. pron.*, he, it.

erbarmen, *tr.*, touch, move to pity, 2094; *refl.* (*with gen.*), take pity on, be merciful to, 111, 143; *impers.* (*with acc. and gen.*), regret, be sorry (for), 2094, 3191.

erbärm=lich, *adj.*, wretched, miserable.

Erbarm=ung, *f.* -en, mercy.

erbauen, *tr.*, build, make.

Erbe, *n.* -s, inheritance.

erbeben, *intr.*, f., tremble, shake.

erben, *intr.*, f. (*with* auf + *acc.*), descend to (*by inheritance*).

erbeuten, *tr.*, capture, (get as booty), win.

Erb=herr, *m.* -n, -en, hereditary lord, sovereign.

Erbin, *f.* -nen, heiress.

erblicken, *tr.*, see, catch sight of, discover.

erbrausen, *intr.*, f., roar, surge up.

erbrechen, erbrach, erbrochen, erbricht, *tr.*, break open (*letter*), open.

Erb=stück, *n.* -(e)s, -e, inheritance (*lands*), 1089.

Erde, *f.* -n, earth, ground; soil, 848; auf —n (*old dat. sg.*), on earth, 1085, 2668; der —n (*old gen. sg.*), 1700.

erdulden, *tr.*, bear, endure, tolerate.

Ereignis, *n.* -sses, -sse, event.

ererben, *tr.*, inherit.

erfaſſen, *tr.*, seize, grasp.

erſtehen, *tr.*, beg, entreat.

erforſchen, *tr.*, investigate, sound, question, 706.

erfrechen, *refl.* (*with gen.*), make bold, (dare) to do.

erfreuen, *tr.*, please, delight.

erfriſchen, *tr.*, refresh.

erfüllen, *tr.*, fill; fulfill, accomplish.

ergeben, ergab, ergeben, ergiebt, *refl.*, submit, yield.

Ergebung, *f.* submission.

ergehen, erging, ergangen, *intr.*, ſ., go forth, be proclaimed, 1229; *with* vor + *acc.*, take place of, 1945.

ergießen, ergoß, ergoſſen, *refl.*, spread, be shed.

ergreifen, ergriff, ergriffen, *tr.*, seize, lay hold of (= *fig.* touch); accept, take, 1295, 1427.

erhalten, erhielt, erhalten, erhält, *tr.*, get, receive; keep, (**hold**) back, restrain, 945; *refl.*, preserve (maintain) itself, 2423.

erheben, erhob (older erhub), erhoben, *tr.*, lift up, raise; *refl.*, rise, arise.

erhellen, *tr.*, brighten, cheer, 2393; light up, 3260.

erinnern, *refl.* (*with gen. or* an + *acc.*), remember.

erjagen, *tr.*, hunt down, get by hunting.

erkennen, erkannte, erkannt, *tr.*, see, recognize, acknowledge; zu — geben, make known, 1203.

Erker, *m.* –ꞩ, —, balcony, bay-window.

erklären, *tr. and refl.*, explain *or* declare (oneself); frei —, set free, 3291.

erkranken, *intr.*, ſ., get (fall) sick.

erkühnen, *refl.*, grow bold, 2004; make bold, dare, 2534.

erkunden, *tr.*, explore, examine.

erlangen, *tr.*, reach.

erlaſſen, erließ, erlaſſen, erläßt, *tr.* (*acc. and dat.*), release, excuse from.

erlauben, *tr.*, allow, permit.

erleben, *tr.*, live to see, meet with, experience.

erledigen, *refl.*, get free, release oneself from (*gen.*).

erleiden, erlitt, erlitten, *tr.*, suffer; tolerate, 1259.

erlöſchen, erloſch, erloſchen, erliſcht, *intr.*, ſ., go out, be extinguished; *as noun*, 2429.

ermächtigen, *refl.* (for bemächtigen), get possession of, seize.

ermorden, *tr.*, murder.

ermüden, *intr.*, ſ., get tired, tire.

erneuern, *tr.*, renew.

ernſt, *adj.*, earnest, grave, solemn.

Ernſt, *m.* –eꞩ, earnestness, seriousness.

ernſt=haft, *adj.*, earnest, serious.

ernten, *tr.*, reap, harvest.

erobern, *tr.*, take, capture.

eröffnen, *tr.*, open, begin.

erquicken, *tr.*, refresh.

erregen, *tr.*, rouse, stir up.

erreichen, *tr.*, reach, get to; attain.

erretten, *tr.,* save, rescue.

Erretter, *m.* -s, —, deliverer.

errichten, *tr.,* set up, **erect.**

erringen, errang, errungen, *tr.,* get by force, win.

ersäufen, *tr.,* flood, drown.

erschaffen, erschuf, erschaffen, *tr.,* create.

erschallen, erscholl, erschollen, *intr.,* f., spread (abroad), *of sound, rumor.*

erscheinen, erschien, erschienen, *intr.,* f., appear.

erschießen, erschoß, erschossen, *tr.,* shoot, kill (*by shot*).

erschlagen, erschlug, erschlagen, erschlägt, *tr.,* **slay,** kill.

erschleichen, erschlich, erschlichen, *tr.,* get by fraud; *part. adj.,* fraudulent, 1253.

erschöpfen, *tr.,* exhaust, tire (wear) out.

erschrecken, erschrak, erschrocken, erschrickt, *intr.,* be startled, alarmed.

erschrecken, *tr.,* frighten, alarm.

ersparen, *tr.,* save, **spare;** *with* an + *dat.,* save at expense of, 775.

erst, *adv.,* first, once (194), only (382), not until, just; *adj.,* first.

erstaunen, *intr.,* f., be surprised.

Erstaunen, *n.* -s, **astonishment.**

erstaunlich, *adj.,* astonishing.

ersteigen, erstieg, erstiegen, *tr.,* climb, scale.

ersticken, *tr.,* stifle, smother, choke.

ertönen, *intr.,* ring.

ertöten, *tr.,* kill, destroy.

ertragen, ertrug, ertragen, erträgt, *tr.,* bear, suffer, stand.

ertrinken, ertrank, ertrunken, *intr.,* f., **drown,** be drowned.

ertrotzen, *tr.,* extort, force from.

erwachen, *intr.,* f., **awake, wake** up.

erwarten, *tr.,* await, expect, look for; *for intr.,* warten, wait, 272, 493.

Erwartung, *f.,* -en, expectation.

erwecken, *tr.,* **awaken,** inspire.

erwehren, *refl.* (*with gen.*), ward off, defend oneself from.

erwerben, erwarb, erworben, erwirbt, *tr.,* get, acquire; produce, 2000.

erzählen, *tr.,* **tell,** relate.

erzeigen, *tr.,* show, do.

erzittern, *intr.,* f., tremble.

erzwingen, erzwang, erzwungen, *tr.,* enforce, extort.

es (*often* 's), *pers. pron. third pers.,* it; *expletive,* there.

Eschenbach. Walther von Eschenbach), one of Emperor Albrecht's murderers.

essen, aß, gegessen, ißt, *tr.,* **eat.**

etlich (-er, -e, -es), *adj. pron., chiefly pl.,* some.

etwas, *indec. adj. and pron.,* some, something.

euer (or **Euer**), *poss. pron.,* **your,** yours; *pers. pron.* (*gen. pl.*), of you, *dat.,* to your friends, 2686.

eurig (or **Eurig**) (der, die, das, -e), *poss. pron.,* **yours.**

ewig, *adj.*, eternal, everlasting; *adv.*, forever.

Ewigkeit, *f.* -en, eternity.

F

fahen (*old and poetic for* fangen), *tr.*, take, seize.

Fahne, *f.* -n, flag, banner.

Fahr (*old and poetic for* Ge= fahr), *f.* -en, danger.

fahrbar, *adj.*, navigable.

Fähre, *f.* -n, ferry.

fahren, fuhr, gefahren, fährt, *intr.*, f., go, row, ride, travel; *Swiss for* treiben, drive, 17; fährt fich, is rowing about, *1; *as noun*, rowing, 2239; mit der Hand —, put one's hand.

Fähr=mann, *m.* -s, "er *or* -leute, ferryman, boatman.

Fahrt, *f.* -en, trip, journey; *pl.* wanderings.

Fahr=zeug, *n.* -s, -e, boat, craft.

Falle, *m.* -n, -n, falcon.

Fall, *m.* -s, "e, fall.

fallen, fiel, gefallen, fällt, *intr.*, f., fall; + in = fall upon, 178; in Straf' —, incur a penalty, 473; ins Land —, invade country, 1385.

fällen, *tr.*, fell, cut down.

Fall=strick, *m.* -s, -e, trap, snare.

falsch, *adj.*, false.

Falsch, *n.* -es (*old and poetic*), deceit, guile.

Falsch=heit, *f.* -en, baseness, falsehood.

falten, *tr.*, fold, wrinkle (*brow*).

Fang, *m.* -(e)s, "e, catch, haul;

— thun, make a catch (haul), 1745.

fangen, fing, gefangen, fängt, *tr.*, catch, take prisoner; *part* as *adj. or noun*, prisoner, cap- tive.

fassen, *tr.*, seize, grasp, take hold of; *refl.*, (come to) compose oneself.

fast, *adv.*, almost.

Fast=nachts=auf=zug, *m.* -s, "e, carnival procession.

faul, *adj.*, lazy, idle.

Faust, *f.* "e, fist, hand.

Favenz. Faenza, town in Italy, near Ravenna. Cf. 912, note.

fechten, focht, gefochten, ficht, *intr.*, fight.

Feder, *f.* -n, feather.

fehlen, *tr.*, miss, *with acc.*, 1890, 1919, *with gen.*, 2063; — auf, miss thing aimed at and hit something else, 1951; *intr.*, fail, be wanting, missing; I shall not be wanting, 446.

Fehler, *m.*, -s, —, fault.

Fehl=sprung, *m.* -s, "e, false leap; — thun, miss one's leap, 1500.

Feier=abend, *m.* -s, -e, quitting (resting) time.

feiern, *intr.*, stop work, be idle.

feig(e), *adj.*, cowardly.

feig=herzig, *adj.*, fainthearted.

feil, *adj.*, for sale, to be bought.

Feind, *m.* -es, -e, enemy.

Feld, *n.* -es, -er, field.

Fels *or* **Felsen**, *m.* -en *or* -ens, -en, cliff, rock.

Felsen=kluft, *f.* "e, rocky gorge.

Felsen=platte, *f.* -n, flat ledge of rock.

Felsen=riff, *n.* -s, -e, ledge *or* reef of rock.

Felsen=steig, *m.* -s, -e, rocky path.

Felsen=thor, *n.* -s, -e, door (gateway) in the rock.

Felsen=ufer, *n.* -s, —, rocky shore.

Felsen=wall, *m.* -s, "e, wall of rock.

Fels(en)=wand, *f.* "e, wall of rock, precipice.

Fenster, *n.* -s, —, window.

fern(e), *adj.*, *adv.*, far, far off, away.

Ferne, *f.* -n, distance.

fern=her, *adv.*, from afar.

Ferse, *f.* -n, heel.

fertig, *adj.*, ready; done, finished.

Fessel, *f.* -n, fetter, bond.

fesseln, *tr.*, fetter, bind.

fest, *adj.*, fast, firm, strong, secure; fortified; *as noun*, 2542.

Fest, *n.* -(e)s, -e, feast, festival; — des Herrn, Christmas, 1401.

Feste, *f.* -n, fortress, stronghold.

fest=halten, hielt, gehalten, hält, *tr.*, hold fast to; *intr.*, hold fast (= unbroken), 2606; *with* an, hold fast (cling) to, 185.

fest=knüpfen, *tr.*, tie (knit) firmly.

feucht, *adj.*, damp.

Feuer, *n.* -s, —, fire.

Feuer=signal, *n.* -s, -e, signal-fire.

Feuer=wächter, *m.* -s, —, night-watchman.

Feuer=zeichen, *n.* -s, —, beacon-fire.

finden, fand, gefunden, *tr.*, find; *refl.*, be found, be.

Finger, *m.* -s, —, finger.

finster, *adj.*, dark, gloomy; *as noun*, darkness, gloom, 595.

Finster=nis, *f.* -sse, darkness.

Firn, *m.* -es, -en, glacier, snow-peak (field).

Fisch, *m.* -es, -e, fish.

fischen, *intr.*, fish.

Fischer, *m.* -s, —, fisherman.

Fischer=kahn, *m.* -s, "e, fisher-man's boat.

Fischer=knabe, *m.* -n, -n, fisher-man's boy.

Flamme, *f.* -n, flame.

flammen, *intr.*, flame, blaze.

Flanke, *f.* -n, flanking (side, corner) wall; cf. 386, note.

Flecken, *m.* -s, —, village, hamlet.

flehen, *intr.*, beseech, entreat; *tr.* (*with* um), beg for, 132; *pres. part. as noun*, suppliant, 1345.

Fleiß, *m.* -es, diligence, in-dustry.

fleißig, *adj.*, diligent, in-dustrious.

fleugt (*old for* fliegt), *pres. ind. 3rd sg. of* fliegen.

fliegen, flog, geflogen, *intr.*, f. *or* h., fly.

fliehen, floh, geflohen, *intr.*, f., flee.

fließen, floß, geflossen, *intr.*, f. *or* h., flow.

Flitter=schein, *m.* –s, tinsel,
(false) glory.

Flöte, *f.* –n, flute.

Fluch, *m.* –es, "e, curse.

Fluch=gebäude, *n.* –s, —, ac-
cursed building.

Flucht, *f.* –en, flight.

flüchten, *tr.*, save by flight,
rescue; *refl.*, flee, escape.

flüchtig, *adj.*, fugitive, fleeting,
transient; wurde —, fled, 569.

Flüchtling, *m.* –s, –e, fugitive.

Flüe (*lit.* cliff, rock wall), *part
of proper name.*

Flüelen. Village in Uri at southern end of Lake Lucerne.

Flug, *m.* –(e)s, "e, flight; im
—e, on the wing, 1950.

Fluh, *f.* –en or "e, rocky wall,
cliff.

Flur=schütz, *m.* –en, –en, ranger,
game-keeper.

Fluß, *m.* –sses, "sse, river.

Flut, *f.* –en, flood, waves.

Föhn, *m.* –(e)s, —, Föhn, south
wind.

folgen, *intr.*, s. (*dat.*), follow;
part. as noun, 2438 *.

Folter=knecht, *m.* –s, –e, tor-
turer.

fordern, *tr.*, demand, claim, call
(ask) for; — lassen, summon.

Form, *f.* –en, form.

forschen, *intr.*, ask, inquire.

fort, *adv. and sep. pref.*, forth,
away, gone; — und —, con-
tinually, 1016; on, 1021.

fort=eilen, *intr.*, s., hurry away.

fort=fahren, fuhr, gefahren, fährt,
intr., continue, keep on.

fort=führen, *tr.*, lead (take,
carry) away (off).

fort=gehen, ging, gegangen, *intr.*,
s., go away; continue, 2798 *.

fort=helfen, half, geholfen, hilft,
intr. (*dat.*), help one get
away.

fort=reißen, riß, gerissen, *tr.*,
tear (carry) away.

fort=setzen, *refl.*, continue.

fort=ziehen, zog, gezogen, *intr.*, s.,
go on, proceed.

fragen, *tr.*, ask (about), inquire
(for, nach); *with* nach, care for,
heed, mind, 1770, 2764.

Frau, *f.* –en, woman, wife; —
Gertrud, Mistress G., 517, *so
also*, 2308; großen —, "Our
Lady," 1364, note.

Fräu=lein, *n.* –s, —, girl of
noble birth, lady; *in address*,
my lady, 1587, 1607.

frech, *adj.*, bold, insolent, shame-
less.

Frech=heit, *f.* –en, insolence.

frei, *adj.*, free; free (= common
property), 2741; voluntary, of
one's own accord; *superl. m.
noun*, 1217; *neut. noun*, open
air (country), 2129, 3087 *.

Freiburg. Capital of Canton
Freiburg.

freien, *intr.* (*with* um), woo; *tr.*,
marry.

Frei=heit, *f.* –en, freedom,
liberty.

Freiheits=brief, *m.* –(e)s, –e,
charter.

Frei=herr, *m.* –n, –en, baron;
Herr —, my lord, 2492.

frei=lich, *adv.*, of course, to be sure, certainly.

frei=willig, *adv.*, of one's own free will, voluntary.

fremd, *adj.*, foreign, strange; — bleiben, remain a stranger, 852; a stranger's, 1037; *as noun*, 950.

Fremde, *f.* strange (foreign)land.

Fremd=ling, *m.* -s, -e, stranger, foreigner.

fressen, fraß, gefressen, frißt, *tr.*, eat (*of animals*), feed on.

Freude, *f.* -n, joy, delight.

Freuden=haus, *n.* -es, "er, house of joy.

Freuden=kunde, *f.* -n, glad tidings.

Freuden=schießen, *n.* -s, —, shooting-match.

Freude=spur, *f.* -en, glad memory.

freudig, *adj.*, glad, joyful.

freuen, *impers. tr.*, please; if you like to, 1979; *refl.*, rejoice, 2070; *as noun*, rejoicing, 2624, 2870.

Freund, *m.* -es, -e, friend.

freund=lich, *adj.*, friendly, kind.

Freund=schaft, *f.* -en, friendship; *older sense*, kindred, 660, 1456.

Frevel, *m.* -s, —, crime, outrage.

freveln, *intr.*, commit crime; *part. as adj.*, outrageous, criminal, 2534.

Frevel=that, *f.* -en, crime, deed of violence.

Friede(n), *m.* -ns, -n, peace.

fried=gewohnt, *adj.*, peaceful.

fried=lich, *adj.*, peaceable, peaceful; *as noun*, 429.

Friedrich. Emperor Friedrich II. (reigned 1212–50).

frisch, *adj.*, *adv.*, **fresh**, brisk, new; quick(ly), 96, 103, 1931, 1964; vigorous(ly) 176, 1485, 2261; sound, good, unhurt, 600, 678; freely, 766, 2056; alertly, 1510; eben —, just now, directly, 522; über —er That, in the very act, 1862; mit —er That, with prompt action, at once, 1971.

Frist, *f.* -en, time.

froh, *adj.*, glad, happy.

fröh=lich, *adj.*, joyful, glad, happy; cheerily, frankly, 2056.

froh=locken, frohlockte, gefrohlockt, *intr.*, exult (rejoice) over (*gen. for*, über + *acc.*), 3069; *as noun*, 3281 *.

fromm (frömmer, frömmst), *adj.*, good, worthy; *adv.*, devoutly; *superl. as noun*, 2683.

Fron=dienst, *m.* -es, -e, (enforced) labor.

Fron=vogt, *m.* -s, "e, overseer, taskmaster.

Frucht, *f.* "e, fruit.

früh, *adj.*, *adv.*, early; untimely, 2989.

Früh=ling, *m.* -s, -e, spring.

Früh=trunk, *m.* -s, morning-drink (cup).

fügen, *tr.*, put (fit) together; submit (yield) to, 474.

fühlen, *tr. and intr.*, feel; —d, groping, 594.

fühl=los, *adj.,* unfeeling, un-sympathetic.

führen, *tr.,* lead, conduct (341), take; handle, manage, wield, carry, 134, 313, 1973; strike (blow), 1774.

Fülle, *f.* fullness, plenty.

füllen, *refl.,* be filled.

fünf, *num.,* five.

fünft(=er, =e, =es), *ord. num.,* fifth.

fünf=und=achtzig, *num.,* eighty-five.

für, *prep.* (*acc.*), for; — **sich,** aside; for itself, independently, 1160; **was —,** what kind (sort) of.

furchen, *tr.,* furrow (*brow*).

Furcht, *f.* fear, **fright;** dread, 2943; respect, 1375.

furcht=bar, *adj.,* fearful, terrible.

fürchten, *tr.,* fear, dread; *refl.,* be afraid (of, **vor** + *dat.*).

fürcht=er=lich, *adj.,* frightful, fearful.

furcht=sam, (*adj.*) *adv.,* timidly.

fürder, *adv.* (*old for* **weiter, mehr**), **further; nicht —,** never again, 384.

Für=seh=ung, *f.* (*old for* **Vorsehung**), providence.

Fürst, *m.* -en, -en, prince.

Fürsten=gunst, *f.* "e, princes' favor.

Fürsten=haus, *n.* -es, "er, princely house (= family).

Fürsten=knecht, *m.* -s, -e, princes' slave.

für=wahr, *adv.,* indeed, verily.

Fuß, *m.* -es, "e, foot; **zu —e,** on foot, 2675; **stehenden —es,** at once, 333.

Fuß=stoß, *m.* -es, "e, (foot) thrust, kick.

G

Gabe, *f.* -n, gift.

gäh=lings, *adv.,* (*Swiss for* **jäh=lings**), abruptly, suddenly.

gäh=stotzig, *adj.,* (*Swiss for* **jäh=stotzig**), steep.

Gang, *m.* -es, "e, course, manner (*of living*).

ganz, *adj.,* whole, all; *adv.,* quite, entirely, wholly; *as noun,* the whole.

gar, *adv.,* quite, very; *with neg.* empathic, at all; even, 2663.

gären, **gor, gegoren,** *tr.,* ferment; *part. adj.,* rankling, 2573.

Garten, *m.* -s, ", garden.

Gasse, *f.* -n, narrow street, road; passage, cf. 1931, note.

Gast, *m.* -es, "e, guest.

Gast=freund, *m.* -es, "e, good (intimate) **friend.**

gast=lich, *adj.,* hospitable.

Gast=recht, *n.* -s, -e, right of hospitality.

Gattin, *f.* —nen, wife.

Gebälk, *n.* -s, -e, (*collect.*), beams, timbers.

gebären, **gebar, geboren, gebiert,** *tr.,* bear, give birth to.

geben, **gab, gegeben, giebt,** *tr.,* give; yield, 1051; furnish, 1129; — + **auf,** put faith in, 883; heed, 2178; **zu erkennen —,** make known, 1203; **was giebt es,** what's the matter, 68;

es giebt (gab, etc.), there is (was, etc.).

gebieten, gebot, geboten, *tr.*, command, govern, rule.

Gebirg(e), *n.* -(e)s, -e, (*collect.*), mountains.

geboren (*past part.* of gebären), born, natural, 1625.

geborgen (*past part. of* bergen), safe, sheltered, hidden.

Gebot, *n.* -s, -e, command, order.

gebrauchen, *tr.*, use.

Gebresten, *n.* -s, —, sorrow, grief, 198, note.

gebühren, *intr.* (*dat.*), be due, belong to; *refl.*, be proper, becoming.

Geburts=land, *n.* -es, "er, native land, country.

Gedächt=nis, *n.* -sses, -sse, memory; zum —, in memory, 3247.

Gedanke, *m.* -ns, -n, thought.

gedeihen, gedieh, gediehen, *intr.*, s., grow, thrive; progress, advance, 353*.

gedenk, *adj.*, (*for* eingedenk), mindful of, 1199.

gedenken, gedachte, gedacht, *intr.* (*gen.*, an + acc.), think of, remember; think (intend) to do, 2274, 3231.

Geduld, *f.* patience.

geduld=ig, *adv.*, patiently.

Gefahr, *f.* -en, danger.

gefähr=lich, *adj.*, dangerous; *neut. noun*, 1517.

gefallen, gefiel, gefallen, gefällt, *intr.* (*dat.*), please.

Gefangene(r) (*past part. as noun*), *m.* -n, -n (*or* -e), prisoner.

Gefängnis, *n.* -sses, -sse, prison.

Gefieder, *n.* -s, (*collect.*), game birds.

Gefolge, *n.* -s, — (*collect.*), retinue, attendants.

Gefühl, *n.* -s, -e, feeling.

gegen, *prep.*, against, towards, about, to (= as compared with), contrary to.

Gegend, *f.* -en, region; scene.

Gegen=teil, *n.* -s, -e, contrary.

gegen=über, *prep.* (*dat.*) *and adv.*, over against, opposite.

gehaben, *refl.*, fare; gehabt Euch wohl, Farewell! 943, 2120, 2685.

gehässig, *adj.*, spiteful; — sein, to hate, 488.

geheim, *adj.*, (secret); intimate.

Geheimnis, *n.* -sses, -sse, secret.

Geheiß, *n.* -es, command, order.

gehen, ging, gegangen, *intr.*, s., go; get loose, fall, 2665; geht nicht, can't be done, 104; hoch —, run high, 109; — um + acc., concern, be a question of, 112; meines Wegs —, go my way, 1570; zu Rate —, take counsel, 287.

Gehöft, *n.* -(e)s, -e, farm.

Gehölz, *n.* -es, -e, woods, forest.

gehorchen, *intr.* (*dat.*), obey.

gehören, *intr.* (*dat.*), belong to.

gehorsam, *adj.*, obedient, dutiful; *pl. as noun*, 400.

Gehorsam, *m.* -s, obedience, allegiance.

Geißel, *f.* –n, scourge.

Geist, *m.* –es, –er, spirit, heart, mind.

Geister-stunde, *f.* –n, ghost (midnight) hour.

Geiz, *m.* –es, greed, avarice.

Geländer, *n.* –s, —, railing.

 gelangen, *intr.*, f., get to, reach.

gelassen, *part. adj.*, *in exclam.* Quiet! 1851.

Geläut(e), *n.* –s, ringing of bells; set of bells, 47, 49.

Geld-not, *f.* "e(n), financial distress.

Gelegen-heit, *f.* –en, opportunity.

Geleit, *n.* –es, –e, escort.

gelenk, *adj.*, supple, agile, nimble.

geliebt, *part. adj.*, loved, dear; *as noun*, 2532.

geloben, *tr.*, promise, vow; *refl.*, pledge oneself, 1225; das ge= lobte (Land), the Promised Land, 3271.

gelten, galt, gegolten, gilt, *intr.*, be worth, be of (have) value (weight, influence); pass, (2054), pass (stand) for, 1111; be at stake, 1921; be worth while, 1938; be a question of, 1990, 2103.

Gelübde, *n.* –s, –, vow.

Gelüsten, *n.* –s (*inf. noun*), desire, purpose.

gemäch-lich, (*adj.*) *adv.*, easily, 141; slowly, 1792.

gemahnen, *tr.* (an + *acc.*), remind of.

gemein, *adj.*, common (= gen-

eral), 435; common (= mean), 830; *as noun*, common good (weal), 737.

Gemeinde, *f.* –n, community; meeting, 1129.

gemein-sam, (*adj.*) *adv.*, together, in common.

Gemse, *f.* –n, chamois.

Gemsen-horn, *n.* –s, "er, chamois-horn.

Gemüt, *n.* –s, –er, mind, heart.

gen, *contraction of* gegen, towards.

genießen, genoß, genossen, *tr.*, enjoy.

Genoß(e), *m.* –en, –en, companion.

Genoß-same, *f.* –n, community, friends.

genug, *adv.*, *indec. adj.*, *noun*, enough.

G(e)nügen, *n.* –s (*inf. noun*), enough; — that, sufficed, 1192.

Genuß, *m.* –sses, "sse, enjoyment.

gerad(e), *adj.*, straight; straightforward, honest, 1014; *adv.*, just, directly.

Gerät, *n.* –s, –e (*collect.*), tools.

gerecht, *adj.*, just, righteous, legitimate, merited; good, worthy, 1069.

Gerechtigkeit, *f.* –en, justice.

Gericht, *n.* –es, –e, judgment; court; zu — sitzen, hold court, 820.

gering, *adj.*, small.

gern(e), *adv.*, gladly, cheerfully; *with verbs*, like to, be glad to.

Gerſau. Village in Schwyz, under the Rigi.

Gerüſt(e), *n.* -(e)s -, scaffolding.

Geſchäft, *n.* -s, -e, business, affair.

Geſchäftig-keit, *f.* -en, activity.

geſchehen, geſchah, geſchehen, geſchieht, *impers. intr.*, ſ., happen, be done (shown, 397); *neut. part. noun*, 993.

Geſchenk, *n.* -s, -e, gift, present.

Geſchick, *n.* -s, -e, fate, future, lot.

Geſchlecht, *n.* -s, -er, generation; sex, 3000.

Geſchmeide, *n.* -s, -, jewels.

Geſchöpf, *n.* -(e)s, -e, creature.

Geſchoß, *n.* -ſſes, -ſſe, arrow, bolt.

geſchwind, (*adj.*) *adv.*, quickly, at once.

Geſchwind-ſein, *n.* -s, quickness.

Geſell(e), *m.* -en, -en, fellow-workman; comrade, 1753.

geſellen, *tr. and refl.*, join (company with).

geſellig, *adv.*, in company, together.

Geſetz, *n.* -es, -e, law.

Geſicht, *n.* -(e)s, -er, **sight**, view; face, look.

Geſindel, *n.* -s, rabble.

geſinnt, *part. adj.*, minded, disposed.

Geſpann, *n.* -s, -e, span, yoke.

geſpannt, *part. adj.*, eager.

Geſpräch, *n.* -(e)s, —e, discourse, conversation.

Geßler-iſch, *proper adj.*, Gessler's, of Gessler.

Geſtade, *n.* -s, —, shore, bank.

Geſtalt, *f.* -en, shape, form.

geſtaltet, *part. adj.*, formed, shaped.

geſtehen, geſtand, geſtanden, *tr.*, confess.

Geſträuch, *n.* -(e)s (*collect.*), bushes.

geſtreng, *adj.*, stern, dread; —er Herr, my lord, 1860, 2737.

geſund, *adj.*, sound, healthy.

Getön, *n.* -(e)s (*collect.*), sound, clang.

getrauen, *refl.* (*dat.*), **trust** oneself, dare.

getreu-lich, *adv.*, faithfully.

getroſt, *adj.*, confident, cheerful, courageous. [fidence.

getröſtet, *part. as adv.*, with con-

gewahren, *tr.*, discover; *with gen.*, become **aware** of, 2253.

gewähren, *tr.*, give, grant; *intr.*, answer (vouch) for (für), 711.

Gewalt, *f.* -en, power, authority, oppression, violence.

Gewalt-beginnen, *n.* -s, act of tyranny.

Gewalt-herrſchaft, *f.* tyranny, despotism.

gewalt-ig, *adj.*, mighty, vast; *adv.*, by violence.

gewalt-ſam, *adj.*, violent; *adv.*, with might, 949.

Gewalt-that, *f.* -en, deed of violence, outrage.

Gewehr, *n.* -s, -e, weapon (= cross-bow).

Geweih, *n.* -(e)s, -e, horns.

VOCABULARY

Gewerbe, *n.* -ß, —, business.

Gewinn, *n.* -ß, -e, gain, profit.

gewinnen, gewann, gewonnen, *tr.*, win, gain, get ; capture, 2875.

gewiß, *adj.*, sure, certain; some.

Gewitter, *n.* -ß, — (*collect.*), storm.

gewöhnen, *tr.*, accustom to.

gewohnt, *part. adj.*, used (accustomed) to (*acc.*, 539; *gen.*, 1913).

gift=geschwollen, *part. adj.*, swollen with poison.

gift=ig, *adj.* (poisonous), malignant.

Gipfel, *m.* -ß, —, height; worst, 640.

Gitter, *n.* -ß, —, grating, cage.

Glanz, *m.* -eß, brightness, splendor; show, 916; glow, 2428.

glänzen, *intr.*, shine, gleam ; *part. adj.*, bright, brilliant.

glanz=voll, *adj.*, radiant, resplendent.

Glarner, *proper adj.*, of Glarus.

Glärnisch. Name of mountain peaks in Glarus.

glatt, *adj.*, smooth, sleek.

Glaube(n), *m.* -(n)ß, —, faith, belief.

glauben, *tr.*, believe, put faith in (*dat.*, *or* an + *acc.*).

glaubens=wert, *adj.*, trustworthy.

gleich, *adj.* like, same; *as noun*, the same, *pl.*, equals; even, 1023; *adv.*, at once, directly (= so=gleich) ; *conj.* (= ob=gleich)), although, 1119-20.

gleichen, glich, geglichen, *intr.* (*dat.*), be like.

gleich=falls, *adv.*, likewise, also.

gleich=förmig, *adv.*, uniformly.

gleich=wie, *conj.*, just (like) as.

gleiten, (usually glitt, geglitten, here weak), *intr.*, j. *or* h., glide, slip.

Gletscher, *m.* -ß, —, glacier.

Gletscher=berg, *m.* -(e)ß, -e, snow-mountain.

Glocke, *f.* -n, bell.

Glöck=lein, *n.* -ß, —, little bell.

glor=reich, *adj.*, glorious.

Glück, *n.* -(e)ß, fortune, prosperity, happiness.

glück=lich, *adj.*, happy, fortunate; *adv.*, successfully, safely; *as noun, pl.* 3275, *sg.* 3284.

glück=selig, *adj.*, happy, successful.

Glücks=stand, *m.* -(e)ß, fortune.

glühen, *intr.*, glow.

Glut, *f.* -en, glow, flame.

Gnade, *f.* -n, mercy, clemency, pardon.

gnäd=ig, *adj.*, gracious, merciful.

gnug = genug.

Gnügen = Genügen.

Gold, *n.* -eß, gold.

Goller (for Koller), *m.* -ß, —, doublet.

gönnen, *tr.*, grant.

gotisch, *adj.*, Gothic.

Gott, *m.* -eß (ᵘer, gods), God.

Gottes=haus, *n.* eß, ᵘer, house of God, monastery.

Gotthard. Name of mountain and pass south of Uri.

Grab, *n.* -eß, ᵘer, grave.

graben, grub, gegraben, gräbt, *tr.*, dig.

grabe = gerade.

Graf, *m.* -en, -en, Count.

Gram, *m.* -s, grief, sorrow.

Gransen, *m.* -s, — (*lit.* beak); der hintere —, stern (*of a boat*).

Gras, *n.* -es, "er, grass.

gräß=lich, *adj.*, terrible, dreadful; *often as noun.*

Grat=tier, *n.* -(e)s, -e, chamois.

grau, *adj.*, gray.

grauen, *impers.intr.*(*dat.*), dread, be afraid (of, vor + *dat.*); *as noun,* terror, 1095.

grauen=voll, *adj.*, terrible, awful.

grau=sam, *adj.*, terrible, cruel.

Grausam=keit, *f.* -en, cruelty.

Grausen, *n.* -s, horror, dread.

grausen=voll, *adj.*, terrible, awful.

greifen, griff, gegriffen, *tr.*, catch, seize (= ergreifen, 73); *with* in + *acc.*, reach, 1278, lay hold of, 1818 *; restrain, stay, 2181; *with* nach + *dat.*, reach out after, 1357; *with* zu + *dat.*, take up, have recourse to, 440, 1291, 1321.

greis, *adj.*, hoary.

Greis, *m.* -es, -e, old man.

Grenze, *f.* -n, border, limit.

grenzen=los, (*adj.*) *adv.*, boundlessly.

Greuel, *m.* -s, —, outrage.

greu=lich, *adj.*, horrible, shocking; *comp. as noun,* 558.

Grimm, *m.* -(e)s, fury.

Groll, *m.* -s, enmity, grudge, *with* auf (= gegen), 259.

grollen, *intr.* (*dat.*), bear a grudge.

groß (größer, größt), *adj.*, great, large; *as noun,* 1055, 3084; astonished, 2336 *.

Groß=vater, *m.* -s, ", grandfather.

Gruft, *f.* "e, crevasse, grave, 1505; dungeon, 2363 (*pl.*).

grün, *adj.*, green; *as noun,* 596.

Grund, *m.* -es, "e, ground, foundation; *pl.*, gorges, 1550; in —, to the bottom, 2707.

gründen, *tr.*, establish.

gründ=lich, (*adj.*) *adv.*, thoroughly.

grünen, *intr.*, grow green; grow, flourish, 2425; *part.adj.*, green, 36.

gruppieren, *tr.*, group; *refl.*, be grouped, 3281 *.

grüßen, *tr.*, greet; *refl.*, exchange greetings.

Gunst, *f.* favor; zu —, in favor of, 1246.

günst=ig, *adj.*, favorable.

Günst=ling, *m.* -s, -e, favorite.

gürten, *tr.*, gird, belt.

gut (besser, best), *adj.*, good; lawful, 82; *often as noun and adv.* (well); Laßt's — sein, never mind, 1107.

Gut, *n.* -es, "er, goods, property, estate, possessions (= 1287, rights).

Güte, *f.* kindness.

güt=ig, *adj.*, kind, gracious; pleasant, 1799.

Gut=that, *f.* -en, kindness, favor.

H

ha, *interj.,* ha! ah!

Habe, *f.* goods, property.

haben, hatte, gehabt, *tr. and aux.,* have, possess; was habt Ihr, what's the matter with you, 70; eilig —, be in a hurry, 773.

Habs=burg. Ancestral castle of the Habsburg family.

Hack=messer (*lit.* hack-knife). One of the jutting cliffs of the Axenberg.

Hafen, *m.* -s, ", haven, harbor.

hageln, *intr. impers.,* hail.

Hahn, *m.* -es, "e, cock.

Hake, *m.* -n (*lit.* hook). Mountain near Schwyz.

halb, *adj.,* half.

Halb=kreis, *m.* -es, -e, half-circle.

Halden (*old dat. of* Halde, slope), part of Melchthal's father's name, 563, note.

Hälfte, *f.* -n, half.

Halle, *f.* -n, hall.

Hals, *m.* -es, "e, neck.

hals=gefähr=lich, *adj.,* dangerous (to life).

halt, *interj.,* halt! hold! stop!

halten, hielt, gehalten, hält, *tr.,* hold, keep (= keep back, 619); *for* zu=halten, keep shut, 802; celebrate, 2653; *often intr.,* hold, keep; halt, wait, 1409, 2853; hold, last, 1514; an sich —, restrain oneself, 1922, 1992*.

Hammer, *m.* -s, ", hammer.

Hand, *f.* "e, hand; auf eigne

—, on one's own account, 232; zur —, at hand, 1122.

Hand=bube, *m.* -n, -n, boy, servant.

handeln, *intr.,* act, take action (2401); *with* an + *dat.,* act toward, treat, 2071, 2343.

hand=haben, handhabte, gehand=habt, to handle.

Hand=langer, *m.* -s, —, laborer.

hand=lich, (*adj.*) *adv.,* vigorously.

hand=los, (*adj.*) *adv.,* inaccessibly.

Hand=schlag, *m.* -s, "e, handclasp.

Hand=schuh, *m.* -s, -e, gauntlet.

Hand=werk, *n.* -s, -e, (handiwork) trade.

hangen, hing, gehangen, hängt, *intr.,* hang.

hängen, (*tr.*) *intr.,* hang.

Hans. Hans, short form of Jo=hann(es).

härmen, *refl.,* grieve.

harm=los, *adj.,* harmless.

harmon=isch, *adj.,* harmonious.

Harnisch, *m.* -es, -e, harness, armor.

Harras, *m.* master of horse.

harren, *intr.* (*gen.,* or auf + *acc.*), wait for, await.

hart, (härter, härtest), *adj.,* hard, harsh; *noun,* 3085; *adv.,* hard (close) by, 3093.

härten, *tr.,* harden, temper.

haschen, *tr.,* snatch, seize

Haß, *m.* -es, hate.

hassen, *tr.,* hate.

Hast, *f.* haste.

Haube, *f.* -n, cap, hood.

Hauch, *m.* –(e)s, breath, air.

Haufe(n), *m.* –ns, –n, troop, body (*of men*).

häufen, *refl.*, be heaped.

Haupt, *n.* –es, "er, head; leader, president.

Haupt=ort, *m.* –es, "er, chief-town.

Haus, *n.* –es, "er, house, home; House (= family); zu —e, at home, 535, 1487; nach —e, home, 2048.

hausen, *intr.*, live; stay, be.

Haus=flur, *f.* –en, *primarily* entrance-hall; room.

Haus=frau, *f.* –en, house-wife, wife.

Haus=gebrauch, *m.* –s, "e, family custom.

Haus=genoß(e), *m.* –ssen, –ssen, (household) companion.

haus=halten, hielt, gehalten, hält, keep house, live.

Häus=lein, *n.* –s, —, little house.

häus=lich, *adj.*, domestic, household.

Haus=recht, *n.* –(e)s, –e, household (family) right.

Haus=thür, *f.* –en, house-door.

Haus=vater, *m.* –s, ", family man, father of a family.

heben, hob, gehoben, *tr.*, lift, raise.

Heer, *n.* –es, –e, army, host.

Heer=macht, *f.* "e, army, armed force.

Heer=weg, *m.* –es, –e, highway, road.

Heer=zug, *m.* –es, "e, host, army.

heftig, *adj.*, violent, vehement, sharp.

Heftig=keit, *f.* –en, vehemence violence.

Heide, *m.* –n, –n, heathen.

Heil (*n.* –es, health), *interj.*, hail!

heilen, *tr.*, heal, cure.

heilig, *adj.*, holy; –er Gott, merciful Heaven! 105.

Heilig=tum, *n.* –s, "er, sanctuary.

heim, *adv. and sep. pref.*, home, homeward.

Heimat, *f.* –en, home, native land, dwelling-place.

heimat=lich, *adj.*, native.

heim=bringen, brachte, gebracht, *tr.*, bring home.

heim=isch, (*adj.*) *adv.*, at home.

Heim=kehr, *f.* return home.

heim=kehren, *intr.*, s., return home.

heim=lich, *adj.*, secret.

heim=sehnen, *refl.*, long for home.

heim=treiben, trieb, getrieben, *tr.*, drive home.

Heinrich. Henry (Melchthal's father).

heischen, *tr.*, ask for.

heiser, *adj.*, hoarse

heiß, *adj.*, hot.

heißen, hieß, geheißen, *intr.*, be called (named); mean, be; es hieß, they said, 2957.

heiter, *adj.*, merry, gay, bright.

Helden=kraft, *f.* "e, heroic strength.

Helden=kühnheit, *f.* heroic courage.

helfen, half, geholfen, hilft, *intr.* (*dat.*), help.

Helfer, *m.* -s, —, helper, accomplice.

hell, *adj.*, clear, bright; shrill.

Helm, *m.* -es, -e, helmet.

her, *adv. and sep. pref.*, here, hither (*toward speaker*); lange —, long since, 1549.

her=ab, *adv. and sep. pref.*, down (from); *after acc.*, down (along), 2695*.

herab=flammen, *intr.*, f., flash down.

herab=reiten, ritt, geritten, *intr.*, f., ride down.

herab=senden, sandte, gesandt, *tr.*, send down.

herab=steigen, stieg, gestiegen, *intr.*, f., climb down.

heran, *adv. and sep. pref.*, here, this way, up.

heran=ziehen, zog, gezogen, *intr.*, f., come on, approach.

her=auf, *adv. and sep. pref.*, up, up here.

her=aus, *adv. and sep. pref.*, out here, from, forth.

heraus=finden, fand, gefunden, *reciprocal refl.*, find out, recognize one another.

heraus=geben, gab, gegeben, giebt, *tr.*, give (deliver) up.

heraus=nehmen, nahm, genommen, nimmt, *tr.*, take out.

heraus=stürzen, *intr.*, f., rush out.

heraus=treten, trat, getreten, tritt, *intr.*, f., step out.

heraus=wachsen, wuchs, gewach-

sen, wächst, *intr.*, f., grow up out of.

herb, *adj.*, bitter.

her=bei, *adv. and sep. pref.*, here, this way, up.

herbei=eilen, *intr.*, f., hasten up.

herbei=kommen, kam, gekommen, *intr.*, f., come up.

Herberg(e), *f.* -en, (*lit.* inn), shelter.

Herd, *m.* -es, -e, hearth.

Herde, *f.* -n, herd.

Herde(n)=glocke, *f.* -n, herdbell.

Herden=reihen, *m.*, -s, —, herdsman's call (= Kuh=reihen).

herein, *adv. and sep. pref.*, in, in here.

herein=dringen, drang, gedrungen, *intr.*, f., press (force way) in, penetrate.

herein=eilen, *intr.*, f., hurry in.

herein=führen, *tr.*, bring (lead) in.

herein=rufen, rief, gerufen, *tr.*, call in.

herein=stürzen, *intr.*, f., rush in; noun, 2797 *; im —, as they rush (come) up.

herein=treten, trat, getreten, tritt, *intr.*, f., step in, enter.

herein=ziehen, zog, gezogen, *tr.*, draw in.

her=finden, fand, gefunden, *refl.* find one's way.

her=führen, *tr.*, lead (bring) here.

her=für (*old for* hervor), *adv. and sep. pref.*, forth, out.

herfür=brechen, brach, gebrochen, bricht (*for* hervor=brechen), *intr.*, f., break out.

herfür=ziehen (*old for* hervor= ziehen), zog, gezogen, *tr.*, draw (take) out.

her=geben, gab, gegeben, giebt, *tr.*, give up.

her=hangen, hing, gehangen, hängt, *intr.*, ſ., hang down over.

Heribann (*for* Heer=bann), *m.* –s, call to arms.

her=kommen, kam, gekommen, *intr.*, ſ., come here.

Herolds=ruf, *m.* –es, –e, herold's call.

Herr, *m.* –n, –en, lord, Lord, master; *old form* Herre, Sir, 1559; husband, 3109.

her=reichen, *tr.*, reach (give) (*hand*).

Herren=bank, *f.* ˮe, nobles' bench.

Herren=burg, *f.* –en, lordly castle.

Herren=knecht, *m.* –(e)s, –e, vas- sal, slave.

Herren=leute, *pl.*, well-to-do cit- izens.

herren=los, *adj.*, without a (feu- dal) lord, 1217; unclaimed, free, 1251.

Herren=schiff, *n.* –(e)s, –e, gover- nor's boat.

herr=lich, *adj.*, splendid, glorious; *noun*, glory, 2423.

Herr=schaft, *f.* –en, authority, rule.

herrschen, *intr.*, rule, reign.

Herrscher, *m.* –s, —, ruler.

her=schicken, *tr.*, send here.

herüber, *adv. and sep. pref.*, across, over here.

herüber=klingen, klang, geklun- gen, *intr.*, ring (sound) over here.

her=überkommen, kam, gekom- men, *intr.*, ſ., come over (across) here.

her=um, *adv. and sep. pref.*, around, about.

herum=gehen, ging, gegangen, *intr.*, ſ., go (be passed) round.

herunter, *adv. and sep. pref.*, down.

herunter=gießen, goß, gegossen, *intr.*, ſ., pour down.

herunter=holen, *tr.*, bring down.

herunter=sinken, sank, gesunken, *intr.*, ſ., sink down.

herunter=steigen, stieg, gestiegen, *intr.*, ſ., descend.

hervor, *adv. and sep. pref.*, forth, out.

hervor=brechen, brach, gebrochen, bricht, *intr.*, ſ., break forth, rush out.

hervor=graben, grub, gegraben, gräbt, *tr.*, dig out from under (unter, 2545).

hervor=kommen, kam, gekommen, *intr.*, ſ., come forth.

hervor=stürzen, *intr.*, ſ., rush (out) forth.

hervor=treten, trat, getreten, tritt, *intr.*, ſ., step forward.

Herz, *n.* –ens, –en, heart.

herz=einig, *adj.*, one at heart.

herz=haft, (*adj.*) *adv.*, boldly.

herz=lich, (*adj.*) *adv.*, heartily, warmly; very.

Herzog, *m.* –s, ˮe, duke.

heulen, *intr.*, howl, roar.

heute, *adv.*, to-day.

hie=dannen (= von dannen), *adv.*, out of this, away from here.

hie=her (*for* hier=her)=kommen, kam, gekommen, *intr.*, f., get hier, *adv.*, here.   [here.

Hilfe, *f.* help; *interj.*, Help! zu —, Help! 1854.

hilf=los, *adj.*, helpless.

hilf=reich, *adj.*, helpful.

Himmel, *m.* –s, —, heaven, sky; climate, 1799.

himmel=hoch, *adj.*, high as heaven.

himmel=schreiend, *part. adj.*, atrocious, outrageous.

Himmels=dach, *n.* –s, sky.

Himmels=gabe, *f.* –n, gift of heaven.

Himmels=glück, *n.* –(e)s, heavenly bliss.

Himmels=licht, *n.* –s, –er, light of heaven.

Himmels=raum, *m.* –es, "e, quarter of heaven, direction (1793).

hin, *adv. and sep. pref.*, hence, thither, away (*from speaker*); over, gone, 16, 24, 2091; wo ... hin, whither, where.

hin=ab, *adv. and sep. pref.*, down (wards).

hinab=dringen, drang, gedrungen, *intr.*, f., penetrate.

hinab=drücken, *tr.*, press down, repress.

hinab=führen, *tr.*, lead down.

hinab=senden, sandte, gesandt, *tr.*, send down.

hinab=sinken, sank, gesunken, *intr.*, f., sink down.

hinab=steigen, stieg, gestiegen, *intr.*, f., descend.

hin=an, *adv.*, up.

hin=auf, *adv. and sep. pref.*, up.

hinauf=greifen, griff, gegriffen, *intr.*, reach up.

hinauf=heben, hob, gehoben, *tr.*, lift up.

hinauf=schwingen, schwang, geschwungen, *tr.*, swing up on.

hinauf=sehen, sah, gesehen, *intr.*, look up.

hinaufsteigen, stieg, gestiegen, *intr.*, f., ascend.

hin=aus, *adv. and sep. pref.*, out, away.

hinaus=eilen, *intr.*, f., hasten out.

hinaus=senden, sandte, gesandt, *tr.*, send out.

hindern, *tr.*, hinder, prevent.

Hindernis, *n.* –sses, –sse, hindrance.

hin=deuten, *intr.*, point towards.

hin=drücken, *tr.*, press towards (against).

hin=durch, *adv.*, through.

hin=eilen, *intr.*, f., run up (there).

hin=ein, *adv. and sep. pref.*, in, into.

hinein=gehen, ging, gegangen, *intr.*, f., go in (*house, another room*).

hinein=werfen, warf, geworfen, *tr.*, throw in.

hin=fahren, fuhr, gefahren, fährt, *intr.*, f., go away; *imper.*, away! 617, 1693; row along, 2249.

hin=fallen, fiel, gefallen, fällt, *intr.*, ſ., fall (kneel) down.

hin=finden, fand, gefunden, *refl.*, find one's way.

hin=flüchten, *refl.*, flee.

hin=fort, *adv.*, henceforth.

hin=führen, *intr.*, lead (run) along.

hin=gehen, ging, gegangen, *intr.*, ſ., go there; wo gehſt du hin, where are you going?

hin=kommen, kam, gekommen, *intr.*, ſ., get to (there); wo kam ... hin, what became of, where ... go? 2709.

hin=leben, *intr.*, live along.

hinnen, *adv.*, in here; von —, away, 2775.

hin=pflanzen, *tr.*, set up.

hin=reichen, *tr.*, reach (hold) out.

hin=reiten, ritt, geritten, *intr.*, ſ., ride along.

Hin=ſcheid, *m.* -ß, death.

hin=ſchiffen, *intr.*, ſ., sail along.

hin=ſehen, ſah, geſehen, *intr.*, look there (that way).

hin=ſenden, ſandte, geſandt, *tr.*, send thither.

hin=ſtehen, ſtand, geſtanden, *intr.*, stand, go stand.

hin=ſtellen, *tr.*, put, *refl.*, take a stand.

hinten, *adv.*, behind, back (there).

hinter (*superl.* hinterſt), *adj.*, hinder; —n Granſen, stern.

hinter, *prep.* (*dat., acc.*), behind,

after; *adv., sep., insep. pref.*, behind, back.

hintergeh'en, hinterging, hinter= gangen, *insep.*, deceive.

Hinter=grund, *m.* -ß, "e, back- ground.

Hinter=halt, *m.* -ß, ambush.

hinter=halten, hinterhielt, hinter= halten, hinterhält, *tr., insep.*, with**hold.**

hinterſt, *adj., superl.* of hinter.

hin=über, *adv. and sep. pref.*, over, across; over = dead, 2304.

hinüber=dringen, drang, gedrun= gen, *intr.*, ſ., reach across.

hinüber=gehen, ging, gegangen, *intr.*, ſ., go over, cross.

hinüber=ſchaffen, *tr.*, take (set) over (across).

hinüber=tragen, trug, getragen, trägt, *tr.*, take (carry) over.

hinüber=ziehen, zog, gezogen, *intr.*, ſ., go (move) over (across).

hin=unter, *adv. and sep. pref.*, down(wards).

hinunter=ſchiffen, *intr.*, ſ., go (sail) down.

hinunter=ſteigen, ſtieg, geſtiegen, *intr.*, ſ., descend.

hin=weg, *adv. and sep. pref.*, away, off, über ... —, over, across.

hinweg=gehen, ging, gegangen, *intr.*, ſ., go (pass) over (**away**).

hinweg=legen, *tr.*, lay aside (**away**).

hinweg=treten, trat, getreten, tritt, *intr.*, ſ., step aside.

hinweg=werfen, warf, geworfen, wirft, *tr.*, throw away, cast off.

hin=werfen, warf, geworfen, wirft, *tr.*, throw (cast) away (down).

hin=ziehen, zog, gezogen, *tr.*, attract.

hin=zu, *adv. and sep. pref.*, towards, up (to).

hinzu=laufen, lief, gelaufen, läuft, *intr.*, f., run up.

Hirsch, *m.* -es, -e, stag.

Hirt, *m.* -en, -en, herdsman.

Hirten=knabe, *m.* -n, -n, herdsman's boy.

hoch (höher, höchst), *adj.* (declined hoher, etc.), high, great, noble; *adv.*, greatly, very.

Hoch=flug, *m.* -s (collect.), large game birds.

hoch=geboren, *part. adj.*, highborn, noble.

Hoch=gewilde (*for* Hoch=wild), *n.* -s (collect.), large game (*animals*); Hochflug und —, large game (bird and beast), 901.

Hoch=land, *n.* -es, -e, highland.

hoch=springen, sprang, gesprungen, *intr.*, f., leap up high.

hoch=verständig, *adj.*, highly intelligent, most sensible.

Hoch=wacht, *f.*, -en, beacon (signal) fire; signal height, observation-point, 2849.

hoch=würdig, *adj. as noun*, the sacrament, 1749.

Hoch=zeit, *f.* -en, wedding (procession).

Hochzeit=gesellschaft, *f.* -en, wedding-party.

Hochzeits=haus, *n.*, -es, "er (*lit.* wedding-house), wedding-feast.

Hof, *m.*, -es, "e, farm(yard), court(yard).

hoffen, *tr.*, hope.

Hoffnung, *f.* -en, hope, expectation.

Hof=statt, *f.* court.

Hof=thor, *n.* -s, -e, yard-gate.

Höhe, *f.* -n, height, top; in die —, up.

Hoheit, *f.* -en, greatness; authority, sovereignty.

hohl, *adj.*, hollow, empty; deep, sunken, 2561.

Höhle, *f.* -n, cave, hole, den; socket, 643.

Hohl=weg, *m.* -s, -e, (sunken) road, narrow pass.

hohn=sprechen, sprach, gesprochen, spricht, *intr.*, mock.

hold, *adj.*, gracious, kind, sweet, propitious; — sein, like, love, 1415.

holen, *tr.*, fetch, get, bring.

Höllen=qual, *f.* -en, (hellish) awful agony.

Höllen=rachen, *m.* -s, —, mouth of hell.

Hol(l)under=strauch, *m.* -s, "e, elder-bush.

Holz, *n.* -es, "er, wood.

horchen, *intr.*, hearken, listen.

Horde, *f.* -n, horde.

hören, *tr.*, hear.

Horn, *n.* -(e)s, "er, horn, peak.

Hornisse, *f.* -n, hornet.

hübsch, *adj.*, pretty, nice; *as noun*, 1583.

Huf, *m.* -es, -e, hoof.

huldigen, *tr.*, give homage (allegiance).

Huldigung, *f.* -en, homage.

hundert, *num.*, hundred.

hurtig, *adj.*, quick; mach' —, make haste, 37.

Hut, *m.* -es, "e, hat.

Hütte, *f.* -n, hut, cottage.

J

Jberg. Father of Stauffacher's wife, Gertrud.

ich, *pron.*, I.

ihr, *pron.*, you, ye (*pl. of* du); Jhr (*old polite address; pl. verb*), you.

ihr, *poss. adj.*, her, its, their; Jhr, your (*polite form*).

Jmifee, Jmmenfee. Village on Lake Zug.

immer, *adv.*, always; auf —, forever.

immer=dar, *adv.*, always; auf —, forever.

in, *prep.* (*dat., acc.*), in, into, to, at, within; ins = in das; im = in dem; in = in den, 305, 2707, 2735.

Jn=brunst, *f.* fervor.

in=dem, *conj.*, while, as, when; *adv.*, meanwhile.

in=des, indeffen, *conj.*, while; *adv.*, meanwhile.

Jnhalt, *m.* -s, substance, contents.

inne, *adv.*, within; — halten, pause, 2500 *.

inner, *adj.* (inner); *as noun*, interior, 2933; heart, soul.

innerst, *adj. as noun*, inmost heart (thoughts), 297; inmost recesses, 505.

Jnfel, *f.* -n, isle.

irdisch, *adj.* (earthly) *as noun*, earthly things.

irr(e), *adj.*, astray.

irren, *intr.*, wander; *refl.*, be mistaken, 1828.

Jrr=tum, *m.* -s, "er, error.

Jtalien, *n.* -s, Italy.

J

ja, *adv.*, yes, surely, you know.

Jagd, *f.* -en, hunt, chase.

Jagd=horn, *n.* -s, "er, hunting-horn.

Jagd=kleid, *n.* -s, -er, hunting-costume.

jagen, *tr. and intr.*, hunt, pursue.

Jäger, *m.* -s, —, hunter.

Jahr, *n.* -es, -e, year.

Jahr=markt, *m.* -s, "e, fair(time).

Jammer, *m.* -s, —, grief, wretchedness.

jammern, *tr., intr., impers.* (*gen.*), pity, grieve, excite pity.

Jammer=ruf, *m.* -s, -e, cry of distress.

je, *adv.*, ever, each time; je der zehnte, every tenth, 1171.

jeder (-e, -es), *adj., pron.*, each (every) one.

jed=weder (-e, -es), *adj., pron.*, *old for* jeder.

jemand, *pron.*, someone (body).

jener (-e, -es), *adj., pron.*, that (one), the former, he.

jen=feits, *adv. and prep.* (*gen.*), beyond, on the other side of.

jetzo, *adv., old for* jetzt.

jetzt, *adv.,* now; bis —, until now.

Joch, –es, –e, **yoke**; (mountain) ridge.

Judas (*gen.* Judä). St. Jude.

Jugend, *f.* **youth.**

jugend=lich, *adj.,* **youthful.**

jung (jünger, jüngst), *adj.,* **young**; jüngst, *adv.,* recently.

Jung=frau. Name of the highest peak in the Bernese Alps.

Jüng=ling, *m.* –s, –e, **young man.**

Junker, *m.* –s, —, **young** noble**man.**

just, *adv.,* **just** (then).

K

Kahn, *m.* –s, "e, **boat.**

Kaiser, *m.* –s, —, **emperor.**

Kaiser=haus, *n.* –es, "er, **imperial house** (family).

Kaiser=hof, *m.* –s, "e, **imperial court.**

Kaiser=krone, *f.* –n, **imperial crown.**

Kaiser=lich, *adj.,* **imperial.**

Kaiser=mord, *m.* –s, –e, **murder** of an emperor.

Kalk, *m.* –es, (–e = kinds of) **lime.**

kalt, *adj.,* **cold.**

Kammer, *f.* –n, **chamber,** room.

Kampf, *m.* –es, "e, **conflict,** battle, struggle.

kämpfen, *intr.,* **fight,** struggle.

karg (*adj.*), *adv.,* sparingly.

Kauf=mann, *m.* –s, Kauf=leute, **merchant.**

Kaufmanns=schiff, *n.* –(e)s, –e, **merchant-ship,** trading-boat.

Kaufmanns=straße, *f.* –n, **commercial highway.**

kaum, *adv.,* scarcely, hardly.

keck, *adj.,* **bold,** daring.

keck=lich, *adv.,* **boldly.**

Kehle, *f.* –n, **throat.**

kehren, *refl.* (*impers.*), return.

Keim, *m.* –es, –e, **germ.**

kein (–e, —), *adj.,* **no,** not a (any), **none.**

kein=er (–e, —), *pron.,* **no one** (man), none.

Keller, *m.* –s, —, **cellar** (= dungeon).

kennen, kannte, gekannt, *tr.,* **know,** — lernen, become acquainted with.   [geon.

Kerker, *m.* –s, —, **prison,** dun-

Kerl, *m.* –s, –e, **fellow.**

Kerns. Village in Unterwalden near Sarnen.

Kernwald. Forest of Kerns.

Kette, *f.* –n, **chain.**

Kind, *n.* –es, –er, **child.**

Kindes=kind, *n.* –es, –er, *pl.,* **children's children.**

Kind=lein, *n.* –s, —, **little child.**

Kissen, *n.* –s, —, **cushion.**

Klage, *f.* –n, **grievance,** complaint.

klagen, *intr.,* **complain of** (wider, über).

Klang, *m.* –es, "e, **sound,** ring.

klar, *adj.,* **clear,** plain.

Kleid, *n.* –s, –er, **dress**; garb.

kleiden, *tr.,* **clothe,** dress.

klein, *adj.,* **little,** petty, trivial.

Kleinod, *n.* -ß, -e, *or* —ien, jewel, treasure.

klimmen, klomm, gekommen (*also weak*), *intr.*, ſ., climb.

klingen, klang, geklungen, *intr.*, sound; *as noun*, 3.

Klippe, *f.* -n, cliff.

klopfen, *intr.*, knock.

Kloſter, *n.* -ß, ", convent, monastery.

Kloſter=leute, *pl.*, people (= serfs) of a monastery.

Kloſter=mei(e)r, *m.* -ß, —, monastery-overseer.

Kluft, *f.* "e, cleft, gorge.

klug (klüger, klügſt), *adj.*, shrewd, wise, prudent.

Knabe, *m.* -n, -n, boy.

Knecht, *m.* -ß, -e, servant, vassal, slave.

Knecht=ſchaft, *f.* bondage, servitude. [tude.

Knie, *n.* -ß, -e, knee.

knieen, *intr.*, kneel.

Köcher, *m.* -ß, —, quiver.

kommen, kam, gekommen, *intr.*, ſ., come, arrive; *with* auf, think of, 1518; zu ſich —, come to (compose) oneself, 2035, 2047.

komm=lich, *adj.* (*Swiss*), comfortable, good.

König, *m.* -ß, -e, king.

König=in, *f.* -nen, queen.

könig=lich, *adj.*, kingly, royal.

Königs=burg, *f.* -en, king's castle.

können, konnte, gekonnt, kann, *tr. and modal aux.*, can, may, be able; *with* bei, get at = hurt, 2708.

Kopf, *m.* -(e)ß, "e, head.

Korn, *n.* -(e)ß, "er, corn, (= wheat) grain.

koſt=bar, *adj.*, costly, precious.

koſten, *tr.*, cost.

köſt=lich, *adj.*, choice, precious.

krachen, *intr.*, crash, crack; *noun*, 36*.

krächzen, *intr.*, croak.

Kraft, *f.* "e, force, strength.

kräftig=lich, *adv.*, strongly, vigorously; *old for* kräftig.

kraft=los, *adj.*, powerless, weak; in vain, 2608.

krähen, *intr.*, crow.

krampf=haft, *adj.*, convulsive.

Kranke (*adj. noun, from* krank), *m.* -n, -n *or* —, sick person.

kränken, *tr.*, hurt (*feelings*), grieve, wrong.

Kranz, *m.* -eß, "e, wreath, crown.

Kränz=lein, *n.* -ß, —, little wreath (garland).

Kraut, *n.* -ß, "er, herb, plant.

Kreis, *m.* -eß, -e, circle; sphere, 762; socket, 678; round, 2402.

kreucht (*old for* kriecht), *pres. ind., 3d sg. of* kriechen.

Kreuz, *n.* -eß, -e, cross.

Kreuz=lein, *n.* -ß, —, little cross.

kriechen, kroch, gekrochen, *intr.*, ſ. *or* h., creep, crawl.

Krieg, *m.* -(e)ß, -e, war.

krieger=iſch, *adj.*, warlike.

Krieges=macht, *f.* "e, military force.

Krieges=not, *f.* "e, distress of war.

Kriegs=dromme'te (*for* —trom=pe'te), war-trumpet.

Krone, *f.* -n, crown.

krönen, *tr.*, crown.

Krümme, *f.* -n, winding, bend.

Kuckuck, *m.* -s, -e, cuckoo.

Kuh, *f.* "e, cow.

kühlen, *tr.*, cool.

kühn, *adj.*, bold.

Kühn=heit, *f.* -en, boldness.

Kuh=reihen. Kuhreihen, the Swiss herdman's cattle-call; cf. *1, note.

Kulm, *m.* -es, -e, peak, crest.

Kummer, *m.* -s, anxiety, grief.

kümmern, *tr.*, concern. [distress.

kummer=voll, *adj.*, sorrowful, anxious.

Kunde, *f.* -n, knowledge, news.

kundig, *adj.*, having knowledge; — sein (*with gen.*), know, be familiar with.

Kund=schaft (*collect.*), *f.* spies.

Kunst, *f.* "e, art, skill.

kunst=geübt, *part. adj.*, practised, skillful.

kurz (kürzer, kürzest), *adj.*, short.

kürz=en, *tr.* (*lit.* shorten), cut off, deprive of (um + *acc.*).

Kurz=weil, *f.* (*also m. and n.* -s), pleasantry, jest.

Küßnacht. Village at north end of Lake Lucerne.

L

laben, *tr.*, refresh (*with food, drink*).

Labung, *f.* -en, refreshment.

lächeln, *intr.*, smile.

lachen, *intr.*, laugh.

laden, lud, geladen (*for ein= laden*), *tr.*, invite, summon.

laden, lud, geladen, *tr.*, load, 357.

Lager, *n.* -s, —, court.

Lamm, *n.* -es, "er, lamb.

Lämmer=geier, *m.* -s, —, lamb's vulture.

Land, *n.* -es, "er *or* -e, land, country; —e, cantons; zu—e, by land, 2280.

Land=ammann, *m.* -s, -e, chief magistrate, landammann.

Land=bedrücker, *m.* -s, —, oppressor.

landen, *intr.*, [.], land.

Landenberg(er). Beringer von Landenberg, governor in Unterwalden.

Landenberg=isch, *proper adj.*, Landenberg's.

Länder=gier, *f.* greed for land.

Länder=kauf, *m.* -s, "e, purchase of land.

Länder=kette, *f.* -n, chain of lands.

Landes=ammann, cf. Landammann.

Landes=feind, *m.* -(e)s, -e, enemy of the country.

Landes=mark, *f.* -en, boundary, border.

Landes=unglück, *n.* -s, -e, national calamity.

Land=leute, *pl.*, peasants, men.

Land=mann, *m.* -(e)s, —leute, country-man, peasant.

Land=mark, *f.* -en, border, boundary.

Land=schaft, *f.* -en, landscape, scene.

Lands=gemeinde, *f.* -n, general assembly.

Lands=gesetz, *n.* -es, -e, law of the land.

Lands=mann, *m.* -s, —leute, fellow-countryman.

Land=straße, *f.* -n, highroad.

Land=sturm, *m.* -s, call (of militia) to arms.

Land=vogt, *m.* -s, "e, governor.

Land=wehr, *f.* -en, bulwark.

lang (länger, längst), *adj.*, long; *adv.* long; *with acc.*, for, during; längst, long (ago) since.

langen, *tr.*, reach, take down.

lang=sam, *adj.*, slow.

längst, *adv.*, long, long ago. Cf. **lang.**

Lanze, *f.* -n, lance.

lassen, ließ, gelassen, läßt, leave, let alone, give up, lose; let, allow; have done; sich — + *infin.*, can (may) be; laßt's gut sein, never mind, 1107.

Last, *f.* -en, load, burden.

lasten, *intr.*, weigh upon, oppress.

lauern, *intr.*, lurk, lie in wait (for, auf).

Lauf, *m.* -(e)s, "e, course; im —, under way, started, 2865.

laufen, lief, gelaufen, läuft, *intr.*, f. *or* h., run, move, pass; ge— kommen, come running.

lauschen, *intr.*, listen, lurk.

laut, *adj.*, aloud.

Laut, *m.* -es, -e, sound.

lauten, *intr.*, sound, run, stand (written).

läuten, *tr. and intr.*, ring; toll (*bell*).

lauter, *adj.*, pure, clear.

Lawine, *f.* -n, avalanche.

leben, *intr.*, live; lebt wohl, Farewell! von etwas —, live on.

Leben, *n.* -s, —, life; ums — gehen, das — gelten, life is at stake.

lebendig, *adj.*, living, alive; *as noun*, 2150.

Lebens=blut, *n.* -s, life-blood.

Lebens=glück, *n.* -s, life-happiness.

leb=haft, (*adj.*) *adv.*, eagerly.

Leb=tag, *m.* -s, -e, life; all the days of my life, 2703.

lechzen, *intr.*, long (languish, thirst) for (nach).

ledig, *adj.*, free, loose.

leer, *adj.*, empty; vain.

leeren, *tr.*, clear.

legen, *tr.*, lay, put.

Leh(e)n, *n.* -s, —, fief; zu — tragen, hold in fief.

Lehen=hof, *m.* -s, "e, feudal court.

Lehens=herr, *m.* -n, -en, feudal (liege) lord.

lehnen, *intr.*, lean (on, auf).

lehren, *tr.*, teach.

Leib, *m.* -es, -er, body, self (1839), life; — und Leben, life and limb, 1925; — und Blut, life, 661.

Leibes=kraft, *f.* "e, bodily strength; *pl.*, all my might, 2263.

leib=lich, *adj.*, one's own.

Leichnam, *m.* -s, -e, (dead) body, corpse.

leicht, (*adj.*), light, easy; frivolous, 794; ready, 300; *adv.*, quickly, easily, promptly.

leicht=fertig, *adj.*, wanton, impudent.

leiden, litt, gelitten, *tr.*, endure, suffer; *intr.*, allow, 2341.

Leiden, *n.* -s, —, suffering.

leider, *interj.*, alas!

leihen, lieh, geliehen, *tr.*, lend.

leisten, *tr.*, do, accomplish; Pflicht —, fulfill duty, 1361; Bürgschaft —, give bail, 1831.

leiten, *tr.*, lead; bring, 1353; Steg —, lay bridge, 1270.

Leiter, *f.* -n, ladder.

lenken, *tr.*, direct, guide.

Lenz, *m.* -es, -e, spring-time = prime.

Leopold. Second son of Emperor Albrecht.

lernen, *tr.*, learn.

lesen, las, gelesen, liest, *tr.*, read.

letzt, *adj.*, last; *as noun*, last, 862; last resort, 1319; worst, 3180.

leuchten, *intr.*, light, shine on, give light; *as noun*, 1443.

Leute, *pl.*, people, men.

Licht, *n.* -es, -er, light.

lichten, *tr.*, light = clear (forest).

lieb, *adj.*, dear, beloved; *comp.* —er, *as adv.*, rather.

Liebe, *f.* love; kindness, favor, 2291.

lieben, *tr.*, love.

lieber (*comp.* of lieb), *adv.*, rather.

lieb=lich, *adj.*, lovely.

Lied, *n.* -es, -er, song, poem.

liegen, lag, gelegen, *intr.*, h. *and* f., lie, be (situated); *with* an + *dat.*, concern, be important, cf. 622, note; an mir —, be my fault, 2904.

Linde, *f.* -n, linden-tree.

link, *adj.*, left; zur Linken, to the left (hand), *1.

links, *adv.*, on the left.

Lippe, *f.* -n, lip.

Lisel. Dim. of Elisabeth.

loben, *tr.*, praise.

Locke, *f.* -n, lock.

locken, *tr.*, entice, attract.

lodern, *intr.*, blaze.

loh, *adv.*, brightly, with a blaze.

Lohn, *m.* -es, "e, reward.

lohnen, *tr.*, reward, repay.

los, *adj.*, loose, (up, 109), free from, rid of, — werden, get rid of; *sep. pref.*, loose, off, free.

Los, *n.* -es, -e, lot, fate.

los=binden, band, gebunden, *tr.*, unloose, unfasten.

lösen, *tr.*, loosen, throw off; acquit, 2048; redeem, 3236.

los=geben, gab, gegeben, giebt, *tr.*, set free.

los=lassen, ließ, gelassen, läßt, *tr.*, let loose.

los=reißen, riß, gerissen, *refl.*, tear oneself away.

Lowerz. Village on Lake Lowerz.

Luft, *f.* "e, air, breeze. [werz.

lugen (*S.G.*, *Swiss*), *intr.*, look (and see).

lügen, log, gelogen, *intr.*, lie; be wrong, 258; das lügst du, that's a lie, 1835.

Luſt, *f.* *e, lust, desire; pleasure; böſe —, malice, 272.

lüſtern, *adj.*, hot, impetuous.

Luxemburg, Graf von. Count Heinrich IV. of Luxemburg, afterwards Emperor Heinrich VII.

Luzern. Lucerne, city on northwest arm of Lake Lucerne.

M

machen, *tr.*, make; fix, 1479; play (part of), 759; mach' hurtig, be quick, 37.

Macht, *f.* *e, might, authority.

mächtig, *adj.*, mighty, strong; *with gen.*, master of.

Mädchen, *n.* -s, —, maiden, girl.

mahnen, *tr.*, remind; *part. as noun*, claimant, 2956.

Mai, *m.* -es (*old* -en), -e (*old* -en), May.

Maien=tau, *m.* -s, May-dew.

maleriſch, *adj.*, picturesque.

man, *indef. pron.*, one, we, you, they, people; *often passive construction.*

mancher (-e, -es), *adj. and pron.*, many (a), many a one.

Mandat, *n.* -s, -e, mandate, order.

Mann, *m.* -es, *er, man, husband.

Männer=wert, *m.* -s, manly worth.

Mannes=wort, *n.* -s, -e, word of a (true) man.

männ=lich (*old form* mann=lich, 2875), manly, brave.

Mantel, *m.* -s, *, mantle, cloak.

Markt, *m.* -es, *e, market (place).

Marter, *f.* -n, pain, torture.

Maß, *n.* -es, -e, measure.

mäßigen, *refl.*, restrain oneself, be moderate.

matt, *adj.*, faint, weak.

Matte, *f.* -n, mead(ow); *S.G. and Swiss for* Wieſe.

Mauer, *f.* -n, wall.

Mauer=ſtein, *m.* -s, -e, stone (*for building*).

Maulwurfs=haufe(n), *m.* -ns, -n, mole-hill (heap).

Maus, *f.* *e, mouse.

Meer, *n.* -(e)s, -e, sea, ocean.

Mehr, *n.* -es, majority.

mehr, *adv.* (*adj.*), more.

mehren, *tr.*, increase, favor.

mehrere, *pl. adj.*, several.

Mehrheit, *f.* -en, majority.

mehrſt, *superl. adj.*, *old for* meiſt, most.

meiden, mied, gemieden, *tr.*, avoid.

Meier, *m.* -s, —, overseer, steward; often proper name.

mein (-er, -e, -es), *poss. adj. and pron.*, my, mine.

meinen, *intr. and tr.*, think, mean, intend.

meinig (der -e, die -e, das -e, *poss. adj., pron.*, mine; *as noun*, my own, 3136.

Meinrad. St. Meinrad, founder of monastery of Einsiedeln.

Meinung, *f.* -en, opinion, wish (396), intentions (2021).

meift (*superl. of* mehr), *adj.*, most; am —en, most.

Meifter, *m.* -8, —, master.

Meifter=fchuß, *m.* -es, "ffe, master-shot.

Melch=thal. Valley of the Melchi in Unterwalden, near Sarnen.

melfen, *tr.*, milk.

Melf=napf, *m.* -8, "e, milk-pail.

Melodie', *f.* -n, melody, air.

Menge, *f.* -n, crowd.

Menfch, *m.* -en, -en, man, human being; fein —, nobody, 98.

Menfchen=denfen, *n.* -8, memory (lit. thinking) of man; feit —, within man's memory, 529.

menfchen=leer, *adj.*, deserted, lonely.

Menfchen=fpur, *f.* -en, human trace.

Menfch=heit, *f.* humanity.

menfch=lich, *adj.*, human; *as noun*, anything (human, *i.e.* accident), 159.

Menfch=lich=feit, *f.* humanity, humaneness.

merfen, *tr.*, notice, mark.

Merf=mal, *n.* -8, -e, mark, sign.

meffen, maß, gemeffen, mißt, *tr.*, measure; mit Augen —, look at closely, 3151; *refl.*, be equal to (2024), vie with.

Metten=glöcflein, *n.* -8, —, matin-bell.

Meute, *f.* -n, pack (*hounds*).

Meuterei', *f.* -en, riot.

Milch, *f.* milk.

mild, *adj.*, mild, gentle, kind.

Milde, *f.* mildness, gentleness.

mild=thätig, *adj.*, benevolent, charitable.

mißbrauchen, *tr. insep.*, misuse, abuse.

Miß=gunft, *f.* ill-will, malice.

mit, *prep.* (*dat.*), *adv.*, *sep. pref.*, with, together; along (too, 2183); by, on, in; — dabei, there too, 1521.

mit=bringen, brachte, gebracht, *tr.*, bring along with = require, 1402.

mit=führen, *tr.*, take (carry) along with.

mit=geben, gab, gegeben, giebt, *tr.*, give to one departing; *with* in + *acc.*, put in with, 864.

mit=fommen, fam, gefommen, *intr.*, f., come along with.

Mit=leid, *n.* -8, pity, sympathy.

mit=nehmen, nahm, genommen, nimmt, *tr.*, take, accept, enjoy.

Mitfchuld, *f.* (joint) guilt.

mit=fchwören, fchwor, gefchwo= ren, *intr.*, swear too (= with others).

Mittag=fonne, *f.* -n, midday-sun = south.

Mittag=ftunde, *f.* -n, midday-hour, noon.

Mitte, *f.* middle, midst.

mit=teilen, *tr.*, tell.

Mittel, *n.* -8, —, means, way, resort.

mitten, *adv.*, in the middle (midst) of, right in.

Mitter=nacht, *f.* "e, midnight; north, 1167.

mit=ziehen, zog, gezogen, *intr.*, f., march along with.

mögen, mochte, gemocht, mag, *tr.*, *and modal aux.,* **may,** can; like (*with acc.*).

mög=lich, *adj.,* possible.

Moment, *n.* -ß, -e, moment.

Mönch, *m.* -ß, -e, monk.

Mond, *m.* -eß, -e, moon; month, 2751.

Mond(en)=nacht, *f.* ̈e, moonlight night; Monden = *old weak gen. sg.*

Mond=licht, *n.* -ß, moonlight.

Mond=regen=bogen, *m.* -ß, ̈, moon rainbow.

Monstranz, *f.* -en, monstrance, sacrament-box. Cf. 1752, note.

Mord, *m.* -ß, -e, murder.

Mörder, *m.* -ß, —, murderer.

mörder=isch, *adj.,* murderous.

Mord=gedanke, *m.* -nß, -n, murderous thought.

Mord=gewehr, *n.* -ß, -e, murderous (deadly) weapon.

Morgen, *m.* -ß, —, morning.

morgen, *adv.,* to-morrow.

Morgen=röte, *f.* -n, morning-red, dawn.

Morgen=strahl, *m.* -ß, -en, morning light.

Mörlischachen. Village near Küssnacht.

Mörtel, *m.* -ß, —, mortar.

müde, *adj.,* tired, weary.

Mühe, *f.* -n, trouble, hardship.

Müller (Johannes). Swiss historian and friend of Schiller.

Mund, *m.* -eß, -e, mouth (= voice, 1054), lips.

munter, *adj.,* lively, brisk; rapid.

Muotta (pronounce Mwótta). Stream entering the lake at Brunnen.

murren, *intr.,* murmur, grumble.

Musik′, *f.* music.

müssen, mußte, gemußt, muß, *intr. and modal aux.,* **must,** have to.

müßig, *adj.,* idle.

mustern, *tr.,* look at intently.

Mut, *m.* -(e)ß, courage, heart; **mood,** desire, 1771.

mutig, *adj.,* brave, courageous; martial, 835; *as noun,* 313.

Mutter, *f.* ̈, mother.

Mütter=chen, *n.* -ß, —, dear (little) mother.

mütter=lich, *adj.,* maternal; *as noun,* mother's estate, 1345.

Mutter=schmerz, *m.* -e(n)ß, -en, [birth-pains.

Mütze, *f.* -n, cap.

Mythen=stein. Mythenstein. Cf. 39, note.

n

nach, *prep.* (*dat.*), *adv., sep. pref.,* after, to, towards, according to, along, about.

Nachbar, *m.* -ß (*or* -n), -n, neighbor.

nach=dem, *conj.,* after.

nach=drängen, *intr.,* press (crowd) after.

nach=dringen, drang, gedrungen, *intr.,* f., (press) follow after.

nach=eilen, *intr.,* f., hurry after.

Nachen, *m.* -ß, —, boat.

nach=folgen, *intr.,* f., **follow** (after).

nach=gehen, ging, gegangen, *intr.*, f., pursue, follow (= be engaged in).

nach=her, *adv.*, afterwards.

nach=jagen, *intr.*, f. *and* h., pursue, rush after.

nach=kommen, kam, gekommen, *intr.*, f., follow; come up.

Nach=richt, *f.* -en, news, report.

nach=setzen, *intr.*, set after, pursue.

nach=sprechen, sprach, gesprochen, spricht, *tr.*, repeat.

nächst, *prep.* (*dat.*), next to, close by; *adj.* (*superl.* of nah), next, first; *as noun*, neighbor, 107.

nach=stürzen, *intr.*, f., hurry after.

Nacht, *f.* "e, night; *strong gen.* nachts, des Nachts *as adv.*, the (at) night, 1781, 2876.

nach=thun, that, gethan, *tr.* (*dat. pers.*), imitate (in), do after.

nächt=lich, *adj.*, nightly, nocturnal; *adv.*, by night.

Nacht=zeit, *f.* -en, night-time.

nach=ziehen, zog, gezogen, *tr.*, draw (up) after.

Nacken, *m.* -s, —, neck.

nackt, *adj.*, naked.

nah(e) (näher, nächst), *adj.*, near (by), close.

Nähe, *f.* (*lit.* nearness), presence.

nahen, *intr.*, come (near), approach.

nähern, *refl.*, draw near, approach.

nähren, *tr.*, nourish, feed, support.

Nahr=ung, *f.* -en, food, nourishment.

Name, *m.* -ns, -n, name; mit —, by name, 531.

närrisch, *adj.*, foolish, queer.

Natu'r, *f.* nature.

natur=vergessen, *part. adj.*, unnatural.

Naue, *f.* -n, boat. *S.G.*, *Swiss.*

Nebel=decke, *f.* -n, veil of fog.

neb(e)licht (*old for* nebelig), *adj.*, misty, foggy.

neben, *prep.* (*dat.*, *acc.*), by, near, beside.

nebst, *prep.* (*dat.*), together with.

Neffe, *m.* -n, -n, nephew.

nehmen, nahm, genommen, nimmt, *tr.*, take (from, *dat. pers.*); accept; überhand —, get the upper hand, 2120.

Neid, *m.* -es, envy.

neid=isch, *adj.*, envious (*dat. for* auf + *acc.*, 260).

nein, *adv.*, no.

nennen, nannte, genannt, *tr.*, name, call; *refl.*, be named (called), 369.

Netz, *n.* -es, -e, net.

neu, *adj.*, new, fresh, recent; *adv.*, anew, afresh; von —em, aufs —e, anew, again.

Neuer=ung, *f.* -en, innovation.

Neu=gier, *f.* curiosity.

Neu=jahrs=geschenk, *n.* -s, -e, New Year's present.

nicht, *adv.*, not; gar —, not at all; noch —, not yet.

nichts, *indec. pron.*, nothing; — als, nothing but.

nid (*Swiss*), *prep.* (*dat.*), below.

nie, *adv.*, never; noch —, never before.

nieder, *adv. and sep. pref.,* down; Down!

nieder=brennen, brannte, ge= brannt, *tr.,* burn down.

nieder=fallen, fiel, gefallen, fällt, *intr.,* f., fall down.

nieder=knieen, *intr.,* kneel (down).

nieder=lassen, ließ, gelassen, läßt, *tr.,* let down.

nieder=quellen, quoll, gequollen, quillt, *intr.,* f. and h., trickle down.

nieder=reißen, riß, gerissen, tear (pull) down.

nieder=schlagen, schlug, geschla= gen, schlägt, *tr.,* strike down.

nieder=schmelzen, schmolz, ge= schmolzen, schmilzt, *intr.,* f., melt down.

nieder=senden, sandte, gesandt, *tr.,* send down.

nieder=sinken, sank, gesunken, *intr.,* f., sink down.

nieder=steigen, stieg, gestiegen, *intr.,* f., descend.

nieder=stoßen, stieß, gestoßen, stößt, *tr.,* strike down.

Nieder=ung, *f.* -en, lowland.

nieder=werfen, warf, geworfen, wirft, *refl.,* prostrate oneself.

nie=mals, *adv.,* never.

niemand, *pron.,* no one, no- body.

nimmer, *adv.,* never.

nimmer=mehr, *adv.,* Never!

nirgend(s), *adv.,* nowhere.

nit, *adv.,* not; *colloq. for* nicht; *especially S.G. and Swiss.*

noch, *adv.,* yet, still, as yet, even,

besides, more, other; *conj.* nor, 1943.

Not, *f.* "e, need, distress; — thun (*or* sein), be necessary; vonnöten haben, have need of (*gen.*), 349.

not=gedrungen, *part. adj. as adv.,* by necessity, under constraint.

Not=gewehr, *n.* -s, -e, means of defense.

Not=wehr, *f.* self-defense.

nun, *adv.,* now; *interj.,* Well!

nur, *adv.,* only; just, do, pray *with imp.*

O

O, *interj.,* Oh!

ob, *conj.,* whether, if; though, 1159; — + schon, gleich, wohl = although; *prep. dat.* (*gen.*), on account of. ob *in com- pounds implies* above, over.

Ob=dach, *n.* -s, lodging, shelter.

oben, *adv.,* above, up there, high up; before.

Ober=haupt, *n.* -s, "er, chief authority (ruler).

ober=herrlich, *adj.,* sovereign.

ob=gleich, *conj.,* although.

Ob=mann, *m.* -s, "er, judge, arbitrator.

Obrig=keit, *f.* -en, authorities, superiors, 472.

Ochs, *m.* -en, -en, ox.

öde, *adj.,* desolate, lonely.

oder, *conj.,* or.

offen, *adj.,* open.

offen=baren, *tr.,* open, disclose.

offen=stehend, *part. adj.,* (stand- ing) open.

öffent=lich, *adj.*, public.

öffnen, *tr.*, **open;** *refl.*, open, (show itself).

oft, *adv.*, often.

Ohm, *m.* -ß, -e, uncle, (*old*).

Oheim, *m.* -ß, -e, uncle.

ohne, *prep.* (*acc.*), without.

ohnmächtig, *adj.*, impotent, vain, powerless.

Ohr, *n.* -eß, -en, ear.

Opfer, *n.* -ß, —, sacrifice, victim.

Orchester, *n.* -ß, orchestra.

ordent=lich, (*adj.*) *adv.*, properly.

Ordnung, *f.* -en, order.

Ort, *m.* -eß, -e (*or* "er), place; *pl.* —e, canton.

Öst(er)reich, *n.* -ß, Austria.

öst=lich, *adj.*, eastern.

P

Paar, *n.* -eß, -e, pair.

Pair (pronounce **Pär**), *m.* -ß, -e (*or* -ß), peer.

Palm. Rudolph von Palm, accomplice of Johannes Parricida.

Papst, *m.* -eß, "e, pope.

Paradies, *n.* -eß, -e, paradise.

Parricida, *m.* (*not declined*), parricide.

Partei=ung, *f.* -en, faction.

Paß, *m.* -ffeß, "ffe, (*mountain*) pass.

Pause, *f.* -n, pause, moment.

Pelz=wams, *n.* -eß, "er, fur coat.

Pergament, *n.* -ß, -e, parchment, charter.

Perle, *f.* -n, pearl.

Perso'n, *f.* -en, person; rôle,

part, 812; *pl.* = dramatis personae.

Peter (Sankt), *m.* -ß, Saint Peter.

Pfad, *n.* -eß, -e, **path.**

Pfaff(e), *m.* -n, -n, priest.

Pfalz, *f.* -en, **palace,** court.

Pfand, *n.* -eß, "er, pledge, security; trust, 2508.

Pfarrer, *m.* -ß, —, pastor.

Pfauen=feder, *f.* -n, peacock-feather.

Pfeife, *f.* -n, (*lit.* pipe), whistle.

Pfeil, *m.* -eß, -e, arrow.

Pferd, *n.* -eß, -e, horse; zu —, on horseback.

Pflanze, *f.* -n, plant.

pflanzen, *tr.*, plant.

Pflege, *f.* care, nursing.

pflegen, *intr.*, be accustomed, used to; **Rats —,** take counsel. 339.

Pflicht, *f.* -en, duty, obligation (= allegiance).

pflicht=gemäß, *adv.*, dutifully, duly.

pflichtig, *adj.*, subject (bound) to.

Pflug, *m.* -eß, "e, plow.

Pflug=stier, *m.* -ß, -e, plow-ox.

Pforte, *f.* -n, gate, door.

Pfosten, *m.* -ß, —, post.

Pike, *f.* -n, pike.

Pilger, *m.* -ß, —, pilgrim.

Pilgers=tracht, *f.* -en, pilgrim dress.

plagen, *refl.*, worry, be troubled.

Platte, *f.* -n, ledge (*of rock*).

Platz, *m.* -eß, "e, **place,** square (ground 964); *interj.*, make way!

plötz=lich, *adj.*, sudden.

Popanz, *m.* -es, -e, bugbear.

Port, *m.* -s, -e, port.

pracht=voll, *adj.*, splendid, spirited.

prangen, *intr.*, shine, be gorgeous; parade.

Pranger, *m.* -s, —, pillory.

praſſeln, *intr.*, crackle.

Preis, *m.* -es, -e, prize.

preiſen, pries, geprieſen, *tr.*, praise; *refl.*, be glad, call . . . fortunate, 1084.

preſſen, *tr.*, trouble, worry (*for usual* drücken), 251.

Prospekt, *m.* -s, -e, prospect, view.

prüfen, *tr.*, prove, weigh, test.

Prüfung, *f.* -en, test, trial.

Puls, *m.* -es, -e, pulse = moment.

Purpur=mantel, *m.* -s, ", purple mantle.

Q

Qual, *f.* -en, torment, pang.

quälen, *refl.*, distress oneself,

Qualm, *m.* -s, smoke. [worry.

Quell, *m.* -es, -e, fountain.

Quelle, *f.* -n, spring, fountain.

R

Rabe, *m.* -n, -n, raven.

Rache, *f.* vengeance, revenge.

Rache=geist, *m.* -es, -er, spirit of vengeance, Fury.

rächen, *tr.*, avenge.

Rächer, *m.* -s, —, avenger.

Rach=gefühl, *n.* -s, -e, thirst for vengeance.

ragen, *intr.*, stand out, loom up, be prominent.

Rand, *m.* -es, "er, edge, verge (= in imminent danger, 2237).

Ränke, *pl.*, tricks, intrigues.

Rappersweil. Town on Lake Zürich.

raſch, *adj.*, quick, prompt; **rash,** impetuous.

raſen, *intr.*, rave, rage, be mad; *part. as adj.*, mad, *as noun*, madman.

raſt=los, *adv.*, restlessly, unceasingly.

Rat, *m.* -es, advice, counsel; *pl.* Räte, councillor; zu —e gehen, —s pflegen, take counsel, 289, 331; — wiſſen, know what to do, 2239.

raten, riet, geraten, rät, *tr.* (*dat. pers.*), advise, counsel.

Rat=haus, *n.* -es, "er, townhall.

Raub, *m.* -es, robbery, prey.

rauben, *tr.*, rob, plunder; carry away, 2532.

Räuber, *m.* -s, —, robber.

Raub=tier, *n.* -(e)s, -e, wild animal, beast of prey.

Rauch, *m.* -(e)s, smoke.

Raum, *m.* -(e)s, "e, **room,** distance.

räumen, *tr.*, quit, leave.

rauſchen, *intr.*, rush, roar; creak, 503; *as noun*, 2098 *.

Rebell', *m.* -en, -en, rebel.

Rechen, *m.* -s, —, rake.

rechnen, *intr.*, count, rely (on, auf).

Rechnung, *f.* -en, reckoning.

recht, *adj.,* **right;** true, real, genuine; decent, respectable, 1470; Rechte, right hand; zur Rechten, to the right, *1; *adv.,* well, thoroughly.

Recht, *n.* −es, −e, **right,** privilege; justice; — sprechen, dispense justice.

rechten, *intr.,* be at law about (um), contest.

recht=fertigen, *tr.,* justify.

recht=los, *adj.,* without rights, outlawed.

rechts, *adv.,* on (to) the **right.**

Rede, *f.* −n, talk, words; — stehen, answer, render account, 75, 1954; zur — kommen, be spoken of, 2301.

reden, *intr. and tr.,* talk, speak.

red=lich, *adj.,* honest, plain, candid; *as noun,* good people, 276; *adv.,* frankly, 292, well, 287; stoutly, 489; steadily, 2249.

Redlich=keit, *f.* integrity.

rege, *adj.,* busy, lively.

regen, *refl.,* stir, move.

Regen, *m.* −s, —, rain.

Regen=bogen, *m.* −s, −, rainbow.

Regent', *m.* −en, −en, **regent,** governor.

regieren, *tr. and intr.,* rule, reign; control, 757.

Regiment, *n.* −s, −e, rule, government; management, 342.

reich, *adj.,* **rich;** *adv.* well, abundantly, richly.

Reich, *n.* −(e)s, −e, empire.

reichen, *tr.,* **reach,** give (extend).

reich=lich, *adv.,* abundantly.

Reichs=bote, *m.* −n, −n, imperial messenger.

Reichs=fürst, *m.* −en, −en, prince of the empire.

Reichs=panier, *n.* −s, −e, imperial **banner.**

Reichs=vogt, *m.* −s, ˣe, imperial bailiff, governor.

Reihe, *f.* −n, row, line; rank.

Reihen, *m.* −s, —, row, procession.

rein, *adj.,* clean, pure, clear of, innocent, free from; *adv.,* clearly, perfectly.

Reis, *n.* −es, −er, twig.

Reis=holz, *n.* −es, ˣer, brushwood.

Reisigen (*pl. of* reisig, *mounted*), trooper.

reißen, riß, gerissen, *tr.,* tear, drag, dash; pull (throw) down, 2766*.

reiten, ritt, geritten, *intr.,* ſ. *and* h., ride; geritten + verb = riding.

Reiter, *m.* −s, —, rider, trooper.

Reiters=mann, *m.* −s, ˣer (−leute), horseman, soldier.

reizen, *tr.,* anger, rouse, irritate; —d, charming, 1712.

rennen, rannte, gerannt, *intr.,* ſ. *and* h., run.

Respekt, *m.* −es, respect.

Rest, *m.* −es, −e, (*pl.*) remains.

retten, *tr.,* save, rescue, deliver.

Retter, *m.* −s, —, rescuer, deliverer.

Rettung, *f.* -en, rescue, deliverance.

rettungs-los, *adv.*, past help.

Rettungs-ufer, *n.* -s, —, shore of safety.

Reue, *f.* repentance.

reuen, *impers.* (*acc.*), regret, repent of.

Reue-thräne, *f.* -n, penitent tear.

Reuß. River flowing through Lake Lucerne.

Reverenz', *f.* -en, homage, obeisance.

Rhein. The river Rhine.

Rheinfeld(en). Town on the Rhine, near Basel.

richten, *tr.*, turn, direct; *refl.*, rise (up, in die Höhe), 2416 *; judge, 3056.

Richter, *m.* -s, —, judge.

richter-lich, *adj.*, judicial.

Richter-spruch, *m.* -s, "e, sentence.

Richt-maß, *n.* -es, -e, rule, measure.

Riegel, *m.* -s, —, bolt. [ure.

Rigi-berg, *m.* -(e)s. The Rigi, mountain on east shore of Lake Lucerne.

Rind, *n.* -es, -er, ox; *pl.* cattle.

Ring, *m.* -es, -e, ring.

ringen, rang, gerungen, *intr.*, writhe, struggle; wring, 180 *; *refl.*, get out of (aus), 1512.

rings, *adv.*, around, — umher (herum), all (around) about.

rings-um, *adv.*, all around.

rinnen, rann, geronnen, *intr.*, s., run, flow.

Riß, *m.* -sses, -sse, rent, crack.

Ritter, *m.* -s, —, knight.

Ritter-fräulein, *n.* -s, —, maid of noble birth.

Ritter-kleidung, *f.* knight's

ritter-lich, *adj.*, knightly. [dress.

Ritter-mantel, *m.* -s, ", knight's mantel.

Ritter-pflicht, *f.* -en, knightly duty.

Ritter-wort, *n.* -s, -e, knightly word.

roh, *adj.*, rough, rude, cruel.

Rohr, *n.* -(e)s, -e *or* "e, reed.

rollen, *intr. and tr.*, roll.

Römer-krone, *f.* -n, Roman crown.

Römer-zug, *m.* -es, "e, journey to Rome.

Roß, *n.* -sses, -sse, horse.

Roßberg. Castle in Unterwalden.

rosten, *intr.*, h. *and* s., rust.

rost-ig, *adj.* rusty.

rot (röter, rötest), *adj.*, red.

rucht-bar (*for* ruch-bar), known, public.

Rücken, *m.* -s, —, back, rear; backing, support, 662, 1844.

rück-springen, sprang, gesprungen, *intr.*, s., leap backward.

Rudenz. The Attinghausen Castle in Flüelen, from which Ulrich von Rudenz is named.

Ruder, *n.* -s, —, oar.

Ruderer, *m.* -s, —, oarsman, rower.

Rudolph. Rudolph of Habsburg, German Emperor, reigned 1273–1291.

Ruf, *m.* –es, –e, report.

rufen, rief, gerufen, *tr. and intr.,* call, summon; cry.

Ruffi (*Swiss*), *n.* –s, landslide.

Ruhe, *f.* rest, peace, quiet; *exclam.,* 1396.

ruhen, *intr.,* rest.

ruhig, *adj.,* quiet, calm, peaceful; *exclam.,* 1299.

Ruhm, *m.* –(e)s, fame, glory.

rühmen, *tr.,* praise; *refl.,* boast (of, *gen.*), glory in, be proud to be.

rühm-lich, *adj.,* laudable.

rühren, *tr.,* stir, move; beat (*drum*), 402 *; touch, 1952.

Ruine, *f.* –n, ruin.

Runse, *f.* –n, gully, run (*of water*).

rüsten, *tr. and refl.,* prepare, 93; arm, equip.

Rütli. The Rütli; meadow on west shore of Lake Lucerne. Cf. 728, note.

S

Saal, *m.* –es, Säle, hall.

Saat, *f.* –en, seed.

Sache, *f.* –en, thing, matter, affair; cause.

säen, *tr.,* sow.

sagen, *tr.,* say, tell; mean.

Salz, *n.* –es, (–e), salt.

sammeln, *tr.,* collect (*money for*), gather.

Sammlung, *f.* (–en), meditation, thought, devotion.

sammt, *prep.* (*dat.*), along (together) with.

sanft (sänfter, sänft(e)st), *adj.,* soft, gentle, kind; — thun, cajole, deal gently with, 2713.

Sankt, *adj.* (*indec.*), holy, **saint.**

Sarnen. Town and castle in Unterwalden.

Sarner, *adj.,* of Sarnen.

Sass(e), *m.* –n, –n, tenant, settler; bondman, 1209.

Sättigung, *f.,* satisfaction, satiation.

sauer, *adj.,* sour, hard, toilsome.

saugen, sog, gesogen, *tr.,* suck, drink in.

Säule, *f.* –n, (pillar), pole.

säumen, *intr.,* delay, hesitate, linger; *as noun,* 2281, 2513.

Säumer, *m.,* –s, —, pack-horse driver.

Saum=roß, *n.* –sses, –sse, pack-horse.

Scene, *f.* –n, scene, stage; in die — rufend, calling to some one behind the scenes; die vordere —, foreground, 1771 *.

Scepter, *n.* –s, scepter.

Schächen, *m.* –s. A river flowing into the Reuss near Attinghausen. See map.

Schächen=thal, *n.* –s. Schächen valley.

Schädel, *m.* –s, —, skull.

Schade(n), *m.* –ns, –n or ″n, harm, damage.

schaden, *intr.,* do harm (damage).

schädigen, *tr.,* injure, hurt, damage.

Schaf, *n.* –es, –e, sheep.

schaffen, *tr.,* do, accomplish; get, find, procure, secure, 1012, 2799; get (= take) away.

across, 1527, 2757; es —, act, 281; produce, 572.

Schaffhaufen. City on the Rhine, near Lake Constance.

Schaff=ner, *m.* -s, —, manager, overseer; — machen, be (play) the overseer, 759.

Schall, *m.* -(e)s, -e, sound.

schallen, scholl, geschollen (*also weak*), *intr.*, h. *and* s., resound.

schalten, *intr.*, rule, hold sway.

Scham, *f.* shame.

schämen, *refl.* (*gen.*), be ashamed of.

Schande, *f.* -n, shame, disgrace.

schänden, *tr.*, dishonor, disgrace.

Schänd=er, *m.* -s, —, despoiler.

Schänd=lich=keit, *f.* -en, shame, disgrace, ignominy.

Schanze, *f.* -n, chance; in die — schlagen, risk, venture.

Schar, *f.* -en, troop, herd; (multitude) forest (*of lances*), 2445.

scharf (schärfer, schärf[e]st), *adj.*, sharp, keen.

scharren, *tr.*, scratch, paw.

Schatte(n), *m.* -ns, -n, shadow.

Schatz, *m.* -es, "e, treasure.

Schau, *f.* show; zur — tragen, display, make show of, 781.

schaudern, *intr.*, shudder.

schauen, *tr.*, see, look at, behold.

schauer=lich, *adj.*, awful, dreadful.

schäumen, *intr.*, foam.

Schau=platz, *m.* -es, "e, scene.

Schau=spiel, *n.* -s, -e, sight, spectacle; drama (*title-page*).

scheel, *adj.* (*lit.*, squint-eyed), envious, malignant.

Scheibe, *f.* -n, target.

scheiden, schied, geschieden, *tr.*, separate; *intr.*, s., go, depart, leave; pass away, 954; depart, die, 2393; dahin —, die, 2463.

Schein, *m.* -(e)s (**shine**), light; excuse, pretext, 306, 310; semblance, appearances, 1636.

scheinen, schien, geschienen, *intr.*, seem.

schellen, *intr.* (*tr.*), ring (*bell*).

schelten, schalt, gescholten, schilt, *tr.*, scold, blame; nickname, call, 826.

schenken, *tr.*, give, grant, bestow on.

Scherz, *m.* -es, -e, jest, fun.

scherzen, *intr.*, jest.

scheu, (*adj.*) *adv.*, timidly, in fear.

scheuen, *tr.*, shun, shrink from; fear.

Scheune, *f.* -n, barn.

scheuß=lich, *adj.*, hideous, horrible.

schicken, *tr. and intr.* (*with* nach), send (for).

Schick=fal, *n.* -s, -e, fate, lot, destiny.

Schickfals=probe, *f.* -n, trial (*of fate*).

Schick=ung, *f.* -en, decree, providence.

Schiefer=decker, *m.* -s, —, (slate-) roofer.

schielen, *intr.*, steal a glance.

schießen, schoß, geschossen, *intr. and tr.*, shoot.

Schieß=zeug, *n.* -(e)s, shooting-things (= bow and arrows).

Schiff, *n.* -(e)s, -e (**ship**), boat.

Schiff=bruch, *m.* –s, "e, ship-wreck.

schiffen, *intr.*, take ship, sail.

Schiffer, *m.* –s, —, boatman.

Schiff=lein, *n.* –s, —, little boat.

Schild, *n.* –es, –e, shield.

Schild=wache, *f.* –n, sentinel, guard.

Schimmer, *m.* –s, —, shimmer, ray.

schimmern, *intr.*, gleam, shimmer.

Schimpf, *m.* –es, (–e), disgrace, insult.

Schirm, *m.* –es, (–e), protection, support; Schutz und —, shield and shelter, 1215.

schirmen, *tr.*, protect, defend; *refl.*, shield oneself, 1058.

Schirmer, *m.* –s, —, protector.

Schlacht, *f.* –en, battle.

Schlacht=schwert, *n.* –s, –er, (battle-)sword.

Schlaf, *m.* –(e)s, sleep.

Schläfer, *m.* –s, —, sleeper.

Schlag=baum, *m.* –s, "e, toll-gate, barrier.

schlagen, schlug, geschlagen, schlägt, *tr.*, strike, smite; fight, 1230; — + um, throw around, 782; 1436, *cf.* Schanze; — + in, cast, put, 2339; *refl.*, fight (force, make) one's way, 1175, 1485; *intr.*, beat, strike (+ an, 1289*, 1684, 2167); rise, 2879.

Schlag=lawi'ne, *f.* –n, avalanche (*of solid ice*).

Schlange, *f.* –n, serpent.

schlank, *adj.*, slender, slight.

schlecht, *adj.*, bad, worthless.

schleichen, schlich, geschlichen, *refl.* (*also intr.*, s.), slink, steal (*one's way*).

schlendern, *intr.*, be slow, loiter.

schleppen, *refl.*, drag (oneself) along.

schleudern, *tr.*, fling, hurl.

schleunig (*adj.*), adv., quickly.

Schlich, *m.* –es, –e, secret path (*old sense*).

schlicht, *adv.*, plainly, frankly.

schlichten, *tr.*, arrange, settle.

schließen, schloß, geschlossen, *tr.*, shut in, enclose; end, conclude; form, establish, 1855*, 2400.

schlimm, *adj.*, bad (*comp.*, 2271).

Schlinge, *f.* –n, noose, snare.

Schloß, *n.* –sses, "sser, lock, 507; castle, stronghold.

schlummern, *intr.*, slumber.

Schlund, *m.* –(e)s, "e, gorge; abyss (*of waters*), 2139.

Schluß, *m.* –sses, "sse, conclusion, decision (*for* Entschluß).

Schmach, *f.* dishonor, shame, outrage.

schmachten, *intr.*, long (yearn) for.

schmeicheln, *intr.* (*dat.*), flatter; coax, 2713.

Schmelz, *m.* –es, enamel.

Schmerz, *m.* –e(n)s, –en, pain, grief.

schmerzen, *tr.*, hurt, pain.

Schmerzens=pfeil, *m.* –s, –e, painful arrow.

Schmerzens=sehn=sucht, *f.* painful (*say* pain and) longing.

schmerz=lich, *adj.*, painful.

ſchmerz=zerriſſen, *part. adj.*, grief-stricken, torn with grief.

Schmi(e)d, *m.* -(e)s, -e, smith.

ſchmieden, *tr.*, forge.

ſchmiegen, *refl.*, cling (to, an).

ſchmuck, *adj.*, nice, pretty.

ſchmücken, *tr.*, adorn.

Schnecke, *f.* -n, snail.

Schnee=gebirg(e), *n.* - (e)s, -e, snow-covered mountains.

ſchneiden, ſchnitt, geſchnitten, (*tr.*) *intr.* (*with* in + *acc.*), cut.

ſchnell, *adj.*, quick; rash, violent, 423.

ſchon, *adv.*, already; surely; even; *often translated by an intonation showing emphasis.*

ſchön, *adj.*, fair, fine, handsome, noble.

ſchonen, *tr. and intr.* (*gen.*), spare.

ſchöpfen, *tr.*, get, find.

Schöpfung, *f.* -en, creation.

Schöpfungs=tag, *m.* - (e)s, -e, day of creation.

Schoß, *m.* -es, ᵘe, lap, bosom.

Schranke, *f.* -n, bound, limit.

Schrecken, *m.* -s, —, fright, terror.

ſchrecken, *tr.*, frighten, terrify.

Schreckens=ſtraße, *f.* -n, road of terror.

Schreck=horn. One of the peaks in the Bernese Alps.

ſchrecklich, *adj.*, fearful, terrible; *superl. as noun*, 3179.

Schreck=nis, *n.* -ſſes, -ſſe, horror.

Schreiben, *n.* -s, —, letter, document.

ſchreien, ſchrie, geſchrieen, *intr.*, cry (call) to, scream; *part. adj.*, shameful, outrageous, 1841.

ſchreiten, ſchritt, geſchritten, *intr.*, ſ., stride, walk; geſchritten, striding, 1563.

Schritt, *m.* -(e)s, -e, step, pace.

ſchroff, *adj.*, steep.

Schuld, *f.* -en, debt; fault, guilt.

ſchuldig, *adj.*, owing, — blieb, owed; *as noun*, guilty one, 2185.

Schulter, *f.* -n, shoulder.

Schurke, *m.* -n, -n, rascal, scoundrel.

ſchürzen, *tr.*, gird.

Schuß, *m.* -ſſes, ᵘſſe, shot.

ſchütteln, *tr.*, shake.

Schutz, *m.* -es, (ᵘe), protection, defense; — und Trutz, defense and defiance, offense and defense, 743, 1485; — und Schirm, protection and defense, 1215.

Schütz(e), *m.* -en, -en, hunter, archer.

ſchützen, *tr.*, protect, defend (from, vor + *dat.*).

Schützen=regel, *f.* -n, archer's rule.

Schwaben, *n.* -s, Swabia.

ſchwäb=iſch, *adj.*, Swabian.

ſchwach (ſchwächer, ſchwächſt), *adj.*, weak; poor, little; *as noun*, 328, 437, 2676.

Schwäher, *m.* -s, —, father-in-law.

ſchwanen, *impers. intr.* (*dat.*), have forebodings.

ſchwank, *adj.*, pliant, 927; swaying, 1417.

ſchwanken, *intr.*, stagger, totter; toss.

Schwarm, *m.* –eß, ⁸e, **swarm.**

ſchwarz (ſchwärzer, ſchwärzeſt), *adj.*, black; *as noun*, black = bull's eye.

Schwarze Berg, der. Black Mountain, *i.e.* the Brünig.

ſchweben, *intr.*, hover.

ſchweigen, ſchwieg, geſchwiegen, *intr.*, be (keep) silent; —b, silently; *as noun*, silence, 421.

Schweiz, *f.* **Switzerland.**

Schweizer, *m.* –ß, —, **Swiss** man.

Schweizer=in, *f.* –nen, **Swiss** woman.

ſchwelgen, *intr.*, feast, revel.

Schwelle, *f.* –n, threshold.

ſchwer, *adj.*, heavy, severe, grievous, hard, grave; *as noun*, hardship, trial, 190; serious things, 546; crime, 2745.

Schwert, *n.* –eß, –er, **sword.**

Schweſter, *f.* –n, sister.

Schweſter=ſohn, *m.* –(e)ß, ⁸e, sister's son, nephew.

ſchwimmen, ſchwamm, geſchwom= men, *intr.*, h. and ſ., swim; *impers.* 1984.

Schwimmer, *m.* –ß, —, swimmer.

ſchwindlicht (*old for* ſchwinb[e]lig), *adj.*, dizzy.

ſchwingen, ſchwang, geſchwungen, *tr.*, swing, wield; *refl.*, swing oneself (leap) up, 2265.

ſchwören, ſchwor (ſchwur), ge= ſchworen, *tr. and intr.*, **swear** (allegiance), vow.

Schwung, *m.* –(e)ß, ⁸e, swing, strain, air (*in music*).

Schwur, *m.* –(e)ß, ⁸e, oath, vow.

Schwyz. Town and canton east of Lake Lucerne.

Schwyzer, *adj.*, of **Schwyz**; *as noun*, **Switzer**, 254, 659.

Schwyzer=land, *n.* –eß, –e, Canton Schwyz; **Swiss** canton, 3039.

ſechß, *num.*, **six.**

ſechſt, *num. adj.*, **sixth.**

See, *m.* –ß, –n, lake.

Seele, *f.* –n, soul.

Segen, *m.* –ß, —, blessing; rich crop, 1801.

ſegen=voll, *adj.*, rich in blessing.

ſegnen, *tr.*, bless.

ſehen, ſah, geſehen, ſieht, *tr. and intr.*, see, look, behold; *as noun*, sight, 587.

Seher, *m.* –ß, —, seer, prophet.

ſehnen, *refl.*, long (yearn) for; Heim —, be homesick for (nach)), 844; *as noun*, longing, 1676.

ſehr, *adv.*, very (much), greatly.

Seide, *f.* –n, silk.

Seil, *m.* –eß, –e, cord, tie.

ſein, war, geweſen, bin, *intr.*, ſ., wie bem . . . ſei, however that may be, 2959; ſei bem wie ihm wolle, be that as it may.

ſein, *poss. adj.*, his, its; bie Seinen, his own people; baß Seine, his own land.

ſeit, *prep.* (*dat.*), since, for; *conj.*, since.

ſeit=bem, *adv.*, since, since then.

Seite, *f.* –n, side.

ſeit=wärts, *adv.*, sideways.

ſelb=ander, *pron.*, together (with another).

ſelber, *pron. indecl.*, self.

ſelbſt, *pron. indecl.*, self; von —, of their own accord, 431; *adv.*, even, 1208.

Selbſt=herr, *m.* -n, -en, one's own master.

ſelig, *adj.*, blessed, happy.

Seliſberg. Mountain and village on west shore of Lake Lucerne.

ſelten, *adj.*, rare; *adv.*, rarely, seldom.

ſeltſam, *adj.*, strange, old, singular; *as noun*, 1907.

ſenden, ſandte, geſandt (*also weak*), *tr.*, send.

Senn(e), *m.* -en, -en, herdsman.

Senn=hütte, *f.* -n, herdsman's [hut.

Senſe, *f.* -n, scythe.

Sente, *f.* -n, herd.

ſeßen, *tr.*, set, put; dran —, stake (on), 906, 2332, 2892; *refl.*, take a seat.

Sewa. Town in Schwyz; Schiller puts it in Unterwalden.

ſich, *indecl. refl. pron. 3d pers.*, him(her, its)self, themselves; with Sie, your(-self, selves); each other.

ſicher, *adj.*, safe, secure; certain.

Sicher=heit, *f.* safety, security.

ſichern, *tr.*, guarantee, assure (of).

ſicht=bar, *adj.*, evident, visible.

ſie, *pers. pron.*, she, it; *pl.*, they; Sie, *2d pers.* (*polite*), you.

Sieg, *m.* -(e)s, -e, victory.

ſieg=berühmt, *part. adj.*, famous as victors.

ſiegen, *intr.*, conquer; *part. adj.*, triumphant, 2447.

Sieger, *m.* -s, —, victor.

ſieg=reich, *adj.*, victorious.

Signal=feuer, *n.* -s, —, signal-fire.

Sigriſt, *m.* -en, -en, sacristan.

Sillinen. Village and castle below Altorf.

Simon. St. Simon. Cf. 146, note.

ſingen, ſang, geſungen, *tr. and intr.*, sing, chant.

ſinken, ſank, geſunken, *intr.*, ſ., sink, fall.

Sinn, *m.* -es, -e, (-en), sense; mind; meaning; bei —en, in his senses, 138; zu — kommen, intend, mean, 1894.

ſinnen, ſann, geſonnen, *tr.*, think (of), intend.

Sitte, *f.* -n, custom, manners, morals.

Siß, *m.* -es, -e, seat, residence.

ſißen, ſaß, geſeſſen, sit; live, have one's seat.

Sklave, *m.* -n, -n, slave.

ſklav=iſch, *adj.*, slavish.

ſo, *adv. and conj.*, so, thus, then (48), well then, as (2756); — wie, just as; — oder —, one way or another, whether or no, 2732.

ſo=eben, *adv.*, just (now).

ſo=gleich, *adv.*, at once.

Sohn, *m.* -es, "e, son.

ſo=lang, *conj.*, so long as.

ſolch (–er, –e, –es), *adj. and pron.*, such.

Söld=ner, *m.* –s, —, hired soldier.

ſollen, *weak; pres. indic.* ſoll; *intr. and modal aux.*, shall, ought, must; be to, be intended, be said to; mean, 391.

Sommer, *m.* –s, —, summer.

ſondern, *conj.* (*with neg.*), but.

Sonne, *f.* –en, sun; —n (= *old gen. sg.*), 1108.·

Sonnen=ſchein, *m.* –s, sunshine.

ſonnen=ſcheu, *adj.*, sun-shy, light-dreading.

ſonnig, *adj.*, sunny.

ſonſt, *adv.*, otherwise, else, besides, once = formerly.

Sorge, *f.* –n, care, anxiety.

ſorgen, *intr.*, fear, care (for); look out for (368), provide for, 3067.

ſorgen=voll, *adj.*, anxious.

Sorg=falt, *f.* care, solicitude.

Späher, *m.* –s, —, spy.

ſpannen, *tr.*, draw, bend (*bow*); + von *or* aus, unyoke, 479, 568.

Spann=ung, *f.* expectation; excitement, 569*.

ſparen, *tr.*, spare, save; put off, 2549.

ſpät, *adj.*, late; distant (*in time*).

Speer, *m.* –(e)s, –e, spear.

ſperren, *tr.*, block up, bar.

Spiegel, *m.* –s, —, mirror.

Spiel, *n.* –(e)s, –e, game, sport; — treiben, make sport of, 407.

ſpielen, *tr.*, play, personate; *intr.*, play; trifle with, 1924.

Spiel=mann, *m.* –(e)s, –männer *or* –leute, minstrel.

Spieß, *m.* –es, –e, spear, pike.

ſpinnen, ſpann, geſponnen, *tr.*, spin; plan, plot, 1107; es ſpinnt ſich etwas, something is on foot (plotting), 1518.

Spitze, *f.* –en, point, peak.

ſpitzen, *tr.*, point (*ears*), prick up.

ſpitz=ig, *adj.*, pointed, sharp.

Spott, *m.* –es, scorn, ridicule.

ſpotten, *intr.* (*gen.*), mock, laugh at.

Sprache, *f.* –n, language.

ſprechen, ſprach, geſprochen, ſpricht, *tr. and intr.*, say, talk, speak; see = speak with, 2309, 2670.

ſprengen, *tr.*, burst, break, shatter.

ſpringen, ſprang, geſprungen, *intr.*, ſ., spring, jump, run; geſprungen + *inf.* running.

Spruch, *m.* –es, ″e, saying; sentence, 1935; judgment, 3056.

ſpülen, *intr.*, wash, play (*of water*).

Spur, *f.* –en, trace, sign (= evidence), trail, path.

ſpur=los, *adj.*, leaving no trace.

ſtaats=klug, (*adj.*) *adv.*, wisely. diplomatically.

Stab, *m.* –(e)s, ″e, staff, stick.

Stachel, *m.* –s, —, sting; goad.

Stadt, *f.* ″e, city, town.

Stahl, *n.* –(e)s, (″e), steel.

Stall, *m.* –(e)s, ″e, stall, stable.

Stall=meiſter, *m.* –s, —, master of horse.

Stamm, m. -(e)§, "e, race, line-age; house (= family), 890.

Stamm=holz, n. -e§, "er, solid (trunk-)wood.

Stand, m. -e§, "e, rank, class; resistance, 1429; estate, district, 2993.

Stange, f. -en, pole.

Stanz. Town in Unterwalden.

stark (stärk=er, stärk=[e]st), adj., strong; as noun, 438, 1843.

stärken, tr., strengthen; refl., gain strenght.

starr, adj., stiff; frozen, 1050; obstinate, 2783.

Statt, f. stead, place.

statt, prep. (gen. or inf. + zu; with daß clause); instead of.

Stätte, f. -n, place.

stattlich, adj., splendid, fine.

Statur, f. (-en), stature.

Staub, m. -e§, dust.

Staub=bach, m. -§, "e, spray-brook, cascade.

stäuben, intr., scatter spray.

stechen, stach, gestochen, sticht, tr. and intr., sting, strike; prompt, impel, 1771.

stecken, tr., stick; put; stecktest zu dir, took, concealed about you, 2050.

Steg, m. -e§, -e, foot-bridge, path.

stehen, stand, gestanden (old form stund), intr., h. (and f.), stand; + um, be, 570, 1719, 1768; with dat. + adv., fit, become, 53; Rede —, answer, give account, 75, 1954; + zu, stand by; —den Fußes, at once, 333.

steifen, refl., be stubborn.

Steig, m. -e§, -e, path.

steigen, stieg, gestiegen, intr., f., climb (up or down), rise, ascend, descend, go.

steil, adj., steep.

Stein, m. -e§, -e, stone.

Stein. Castle at Baden.

Steinen. Village in Schwyz.

stein=ern, adj., stony.

Stein=metz, m. -en, -e, stone-cutter.

Stelle, f. -n, place; zur — schaffen, produce, 572.

stellen, tr., put, station; refl., take one's stand; stand at bay, 648.

Stell=ung, f. -en, position.

sterben, starb, gestorben, stirbt, intr., f., die; part. as noun, 2809 *.

Stern, m. -e§, -e, star; pupil (of eye), 642, 675.

Sternen=himmel, m. -§, —, starry heaven.

stets, adv., always.

Steuer, n. -§, —, helm, rudder.

Steuer=leute, pl., steersmen.

Steuer=mann, m. -§, -männer or -leute, steersman.

steuern, tr. and intr., steer.

steuern, intr., pay taxes.

Steuer=ruder, n. -§, —, helm, rudder.

Steu(e)rer, m. -§, —, steerer.

Stier, m. -(e)§, -e, bull, ox.

stiften, tr., found, establish.

Stifter, m. -§, —, founder.

still, adj., adv., still, quiet, silent, secret; im —en, quietly, secretly; *interj.*, be still, silence! 392.

Stille, *f.* silence.

stillen, *tr.*, still, quench, slake.

Stimme, *f.* –n, voice; vote.

stimmen, *intr.*, vote, 1147; accord, suit, 2658.

Stirne, *f.* –n, brow; face, front, 2124.

stolz, *adj.*, proud, haughty.

Stolz, *m.* –es, pride.

stören, *tr.*, disturb.

stoßen, stieß, gestoßen, stößt, *tr. and intr.*, thrust, exclude (aus), 1304; strike (*with eye*), see, 2724.

Strafe, *f.* –n, punishment; in — fallen, become liable to punishment, 473.

strafen, *tr.*, punish.

sträf-lich, *adj.* (*as noun*), punishable, criminal, 465.

straf=los, *adj.*, unpunished.

Strahl, *m.* –(e)s, –en, beam, ray, gleam.

Strang, *m.* –es, "e, string, cord.

Straße, *f.* –n, way; road, highway.

Strauß, *m.* –es, "e, struggle.

streben, *intr.*, strive; *as noun*, 1677, 1682.

Strebe=pfeiler, *m.* –s, —, buttress.

strecken, *tr.*, stretch (reach) out.

Streich, *m.* –s, –e, stroke, blow.

streifen, *intr.*, f. *and* h., rove, wander.

Streit, *m.* –(e)s, –e, fight, struggle; question (2714), dispute.

Streit=axt, *f.* "e, battle-**axe**.

streiten, stritt, gestritten, *intr.*, contend, **strive** (fight) for.

streng, *adj.*, strict, stern, severe.

Strenge, *f.* severity, sternness; cold, rigor, 2638.

streuen, *tr.*, **strew**, scatter.

Strich, *m.* –es, –e, track, direction.

Strick, *m.* –es, –e, cord; snare,

Stroh *m.* –(e)s, straw.   [998.

Strom, *m.* –(e)s, "e, **stream**, current, flood, river.

stumm, *adj.*, dumb, silent.

Stunde, *f.* –n, hour, time.

Sturm, *m.* –es, "e, storm.

stürzen, *intr.*, f., fall, rush; *tr.*, tear down; plunge, cast; *refl.*, throw (cast) oneself.

stützen, *tr.*, support; *past part.* leaning (on, auf), 1150*.

suchen, *tr.*, seek, look for; want (from, an), 2692.

Sumpf, *m.* –es, "e, swamp.

Sumpfes=luft, *f.* "e, swamp-air.

Sünde, *f.* –n, sin.

Sündflut, *f.* flood.

Surennen. Mountains between Uri and Unterwalden.

süß, *adj.*, sweet.

T

Tadel, *m.* –s, —, blame, reproach.

Tafel, *f.* –n, table.

Tag, *m.* –es, –e, day; Tage lang, for days, 2637; assembly, meeting, 1146.

Tag=dieb, *m.* –(e)s, –e, idler, loiterer.

tagen, *intr.*, dawn, 752; hold a meeting, meet.

Tages=anbruch, *m.* -8, "e, daybreak.

Tages=ordnung, *f.* -en, order of the **day,** regular business.

Tage=werk, *n.* -(e)8, -e, (**day**) labor.

tapfer, *adj.*, brave.

tauchen, *intr.*, dive.

taumeln, *intr.*, reel.

täuschen, *tr.*, deceive, escape.

tausend, *num.*, thousand.

tausend=jährig, *adj.*, of a thousand years.

tausend=mal, *adv.*, a thousand times.

Teger=feld(en), Konrad von, one of Emperor Albrecht's murderers.

Teil, *m.* (*or n.*), -e8, -e, part, share; zu teil werden = become share of = be given to, 1136.

teilen, *tr.*, divide, share; have in common, 3184.

teil=haft, teil=haftig, *adj.*, having part (share) in; *with* fein, to share.

teuer, *adj.*, **dear,** beloved; precious, 1041.

Teufel, *m.* -8, —, **devil** (in exclam).

teufel=isch, *adj.*, **devilish.**

Teufels=münster (Devils Minster), a dangerous rock on the west shore of Lake Lucerne, below Selisberg.

Teu(e)rung, *f.* -en, famine.

Thal, *n.* -(e)8, "er, valley.

Thal=grund, *m.* -(e)8, "e (bottom of a) valley.

Thal=vogt, *m.* -(e)8, "e, dalegovernor, lord of the valley (*storm-clouds*).

That, *f.* -en, **deed,** action, act; über frischer —, in the very act, 1862; mit frischer —, at once, 1971.

Thäter, *m.* -8, —, **doer,** perpetrator.

Thor, *n.* -(e)8, -e, gate(way).

thöricht (*adj.*), *adv.*, foolishly.

Thräne, *f.* -n, tear.

Thron, *m.* -e8, -e, throne.

thun, that, gethan, *tr. and intr.*, do, act, make; gut —, be well, 286; not —, be necessary, 506; fanft —, deal gently with, 2713; wohl — + *dat.*, does them good, they like to, 807.

Thür(e), *f.* -en, **door.**

Thurgau. The Canton Thurtief, *adj.*, **deep.** [gau.

Tiefe, *f.* -n, **depth(s), deep;** background (*of stage*).

Tier, *n.* -e8, -e, animal, beast.

Tiger, *m.* -8, —, tiger.

toben, *intr.*, rage, struggle.

Tochter, *f.* ", daughter.

Tod, *m.* -e8, (-e) and Todes=fälle, death; am —, at point of death, 2116; auf — und Leben, for life and death, 744.

Tod=feind, *m.* -e8, -e, mortal enemy.

Ton, *m.* -(e)8, "e, tone.

tosen, *intr.*, rage, roar; *as noun*, 2098*.

tot, *adj.*, **dead**; *as noun often.*

töten, *tr.*, kill, put to **death**; tötet, is deadly, means death, 106.

Toten=hand, *f.* ʺe, dead hand.

Trachten (*inf. as noun*), *n.* –s, thought, purpose, intention.

tragen, trug, getragen, trägt, *tr.*, carry; bear; endure; hold in fief, 263, 1360; feel, have, cherish, 549, 3043.

trauen, *intr.*, trust in, rely on.

trauern, *intr.*, grieve, be sad; mourn (for, um).

trau=lich, *adj.*, familiar.

träumen, *tr.*, dream.

Träum=er, *m.* –s, —, dreamer.

traun, *interj.*, faith! really!

traur=ig, *adj.*, sad, sorrowful.

treffen, traf, getroffen, trifft, *tr.*, strike, hit.

treff=lich, *adj.*, fine, good; *as noun*, 2338.

Treib. Village on west shore of the Lake, opposite Brunnen.

treiben, trieb, getrieben, *tr.*, drive, impel; do (conduct things), carry on, 407, 542, 724; *real intr.* (h. and f.), toss, drift; *apparent intr.*, 62, 540.

trennen, *tr. and refl.*, separate, part from, leave.

treten, trat, getreten, tritt, *intr.*, f. and h., step, go; *with prep.* + *acc.* enter; *tr.*, trample.

treu, *adj.*, **true**, faithful. [2770.

Treue, *f.* faithfulness, loyalty.

treu=lich, *adv.*, faithfully, loyally.

treu=los, *adj.*, faithless, untrue (to).

Trieb, *m.* –es, –e, natural impulse; love (*of country*), 849.

triefen, troff, getroffen, *intr.*, drip.

trinken, trank, getrunken (*tr.*), *intr.*, drink.

Trommel, *f.* –n, drum.

Trost, *m.* –es, consolation, comfort; hope, 6093.

trösten, *tr.*, console, comfort; *refl.*, find consolation.

trost=los, *adj.*, disconsolate, wretched, despairing.

Trotz, *m.* –es, defiance.

trotz, *prep.* (*dat.*), in spite of.

trotzen, *intr.*, defy.

trüben, *tr.*, disturb.

Trüb=finn, *m.* –s, melancholy, care.

trüg=er=isch, *adj.*, treacherous.

Trümmer, *pl.*, ruins.

Trupp, *m.* –s, –e (–s), troop (*of horse*).

Trutz, *m.* –es, defiance; Schutz und —, defense and defiance = offense and defense, 744, 1485.

trutz=ig=lich (*old for* trotzig), *adv.*, defiantly.

Tübingen, an important German city, home of great publishing interests.

Tugend, *f.* –en, virtue; quality, 853.

tugend=haft, *adj.*, virtuous.

tumult=u=arisch, *adv.*, tumultuously.

Turm, *m.* –(e)s, ʺe, tower; prison.

Turnier, *n.* –s, –e, tournament

Twing, *m.* -(e)ß, -e, prison, dungeon.

Twing=hof, *m.* -(e)ß, ⁗e, prison.

Tyrann, *m.* -en, -en, tyrant.

Tyrannei, *f.* -en, tyranny.

Tyrannen=joch, *n.* -(e)ß, -e, tyrant's yoke.

Tyrannen=macht, *f.* ⁗e, tyrant's power, tyranny.

Tyrannen=schloß, *n.* -ffeß, ⁗ffer, tyrant's castle.

Tyrannen=schwert, *n.* -eß, -er, tyrant's sword.

tyrann=isch, *adj.*, tyrannical.

u

übel (*adj.*), *adv.*, ill, wrong.

Übel, *n.* -ß, —, evil, wrong.

üben, *refl.*, practice.

über, *prep.* (*dat. and acc.*), *adv.*, *sep. and insep. pref.*, over, above; beyond, across; of, about, concerning; by way of, 520, 2279, 2284, 2286; drüber, more than that, 1228, 1367; die Zeit —, during, etc., 1992*. überm = über dem; übern = über den.

über=all, *adv.*, everywhere.

überde'nken, überda'chte, überda'cht, *insep. tr.*, think over (of).

Über=druß, *m.* -ffeß, disgust, disdain.

Über=fahrt, *f.* -en, passage; um die —, to take him across, 132.

über=hand, *adv.* in — nehmen, get upper hand, get worse, 2120.

überla'ffen, überli'eß, überla'ffen, überlä'ßt, *insep. tr.*, give up to.

überlie'fern, *insep. tr.*, give up, hand over.

Über=mut, *m.* -ß, insolence.

überne'hmen, überna'hm, überno'mmen, überni'mmt, *insep. tr.*, overcome, get best of, 482; undertake, 1414.

überra'schen, *insep. tr.*, surprise.

ü'ber=schwellen, schwoll, geschwollen, schwillt, *sep. intr.*, ſ., overflow.

ü'ber=setzen, *sep. tr.*, set (take) over (across).

überste'hen, übersta'nd, übersta'nden, *insep. tr.*, stand, overcome; part., over, past, 2260.

ü'ber=treten, trat, getreten, tritt, *sep. intr.*, ſ., go over to.

übrig, *adj.*, over, left (over); die —en, the others; — bleiben, be left (over), remain, 1352.

Ücht=land. Old name of the region between the Jura and the Bernese Alps.

Ufer, *n.* -ß, —, shore, bank.

Uhr, *f.* -en, clock. Cf. 2568, note.

Uli. Diminutive of Ulrich.

um, *prep.* (*acc.*), *adv.*, *sep. and insep. pref.*, round, about, over; for, concerning (570), at; um . . . willen, for sake of, because of, for; + zu + *inf.*, in order, so as (to); *with* verdienen, at hands of, from; umß = um das.

uma'rmen, *insep. tr.*, embrace.

umdrä'ngen, *insep. tr.*, crowd around.

umfa′ffen, *insep. tr.*, embrace.

umga′rnen, *insep. tr.*, surround.

umge′ben, umga′b, umge′ben, umgie′bt, *insep. tr.*, surround, enclose.

u′m=gehen, ging, gegangen, *sep. intr.*, f., go round.

um=he′r, *adv. and sep. pref.*, around, round about; um (*acc.*) her, around.

umhe′r=bliden, *sep. intr.*, look around.

umhe′r=merfen, *sep. intr.*, look about.

umhe′r=fiten, faß, gefeffen, *sep. intr.*, f., sit around.

umhe′r=ftehen, ftand, geftanden, *sep. intr.*, f., stand around.

umhe′r=fpähen, *sep. intr.*, look about.

umhül′len, *insep. tr.*, cover, veil.

u′m=fehren, *sep. intr.*, f., and *refl.*, turn round; come back, return.

U′m=freis, *m.* -es, -e, circuit.

umrin′gen, *insep. tr.*, surround.

umfchlie′ßen, umfchlo′ß, umfchlo′f=fen, *insep. tr.*, enclose, surround.

u′m=fehen, fah, gefehen, fieht, *sep. refl.*, look (around) about.

umfonft′, *adv.*, in vain; for nothing.

umfte′hen, umfta′nd, umfta′nden, umfte′ht, *insep. tr.*, surround, stand around.

u′m=wandeln, *sep. tr.* (in + *acc.* or zu + *dat.*, 1264), change, turn into.

U′m=weg, *m.* -(e)s, -e, roundabout **way**, circuit.

umwe′rben, umwa′rb, umwo′r=ben, umwi′rbt, *insep. tr.*, woo, pay court to.

U′nbedacht, (*adj. as noun*), *m.* -s, thoughtlessness.

un=befannt, *part. adj.*, **unknown**, unfamiliar.

un=bequem, *adj.*, inconvenient, disagreeable; *as noun*, 2722.

un=bewaffnet, *part. adj.*, unarmed.

un=bezahlt, *part. adj.*, unpaid.

un=billig, *adj.*, unjust; *as noun*, injustice, 317.

und, *conj.*, and.

un=durch=bringlich, *adj.*, impenetrable, inaccessible, 2601.

un=entdedt, *part. adj.*, undiscovered.

un=erhört, *part. adj.*, **unheard** of; *as noun*, outrage, 403.

un=erfättlich, *adj.*, insatiable.

un=erträglich, *adj.*, unbearable, insufferable.

Ungar, *m.* -n, -n, **Hungarian**.

un=geboren, *part. adj.*, unborn.

U′n=gebühr, *f.* wrong.

un=gebühr=lich, *adj.*, improper; *as noun*, improper proposal,

Un=geduld, *f.* impatience. [94.

un=gebuldig, *adj.*, impatient.

un=geheuer, *adj.*, great, terrible; *as noun*, 1891.

un=gefränkt, *part. adj.*, undisturbed, 1928; in peace, 2682.

un=gerecht, *part. adj.*, unjust.

un=gereizt, *part. adj.*, unprovoked.

un=gefeßlich, *adj.*, illegal, irregular.

un=getröftet, *part. adj.*, uncomforted.

U'n=gewitter, *n.* -$, —, (severe) storm.

un=gezügelt, *part. adj.*, unrestrained.

U'n=glimpf, *m.* -$, harsh treatment, cruelty.

U'n=glück, *n.* -$, -e, disaster, misfortune.

un=glücklich, *adj.*, unhappy, wretched.

un=glückfelig, *adj.*, unhappy; *as noun*, 501, 2887.

Unglücks=that, *f.* -en, unhappy deed.

U'nheil, *n.* -$, mischief, evil.

un=leidlich, *adj.*, unbearable, intolerable.

un=menfchlich, *adj.*, inhuman.

un=möglich, *adj.*, impossible.

Un=mündigkeit, *f.* minority, dependence.

U'n=mut, *m.* -$, ill-will, anger.

un=nüß, *adj.*, useless.

U'nrecht, *n.* -$, wrong; guilt, crime, 982.

un=ruhig, *adj.*, restless, impatient.

U'n=fchuld, *f.* innocence.

un=fchuldig, *adj.*, innocent.

unfer (-e, —), *poss. adj. pron.*, our, ours.

unten, *adv.*, down, below.

unter, *prep.* (*dat. and acc.*), *adv.*, *sep. and insep. pref.*, **under**, below; among, in, amid = during; — ... hervor, out

from under; unterm = unter dem; unters = unter das.

unterbre'chen, unterbra'ch, unter= bro'chen, unterbri'cht, *insep. tr.*, interrupt, break.

unter=deffen, *adv.*, meanwhile.

unterdrü'cken, *insep. tr.*, oppress; *as noun*, 1618.

Unterdrücker, *m.* -$, —, oppressor.

Unter=gang, *m.* -$, "e, destruction, ruin.

unterne'hmen, unterna'hm, un= terno'mmen, unterni'mmt, *in= sep. tr.*, undertake.

unterfte'hen, unterfta'nd, unter= fta'nden, *insep. refl.*, dare, venture; take upon oneself, 234.

unter=tauchen, *intr. sep.*, dive under.

Unter=walden. The Canton Unterwalden.

Unter=waldner, *m.* -$, —, **Un**terwaldener.

unter=wegs, *adv.*, on the **way**.

unterwe'rfen, unterwa'rf, unter= wo'rfen, unter=wi'rft, *insep. tr.*, subdue; *refl.* (*dat.*), submit, yield.

unterwü'rfig, (*adj.*) *adv.*, respectfully.

U'n=that, *f.* -en, evil deed, crime.

un=verändert, *part. adj.*, unchanged.

un=veräußerlich, *adj.*, inalienable.

un=verdächtig, *adj.*, without exciting suspicion.

un=verleßt, *part. adj.*, uninjured, safe.

Un-vernunft, f. folly, senseless-
ness.

un-vernünftig, adj., unreasoning.

un-verschämt, part. adj., insolent;
· as noun, 476.

un-versehrt, part. adj., unhurt.

un-wandelbar, (adj.) adv., in-
variably.

un-weit, prep. (gen. or dat.), not
far from.

Un-wille(n), m. -ns, anger, indignation.

un-willkürlich, (adj.) adv., in-
voluntarily.

un-wirtlich, adj., inhospitable.

un-zerbrechlich, adj., indestruc-
tible.

ur-alt, adj., very old, ancient.

ur-alters, adv., of old; von —
her, from (of old) time im-
memorial.

Uri. The Canton Uri.

Urner, m. -s, —, man of Uri,
Urner.

Ur-fehde, f. -n, sacred oath (to
keep the peace).

U'r-sache, f. -n, cause, reason.

U'r-sprung, m. -s, "e, origin.

U'r-stand, m. -s, "e, original
condition.

U'rteil, n. -s, -e, judgment.

ur-teilen, intr., judge.

v

Variation, f. -en, variation.

Vater, m. -s, ", father.

Vater-land, n. -(e)s, fatherland.

väter-lich, adj., fatherly; pater-
nal; native; of our fathers,
1100.

vater-los, adj., fatherless.

Vater-mord, m. -s, parricide.

Väter-tugend, f. -en, ancestral
(inherited) virtue.

verabscheuen, tr., abhor, despise.

verachten, tr., despise; disobey,
402.

Veracht-ung, f. contempt, dis-
regard.

verachtungs-wert, adj., worthy
of contempt.

verändern, refl., change.

veräußern, tr., alienate (by sale)

verbergen, verbarg, verborgen,
verbirgt, tr. and refl., hide,
conceal; as noun, 612.

verbieten, verbot, verboten, tr.,
forbid, deny.

verbinden, verband, verbunden,
tr., unite; bind, blindfold,
1960.

verblassen, intr., turn pale.

verblenden, tr., blind; delude;
part. as noun, 840.

verbluten, intr. and refl., bleed
to death.

Verbrechen, n. -s, —, crime.

verbreiten, tr., spread.

verbrennen, verbrannte, ver-
brannt, intr., burn up (to
death).

Verdammnis, f. condemnation;
damnation (exclam.), 2818.

verdanken, tr., owe, thank one
for.

verderben, verdarb, verdorben,
verdirbt, tr., ruin, destroy.

verdienen, tr., deserve (at the
hands of, um + acc.).

Verdrieß (old for **Verdruß**), m.

-ſſes, vexation; zum -ſſe, to
worry, 1739.

verdrießen, verdroß, verdroſſen,
tr., worry; ſich — laſſen, hesitate to, 2637.

Verdruß, *m.* -ſſes, vexation; zum
—ſſe, to vex, 1966.

verehren, *tr.*, honor, respect.

vereiden, *tr.*, bind by oath.

vereinen, *tr.*, unite; combine.

vereinigen, *tr.*, unite.

verfallen, verfiel, verfallen, ver=
fällt, *intr.*, ſ., be forfeited to.

verfangen, verfing, verfangen,
verfängt, *intr.*, avail, 1286;
refl., be caught, 2165.

verfehlen, *intr.*, fail (in, of, *gen.*).

verfluchen, *tr.*, curse.

verfolgen, *tr.*, pursue.

Verfolger, *m.* -s, —, pursuer.

verführen, *tr.*, mislead, deceive.

Verführung, *f.* -en, temptation.

vergeben, vergab, vergeben, ver=
giebt, *tr.*, forgive.

vergebens, *adv.*, in vain, for
nothing.

vergeb=lich, *adj.*, useless.

Vergelt=ung, *f.* retribution,
vengeance.

vergeſſen, vergaß, vergeſſen, ver=
gißt, *tr.*, forget.

vergiften, *tr.*, poison.

vergleichen, verglich, verglichen,
tr., arrange, settle.

vergraben, vergrub, vergraben,
vergräbt, *tr.*, bury.

vergrößern, *tr.*, increase, add to.

vergüten, *tr.*, make good, atone.

verhaften, *tr.*, arrest.

verhalten, verhielt, verhalten, ver=

hält, *tr.* (*for* vorenthalten),
conceal, keep back from, 532;
refl., be (stand) thus (as), 1243.

verhandeln, *tr.*, transact, do.

verhängen, *tr.*, ordain.

verhaßt, *part. adj.*, hated.

verhehlen, *tr.*, hide, conceal.

verhindern, *tr.*, hinder, prevent.

verhüllen, *tr. and refl.*, cover;
hide the face.

verhüten, *tr.*, prevent; verhüt
(e)s Gott, God forbid! 1536,
1894.

verirren, *intr. and refl.*, get lost;
part., lost, 1499, 3106.

verjagen, *tr.*, drive out.

verkaufen, *tr.*, sell.

verkleiden, *tr.*, disguise.

verkümmern, *intr.*, wither, languish.

verkünden, *tr.*, tell, 2292; announce, 2680.

verkündigen, *tr.*, show, manifest
itself, 2072; proclaim, 2786.

verlangen, *tr.*, demand.

Verlangen, *n.* -s, —, longing,
wish.

verlaſſen, verließ, verlaſſen, ver=
läßt, *tr.*, leave, forsake; *refl.*
(auf + *acc.*), rely on.

verlaufen, verlief, verlaufen, ver=
läuft, *refl.*, stray away.

verlauten, *intr. impers.*, be said
(reported).

verlegen, *part. adj.*, embarrassed.

verleihen, verlieh, verliehen, *tr.*,
give, grant.

verletzen, *tr.*, hurt; disobey,
1820.

verlieren, verlor, verloren, *tr.*,

lose; *refl.*, lose oneself, disappear, 1780.

vermauern, *tr.*, wall up.

vermehren, *tr.*, increase.

vermeiden, vermied, vermieden, *tr.*, avoid.

vermengen, *tr.*, confound, confuse.

vermögen, *tr.*, be able (to do); *as noun*, ability, 1525.

vernehmen, vernahm, vernommen, vernimmt, *tr.*, hear; learn.

Vernunft, *f.* reason.

vernünft-ig, *adj.*, sensible.

veröden (*tr. and*) *intr.*, lay waste; be deserted.

verpfänden, *tr.*, mortgage.

Verrat, *m.* –s, treachery (towards, an).

verraten, verriet, verraten, verrät, *tr.*, betray.

Verräter, *m.* –s, —, traitor.

verrinnen, verrann, verronnen, *intr.*, f., pass (away).

versagen, *tr.*, deny, refuse; fail, 1564.

versammeln, *refl.*, meet, gather (come) together.

Versamm-lung, *f.* –en, meeting, assembly.

verschaffen, *tr.*, secure, get, obtain.

verscheiden, verschied, verschieden, *intr.*, f., die.

verschenken, *tr.*, give away.

verscheuchen, *tr.*, scare away.

verschieben, verschob, verschoben, *tr.*, postpone, put off.

verschieden, *adj.*, different.

verschleiern, *tr.*, veil.

verschließen, verschloß, verschlossen, *tr.*, shut (lock) up; *part.*, retired, hidden, 1689.

verschlingen, verschlang, verschlungen, *tr.*, swallow up.

verschmähen, *tr.*, despise.

verschulden, *tr.*, do, be guilty of.

verschütten, *tr.*, bury, overwhelm.

verschwinden, verschwand, verschwunden, *intr.*, f., disappear.

Verschwörung, *f.* –en, conspiracy.

versehen, versah, versehen, versieht, *refl.* (+ zu *or dat. pers.*, *gen. thing, or* daß *clause*), expect of, look to for.

versenden, versandte, versandt (*also weak*), *tr.*, **send** (= shoot).

versetzen, *tr.*, put, throw, 3038; reply, 229.

versöhnen, *refl.*, be reconciled, make one's peace (with).

versprechen, versprach, versprochen, verspricht, *tr.*, promise.

verständig, *adj.*, wise, prudent; *as noun*, 248.

versteckt, *part. adj.*, hidden, remote.

verstehen, verstand, verstanden, *tr.*, understand, mean, 216; *refl.* + auf + *acc.*, understand, know, 1635; + mit + *dat.*, have understanding with, 1397.

verstocken, *refl.*, be stubborn.

verstohlen, (*part. adj.*) *adv.*, by stealth.

versuchen, *tr.*, try, attempt; tempt, 1532, 2046.

verteidigen, *tr.,* defend.

Verteidiger, *m.* -s, —, defender.

vertilgen, *tr.,* destroy, annul.

vertrauen, *intr.* (*dat.* or auf + *acc.*), trust (confide) in, rely on; *tr.,* confide, trust, 199, 1439; *as noun,* 2483.

vertraut, *part. adj.,* trusted, intimate.

vertreiben, vertrieb, vertrieben, *tr.,* drive out, expel; *part. as noun,* 2931.

verüben, *tr.,* do, commit.

verwahren, *tr.,* guard; lock up.

verwalten, *tr.,* administer.

verwandeln, *tr. and refl.,* change.

verwandt, *part. adj., as noun,* relative.

verwegen, verwog, verwogen, *refl.* (*gen.*), dare, be bold to do.

verwegen, *adj.,* bold, daring; *as noun,* 2022.

verweigern, *tr.,* deny.

verweilen, *intr.,* remain, stop.

verwirken, *tr.,* forfeit.

verwünschen, *tr.,* curse; *part. as interj.,* curse (confound) it! 177.

verzagen, *intr.,* despair (of).

verzeihen, verzieh, verziehen, *tr.* (*dat. of person*), pardon, forgive.

verzieren, *tr.,* decorate.

verzweifeln, *intr.,* despair.

Verzweifl=ung, *f.* despair.

Verzweiflungs=angst, *f.* ᵘe, anxiety of despair.

verzweiflungs=voll, *adj.,* desperate, in despair.

Vetter, *m.* -s, —, cousin; kinsman, 1035.

Vieh, *n.* -s, *collect.,* cows, cattle; beast.

viel, *adj.,* much, a great deal, many; *adv.,* very.

viel=erfahren, *part. adj.,* of great experience, wise; *as noun,* 665.

viel-leicht, *adv.,* perhaps, possibly, may be.

viel=mehr (*adv.*), *conj.,* but rather.

vier, *num.,* four.

viert(e), *num.,* fourth.

Vierwaldstätter=see, *m.* -s, Lake of the Four Forest Cantons = Lake Lucerne.

Vogel, *m.* -s, ᵘ, bird.

Vogt, *m.* -(e)s, ᵘe, bailiff, governor.

Volk, *n.* -es, ᵘer, folk, people, nation.

voll (voller, vollst), *adj., adv., sep. and insep. pref.,* full, complete; great, 65; Jahre — haben, reach full age, be of age, 1346.

vollbri'ngen, vollbra'chte, vollbr'acht, *insep. tr.,* finish, accomplish, carry out; *part. as noun,* 218.

vollen'den, *insep. tr.,* end, finish, accomplish; go on, 565.

völl=ig, *adj.,* full; *adv.,* perfectly.

Voll=macht, *f.* -en, authority.

von, *prep.* (*dat.*), of, from, by, because (on account) of, through; *in names and titles,* of (from); vom = von dem.

vonnöten (= von Nöten), *adv.,* needful; — haben, need, **349**

vor, *prep.* (*dat. and acc.*), *adv. and sep. pref.*, before; from, 2354; **for** (= because of), 2239, 3130; of, 133; in front of, 182 *, 217; + *dat.* (*time*), ago.

voran, *adv. and sep. pref.*, in front, in advance.

voran-ziehen, zog, gezogen, *intr.*, ſ., precede, go ahead of.

vor-aus, *adv.*, on ahead, in advance.

vor-bauen, *intr.*, take precautions (against).

vor-bei, *adv. and sep. pref.*, (by) past, over, 2087, 3097; an —, past, 1771 *, 2187, 3093.

vorbei-gehen, ging, gegangen, *intr.*, ſ., go (pass) by.

vor-biegen, bog, gebogen, *tr.*, bend over (forward).

vorder, *adj.*, forward, front; —e Scene, front of stage.

Border-grund, *m.* –s, foreground.

vorderst, *adj.*, foremost; die —en, those in front.

vor-gehen, ging, gegangen, *intr.*, ſ., go on, take place.

vor-halten, hielt, gehalten, *tr.*, hold out against, present.

Vor-hang, *m.* –s, "e, curtain.

Vor-hut, *f.* picket, sentinel.

vor-ig, *adj.*, preceding, former; *as noun*, 2452 *.

vor-kommen, kam, gekommen, *intr.*, ſ., come forward.

vorn, *adv.*, in the foreground.

Vor-schub, *m.* –s, help, aid; — thun, render aid, 3046.

Vor-ſehung, *f.* providence, cf. Für-ſehung.

Vor-ſicht, *f.* foresight; caution.

vor-ſpringen, ſprang, geſprungen, *intr.*, ſ., project.

Vor-ſprung, *m.* –s, "e, projecting ledge (*of rock*).

vor-ſtellen, *tr.*, stand for, represent.

Vor-teil, *n.* –s, –e, profit; opportunity, 2252.

vor-treten, trat, getreten, tritt, *intr.*, ſ., stand forth, step forward.

vor-über, *adv. and sep. pref.*, by, past.

vorüber-gehen, ging, gegangen, *intr.*, ſ., go (pass) by (on).

vorüber-lenken, *tr.*, steer past.

vorüber-treiben, trieb, getrieben, *refl.*, hasten past (an + *dat.*), 2613.

vor-wärts, *adv.*, forward, to the front.

Vor-wurf, *m.* –s, "e, reproach.

w

Wache, *f.* –n, watch, guard; — halten, stand guard, 1732 *.

wachſen, wuchs, gewachſen, wächſt, *intr.*, ſ., grow, advance.

Wächter, *m.* –s, —, Watch (*dog's name*), 43; guard, 1861.

wacker, *adj.*, brave, good, worthy; *as noun*, 169.

Waffe, *f.* –n, weapon; *pl.*, arms.

Waffen-dienſt, *m.* –(e)s, –e, military service.

Waffen-freund, *m.* –(e)s, –e, comrade.

Waffen=knecht, *m.* –(e)ß, –e, man-at-arms, soldier.

waffnen, *tr.*, arm.

Wage=fahrt, *f.* –en, daring trip.

wagen, *tr.*, dare, risk.

Wage=sprung, *m.* –(e)ß, "e, daring leap.

Wage=that, *f.* –en, deed of daring.

Wag=stück, *n.*, –(e)ß, –e, daring deed (thing).

Wahl, *f.* –en, choice.

wählen, *tr.*, choose.

Wahl=freiheit, *f.* –en, freedom of (choice) election.

Wahn, *m.* –ß, dream, delusion.

wahn=sinnig, *adj.*, mad, insane.

Wahnsinns=that, *f.* –en, deed of madness.

wahr, *adj.*, true, real.

während, *prep.* (*gen.*), during.

Wahr=heit, *f.* –en, truth.

wahr=lich, *adv.*, truly, really, certainly.

Währ=ung, *f.*, worth, value.

Waibel, *m.* –ß, —, bailiff.

Waise, *f.* –n, orphan.

Wald, *m.* –eß, "er, wood(s), forest.

Wald=gebirg(e), *n.* –ß, –e, (forest-)mountains.

Wald=gegend, *f.* –en, forest-region.

Wald=kapelle, *f.* –n, forest-chapel.

Wald=stätte, *pl.*, Forest-Cantons.

Wald=ung, *f.* –en, woods, forest.

Wald=wasser, *n.* –ß, —, forest-stream.

Wall, *m.* –eß, "e, wall.

wallen, *intr.*, ſ., make pilgrimage, go, come.

walten, *intr.*, rule; control (über + *acc.*), *as noun*, 2819.

Wälti. Dim. of Walther.

wälzen, *tr.*, roll.

Wand, *f.*, "e, wall; face (side) of a cliff.

wandeln, *intr.*, ſ. *and* h., walk, 2460; *tr.* (*cognate object*), go (*way, road*), 3188, 3281.

wandern, *intr.*, ſ., wander, go, travel.

Wanders=mann, *m.* –(e)ß, –leute, traveler.

Wand(e)rer, *m.*, –ß, —, traveler.

wanken, *intr.*, ſ. *and* h., shake, totter.

wann, *adv.*, when.

Wappen=schild, *n.* –(e)ß, –er, coat-of-arms.

wappnen, *tr.*, arm.

warm, *adj.*, warm.

warnen, *tr.*, warn.

Warn=ung, *f.* –en, warning.

Wart. Rudolph von (der) Wart, one of Emperor Albrecht's murderers.

warten, *intr.* (*gen. or* auf + *acc.*), wait, wait for; tend, 1182 (*gen.*).

warum, *adv.*, why.

was, *interrog. pron.*, what; *rel. pron.*, what = that which, whatever; *for* warum, why; *for* etwaß, something, anything; those who, whoever, 1482, 1740; waß für ein, what (sort of) a, 390, 613; waß ... auch, whatever.

Waſſer, *n.* -s, —, water.

Waſſer=huhn, *n.* -s, "er, water-fowl.

Waſſer=kluft, *f.* "e, gorge of water.

Waſſer=wüſte, *f.* -n, waste of waters.

wechſeln, *intr. (and tr.)*, change.

wecken, *tr.*, wake, rouse, stir up.

weder, *conj.*, neither, — ... noch, neither ... nor.

Weg, *m.*, -es, -e, way, road, path; des —es fahren, go along road, 348.

weg, *adv. and sep. pref.*, away, off; über ... weg, from off, 2740.

weg=bleiben, blieb, geblieben, *intr.*, ſ., stay away.

wegen, *prep. (gen.)*, for, on account of.

weg=fahren, fuhr, gefahren, fährt, *intr.*, ſ., set out; go along.

weg=führen, *tr.*, lead away.

weg=gehen, ging, gegangen, *intr.*, ſ., go away; go (roll) over (drüber), 167.

weg=rauben, *tr.*, carry away.

weg=treiben, trieb, getrieben, *tr.*, drive away.

weg=wenden, wandte, gewandt (*also weak*), *tr. and refl.*, turn away, avert.   [mel

weh(e), *interj.*, woe; — mir, Oh

Weh=geſchrei, *n.* -s, cry of distress.

wehklagen, *insep. intr.*, lament.

wehren, *tr. (dat. of person)*, keep, prevent (*from doing*), 234; hinder, 2566.

wehr=los, *adj.*, unarmed, defenseless.

Weib, *n.* -es, -er, woman, wife.

weib=lich, *adj.*, womanly.

weichen, wich, gewichen, *intr.*, ſ. yield, give way; + aus *or* von, leave.

Weide, *f.* -n, pasture.

weiden, *tr.*, pasture, graze; feast (*eyes*) on, 2814.

Weid=geſell(e), *m.* -en, -en, hunter.

Weid=mann, *m.* -(e)s, "er *or* =leute, hunter.

Weid=werk, *n.* -s, game.

weigern, *tr.*, deny, refuse.

Weih(e), *m.* -en, -en, eagle.

weihen, *refl.*, be devoted to.

weil, *conj.*, because, since; *old sense*, while, 341.

weilen, *intr.*, stay, linger.

Weiler, *m. and n.* -s, — (*lit.* village), part of proper name, Joſt von —; in 1077 = Öd=weiler near Rossberg.

weinen, *intr.*, weep.

weiſe, *adj.*, wise.

Weiſe, *f.* -n, way, manner.

weiſen, wies, gewieſen, *tr.*, direct refer, 1333; show, 2162; reprove, 1398.

weis=lich, *adv.*, prudently.

weiß, *adj.*, white.

Weiß=land. *Lit.* Whiteland = Oberhasli Valley.

weit, *adj.*, wide, broad; long, far, distant; das Weite, distance, space, 1475, 1676; ein Weitres, something further, 2299; comp. —er, further, on.

Weite, *f.* –n, distance.

weit=schichtig, *adj.*, far-reaching, vast.

weit=schmettern, *intr.*, resound afar.

welch(=er, =e, =es), *interrog. adj. and pron.*, which, what, what a; *rel. pron.*, who, which, that.

Welle, *f.* –n, wave.

welsch, *adj.*, foreign (Italian).

Welsch=land, *n.* –s, Italy.

Welt, *f.* –en, world, earth.

wenden, wandte, gewandt (*also weak*), *refl.*, turn (to).

wenig, *adj.*, little, few.

wenn, *conj.*, if, when; — auch, whenever, though.

wer, *interrog. pron.*, who; *rel. pron.*, who = whoever, he who.

werben, warb, geworben, wirbt, *tr.*, get, make, win; *intr.*, sue for, woo; *as noun*, request, 1314.

werden, ward, geworden, wird, *intr.*, s., become, get (to be), grow; *aux.*, shall, will; *pass.*, be; *with dat. or* zu teil, be given to, 149, 646, 1136; im Werden, in progress, 2728; mir wird, I feel, 514.

werfen, warf, geworfen, wirft, *tr.*, throw, cast.

Werk, *n.* –(e)s, –e, work; im —, planned, on foot, 2728.

Werk=leute, *pl.*, workmen.

Werk=zeug, *n.* –(e)s, –e, tool.

wert, *adj.*, worthy, dear.

Wert, *m.* –es, –e, worth.

Wesen, *n.* –s, —, creature.

Westen, *m.* –s, west.

Wetter, *n.* –s, —, lightning (*lit.* weather); —s Strahl, thunderbolt.

Wetter=loch, *n.* –s, "er, weather-hole.

Wett=streit, *m.* –s, dispute.

wetzen, *tr.*, whet.

wider, *prep.* (*acc.*), *adv. and insep. pref.*, against, contrary to.

Wider=part, *m.* –s, –e, opponent.

widerpra'llen, *insep. intr.*, s., rebound.

widerse'tzen, *insep. refl.*, resist.

widerste'hen, widerstand, widerstanden, *intr.* (*dat.*), withstand.

widerstre'ben, *insep. intr.* (*dat.*), oppose, resist.

widerstrei'ten, widerstritt, widerstritten, *insep. intr.* (*dat.*), be contrary to.

wie, *adv.*, how; *conj.*, as, as if, when, like.

wieder, *adv.*, *sep. and insep. pref.*, again; back.

wiederho'len, *insep. tr.*, repeat.

wieder=kehren, *sep. intr.*, s., return; *impers.*, one returns, 64.

wie'der=kommen, kam, gekommen, *sep. intr.*, s., come back.

wie'der=sehen, sah, gesehen, sieht, *sep. tr.*, see again.

Wiege, *f.* –n, cradle.

wiegen, *tr.*, rcck.

Wiese, *f.* –n, meadow.

Wild, *n.* –es, wild animals. [game.

wild, *adj.*, wild.

wild=bewegt, *part. adj.*, stormy.

Wild=heuer, *m.* –s, —, wild-hayer.

Wildnis, *f.* -ſſe, wilderness.

Wille(n), *m.* -ns, -n, will, wish, purpose; um —, for sake of, because of.

willkō'mmen, *adj.*, welcome.

Wimper, *f.* -n, eye-lash.

Wind, *m.* -es, -e, wind.

Windes=wehe, *f.* -n, snow-drift.

Wind=lawine, *f.* -n, wind-avalanche.

Wind=licht, *n.* -(e)s, -er, torch.

winken, *intr.*, make a sign to.

Winter, *m.* -s, —, winter.

wintern, *intr.*, winter.

Winter=ung, *f.* wintering.

wir, *pers. pron.*, *pl.* of ich, we.

Wirbel, *m.* -s, —, whirlpool; — ziehen, whirl, eddy, 116.

wirken, *intr.*, work.

wirk=lich, (*adj.*) *adv.*, really.

Wirt, *m.* -(e)s, -e, host.

Wirtin, *f.* -nen, hostess; wife, 187.

wirt=lich, *adj.*, hospitable.

wiſſen, wußte, gewußt, weiß, *tr.*, know (how); weiß Gott, Heavens! 171.

Wittwen=leid, *n.* -s, widow's grief.

wo, *adv. and conj.*, where, when, if; from whom, 1219.

wo=fern, *conj.*, if, in case.

wogen, *intr.*, surge, seethe.

wo=her, *adv.*, whence, where.

wo=hin, *adv.*, whither, where.

wohl, *adv.*, well; true, no doubt, to be sure; + leben, farewell! — thun, gratify, 807.

Wohl, *n.* -s, weal, welfare.

wohl=an, *interj.*, well then!

wohl=bestellt, *part. adj.*, duly appointed.

wohl=bewahrt, *part. adj.*, well kept.

wohl=feil, (*adj.*) *adv.*, cheap.

wohl=genährt, *part. adj.*, well-fed.

wohl=gepflegt, *part. adj.*, well cared for.

Wohl=that, *f.* -en, good deed, kindness.

wohnen, *intr.*, live, dwell; stay, 3162.

wohn=lich, *adj.*, comfortable, home like.

Wohn=stätte, *f.* -n, dwelling, home.

Wohn=ung, *f.* -en, habitation, abode, home.

Wolf, *m.* -es, "e, wolf.

Wolfen=schieß(en). Noble family in Unterwalden.

Wolke, *f.* -n, cloud.

Wolle, *f.* wool.

wollen (*weak*; *pres. indic.* will), *tr. and modal aux.*, will, wish, intend; be about to; mean, 390; wollte gern, would like to, 118; was will, what may, 492; wollt's Gott, would to God, 1767.

worauf, *adv.*, for (upon) which, whereupon.

worein, *adv.*, into which.

Wort, *n.* -es, "er *or* -e, word.

wozu, *adv.*, for which, for what purpose.

Wucht, *f.* weight.

Wunder, *n.* -s, —, wonder, miracle.

wunder=bar, *adj.*, wonderful.

Wunder=ding, *n.* -ß, -e, strange thing.

wundern, *intr., impers. (acc.)*, wonder; surprise.

Wunder=zeichen, *n.* -ß, —, miraculous sign.

Wunsch, *m.* -es, "e, wish.

wünschen, *tr.*, wish.

würdig, *adj.*, worthy; *as noun*, 954, 1145.

Wurzel, *f.* -n, root.

Wüste, *f.* -n, waste, wilderness.

Wut, *f.* rage, anger.

wüten, *intr.*, rage, be furious.

Wüter=ei, *f.* tyranny.

Wüt(e)rich, *m.* -ß, -e, tyrant.

wütig, *adj.*, raging, stormy.

3

Zacke, *f.* -n, peak.

zagen, *intr.*, be afraid.

Zahl, *f.* -en, number.

zahlen, *tr.*, pay (for).

zählen, *tr.*, count; + auf, rely on.

zähmen, *tr.*, tame, overcome.

zart (zärter, zärtest), *adj.*, tender, gentle.

Zauber, *m.* -ß, —, charm.

zaudern, *intr.*, hesitate.

zeh(e)n, *num.*, ten.

zehn=fach, *adj.*, tenfold.

zehnt, *num. adj.*, tenth.

Zeichen, *n.* -ß, —, sign, token; symbol, 2923.

zeigen, *tr.*, show; *refl.*, appear; *intr.* + auf, nach, point at (to); + in, give view of, 3087 *.

Zeile, *f.* -n, line, verse.

Zeit, *f.* -en, time; eine — lang, for a while.

zeitig, *adv.*, early.

zeit=lich, *adj.*, worldly, temporal.

Zell(e), *f.* -en, cell, hermitage.

zerbrechen, zerbrach, zerbrochen, zerbricht, *tr.*, break down (to pieces), storm.

zerknicken, *tr.*, break off.

zerlumpt, *part. adj.*, ragged.

zernagen, *tr.*, gnaw.

zerreißen, zerriß, zerrissen, *tr.*, tear (away), break.

zerschmettern, *tr.*, kill, dash to pieces.

zerspalten, *tr.*, split open.

zerspringen, zersprang, zersprungen, *intr.*, s., break.

zerstören, *tr.*, destroy, ruin; *part. as adj.*, distorted, 3104 *.

zertreten, zertrat, zertreten, zertritt, *tr.*, tread under foot.

Zeuge, *m.* -n, -n, witness.

zeugen, *intr.*, tell, be witness.

Zeug=ung, *f.* -en, generation.

ziehen, zog, gezogen, *tr.*, pull, draw, attract; Wirbel —, eddy, whirl, 116; *intr.* + an, pull, 477; come from, 1162; flow, 1792; move, 877; go, 2967; pass, 2651; *refl.*, go, 2284; gezogen kommen, come along, 1469, 3280 *.

Ziel, *n.* -ß, -e, end, goal; mark, aim.

zielen, *intr.*, aim, aim at (auf + acc.).

ziemen, *intr. (dat.)*, behove, become.

Zier, *f.* -en, ornament.

Z

Zimmer=agt, *f.* "e, carpenter's axe.

Zimmer=mann, *m.* -s, "er *or* =leute, carpenter.

zimmern, *tr.*, build.

zinsen, *intr.*, pay tribute.

zittern, *intr.*, tremble.

zollen, *intr.*, pay toll.

Zorn, *m.* -(e)s, anger, wrath.

zu, *prep.* (*dat.*), *adv., sep. pref.*, to, at, in, with, for, towards, besides, on, too, as; Reit zu, ride on! 175; schieß' zu, shoot ahead! 1992.

zu=bringen, brachte, gebracht, *tr.*, bring to.

Zucht, *f.* (-en), breed, herd.

Züchtig=ung, *f.* -en, punishment.

zucken, *intr.*, quiver, twitch.

zu=drücken, *tr.*, shut.

zu=erst, *adv.*, first.

zu=fahren, fuhr, gefahren, fährt, *tr.*, bring (carry) up; *intr.*, approach.

zu=fallen, fiel, gefallen, fällt, *intr.*, f., fall to, devolve on.

Zug, *m.* -es, "e, procession, march; *pl.*, features, 2307, 3122.

zu=geben, gab, gegeben, giebt, *tr.*, grant, allow.

zuge'gen, *adv.*, present.

zu=gehen, ging, gegangen, *intr.*, f., go towards (auf, *acc.*); go on, 2258, cf. note.

Zügel, *m.* -s, —, bridle, rein.

zu=gleich, *adv.*, likewise, also, at the same time, both … and, 2009.

zu=kehren, *tr.*, turn towards.

Zu=kunft, *f.* future.

zu=letzt, *adv.*, last, at last.

zu=nächst, *adv.*, next, close by.

Zunft, *f.* "e, guild.

Zunge, *f.* -n, tongue; language.

zu=reiten, ritt, geritten, *intr.*, f., ride on.

Zür(i)ch. The city of Zürich.

zürnen, *intr.*, be angry.

zurück, *adv. and sep. pref.*, back, backwards; *interj.*, back!

zurück=bleiben, blieb, geblieben, *intr.*, f., stay behind.

zurück=fahren, fuhr, gefahren, fährt, *intr.*, f., start back (*in surprise*).

zurück=fallen, fiel, gefallen, fällt, *intr.*, f., fall back.

zurück=führen, *tr.*, bring back.

zurück=geben, gab, gegeben, giebt, *tr.*, give back.

zurück=halten, hielt, gehalten, hält, *tr.*, hold back.

zurück=kehren, *intr.*, f., return.

zurück=kommen, kam, gekommen, *intr.*, f., come back.

zurück=lassen, ließ, gelassen, läßt, *tr.*, leave behind.

zurück=springen, sprang, gesprun=gen, *intr.*, f., fly back.

zurück=stehen, stand, gestanden, *intr.*, f., stand back.

zurück=treten, trat, getreten, tritt, *intr.*, f., step (draw) back.

zurück=werfen, warf, geworfen, wirft, *tr.*, throw back.

zu'=sagen, *tr.*, promise.

zusammen, *adv. and sep. pref.*, together.

zusammen=brechen, brach, gebrochen, bricht, *intr.*, ſ., break down.

zuſammen=flechten, flocht, geflochten, flicht, *tr.*, clasp, entwine.

zuſammen=führen, *tr.*, bring together.

zuſammen=grenzen, *intr.*, meet, come together.

zuſammen=halten, hielt, gehalten, hält, *intr.;* hold together.

zuſammen=laufen, lief, gelaufen, läuft, *intr.*, ſ., run together.

zuſammen=raffen, *refl.*, rouse (control) oneself.

zuſammen=rufen, rief, gerufen, *tr.*, call together.

zuſammen=ſinken, ſank, geſunken, *intr.*, ſ., fall, sink down.

zuſammen=ſteh(e)n, ſtand, geſtanden, *intr.*, ſ., stand together.

Zu=ſchauer, *m.* –s, —, spectator.

zu=ſchleudern, *tr.*, hurl towards.

zu=ſchließen, ſchloß, geſchloſſen, *tr.*, shut, lock.

zu=ſchnüren, *tr.*, oppress.

zu=ſehen, ſah, geſehen, ſieht, *intr.*, look on.

Zuſtand, *m.* –s, ″e, state, condition.

zu=tragen, trug, getragen, trägt, *tr.*, bring up; *refl.*, happen, 2796.

zu=traulich, *adv.*, trustingly.

zu=vor, *adv.*, before.

zu=zählen, *tr.*, count out to.

Zwang, *m.* –es, oppression.

zwanzig, *num.*, twenty.

Zweck, *m.* –s, –e, object, purpose.

Zwei, *num.*, two.

Zweifel, *n.* –s, —, doubt.

zweifeln, *intr.*, doubt.

zwei=mal, *adv.*, twice.

zweit, *num. adj.*, second.

Zwie=tracht, *f.* discord.

Zwing, *m.* –es (–e), prison, keep.

zwingen, zwang, gezwungen, *tr.*, force, compel, keep down, 373; *part.*, under compulsion, 2320.

zwiſchen, *prep (dat. and acc.)*, between, among.

zwölf, *num.*, twelve.

BIBLIOGRAPHY.

The following list does not claim to be in any sense complete. It has been purposely limited to some of the latest and best literature, in the belief that only such will be of real, practical value to those for whom this book is designed. For fuller bibliography, the reader is referred to the works of Dierauer and Hettler, cited at the end of this list.

EDITIONS.

The first edition of Tell and the only one which received Schiller's corrections was:

Wilhelm Tell. Schauspiel von Schiller. Zum Neujahrsgeschenk auf 1805. Tübingen. Cotta. 1804.

CRITICAL EDITIONS.

Important among modern critical editions are those by:

M. Carriere. In Brockhaus' 'Bibliothek der deutschen Classiker des 18. und 19. Jhdts.' Leipzig, 1871.

H. Oesterley. In Goedeke's 'Historisch-kritische Ausgabe,' vol. XIV. Stuttgart, 1872.

W. Vollmer. Stuttgart, 1879.

W. v. Maltzahn. In Hempel's 'Deutsche Classiker.' Schillers Werke, vol. VI. New ed. 1889.

A. Birlinger. In Kürschner's 'Deutsche National-Literatur,' vol. 145. Stuttgart, 1890.

L. Bellermann. Schillers Werke. Kritisch durchgesehene und erläuterte Ausgabe. Leipzig, 1895–97.

SCHOOL EDITIONS.

As among the latest and best of the numerous German and English school editions, with introduction and notes, may be mentioned those of:

German.

Jul. Naumann. Leipzig, 2d ed. 1884. Map.
O. Kallsen. Gotha, 1884.
J. Pölzel. Vienna, 2d ed. 1888. Map.
A. Funke. Paderborn, 7th ed. 1895. Map.
E. Kuenen. Leipzig, 3d ed. 1889.
A. Thorbecke. Bielefeld and Leipzig, 1889. Map.
A. Florin. Tell-Lesebuch. Davos, 1891. Map.
Denzel. Stuttgart, 1892.
Friedrich Schwörer. Wilhelm Tell etc. München, Th. Stroefers Kunstverlag. Richly illustrated.

English.

H. Müller–Strübing and **R. H. Quick.** London, 2d ed. 1874. Map.
C. A. Buchheim. Oxford, 7th ed. 1886. Map.
    Same abridged. Oxford, 2d ed. 1887. Map.
G. E. Fasnacht. London, 1887. Map.
K. Breul. Cambridge, 1890. 2 Maps.
    Same abridged. Cambridge, 1890. Map.
A. H. Palmer. New York, 1898. Map. Vocabulary.
W. H. Carruth. New York, 1899. Map. Vocabulary.

COMMENTARIES.

Valuable among detailed commentaries of Tell are those of:

J. Meyer. Schillers Wilhelm Tell auf seine Quellen zurückgeführt und sachlich und sprachlich erläutert. New ed. revised and enlarged by Barbeck. Nürnberg, 1876.
C. Gude. Erläuterungen deutscher Dichtungen. Leipzig, 7th ed. 1881.
H. Düntzer. Wilhelm Tell erläutert. Leipzig, 5th ed. 1892.
E. Kuenen. Die deutschen Classiker erläutert und gewürdigt. 1 Bdchen. 3d ed. Leipzig, 1889.
A. Florin. Die unterrichtliche Behandlung von Schillers Wilhelm Tell. Davos, 1891.

Böhme. Erläuterungen zu den Meisterwerken der deutschen Dicht-
kunst. Berlin, 1891.

L. Bellermann. Schillers Dramen, Beiträge zu ihrem Verständnis.
Berlin, 1888–91. 2 vols.

H. Gaudig. Aus deutschen Lesebüchern etc. 5ter Band. Weg-
weiser durch die klassischen Schuldramen. 3te Abteilung.
Friedrich Schillers Dramen. Gera and Leipzig, 1894.

LIVES OF SCHILLER.

Th. Carlyle. Life of Friedrich Schiller. Ed. of 1845, with Supple-
ment of 1872. London, 1873.

H. Viehoff. Schillers Leben etc. Stuttgart, 1874–75. 3 vols.

H. Düntzer. Schillers Leben. Leipzig, 1881.

——. The Life of Schiller. Transl. London, 1883.

Karoline von Wolzogen. Schillers Leben. 6th ed. Stuttgart, 1884.

R. Weltrich. Friedrich Schiller etc. Stuttgart, 1885–89. (Not
yet finished.)

O. Brahm. Schiller. Berlin, 1888–92. (As yet incomplete.)

J. Minor. Schiller. Berlin, 1890 ff. (About half finished.)

J. Wychgram. Schiller dem deutschen Volke dargestellt. Bielefeld and Leipzig, 1896. (Well illustrated.)

C. Hepp. Schillers Leben und Dichten. Leipzig, 1885.

E. Palleske. Schillers Leben und Werke. 13th ed. Stuttgart, 1891.

——. Schiller's Life and Works. Transl. London. 2 vols.

J. Sime. Schiller. London, 1882.

H. H. Boyesen. Goethe and Schiller, etc. New York, 1879.

H. W. Nevinson. Life of Friedrich Schiller. London, 1889.

Brief mention is made of Tell in the well-known histories of
German literature by Wilhelm Scherer, Vilmar, Julian Schmidt,
Gervinus, and Hettner.

MISCELLANEOUS.

K. Lucae. Aus deutscher Sprach- und Litteraturgeschichte.
Marburg, 1899.

M. Mühlenbach. Die dramatische Idee in Schillers Wilhelm Tell.
Ratibor, 1883.

H. Bulthaupt. Dramaturgie der Klassiker. Oldenburg–Leipzig,
1889.

——. Dramaturgie des Schauspiels. Leipzig, 1897.

G. Roethe. Die dramatischen Quellen des Schillerschen Tells. In 'Forschungen zur deutschen Philologie.' 1894.

E. Vogt. Schulwandkarte zu Schillers Wilhelm Tell. Breslau, 1896. Large map in six colors.

B. Rein. Karte zu Schillers Wilhelm Tell. Gotha, F. A. Perthes.

The historical and legendary phases of the subject are exhaustively treated in:

W. Vischer. Die Sage von der Befreiung der Waldstädte etc. Leipzig, 1867.

W. Gisi. Quellenbuch zur Schweizergeschichte. Bern, 1869.

H. Hungerbühler. Etude critique sur les traditions relatives aux origines de la Confédération Suisse. Geneva, 1869.

A. Rilliet. Les Origines de la Confédération Suisse. 2d ed. Geneva, 1869.

G. Meyer von Knonau. Die Sage von der Befreiung der Waldstätte. Basel, 1873.

Kopp. Geschichte der eidgenössischen Bünde etc. Luzern, 1874.

F. Vetter. Über die Sage von der Herkunft der Schweizer etc. Bern, 1877.

E. L. Rochholz. Tell und Gessler in Sage und Geschichte. Heilbronn, 1877.

P. Vaucher. Esquisse d'histoire Suisse. Lausanne, 1882.

W. Oechsli. Die Anfänge der Schweizerischen Eidgenossenschaft. Zürich, 1891.

Ed. Heyck. Geschichte der Herzöge von Zähringen. Freiburg i. B., 1891.

J. M. Vincent. State and Federal Government in Switzerland. Baltimore, 1891.

J. Dierauer. Geschichte der Schweizerischen Eidgenossenschaft. Vol. I. Gotha, 1887. Vol. II. Gotha, 1892. Gives very full bibliography.

K. Dändliker. Geschichte der Schweiz. Zürich, 1893.

——. A Short History of Switzerland. Translation. New York, 1899.

A. Gisler. Die Tellfrage. Versuch ihrer Geschichte und Lösung. Bern, 1895.

For full lists of older works, cf.

Aug. Hettler. Schillers Dramen. Eine Bibliographie. Berlin, 1885.

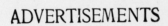

ADVERTISEMENTS

GERMAN GRAMMARS AND READERS.

Nix's Erstes deutsches Schulbuch. For primary classes. Illus. 202 pp. 35 cts

Joynes-Meissner German Grammar. Half leather. $1.15.

Joynes's Shorter German Grammar. Part I of the above. 80 cts.

Alternative Exercises. Two sets. Can be used, for the sake of change, instead of those in the *Joynes-Meissner* itself. 54 pages. 15 cts.

Joynes and Wesselhoeft's German Grammar. $1.15.

Fraser and Van der Smissen's German Grammar. $1.10.

Harris's German Lessons. Elementary Grammar and Exercises for a short course, or as introductory to advanced grammar. Cloth. 60 cts.

Sheldon's Short German Grammar. For those who want to begin reading as soon as possible, and have had training in some other languages. Cloth. 60c.

Ball's German Grammar. 90 cts.

Ball's German Drill Book. Companion to any grammar. 80 cts.

Spanhoofd's Lehrbuch der deutschen Sprache. Grammar, conversation, and exercises, with vocabularies. $1.00.

Foster's Geschichten und Märchen. For young children. 25 cts.

Guerber's Märchen und Erzählungen, I. With vocabulary and questions in German on the text. Cloth. 162 pages. 60 cts.

Guerber's Märchen und Erzählungen, II. With Vocabulary. Follows the above or serves as independent reader. Cloth. 202 pages. 65 cts.

Joynes's Shorter German Reader. 60 cts.

Deutsch's Colloquial German Reader. 90 cts.

Spanhoofd's Deutsches Lesebuch. 75 cts.

Boisen's German Prose Reader. 90 cts.

Huss's German Reader. 70 cts.

Gore's German Science Reader. 75 cts.

Harris's German Composition. 50 cts.

Wesselhoeft's Exercises. Conversation and composition. 50 cts.

Wesselhoeft's German Composition. 40 cts.

Hatfield's Materials for German Composition. Based on *Immensee* and on *Höher als die Kirche*. Paper. 33 pages. Each, 12 cts.

Horning's Materials for German Composition. Based on *Der Schwiegersohn*. 32 pages. 12 cts. Part II only. 16 pages. 5 cts.

Stüven's Praktische Anfangsgründe. Cloth. 203 pages. 70 cts.

Krüger and Smith's Conversation Book. 40 pages. 25 cts.

Meissner's German Conversation. 65 cts.

Deutsches Liederbuch. With music. 164 pages. 75 cts.

Heath's German Dictionary. Retail price, $1.50.

ELEMENTARY GERMAN TEXTS.

Grimm's Märchen and Schiller's Der Taucher (van der Smissen). With vocabulary. *Märchen* in Roman Type. 45 cts.

Andersen's Märchen (Super). With vocabulary. 50 cts.

Andersen's Bilderbuch ohne Bilder (Bernhardt). Vocabulary. 30 cts.

Campe's Robinson der Jüngere (Ibershoff). Vocabulary. 40 cts.

Leander's Träumereien (van der Smissen). Vocabulary. 40 cts.

Volkmann's Kleine Geschichten (Bernhardt). Vocabulary. 30 cts.

Easy Selections for Sight Translation (Deering). 15 cts.

Storm's Geschichten aus der Tonne (Vogel). Vocabulary. 40 cts.

Storm's In St. Jürgen (Wright). Vocabulary. 30 cts.

Storm's Immensee (Bernhardt). Vocabulary. 30 cts.

Storm's Pole Poppenspäler (Bernhardt). Vocabulary. 40 cts.

Heyse's Niels mit der offenen Hand (Joynes). Vocab. and exercises. 30 cts.

Heyse's L'Arrabbiata (Bernhardt). With vocabulary. 25 cts.

Von Hillern's Höher als die Kirche (Clary). Vocab. and exercises. 30 cts.

Hauff's Der Zwerg Nase. No notes. 15 cts.

Hauff's Das kalte Herz (van der Smissen). Vocab. Roman type. 40 cts.

Ali Baba and the Forty Thieves. No notes. 20 cts.

Schiller's Der Taucher (van der Smissen). Vocabulary. 12 cts.

Schiller's Der Neffe als Onkel (Beresford-Webb). Notes and vocab. 30 cts.

Goethe's Das Märchen (Eggert). Vocabulary. 30 cts.

Baumbach's Waldnovellen (Bernhardt). Six stories. Vocabulary. 35 cts.

Spyri's Rosenresli (Boll). Vocabulary. 25 cts.

Spyri's Moni der Geissbub. With vocabulary by H. A. Guerber. 25 cts.

Zschokke's Der zerbrochene Krug (Joynes). Vocab. and exercises. 25 cts.

Baumbach's Nicotiana (Bernhardt). Vocabulary. 30 cts.

Elz's Er ist nicht eifersüchtig. With vocabulary by Prof. B. Wells. 20 cts.

Carmen Sylva's Aus meinem Königreich (Bernhardt). Vocabulary. 35 cts.

Gerstäcker's Germelshausen (Lewis). Notes and vocabulary. 30 cts.

Wichert's Als Verlobte empfehlen sich (Flom). Vocabulary. 25 cts.

Benedix's Nein (Spanhoofd). Vocabulary and exercises. 25 cts.

Benedix's Der Prozess (Wells). Vocabulary. 20 cts.

Lambert's Alltägliches. Vocabulary and exercises. 75 cts.

Der Weg zum Glück (Bernhardt). Vocabulary. 40 cts.

Mosher's Willkommen in Deutschland. Vocabulary and exercises. 75 cts.

Blüthgen's Das Peterle von Nürnberg (Bernhardt). Vocabulary. 35 cts.

Münchhausen: Reisen und Abenteuer (Schmidt). Vocabulary. 30 cts.

Heath's Modern Language Series.

INTERMEDIATE GERMAN TEXTS.   (Partial List.)

Baumbach's Das Habichtsfräulein (Bernhardt).   Vocabulary.   40 cts.

Heyse's Hochzeit auf Capri (Bernhardt).   Vocabulary.   30 cts.

Hoffmann's Gymnasium zu Stolpenburg (Buehner).   Vocabulary.   35 cts

Grillparzer's Der arme Spielmann (Howard).   Vocabulary.   35 cts.

Seidel: Aus Goldenen Tagen (Bernhardt).   Vocabulary.   35 cts.

Seidel's Leberecht Hühnchen (Spanhoofd).   Vocabulary.   30 cts.

Auf der Sonnenseite (Bernhardt).   Vocabulary.   35 cts.

Frommel's Mit Ränzel und Wanderstab (Bernhardt).   Vocabulary.   35 cts

Frommel's Eingeschneit (Bernhardt).   Vocabulary.   30 cts.

Keller's Kleider machen Leute (Lambert).   Vocabulary.   35 cts.

Liliencron's Anno 1870 (Bernhardt).   Vocabulary.   40 cts.

Baumbach's Die Nonna (Bernhardt).   Vocabulary.   30 cts.

Riehl's Der Fluch der Schönheit (Thomas).   Vocabulary.   30 cts.

Riehl's Das Spielmannskind; Der stumme Ratsherr (Eaton).   Vocabulary and exercises.   35 cts.

Ebner-Eschenbach's Die Freiherren von Gemperlein (Hohlfeld).   30 cts.

Freytag's Die Journalisten (Toy).   30 cts.   With vocabulary.   40 cts.

Wilbrandt's Das Urteil des Paris (Wirt).   30 cts.

Schiller's Das Lied von der Glocke (Chamberlin).   Vocabulary.   20 cts.

Schiller's Jungfrau von Orleans (Wells).   Illus.   60 cts.   Vocab., 70 cts.

Schiller's Maria Stuart (Rhoades).   Illustrated.   60 cts.   Vocab., 70 cts.

Schiller's Wilhelm Tell (Deering).   Illustrated.   50 cts.   Vocab., 70 cts.

Schiller's Ballads (Johnson).   60 cts.

Baumbach's Der Schwiegersohn (Bernhardt).   30 cts.   Vocabulary, 40 cts.

Arnold's Fritz auf Ferien (Spanhoofd).   Vocabulary.   25 cts.

Heyse's Das Mädchen von Treppi (Joynes).   Vocab. and exercises. 30 cts

Stille Wasser (Bernhardt).   Three tales.   Vocabulary.   35 cts.

Sudermann's Teja (Ford).   Vocabulary.   25 cts.

Arnold's Aprilwetter (Fossler).   Vocabulary.   35 cts.

Gerstäcker's Irrfahrten (Sturm).   Vocabulary.   45 cts.

Benedix's Plautus und Terenz; Der Sonntagsjäger (Wells).   25 cts.

Moser's Köpnickerstrasse 120 (Wells).   30 cts.

Moser's Der Bibliothekar (Wells).   Vocabulary.   40 cts.

Drei kleine Lustspiele. *Günstige Vorzeichen, Der Prozess, Einer muss heiraten.*   Edited with notes by Prof. B. W. Wells.   30 cts.

Helbig's Komödie auf der Hochschule (Wells).   30 cts.

Stern's Die Wiedertäufer (Sturm).   Vocabulary.   90 cts.

Heath's Modern Language Series.

INTERMEDIATE GERMAN TEXTS. (Partial List.)

Schiller's Geschichte des dreissigjährigen Krieges. Book III. With notes by Professor C. W. Prettyman, Dickinson College. 35 cts.

Schiller's Der Geisterseher (Joynes). Vocabulary. 30 cts.

Arndt, Deutsche Patrioten (Colwell). Vocabulary. 30 cts.

Selections for Sight Translation (Mondan). 15 cts.

Selections for Advanced Sight Translation (Chamberlin). 15 cts.

Aus Herz und Welt. Two stories, with notes by Dr. Wm. Bernhardt. 25 cts.

Novelletten-Bibliothek. Vol. I, five stories. Vol. II, six stories. Selected and edited with notes by Dr. Wilhelm Bernhardt. Each, 35 cts.

Unter dem Christbaum (Bernhardt). Notes. 35 cts.

Hoffmann's Historische Erzählungen (Beresford-Webb). Notes. 25 cts.

Benedix's Die Hochzeitsreise (Schiefferdecker). 25 cts.

Stökl's Alle Fünf (Bernhardt). Vocabulary. 30 cts.

Till Eulenspiegel (Betz). Vocabulary. 30 cts.

Wildenbruch's Neid (Prettyman). Vocabulary. 35 cts.

Wildenbruch's Das Edle Blut (Schmidt). Vocabulary. 25 cts.

Wildenbruch's Der Letzte (Schmidt). Vocabulary. 30 cts.

Wildenbruch's Harold (Eggert). 35 cts.

Stifter's Das Haidedorf (Heller). 20 cts.

Chamisso's Peter Schlemihl (Primer). 25 cts.

Eichendorff's Aus dem Leben eines Taugenichts (Osthaus). Vocab. 45 cts

Heine's Die Harzreise (Vos). Vocabulary. 45 cts.

Jensen's Die braune Erica (Joynes). Vocabulary. 35 cts.

Lyrics and Ballads (Hatfield). 75 cts.

Meyer's Gustav Adolfs Page (Heller). 25 cts.

Sudermann's Johannes (Schmidt). 35 cts.

Sudermann's Heimat (Schmidt). 35 cts.

Sudermann's Der Katzensteg (Wells). Abridged. 40 cts.

Dahn's Sigwalt und Sigridh (Schmidt). 25 cts.

Keller's Romeo und Julia auf dem Dorfe (Adams). 30 cts.

Hauff's Lichtenstein (Vogel). Abridged. 75 cts.

Böhlau Ratsmädelgeschichten (Haevernick). Vocabulary. 40 cts.

Keller's Fähnlein der sieben Aufrechten (Howard). Vocabulary. 40 cts

Riehl's Burg Neideck (Jonas). Vocabulary and exercises. 35 cts.

Lohmeyer's Geissbub von Engelberg (Bernhardt). Vocabulary. 40 cts

Zschokke's Das Abenteuer der Neujahrsnacht (Handschin). Vocab. 35 cts.

Zschokke's Das Wirtshaus zu Cransac (Joynes). Vocabulary. 30 cts.

Heath's Modern Language Series.

ADVANCED GERMAN TEXTS.

Scheffel's Trompeter von Säkkingen (Wenckebach). Abridged. **50** cts.

Scheffel's Ekkehard (Wenckebach). Abridged. 55 cts.

Mörike's Mozart auf der Reise nach Prag (Howard). 35 cts.

Freytag's Soll und Haben (Files). Abridged. 55 cts.

Freytag's Aus dem Staat Friedrichs des Grossen (Hagar). 25 cts.

Freytag's Aus dem Jahrhundert des grossen Krieges (Rhoades). 35 cts.

Freytag's Rittmeister von Alt-Rosen (Hatfield). 50 cts.

Fulda's Der Talisman (Prettyman). 35 cts.

Körner's Zriny (Holzwarth). 35 cts.

Lessing's Minna von Barnhelm (Primer). 60 cts. With vocabulary, 65 cts.

Lessing's Nathan der Weise (Primer). 80 cts.

Lessing's Emilia Galotti (Winkler). 60 cts.

Schiller's Wallenstein's Tod (Eggert). 60 cts.

Goethe's Sesenheim (Huss). From *Dichtung und Wahrheit*. 30 cts.

Goethe's Meisterwerke (Bernhardt). $1.25.

Goethe's Dichtung und Wahrheit. (I-IV). Buchheim. 90 cts.

Goethe's Hermann und Dorothea (Hewett). 75 cts.

Goethe's Hermann und Dorothea (Adams). Vocabulary. 65 cts.

Goethe's Iphigenie (Rhoades). 60 cts.

Goethe's Egmont (Hatfield). 60 cts.

Goethe's Torquato Tasso (Thomas). 75 cts.

Goethe's Faust (Thomas). Part I, $1.15 Part II, $1.50.

Goethe's Poems. Selected and edited by Prof. Harris, Adelbert College. 90 cts.

Grillparzer's Der Traum, ein Leben (Meyer). 40 cts.

Ludwig's Zwischen Himmel und Erde (Meyer). 55 cts.

Heine's Poems. Selected and edited by Prof. White. 75 cts.

Tombo's Deutsche Reden. 90 cts.

Walther's Meereskunde. (Scientific German). 55 cts.

Thomas's German Anthology. $2.25.

Hodges' Scientific German. 75 cts.

Kayser's Die Elektronentheorie (Wright). 20 cts.

Lassar-Cohn's Die Chemie im täglichen Leben (Brooks). 45 cts.

Wagner's Entwicklungslehre (Wright). 30 cts.

Helmholtz's Populäre Vorträge (Shumway). 55 cts.

Wenckebach's Deutsche Literaturgeschichte. Vol. I (to 1100 A.D.) 50 cts.

Wenckebach's Meisterwerke des Mittelalters. $1.26.

Dahn's Ein Kampf um Rom (Wenckebach). Abridged. 55 cts.

Heath's Modern Language Series.

FRENCH GRAMMARS AND READERS.

Bruce's Grammaire Française. $1.15.

Clarke's Subjunctive Mood. An inductive treatise, with exercises. 50 cts.

Edgren's Compendious French Grammar. $1.15. Part I. 35 cts.

Fontaine's Livre de Lecture et de Conversation. 90 cts.

Fraser and Squair's French Grammar. $1.15.

Fraser and Squair's Abridged French Grammar. $1.10.

Fraser and Squair's Elementary French Grammar. 90 cts.

Grandgent's Essentials of French Grammar. $1.00.

Grandgent's Short French Grammar. 75 cts.

Roux's Lessons in Grammar and Composition, based on *Colomba*. 18 cts.

Hennequin's French Modal Auxiliaries. With exercises. 50 cts.

Houghton's French by Reading. $1.15.

Mansion's First Year French. For young beginners. 50 cts.

Méthode Hénin. 50 cts.

Bruce's Lectures Faciles. 60 cts.

Bruce's Dicteés Françaises. 30 cts.

Fontaine's Lectures Courantes. $1.00.

Giese's French Anecdotes. 00 cts.

Hotchkiss' Le Primer Livre de Français. Boards. 35 cts.

Bowen's First Scientific Reader. 90 cts.

Davies' Elementary Scientific French Reader. 40 cts.

Lyon and Larpent's Primary French Translation Book. 60 cts.

Snow and Lebon's Easy French. 60 cts.

Super's Preparatory French Reader. 70 cts.

Bouvet's Exercises in Syntax and Composition. 75 cts.

Storr's Hints on French Syntax. With exercises. 30 cts.

Brigham's French Composition. 12 cts.

Comfort's Exercises in French Prose Composition. 30 cts.

Grandgent's French Composition. 50 cts.

Grandgent's Materials for French Composition. Each, 12 cts.

Kimball's Materials for French Composition. Each, 12 cts.

Mansion's Exercises in Composition. 160 pages. 60 cts.

Marcou's French Review Exercises. 25 cts.

Prisoners of the Temple (Guerber). For French Composition. 25 cts.

Story of Cupid and Psyche (Guerber). For French Composition. 18 cts.

Heath's French Dictionary. Retail price, $1.50.

Heath's Modern Language Series.

ELEMENTARY FRENCH TEXTS.

Easy Selections for Sight Translation (Mansion). 15 cts.

Ségur's Les Malheurs de Sophie (White). Vocabulary. 45 cts.

French Fairy Tales (Joynes). Vocabulary and exercises. 35 cts.

Saintine's Picciola. With notes and vocabulary by Prof. O. B. Super. 45 cts

Mairêt's La Tâche du Petit Pierre (Super). Vocabulary. 35 cts.

Bruno's Les Enfants Patriotes (Lyon). Vocabulary. 25 cts.

Bruno's Tour de la France par deux Enfants (Fontaine). Vocabulary. 45 cts

Verne's L'Expédition de la Jeune Hardie (Lyon). Vocabulary. 25 cts.

Gervais Un Cas de Conscience (Horsley). Vocabulary. 25 cts.

Génin's Le Petit Tailleur Bouton (Lyon). Vocabulary. 25 cts.

Assolant's Aventure du Célèbre Pierrot (Pain). Vocabulary. 25 cts.

Assolant's Récits de la Vieille France. Notes by E. B. Wauton. 25 cts.

Muller's Grandes Découvertes Modernes. 25 cts.

Récits de Guerre et de Révolution (Minssen). Vocabulary. 25 cts.

Bedollière's La Mère Michel et son Chat (Lyon). Vocabulary. 25 cts.

Legouvé and Labiche's Cigale chez les Fourmis (Witherby). 20 cts.

Labiche's La Grammaire (Levi). Vocabulary. 25 cts.

Labiche's Le Voyage de M. Perrichon (Wells). Vocabulary. 30 cts.

Labiche's La Poudre aux Yeux (Wells). Vocabulary. 30 cts.

Lemaitre, Contes (Rensch). Vocabulary. 30 cts.

Dumas's Duc de Beaufort (Kitchen). Vocabulary. 30 cts.

Dumas's Monte-Cristo (Spiers). Vocabulary. 40 cts.

Berthet's Le Pacte de Famine. With notes by B. B. Dickinson. 25 cts.

Erckmann-Chatrian's Le Conscrit de 1813 (Super). Vocabulary. 45 cts.

Erckmann-Chatrian's L'Histoire d'un Paysan (Lyon). 25 cts.

France's Abeille (Lebon). 25 cts.

Moinaux's Les deux Sourds (Spiers). Vocabulary. 25 cts.

La Main Malheureuse (Guerber). Vocabulary. 25 cts.

Enault's Le Chien du Capitaine (Fontaine). Vocabulary. 35 cts.

Trois Contes Choisis par Daudet (Sanderson). Vocabulary. 20 cts.

Desnoyer's Jean-Paul Choppart (Fontaine). Vocabulary. 40 cts.

Selections for Sight Translation (Bruce). 15 cts.

Laboulaye's Contes Bleus (Fontaine). Vocabulary. 35 cts.

Malot's Sans Famille (Spiers). Vocabulary. 40 cts.

Meilhac and Halévy's L'Été de la St.-Martin (François). Vocab. 25 cts.

INTERMEDIATE FRENCH TEXTS. (Partial List.)

Beaumarchais's Le Barbier de Seville (Spiers). 25 cts.

Erckmann-Chatrian's Waterloo (Super). 35 cts.

About's Le Roi des Montagnes (Logie). 40 cts. Vocabulary, 50 cts.

Pailleron's Le Monde où l'on s'ennuie (Pendleton). 30 cts.

Historiettes Modernes (Fontaine). Vol. I. 60 cts.

Historiettes Modernes. Vol. II. 35 cts.

Fleurs de France (Fontaine). 35 cts.

French Lyrics (Bowen). 60 cts.

Loti's Pêcheur d'Islande (Super). 40 cts.

Loti's Ramuntcho (Fontaine). 30 cts.

Sandeau's Mlle. de la Seiglière (Warren). 30 cts.

Souvestre's Le Mari de Mme. Solange (Super). 20 cts.

Souvestre's Les Confessions d'un Ouvrier (Super). 25 cts.

Souvestre's Un Philosophe sous les Toits (Fraser). 50 cts. Vocab., 55 cts.

Augier's Le Gendre de M. Poirier (Wells). 25 cts.

Scribe's Bataille de Dames (Wells). 25 cts.

Scribe's Le Verre d'eau (Eggert). 30 cts.

Merimée's Colomba (Fontaine). 35 cts. With vocabulary. 45 cts.

Merimée's Chronique du Règne de Charles IX (Desages). 25 cts.

Musset's Pierre et Camille (Super). 20 cts.

Verne's Tour du Monde en quatre vingts jours (Edgren). 35 cts.

Verne's Vingt mille lieues sous la mer (Fontaine). Vocabulary. 45 cts.

Sand's La Mare au Diable (Sumichrast). Vocabulary. 35 cts.

Sand's La Petite Fadette (Super). Vocabulary. 35 cts.

Sept Grands Auteurs du XIXᵉ Siècle (Fortier). Lectures, 60 cts.

Vigny's Cinq-Mars (Sankey). Abridged. 60 cts.

Vigny's Le Cachet Rouge (Fortier). 20 cts.

Vigny's Le Canne de Jonc (Spiers). 40 cts.

Halévy's L'Abbé Constantin (Logie). 30 cts. Vocab. 40 cts.

Halévy's Un Mariage d'Amour (Hawkins). 25 cts.

Renan's Souvenirs d'Enfance et de Jeunesse (Babbitt). 75 cts.

Thier's Expédition de Bonaparte en Egypte (Fabregou). 30 cts.

Gautier's Jettatura (Schinz). 30 cts.

Guerber's Marie-Louise. 25 cts.

Zola's La Débâcle (Wells). Abridged. 60 cts.